Object-Oriented Programming Featuring Graphical Applications in Java

Michael J. Laszlo
Nova Southeastern University

Boston San Francisco New York
London Toronto Sydney Tokyo Singapore Madrid
Mexico City Munich Paris Cape Town Hong Kong Montreal

Senior Acquisitions Editor	Maite Suarez-Rivas
Project Editor	Katherine Harutunian
Executive Marketing Manager	Michael Hirsch
Production Services	Marilyn Lloyd/Pre-Press Company, Inc.
Copyeditor	Bernadette Murphy Bentley
Technical Art	Pre-Press Company, Inc.
Proofreader	Michelle Lulos Livingston
Text Design	Pre-Press Company, Inc.
Cover Design	Gina Hagen
Cover Image	© Corbis Images/PictureQuest
Design Manager	Gina Hagen
Prepress and Manufacturing	Caroline Fell

Access the latest information about Addison-Wesley titles from our World Wide Web site:
http://www.aw.com/cs

Library of Congress Cataloging-in-Publication Data

Laszlo, Michael Jay.
Object-oriented programming featuring graphical applications in Java / Michael J. Laszlo.
p. cm.
Includes index.
ISBN 0-201-72627-0
1. Object-oriented programming (Computer science) 2. Java (Computer program language) I. Title.

QA76.73.C153 L396 2001
005.13'3--dc21

2001024931

1 2 3 4 5 6 7 8 9 10—MA—04 03 02 01

Dedication

For Elisa, with love

TABLE OF CONTENTS

PREFACE

The goal of this book is to explore the principal ideas of object-oriented programming using the Java programming language. Object-oriented programming is based on the object model, under which knowledge and behaviors are encapsulated in objects. This programming model has taken hold in recent years due to its effectiveness for coping with program complexity (when used properly), and due to the proliferation of languages such as Java, C++, and Smalltalk, that support the object model.

Although object-oriented programming has been around for several decades, embodied in such early languages as Simula and Smalltalk, new programmers often first encounter the object model while learning Java. We use Java in this book to connect the rich but often-abstract ideas of object-oriented programming to concrete examples. Java provides a clear notation for expressing these ideas, a complement to English prose. Moreover, because you can code, compile, and run Java programs, the language serves as a vehicle for exploring and experimenting. Most of the book's examples and exercises involve two-dimensional computer graphics, and many lead to programs that produce images that are interesting and sometimes unexpected. The book's emphasis on 2-D graphics is intended both to engage the reader and to serve as a concrete setting in which to apply new concepts. New material is put to use in the incremental development, over the course of the book, of a new package of graphics-oriented classes and interfaces.

In writing this book, I have assumed that you have a basic knowledge of Java. If this is not the case, you can gain the requisite background by working through any of a number of introductory texts on this programming language. Whereas the present text does not purport to teach Java, it does explain all but the language's most elementary features as each is first used. The book also relies on two additional resources. First, Java's 2D application programming interface (the Java 2D API), which is a part of Java 2, is used to produce two-dimensional graphics. Second, we'll make use of a small subset of the Unified Modeling Language (UML), a notation for representing system designs; specifically, we use class diagrams to show the static structure of systems and sequence diagrams to show object interactions. Features of the Java 2D API and of UML will be introduced as they are needed, and I do not assume that you are familiar with either.

Structure of This Book

Chapter 1 introduces the basic concepts of the object model: objects and classes, message passing and methods, and four fundamental mechanisms for software reuse—composition, inheritance, design patterns, and application frameworks. The object model is also placed in the context of other prominent programming models.

Chapter 2 discusses procedural abstraction, whereby a procedure is viewed as an operation whose implementation is hidden. The chapter also covers Java's exception mechanism, and explores two standard programming techniques that rely on procedural abstraction: procedural decomposition (in which a procedure is defined in terms of other operations), and recursion (in which a procedure is defined in terms of the very operation it realizes). Procedures are treated early in this book because of their central role in the object model.

Chapter 3 treats data abstraction, which views a data value as a set of associated operations and a protocol for using these operations, while hiding the data value's internal structure. Under the object model, a data value viewed in this way is an object. The chapter also discusses encapsulation—the practice of grouping together related software elements—and information hiding. The chapter concludes by introducing 2-D computer graphics in Java and by developing a program template for computer graphics applications in Java.

Chapter 4 covers composition, a primary mechanism for software reuse. Using composition, you can define a new class that is composed of other classes, known as its components. Every instance of the composite class owns its components. The chapter also presents a program template for *interactive* computer graphics applications, for writing programs with which the user interacts in real time.

Chapter 5 covers inheritance, which is used to define a new class that acquires (or inherits) the attributes and behaviors of an existing class, its parent class. The new class is a child class of its parent class. The chapter discusses the three principal forms of inheritance: inheritance for extension (the child class adds new attributes or behaviors to those it inherits); inheritance for specialization (the child class overrides one or more behaviors it inherits); and inheritance for specification (the child class implements one or more behaviors specified, but not implemented by, its parent class). The chapter also treats the use of inheritance in building a family of related types, as well as the related topic of polymorphism.

Chapter 6 discusses design patterns, which are descriptions of good design solutions to problems that tend to recur. A design pattern describes the set of software elements that comprise the solution, and how to arrange the software elements. Of the rich array of design patterns developed by the software community, this chapter focuses on three. The iterator pattern provides access to a collection or aggregate while hiding its internal structure. The template method pattern defines an algorithm made up of both concrete and abstract steps; subclasses "flesh out" the algorithm by implementing the abstract steps. And the composite pattern is used to combine objects into hierarchies of primitives and composites, while enabling clients to treat both primitives and composites uniformly. This chapter applies these design patterns to several graphics projects, such as triangulating finite point sets; building constructive area geometry (CAG) trees, which are binary trees that combine 2-D shapes under the Boolean set operations of union, intersection, and difference; and building scene graphs, which are hierarchies of primitive and complex graphical figures. (Although such terse descriptions might make these graphics projects seem abstruse and difficult, this chapter explains these concepts and supplies figures that, you may find, are worth a million words.) This chapter also introduces several additional design patterns and presents a standard scheme for classifying patterns.

Chapter 7 covers application frameworks, whose purpose is to simplify the development of applications in a particular application domain. The programmer develops a custom program by extending and implementing the classes and interfaces supplied by the framework, according to the framework's conventions. This chapter explores the Abstract Window Toolkit (AWT), Swing, and Java's event model, which together make up Java's framework for building applications with graphical user interfaces (GUIs). The chapter closes with the development of a GUI-based program for drawing and editing graphical figures.

How to Read This Book

The exercises are an integral part of the book. Some exercises challenge you to implement classes relating to recent material. Other exercises ask you to devise programs that employ recently introduced classes and concepts. Most of the material is cumulative—classes developed in earlier chapters are used in later chapters, and many of the classes and interfaces are incorporated into the graphics-oriented package developed over the course of the book. In some cases, the definition of a class is revised in stages as the book proceeds, in order to put new concepts to use.

Supplements

Exercises range from relatively easy questions, to self-contained programming assignments, to fairly involved programming projects. Exercises that are especially important or that introduce material required later in the book are indicated as essential. If you don't attempt to solve the exercises, at least read the important ones.

The graphics package developed in this book is available in its final form from the site `http://www.aw.com/cssupport`. The Java programs presented in the body of the text are also available from this site, arranged by chapter. The site includes instructions on how to download and install these files. PowerPoint slides of all the figures may be obtained here. Answers to all exercises are available only to instructors through your Addison Wesley Longman sales representative.

Acknowledgements

The Graduate School of Computer and Information Sciences (SCIS), Nova Southeastern University, provided both the opportunity to write this book and a congenial, supportive environment. In particular, I am grateful to the dean of SCIS, Edward Lieblein, and to my colleagues, especially Maxine Cohen, Sumitra Mukherjee, and Junping Sun, for their encouragement and support.

I am fortunate to have had the chance to teach courses at SCIS relating to themes in this book, such as object-oriented design, theory of programming languages, and computer graphics. Much of the material that appears in this book was developed for these courses. I am indebted to more students than I can name for their questions and insights. I also wish to thank colleagues and students at the Institute for Mathematics and Computer Science (IMACS).

I am grateful for the reviews prepared by D. Robert Adams (Grand Valley State University), Manuel E. Bermudez (University of Florida), James R. Connolly (California State University, Chico), Frank Coyle (Southern Methodist University), Prasun Dewan (University of North Carolina at Chapel Hill), John R. Glover (University of Houston), Chung Lee (California State University, Pomona), Ronald McCarty (Penn State Erie, The Behrend College), Jong-Min Park (San Diego State University), Shih-Ho Wang (University of California, Davis), and Marvin V. Zelkowtiz (University of Maryland). Writing a careful review requires considerable time and effort, and I am appreciative. I used many of their suggestions in the final manuscript.

I wish to thank Maite Suarez-Rivas, my editor at Addison Wesley, for her insightfulness and steady support. I am also grateful to Jarrod Gibbons (Marketing Coordinator), Gina Hagen (Design Manager), Katherine Harutunian (Project Editor), Michael Hirsch (Marketing Manager), Marilyn Lloyd (Project Manager), and Patty Mahtani (Associate Managing Editor).

Finally, I wish to thank my family: my wife Elisa, our children Arianna Hannah and David Joshua, and my parents Maurice and Phyllis. Without their love, encouragement, and patience, I could not have written this book.

CHAPTER

1

The Object Model

It is common knowledge that computers manipulate 0s and 1s. Indeed, computers operate on bits in order to carry out low-level processes such as fetching and decoding instructions, adding numbers, and storing values. Yet when we use computers, we generally view them quite differently, at levels far removed from 0s and 1s. We draw figures into on-screen canvases, type text into windows, select objects with mouse clicks, even bring into being virtual 3-dimensional worlds using powerful graphics programs. We are insulated from and connected to the computer's low-level processes by layers of abstraction designed to enhance the power of our thought and expression, while hiding the details of the computer's inner workings. Today's software turns computers into virtual machines that define their own rules of operation and have little apparent connection to the computers' internal processes.

We make use of abstraction not only when we use computers, but also when we write computer programs. We use the high-level features found in most computer languages, such as iteration, recursion, conditional expressions, and procedure calls, to avoid having to program in machine language, the computer's native language. Programmers use abstractions to think in terms appropriate to the problem at hand, without being bothered by the details and intricacies of the computer's low-level logic. Without abstractions of any sort, programmers would be reduced to programming at the machine level of bits, and few if any of the remarkable computer applications we have come to enjoy today would be possible in practice.

What is abstraction? *An abstraction is an idealized model of something, one that presents the thing's essential characteristics while omitting its inessential ones.* We use abstractions to more easily use or understand something in terms of its key aspects, without being distracted by its inessential aspects. We use abstractions to cope with complexity. When you drive a car, you treat the car as an abstraction that includes certain elements that are important from the driver's perspective: the gas pedal is used to accelerate, the brake to decelerate, the steering wheel to steer, the radio to play music, and so forth. The fuel injectors, the tires, the spark plugs, and the axles are not elements of a driver's abstraction because they are not directly manipulated by the driver. As a driver, your view of a car enables you to drive almost any car with little need to reorient yourself, without regard for the car's internal structure.

By way of another example, an object in Java is an abstraction. An object represents and behaves like some real thing (where *real* is defined quite broadly), yet the object captures only those aspects of the real thing that are essential to the task at hand. In a system for registering students in school, every student is represented by an object. The system may ask a student–object for its name or address, or update the student–object's phone number, or inform it that it has been admitted to a certain course. Yet, of course, such student–objects are mere shadows of the real students they represent. Such objects cannot eat pizza, or attend dances, or read books; they behave only in such ways as the registration system requires.

Object-oriented programming languages such as Java provide features for creating and using different kinds of abstractions. These language features support a set of principles that together make up the **object-oriented programming model,** known more conveniently as the **object model.** This introductory chapter sets the stage for our inquiry into the object model. Section 1.1 presents the basic concepts of the object model. Other programming models, such as the imperative and the functional programming models, support other kinds of abstractions and are realized by other programming languages. Section 1.2 places the object model and the Java language in the context of several other prominent programming models.

1.1 Object Model Concepts

A Java program describes a community of objects arranged to interact in well-defined ways for a common purpose. None of the objects is sufficient on its own, but when associated with one another correctly, they collaborate to fulfill the program's promise. Every object provides specific services required by other objects in the community. When an object requires a specific service, it sends a request (called a **message**) to another object capable of providing that service. The object that receives the message responds by performing actions that often involve additional messages being sent to other objects. What results is a vibrant cascade of messages among a network of objects. This is the form of computation under the object model. This is what we imagine happens when a Java program runs.

Where do the objects come from? How is each object's behavior specified? How are their collaborations orchestrated? This is all accomplished by a Java program. *A Java program consists of a collection of class and interface definitions.* Every object belongs to some class. The behaviors of each object are guided by the definition of the class to which the object belongs and the interfaces it implements. Through their behaviors, objects cause new objects to be created and existing objects to be destroyed. Also through their behaviors, objects perform actions and, by sending messages, cause other objects to perform actions as well.

The remainder of this section presents the basic elements of the object model—objects, messages, classes, methods, and various forms of collaboration and of reuse. The section also presents an overview of how these elements fit together into a coherent picture.

1.1.1 Objects

An **object** is a software element that can receive and respond to messages. Objects represent real things, where *real* should be interpreted very broadly. Objects may represent tangible things such as airplanes or apples, or concepts such as colors or graphical figures. They may represent active things that initiate or control processes such as timers, sensors, or people, or passive things that respond only to requests for services such as elevators or dictionaries. Objects may be artifacts in an implementation such as the nodes in a linked list, or user-interaction elements such as buttons or menus. What makes for a good object is a matter of program design and depends in large part on the problem at hand. Generally, objects are chosen that have a role to play in the problem domain addressed by the program or in the program's implementation.

An object's **behavior** refers to how it responds to the messages it receives. In fact, an object is capable of different kinds of **defined behaviors,** corresponding to the different kinds of messages it can understand. Each kind of message evokes a specific defined behavior. The set of defined behaviors associated with an object, and hence the kinds of messages that the object understands, is determined by the object's class.

When an object receives a message, its response is determined jointly by the specific defined behavior evoked by the message and by the object's current **state.** An object has any number of **instance fields,** known more simply as **fields.** The object's state corresponds to the values stored in its fields. As an object responds to messages, it undergoes changes in state, called **state transitions,** meaning that its fields assume new values. The state of an object captures all that is relevant about what the object has undergone from the time it was created to the present. In other words, an object's state captures those aspects of its history that are relevant to its behavior.

Besides behavior and state, an object has an **identity** which serves to distinguish it from other objects. Identity does not depend on an object's state, nor does it change as the object's state changes any more than you become a different person when your state changes (such as when you age, or eat popcorn, or understand a new idea). Two objects of the same class whose states happen to be equivalent remain distinct objects.

Thus we've identified the three defining characteristics of objects: defined behaviors, state, and identity. How an object responds to the messages it receives is determined both by its set of defined behaviors and by its state. For the object to receive messages in the first place, it must be distinguishable from other objects—it must have an identity.

To illustrate these concepts in terms of Java, we'll assume a class for representing points in the Cartesian plane (see Figure 1.1). The `Point` class possesses two fields corresponding to a point's *x* and *y* coordinates. The instruction

```
Point p = new Point(3, 2);
```

accomplishes the following:

- creates a new object belonging to class `Point`,
- initializes this point's *x* coordinate with the value 3 and *y* coordinate with the value 2,
- declares a new reference variable `p`, and
- assigns to the variable `p` a reference to this new `Point` object.

As compact as it is, the preceding instruction creates a new object, initializes its state, and captures a reference to it. This new `Point` object can subsequently be sent messages through the reference stored in the variable `p`, or through copies of this reference.

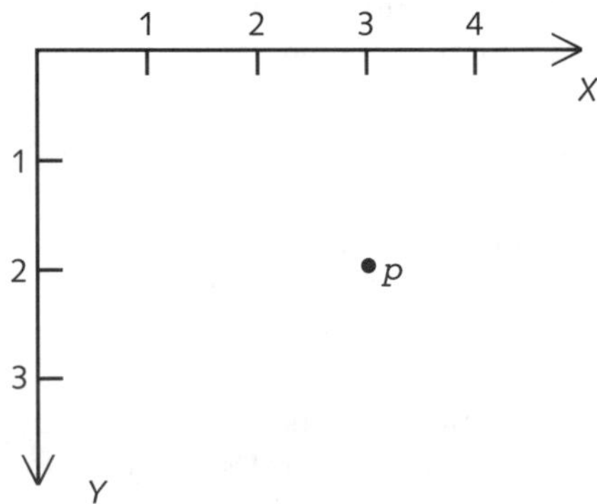

FIGURE 1.1 The plane and the point p=(3,2).

1.1.2 Messages

Objects interact by sending **messages** to one another. The object that sends the message is known as the **sender** or **client**, and the object that receives the message is known as the **receiver** or **server.** The *client–server* terminology is suggested when the sender is viewed as a client that requests another object's services, and the receiver of its request provides those services. To provide the services it promises, an object often relies on the services of still other objects, so at times an object plays the role of server and at times the role of client. In general, an object's role is relative to a message: An object that is a server with respect to some message it receives may respond—in order to carry out the requested service—by sending messages of its own with respect to which it is the client.

A message consists of three elements:

- a message name, also known as a selector,
- a list of zero or more arguments, which provide additional data required by the receiving object, and
- a reference indicating the receiving object.

The arguments may be references to objects or primitive-type values such as integers. Note that a message does not include a reference to the sender, although the sender may include itself as an argument.

You are probably already familiar with Java's syntax for messages. Where `p` is an object that represents a point in the plane, the statement

```
p.setCoordinates(8, 9);
```

is a message consisting of the selector `setCoordinates`, the two arguments 8 and 9, and the receiving object `p`. In response to this message, point `p` updates its location to (8,9).

What object sends the message `p.setCoordinates(8,9)`? The answer is not evident from this brief example. This message appears as code within the body of some defined behavior (method) owned by some object. In the process of executing the method, this object sends the message.

It often happens that an object sends a message to itself. In this case, the message's receiver—which is identical to the sender—is omitted from the message. Thus point `p` may use this statement

```
setY(4);
```

to change its own *y* coordinate to 4. This message consists of the selector `setY` and the argument 4. The receiving object, which is the sender, is implicit. However, because the keyword `this` always refers to the sender of a message (whose code is executing), the message may also be written like this:

```
this.setY(4);
```

thereby making the receiver explicit.

The keyword `this` can also be used as an argument, whereby an object can send a message that identifies itself as the sender. For example, where `p` and `q` are both `Point` objects, `p` can send this message:

```
q.setCoordinates(this);
```

to tell `q` to change its coordinates such that they equal `p`'s coordinates in both *x* and *y*. Here the receiver, point `q`, expects the argument to the *setCoordinates* message to be a `Point` object; in this message, the argument is in fact a `Point` object—it is the sender, point `p`, identified by the keyword `this`.

When an object receives a message, it responds by carrying out a defined behavior. These behaviors are specified by the receiving object's *methods*, which we will consider shortly. There are only three possible net effects that result from carrying out a defined behavior:

- a value is returned to the sender of the message, or
- the receiver undergoes a change in state, or
- objects passed to the receiver as arguments undergo changes in state.

These effects can occur in combinations of one, two, or all three, depending on the specific behavior. It sometimes happens that state changes in the receiver object are due to state changes in one or more of its *object* attributes. If some of these attributes are shared by other objects, the effects of the behavior may be far reaching, extending well beyond the sender and the receiver. The effects of behavior can be difficult to understand and are often the cause of unexpected and incorrect behavior.

1.1.3 Object Interfaces

The set of messages to which an object can respond is determined by the object's interface. The object's interface is presented as a set of operations, each of which corresponds to a defined behavior that the object carries out in response to certain messages. An object's interface is determined by its **type;** in turn, an object's type is determined by the class to which it belongs.

Clients refer to an object's interface to understand the kinds of behaviors it supports. For example, we might express the object interface for `Point` objects using the following Java-like syntax:

```
public class Point {
  // constructs a new point at position (x,y)
  public Point(int x, int y)

  // constructs a new point that is a copy of point p
  public Point(Point p)
```

```
    // constructs a new point at (0,0)
    public Point()

    // returns the x coordinate of this point
    public int getX()

    // changes the x coordinate of this point to newX
    public void setX(int newX)

    // returns the y coordinate of this point
    public int getY()

    // changes the y coordinate of this point to newY
    public void setY(int newY)

    // changes the position of this point to (newX,newY)
    public void setCoordinates(int newX, int newY)

    // changes the position of this point
    // to (p.getX(),p.getY())
    public void setCoordinates(Point p)

    // translates this point by dx along x and dy along y
    public void moveBy(int dx, int dy)

    // returns a string-descriptor for this point: "(x,y)"
    public String toString()
}
```

There are certain rules guiding the use of an object's operations. These rules, referred to as the object's **protocol,** describe how each operation is used. For a client to interact correctly with an object, the client must abide by the object's interface and protocol. For example, when a `Point` object receives a *setCoordinates* message with one argument, the argument must be a `Point`; hence the following message violates the object's protocol:

```
p.setCoordinates(null);
```

The interface for `Point` objects is rather simple, but we'll see objects with more interesting interfaces and protocols later in this book.

The interface that I've been describing is the object's **public interface.** The adjective *public* emphasizes that the operations are available to all objects regardless of their type. In other words, the public interface defines the set of messages that may be sent by any object whatsoever. In addition to the operations that compose its public interface, an object may provide additional operations that only a restricted category of clients may use. The set of operations available to a restricted category of clients is called a **restricted**

interface. The **private interface** is the most restrictive form of interface, and the public interface is the least restrictive. The private interface is a superset of the public interface—it includes all the operations of the public interface, to which it adds private operations available only to objects of the same type.

Java provides two other kinds of restricted interfaces: **protected interfaces** and **package interfaces.** As we move through the spectrum of interfaces—from public, to protected, to package, to private—the interface becomes less accessible but more capable. Interfaces of varying restriction allow privileged clients to manipulate an object in ways that less privileged clients may not.

1.1.4 Methods and Procedures

A **procedure** *is a piece of code that implements an operation.* A procedure describes a computational process that, when executed, carries out the behavior promised by the operation. Viewed as an operation, a procedure maps inputs to outputs and side effects. A procedure receives input through a list of typed parameters. It returns its output to the client code; specifically, to the procedure that calls it. The side effects it produces are changes in the state of objects and actions such as reading input and writing output.

The number and types of a procedure's parameters, together with its name, are jointly referred to as the procedure's **signature.** For example, the signature of class `Point's` two-argument `setCoordinates` method

```
void setCoordinates(int newX, int newY)
```

consists of the procedure name *setCoordinates* and the two-parameter list of types `int` and `int`. The method

```
void setCoordinates(Point p)
```

has a different signature because it declares a one-parameter list of type `Point`, which differs from the parameter list declared by the two-argument version of `setCoordinates`. A procedure's return type is not part of its signature.

A ***method*** *is a procedure associated with an object.* When an object receives a message, it responds by executing one of its methods. The message's arguments are passed as inputs to the method.

Any number of methods may be associated with an object. The process of deciding which method to invoke in response to a particular message is known as **method binding.** Method selection depends on the elements of the message—the selector (name) of the message and the number and types of its arguments. Specifically, method binding finds the object's method whose signature matches the elements of the message—the method's name matches the message's name, and the method's parameter list matches the message's argument list in type and number. To set the *x* and *y* coordinates of a `Point` object `p`, we may send `p` a *setCoordinates* message with the new coordinates

```
p.setCoordinates(3, 4);
```

In response to this message, the point `p` invokes its method whose signature matches

```
void setCoordinates(int newX, int newY)
```

A method name is said to be **overloaded** if it serves as the name of more than one method in the same object. Every method sharing the same overloaded name must have a distinct signature. To resolve a message whose name is overloaded, method binding matches the message's argument list to the parameter lists of the candidate methods. Thus in response to the message

```
p.setCoordinates(new Point(5, 6));
```

the point `p` executes its method having this signature:

```
void setCoordinates(Point p)
```

Here the method name *setCoordinates* is overloaded, so a message's argument list is used to determine which `setCoordinates` method is executed.

The distinction between an operation and a method is important. An operation describes a behavior—a mapping of inputs to outputs and side effects—as viewed from the client that calls the operation. In contrast, a method is the *implementation* of an operation in the form of a procedure. *An operation specifies a behavior; a method describes how the operation is carried out*. It follows that an operation is the abstraction of a method. The operation exhibits what the method does while hiding how it does it.

1.1.5 Encapsulation

Encapsulation is the practice of grouping together a set of related software elements. The word itself, *encapsulation*, suggests elements enclosed by a capsule. Java provides packages for encapsulating a set of related classes. However, the key form of encapsulation occurs at the level of individual objects: an object encapsulates a set of related data and methods.

Encapsulation is also used to compartmentalize the elements that make up an object, thereby making it possible to distinguish between the object's interface and its implementation. We can picture the object as being enclosed by an outer membrane, representing its public interface. Nested inside may be zero or more additional membranes representing interfaces of increasing restriction (see Figure 1.2).

The use of encapsulation to conceal those software elements that are not part of an object's public interface is known as **information hiding.** Java provides four levels of access control—public, protected, package, and private—for distinguishing between those elements that are part of an

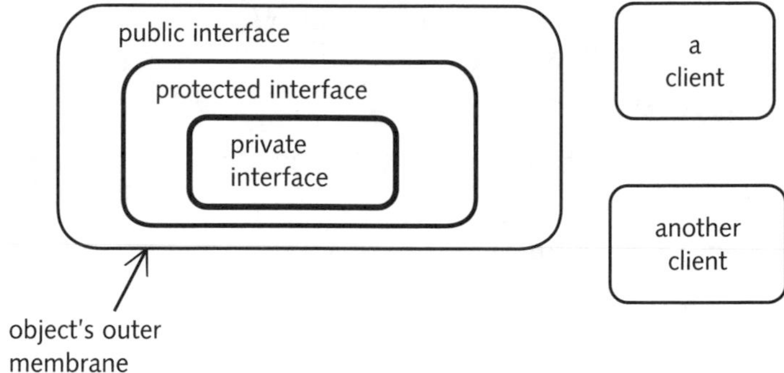

FIGURE 1.2 An object encapsulates a set of interfaces.

object's public interface and those that are not, and for specifying the extent to which the latter elements are hidden.

Information hiding and abstraction are complementary concepts. Abstraction reveals what a client needs to know about an object to use it. Information hiding conceals what a client must not know about an object to prevent its misuse. Abstraction and information hiding work together to reveal the services an object provides—the object's interface—while hiding how it performs those services—the object's implementation.

1.1.6 Classes and Object Instantiation

Every object belongs to some class. The class determines not only the object's type but also its fields and methods. These fields and methods appear within a **class definition.** Whenever a new object is created, the class definition corresponding to the object's type determines the object's structure and behaviors.

As an example we'll consider a `Point` class. So far we've seen a number of code fragments that refer to `Point` objects and, in Section 1.1.3, a description of a `Point` object's defined behaviors. Based on these elements you probably already have a good idea of how to use a point's operations, which puts us in a position to implement the `Point` class. We'll store a point's *x* and *y* coordinates in fields of the same name. Here is its class definition:

```
public class Point {

  // fields
  protected int x, y;

  // constructors
  public Point(int newX, int newY) {
    x = newX;
    y = newY;
  }
```

```
    public Point(Point p) {
      this(p.getX(), p.getY());
    }

    public Point() {
      this(0, 0);
    }

    // other methods
    public int getX() { return x; }

    public void setX(int newX) { x = newX; }

    public int getY() { return y; }

    public void setY(int newY) { y = newY; }

    public void setCoordinates(int newX, int newY) {
      setX(newX);
      setY(newY);
    }

    public void setCoordinates(Point p) {
      setCoordinates(p.getX(), p.getY());
    }

    public void moveBy(int dx, int dy) {
      setCoordinates(getX() + dx, getY() + dy);
    }

    public String toString() {
      String res = "(" + getX() + "," + getY() + ")";
      return res;
    }
}
```

Because all of the methods are declared `public`, together they make up the public interface of `Point` objects. In contrast, the `x` and `y` fields are declared `protected`, so they belong to the restricted interface of `Point` objects. Specifically, the `x` and `y` fields can be directly accessed only by clients whose class belongs either to the same package as `Point` or to a subtype of `Point`. In this book, elements of restricted interfaces will be declared `protected`.

The process of creating a new object from a class is called **instantiating** the class, and an object is said to be an **instance** of its class. When you instantiate a class using the keyword `new`, one of the class' constructors is called. The constructor call obtains memory for the object, establishes its type (or connection to its class), and initializes the values of its fields. The constructor returns a reference to the new object. Subsequently, messages are sent to the object through this reference or through copies of this reference. Here is an example:

```
Point p;
p = new Point(4, 2);
System.out.println("x: " + p.getX());   // x: 4
```

In the preceding code segment, a new `Point` object is created and initialized to represent the point (4,2). A reference to this new object is captured in the variable `p`. Then the point is sent the message *getX* that queries the value of its *x* coordinate (4), which is printed.

An object can be referenced any number of times. In the following code fragment, which continues the one just given, the reference to the point that is stored in the variable `p` is copied into a second variable `q`:

```
Point q;
q = p;
q.setCoordinates(6, 8);
System.out.println("x: " + p.getX());  // x: 6
System.out.println("y: " + p.getY());  // y: 8
```

Once the assignment `q=p` is performed, there are two references to the same point, stored in the variables `p` and `q`. That these two variables reference the same point object is emphasized by the final three instructions. The instruction

```
q.setCoordinates(6, 8);
```

changes the point's *x* and *y* coordinates through the reference stored in the variable `q`. The final two instructions access and print the point's current *x* and *y* coordinates through the reference stored in the variable `p`. The output makes clear that the point referenced by `p` was changed by the *setCoordinate* message sent via the reference in `q`: The variables `p` and `q` reference the same `Point` object. In Figure 1.3, each arrow originates in a reference variable and points to the object being referenced.

1.1.7 Classes and Interfaces

A class serves three primary purposes. First, a class defines a type. Second, a class provides an implementation for its type—it defines how instances are represented and implements the methods in terms of the chosen representation. Lastly, a class provides constructors for initializing instances of its type; in the case of *concrete* classes, constructors are used to both construct and initialize new instances of its type.

Java distinguishes between two kinds of classes: **abstract classes** and **concrete classes.** Both kinds of classes define a type. However, they differ

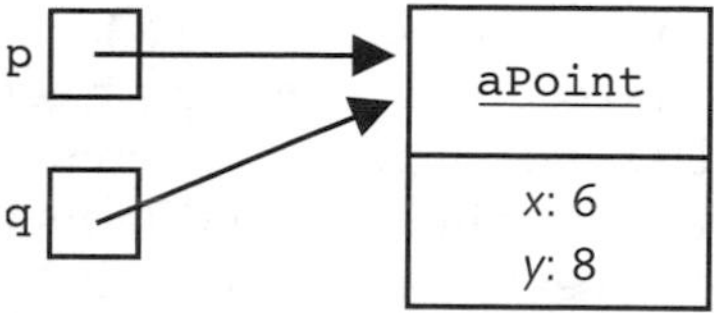

FIGURE 1.3 This `Point` object is referenced twice.

in the extent to which they *implement* their type: Concrete classes provide a complete implementation whereas abstract classes generally provide only a partial implementation. An abstract class may declare more methods than it actually implements (those methods that it declares without implementing are called **abstract methods**). It is not possible to instantiate an abstract class—indeed, if an instance of an abstract class were to receive a message that matches one of its abstract methods, the sender would expect a behavior that the receiver would not know how to carry out.

Java also provides a structure known as an **interface,** which defines a type without providing an implementation for it. All of the methods declared by an interface are implicitly abstract and, as you might expect, interfaces cannot be instantiated. Both abstract classes and interfaces are intended to serve as supertypes for other classes. When a class **extends** an abstract class, it inherits the specification of behaviors and partial implementation of the abstract class. The new class is concrete only if it completes the implementation it inherits. A class **implements** an interface by implementing the abstract methods declared by the interface. The new class is concrete only if it implements all of the methods promised by the interface.

Classes are an essential element of Java, but their role varies across object-oriented programming languages. In the Smalltalk language, classes are objects. To create a new object in Smalltalk, you send a message to a class telling it to instantiate itself. In Java, classes are not objects, but they do have some of the characteristics of objects. Like objects, Java classes have fields (known as **class fields** or **static fields**) and methods (known as **class methods** or **static methods**); unlike objects, classes are not instances of a type. There are also programming languages that make no use of classes whatsoever. The Self programming language is a prototype-based language, which means that new objects are made by copying existing objects (prototypes) and then specifying differences.

1.1.8 Associations

An **association** exists between two classes `A` and `B` if instances of `A` can send messages to instances of `B`. When an object `a` (of class `A`) can send messages to an object `b` (of class `B`), the two objects are said to be **linked.** For this to be possible, the object `a` requires a reference to the object `b`. The most common way is for `a` to store its reference to `b` in a field. For example, a line segment contains two endpoints (`Point` objects). A line segment object would contain two fields, each holding a reference to one of its endpoints. To report or update the coordinates of one of its endpoints, the line segment sends a message to the endpoint through the reference stored in its field.

Other mechanisms, besides the use of fields, may be used to realize an association between two classes. An object `a` may create a new instance of class `B` for a one-time use, without retaining the reference to the new object beyond this use. Another mechanism for linking two objects occurs when an object `a` receives an object `b` as part of a message, specifically, as one of the message's arguments. For example, a `Graphics2D` object, which defines methods for drawing various kinds of graphical figures, may be sent a *draw* message with a reference to the rectangle to be drawn:

```
aGraphics2D.draw(aRectangle);
```

In response to receiving this *draw* message, `aGraphics2D` sends messages to `aRectangle` to determine its position and dimensions. The objects `aGraphics2D` and `aRectangle` are linked while the `draw` method executes.

Navigability refers to the direction in which messages travel between two linked objects. A line segment stores a reference to each of its two endpoints, but the endpoints do not reference the line segment. In this case navigability is one-way—the line segment can send messages to its endpoints but not vice versa. Two-way navigability is also common. An example is the association between students and courses in a school's registration system. A student–object maintains references to the courses she takes so that the system can track her progress. Likewise, a course–object maintains references to the students enrolled in the course so that the system can produce student rolls, grade sheets, and the like. The link between a student–object and a course–object is bidirectional—each is able to send messages to the other.

An association between two classes reflects a relevant relationship between two concepts. That a line segment has two endpoints is captured by the association between the classes `LineSegment` and `Point`. That a student takes a course is captured by the association between the classes `Student` and `Course`. It is important to understand how classes are associated for two reasons. First, associations indicate dependencies between objects. Because objects interact, changes to one part of the system may affect other parts. Specifically, when an object's interface changes, it is necessary to understand the effects on the clients that depend on it. Secondly, the associations between classes provide a high-level view of the system's elements and their relationships; they present the system's overall design while concealing a myriad of implementation details.

Classes and their associations can be depicted using **class diagrams.** The class diagrams used in this book follow **Unified Modeling Language**

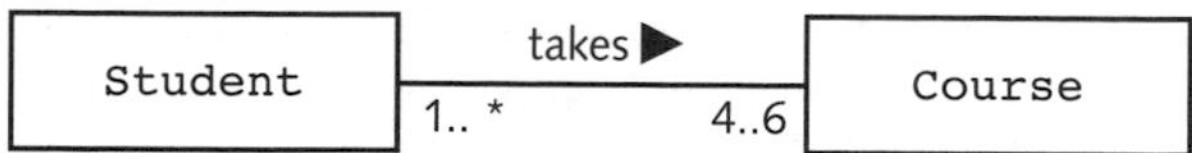

FIGURE 1.4 An association exists between the `Student` and `Course` classes.

(UML) notation, which depicts classes as boxes and associations as lines connecting boxes. Figure 1.4 presents a class diagram that captures the association between the `Student` and `Course` classes. Each class is represented by a named box, and the fact that an association exists between them is indicated by the line linking the boxes. In this example, the association is named (*takes*) and assigned a direction by the solid triangle, which tells us how to "read" the association: *A student takes courses,* or *a course is taken by students.* The notations at each end of the line indicate the *multiplicities* of the association, that is, the number of objects involved in the association. The class diagram informs us that a student may take between four and six courses, and that a course may be taken by one or more students.

Class diagrams may include adornments for naming classes, indicating their behaviors and providing additional details. Appendix C summarizes the elements of the UML that we make use of in this book.

1.1.9 Composition

One of the key benefits of object-oriented programming is that it supports reuse of software elements. In particular, it provides several mechanisms for defining new classes in terms of existing classes. The new classes acquire access to the fields, behaviors, and implementations of the existing classes, thereby effectively reusing the existing classes. Two of the principal mechanisms for reuse are **composition** and **inheritance.**

An association exists between two classes if instances of the two classes can communicate. Composition is a kind of association in which an instance of one of the classes *owns* one or more instances of the second class. Composition captures the *has-a* relationship between two objects, in which one object contains or owns a second object. The owning object is called the **composite,** and the object or objects it owns are its **components.** This kind of relationship is quite common in the real world: cars contain engines, houses contain windows, and plants contain leaves.

A composite object has a special relationship with its components: The composite directly communicates with its components and controls the lifetime of its components, and is the only object to do so. *A composite object uses the services of its components to carry out its own behaviors.* By way of example, consider an object that represents a line segment connecting two points (its endpoints) in the plane. A line segment object is a composite with two components, point objects corresponding to its endpoints. A line segment creates its endpoints at the time of its own creation. When a line segment is asked to move one of its endpoints to a new location, it does so by sending that endpoint a *moveBy* or *setCoordinates* message. No other object can send messages to a line segment's endpoints besides the line segment itself. Moreover, when a line segment's lifetime ends, its two endpoints perish as well.

A composite object generally contains fields that reference its components. For instance, our line segment class might be defined in part like this:

```
public class LineSegment {

  // fields: this line segment's components
  protected Point endpoint0, endpoint1;

  // constructor
  public LineSegment(int x0, int y0, int x1, int y1) {
    endpoint0 = new Point(x0, y0);
    endpoint1 = new Point(x1, y1);
  }

  // move endpoint0 to a new location
  public void moveEndpoint0(int newX, int newY) {
    endpoint0.setCoordinates(newX, newY);
  }

  // other methods
  ...
}
```

The class diagram in Figure 1.5 depicts the association between the `LineSegment` and `Point` classes. The line linking the two labeled boxes indicates the association; the filled diamond at `LineSegment`'s end of the line further specifies the association—it is one of composition in which `LineSegment` is the composite. The multiplicity value of 2 at `Point`'s end of the line indicates that a `LineSegment` is composed of exactly two points.

Sometimes the number of components belonging to a composite is not known in advance, or the number of components is expected to vary over the composite's lifetime. In such cases the composite may own a **collection** that contains its components. The collection provides services that the composite uses to manage its components; to order them, insert new ones, delete existing ones, and others. An example is a polygon, which is a closed path of

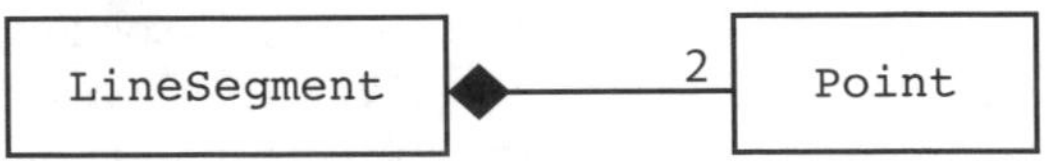

FIGURE 1.5 A line segment is composed of two points.

straight line segments (its **edges**). The endpoints of these edges, where two adjacent edges meet, are called **vertices.** Polygons allow clients to do such operations as insert new vertices, delete existing vertices, and traverse from vertex to adjacent vertex in clockwise or counterclockwise rotation. To support these operations, a polygon could store its vertices in a circular list, ordered as the vertices occur along the polygon. This circular list provides services used by the polygon to perform its own operations. For instance, the circular list allows new elements to be inserted at any position, a service that the polygon uses whenever asked to insert a new vertex.

1.1.10 Inheritance

Inheritance is a second principal mechanism for software reuse. When a new class is defined using inheritance, it acquires the fields and behaviors of an existing class. The new class is known as a **subclass** or **child class** of the existing class, and the existing class is called its **superclass** or **parent class.** In turn, the subclass may serve as a superclass to any number of other classes (its subclasses). What results is an **inheritance hierarchy,** such as the one pictured in the class diagram of Figure 1.6. In this class diagram, a line connects every parent class to each of its child classes, where a hollow triangle appears on the side of the parent class. The `Figure` class lies at the root of the hierarchy, and the `LineSegment`, `Point`, and `Region` classes are its subclasses. In turn, the `Ellipse` and `Rectangle` classes are subclasses of the `Region` class. (These classes are introduced only for this introductory chapter, whereas the classes and associations we'll develop in later chapters will be quite different.)

Every class has any number of child classes, and every class has exactly one parent class, except for the `java.lang.Object` class which has no parent class. In fact, the `Object` class lies at the root of a (very large) global

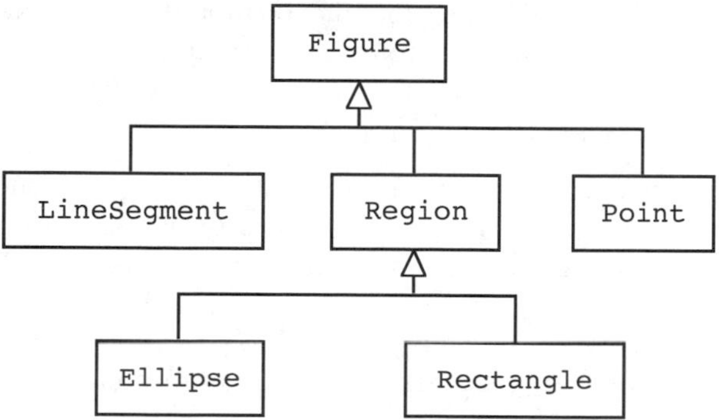

FIGURE 1.6 A class diagram showing inheritance relationships.

inheritance hierarchy to which every class belongs. A class diagram serves as a window into this global inheritance hierarchy, showing the associations among a small set of relevant classes. The `Object` class does not appear in Figure 1.6 because it is not relevant to the task at hand.

You are probably already familiar with the syntax for creating new subclasses. The class definition for the `Ellipse` class takes this form:

```
public class Ellipse extends Region {
   ...
}
```

When a class definition omits the `extends` clause, the new class becomes a child of the `Object` class.

At its simplest, a class corresponds to a concept, and its subclasses correspond to specialized versions of the concept. Two classes related in this way partake in the *is-a* relationship: Every instance of the subclass is an instance of the superclass. Referring to Figure 1.6, every ellipse is a region, and every region is a figure.

Unfortunately, using inheritance properly cannot be reduced to discovering whether two concepts are related by the *is-a* relationship. This is because we use inheritance to reuse behaviors rather than static properties. Inheritance is used in three different ways:

- A subclass may define new fields and methods that supplement those it inherits.
- A subclass may provide new implementations for one or more of the methods it inherits. A method that is redefined by a child class is said to be **overridden;** the child class **overrides** that particular method. This represents a change in behavior. In response to the same message, an instance of the child class and an instance of its superclass invoke different methods, giving rise to different behaviors.
- A subclass may implement one or more methods that its superclass declares but does not implement. In this case, the superclass is an abstract class and those methods it declares without implementing are its abstract methods.

Inheritance is used to create a family of types. The members of the family share the operations defined by the **supertype** at the root of the inheritance hierarchy. Each type in the family is a **subtype** of its supertypes. In Figure 1.6, the `Ellipse` type is a subtype of three types: the `Figure` type, the `Region` type, and its own type (`Ellipse`). All of the types in this figure support the operations defined by their common supertype, `Figure`, and some of the subtypes may support additional operations of their own.

An interface `A` can also serve as the supertype for a family of types. Its subtypes consist of classes that implement `A` and interfaces that extend `A`, plus *their* subtypes. In Figure 1.7, the `Figure` class implements the `Geometry`

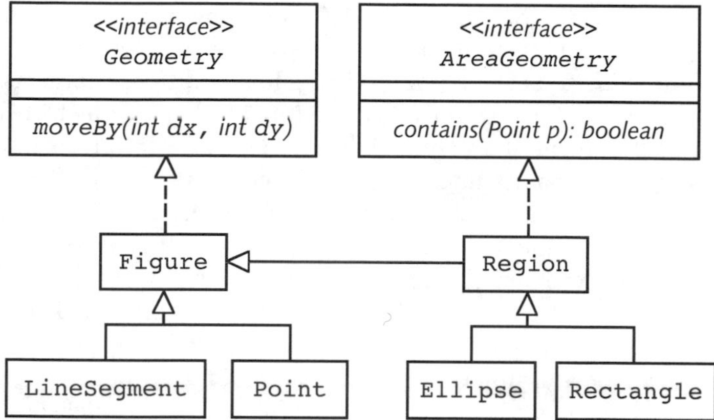

FIGURE 1.7 A class diagram with implementation of interfaces.

interface, which promises the `moveBy` operation for translating a geometry. Every subtype of `Geometry` supports the `moveBy` operation. Similarly, the `Region` class implements the `AreaGeometry` interface, which declares the operation `contains` for deciding whether an area-enclosing geometry contains the input point p. A type presents each of the interfaces promised by its supertypes. Thus an `Ellipse` object can be treated as an ellipse, a region, an area geometry, a figure, or a geometry, depending on the client's needs.

Clients interact with an object through any of the object's supertypes. The supertype defines the object's apparent interface, but the object's actual type determines its behavior. This means that clients can use an object without knowing its actual type, while trusting the object to carry out an appropriate behavior. For example, based on Figure 1.7, a client can handle various kinds of geometries—line segments, points, ellipses, and rectangles—by treating them all as realizations of their common `Geometry` supertype. For example, we can define a procedure that gets called with an array of geometries and the integers `dx` and `dy`, and translates each of the geometries by `dx` along the x axis and `dy` along the y axis:

```
static void translateAll(Geometry[] geometries,
                         int dx, int dy) {
  for (int i = 0; i < geometries.length; i++) {
    Geometry geom = geometries[i];
    geom.moveBy(dx, dy);
  }
}
```

The `translateAll` procedure is able to send the *moveBy* message to the geometry `geom` because `moveBy` is included in the interface of every `Geometry` subtype. Although the actual type of each `geom` is unknown, its behavior is expected to be correct regardless of whether it's a point, rectangle, ellipse, or any other type of geometry. **Polymorphism,** which strictly speaking means *many forms*, is the ability to interchange different objects without affecting clients. In effect, it is a supertype that assumes many forms—a supertype can take the form of any of its various subtypes. In our example, the `Geometry` supertype can assume the form of any of its subtypes.

When inheritance is used to define a new class, the new child class becomes available for use by clients—the software system is extended by a new type. Yet even with the availability of this new class, the system works as it did before. Neither the class' superclass nor clients of this superclass are affected or changed by the introduction of the new subclass. This is a remarkable aspect of inheritance: You can extend or modify a class by subclassing it, yet the class itself remains unaffected. Every class is open for modification through inheritance, yet remains closed and fixed from the viewpoint of its clients. Inheritance permits a class to be reused without affecting the class or any of its dependents.

1.1.11 Design Patterns and Frameworks

Whenever you approach a new programming problem, you bring your experience to bear: You look for similarities to problems you've encountered in the past and attempt to apply solutions that have worked before. In other words, you attempt to reuse good solutions. A design pattern represents a generic solution to a common, recurring problem. The design pattern names and describes the set of software elements that compose the solution and explains how to arrange the software elements. It also describes the class of problems to which the solution applies and the consequences and tradeoffs of applying the solution.

As an example of a design pattern, consider a program that maintains a collection of regions (rectangles and ellipses) and displays them in different ways: in a window that renders them filled, in a second window that renders only their outlines, in a text window that lists each region's dimensions, and so forth. The problem is as follows: Whenever the state of the collection changes—regions are added or removed, or some region in the collection is resized or repositioned—the windows in which they're displayed must be updated. We can use the **observer design pattern** to solve this problem. The collection of regions is known as the **subject,** and the various display windows are its **observers.** Whenever the state of the collection changes, it notifies each of the display windows (its observers) so that each can update itself accordingly. This design pattern minimizes the interdependence (or coupling) between the collection and its observers: The collection knows nothing about how the display windows update themselves. Moreover, new observers can be registered with the collection, and existing observers can be removed, without affecting the collection itself.

Design patterns capture the expertise of the software design community and make successful designs available for reuse. Applications based on design patterns are generally easier to extend, modify, maintain, and understand than those that are not. Design patterns also provide software developers with a shared vocabulary with which to think about and communicate ideas. What results is an evolving catalog of shared patterns representing design solutions to problems that tend to arise again and again.

Like design patterns, **application frameworks,** also known more simply as **frameworks,** are a form of design reuse. A framework is a set of classes and interfaces intended to be extended and implemented in prescribed ways, to serve as the skeleton of an application that the programmer customizes as desired. The goal is to simplify the development of applications in a particular application domain. An example is Java's Abstract Window Toolkit (AWT), Swing, and event model, which together form a framework for developing applications with graphical user interfaces (GUIs). Because frameworks are usually tied to a system or a programming language, they are less abstract than design patterns. However, frameworks are usually large in scope and often contain design patterns as their architectural elements.

Exercises

1.1 When you drive a car, you employ an abstraction that includes the gas pedal, brake pedal, and steering wheel, but not the fuel injectors, engine, and cooling system. However, when your car breaks down, you cope by adopting a different abstraction, one that includes the fuel injectors, engine, cooling system, tires, and other components by which the driver's commands are translated into propulsion. A mechanic's view of a car is useful for repairing a broken car, whereas a driver's view is useful for driving a functioning car. It is common for complex things (such as cars) to admit different abstractions, based on the various ways they are used or understood.

People are viewed by a much wider range of abstractions than cars, perhaps owing to our greater complexity. Consider the behaviors expected of people in a number of different roles: parent, sibling, child, friend, waiter, bank teller, salesperson, or doctor. When you encounter a person in a specific role, do you have certain expectations of how they will behave? Are there certain sets of messages that you are free to send, and other messages that are inappropriate?

1.2 A satire of promotional material for a bank makes this boast: "At our bank, you're not just a number. You're three numbers, followed by a dash, followed by four more numbers, a second dash, and three more numbers." Do you think that people and companies were engaged in "object-oriented thinking" even before there were any object-oriented programming languages? What are some occupations that tend to "objectify" people—the practitioners or those they serve—and how do they do so?

1.3 Why can't we use a circular list in place of a polygon? Can you think of services that a polygon provides that a circular list does not?

1.4 Based on the class diagram of Figure 1.7 and our definition of the `Point` class, write a procedure that takes an array of area geometry objects and a point `p`, and returns `true` if and only if point `p` is contained in every one of the area geometries. The procedure's header looks like this:

```
static boolean
  containsInIntersection(AreaGeometry[] g, Point p)
```

1.2 The Object Model and Other Programming Models

At the beginning of this chapter, I stressed the importance of abstraction for managing the complex task of programming. Few programmers today write programs in machine language, at the level of 0s and 1s. Instead, programming is usually carried out using higher-level programming languages. Each such language employs a set of abstractions known as a **programming model.** The kinds of abstractions supported by a programming model are generally far removed from, and much higher than, the computer's low-level processes, and they are responsible for the programming model's power. Common programming models include the imperative model (exemplified by such languages as C, Pascal, and Fortran), the functional model (Lisp, Scheme, and ML), and the declarative model (Prolog). In this book we study the **object-oriented programming model,** also known more simply as the **object model.** This is the programming model supported by such languages as Simula, Smalltalk, C++, and Java. The remainder of this section summarizes the programming models most widely used today.

Programming models date to the mid-1950s with the advent of Fortran, an example of an imperative programming language. Under the **imperative programming model,** a program consists of a sequence of statements or commands. The execution of each statement changes the state of the computer by modifying the contents of memory locations and by producing other side effects such as reading input and writing output. The execution of a program carries the computer through a series of state changes and side effects.

Imperative languages provide the assignment statement for associating a name (called a variable) with a value. A given variable can be assigned different values at different times. Compound storage structures such as arrays and records (also sometimes known as structures) are also usually supported. Given the importance of the flow of execution, imperative languages usually provide an assortment of control structures. These include sequencing (i.e., do this, then do that), alternation (*if* and *switch* commands), iteration (*for*, *do*, and *while* commands), and recursion (the ability for procedures to call themselves). Imperative languages also allow you to define new procedures and to invoke procedures. Under the imperative model, the emphasis is on describing processes to manipulate data in storage structures. The imperative model is supported by such languages as Fortran, PL/1, Algol, Pascal, and C.

Under the **functional programming model,** also known as the **applicative model,** expressions are evaluated for their value, rather than for their side effects. The functional model treats procedures as abstract functions that map input values to output values. Functional programming dates to the late 1950s with the appearance of Lisp, whose name is an acronym for *LISt Processing language*. Lisp was originally used mainly for artificial intelligence because of its ability to handle symbolic data and to treat programs as data, enabling it to create new programs on the fly. The language is now used in many problem domains and has given rise to numerous derivative languages, notably ML, Scheme, Haskell, and the object-oriented CLOS language. Functional programming languages provide control structures similar to those of imperative languages, but tailored to the definition of expressions. For example, instead of providing an *if* statement, functional languages provide a conditional expression whose value depends on the value of a test expression. Moreover, iteration is usually achieved using recursion. Functional languages also treat procedures as first-class objects, meaning that procedures can be passed as arguments, returned as values, and stored in data structures. This blurs the distinction between procedures and data that is so important in the imperative programming model.

Functional programs are easier to reason about and more amenable to correctness proofs than imperative programs for two reasons: they employ functions, which are well understood by mathematics; and they avoid side effects, which require that one be concerned with the order in which things are done. However, standard versions of Lisp, ML, and Scheme are not purely functional—practicality requires that these languages provide certain operations that entail side effects such as assignment, input, and output.

Under the **declarative model,** also known as the **rule-based programming model,** a program consists of a collection of rules and axioms. A declarative program provides the basic information (axioms) and the means for making inferences (rules), but does not specify *how* to obtain the desired result. In an imperative program, the program's logic is closely linked to the order in which statements are executed. In contrast, the logic in a declarative program is determined by the logical relationships that hold among its axioms and rules. Thus declarative programming achieves a separation between logic and control not possible in imperative programming. The programmer is concerned not with control—the order in which rules should be applied—but with logical relationships. The canonical rule-based programming language is Prolog, used for logic programming. Rule-based languages lack the control structures of imperative languages. Nonetheless, because the structure of a Prolog program affects its efficiency, Prolog provides some control structures for improving performance.

The **object model** represents the problem domain as a collection of objects that collaborate. Java is not the first object-oriented programming language; it is preceded by a number of programming languages also based on the object model. Object-oriented programming originated with the programming language Simula. Developed in Norway in the 1960s to handle simulation problems, Simula borrowed the block structure and control structures from Algol-60 and added support for coroutines. (A coroutine is a procedure that can be stopped and later restarted where it left off.) Simula-67, the successor to Simula, introduced support for classes and objects, but the language never achieved widespread use.

The Smalltalk programming language was developed at Xerox's Palo Alto Research Center in the early 1970s. It was designed from the ground up to be a pure object-oriented language in which everything is an object or a method, with an inheritance hierarchy rooted in a single class. The language is designed to encourage an object-oriented mind-set. In an imperative language, you evaluate the expression `3+4` by adding `3` and `4` to obtain the result `7`. However, in Smalltalk the expression `3+4` is viewed as a message: The object `3` is the receiver, `+` is the message name, and the object `4` is the argument. To evaluate `3+4`, you send the message `+ 4` to the object `3`, thereby obtaining the object `7` as the result. This is an example of a *binary message* expression. Smalltalk defines only two other forms of message expression. A *unary message* is used for messages that take no arguments; for example, the expression `4 factorial` says to send the message `factorial` to the object `4`, thus obtaining the object `24`. A *keyword message* is used for messages whose arguments are identified by keyword. For example, the expression `anArray at: 2 put: 5` is used to put the object `5` at index `2` of the array `anArray`. This message is handled by a method named `at:put:` of `anArray`, and the keywords `at:` and `put:` match the arguments `2` and `5` with the method's parameters.

Smalltalk was intended as a language easy enough to be used not just by professional programmers, but also by nonspecialists and children. The syntax for sending messages and defining methods is straightforward, and the language avoids much of the complexity of other languages (e.g., there is no need for operator precedence and associativity, or for many of the complicated control structures found in imperative languages). As in Java, objects are allocated from the heap and handled through references, and objects are deallocated automatically when they are no longer referenced.

Traditionally, Smalltalk appears as an integrated development environment that includes editor windows, graphics windows, browser windows for exploring the class hierarchy, an interpreter, and other features, all capable of running on a personal computer.

The C++ language, developed by Bjarne Stroustrup at Bell Laboratories in the 1980s, originated with the C programming language. The first step from C to C++ was called C with Classes, a language that blends some of the object-oriented features of Simula with the syntax of C. C with Classes evolved into C++ by adding a mechanism for dynamic method binding (virtual functions), function and operator overloading, and reference types; these first appeared in Release 1.0 of C++ in 1985. Between 1985 and 1990, C++ continued to evolve based in large part on input from users. Release 3.0 of C++, distributed in 1990, included templates and exception handling.

C++ has become a popular language in recent years. Because it is backward compatible with the C language, C programs can be compiled as C++ programs, enabling C programmers to learn and adopt features of C++ at their own pace. Moreover, the syntactic and semantic similarities between the two languages make C++ easier to learn for those who already know C, itself a popular language. C++ has a number of features not found in other object-oriented languages. *Templates* provide a way of defining a type-generic class to serve as the pattern for a family of type-specific classes; for example, you can define a collection template from which can be derived any number of collection classes for storing values of a specific type (e.g., a collection class for storing integers, a collection class for storing points). *Operator overloading* enables you to associate user-defined procedures with a wide range of operators such as +, *, and <. *Multiple inheritance* allows a new class to inherit both implementation and interface from any number of other classes, its parent classes (in contrast, Java supports multiple inheritance of interface but not implementation). C++ is rich with powerful features, but on the downside, it is a complex language that is difficult to use correctly.

Java dates to 1991 when a group of Sun Microsystems engineers led by James Gosling began developing a language for programming consumer devices such as cable TV boxes, VCRs, and microwave ovens. By 1994 the engineers realized that their evolving language possessed the properties of a good Internet language—it is object-oriented, secure, architecture-neutral, interpreted, and multithreaded. They used Java to develop a Web browser called HotJava, first demonstrated publicly in 1995. When released by Sun in late 1995, Java was primarily used to create applets, small programs that can be embedded in Web pages and executed by browsers. However, in the years since its introduction, Java has become a first-class programming language used in a wide range of systems, from embedded devices through large-scale applications. The most recent version, Java 2, was released in 1999 and includes new features such as Java 2D for two-dimensional graphics, of which we make use in this book.

One reason for Java's widespread adoption is its platform independence, captured by the phrase *write once, run everywhere*. When Java code is compiled, the resulting executable is a set of instructions in **Java bytecode**. This is the language processed by the Java interpreter, also known as **Java Virtual Machine (JVM).** Java executables can run on any machine for which a JVM has been developed. Because JVMs have been written for all popular operating systems, compiled programs can be posted on the Internet and then downloaded and executed on all common platforms, making Java a near-universal language for sharing dynamic content across the Internet. Moreover, because Java includes an extensive set of standard classes, many or most of the classes a Java program requires will already reside on the local machine executing the program. To share a Java program, it is not necessary to transfer all the classes that compose the program, but only those classes that account for the program's distinctiveness. A small Java program can pack a big punch.

CHAPTER

2

Procedural Abstraction

Procedures are important for two reasons. First, because methods are procedures associated with objects, one cannot fully understand objects without understanding procedures. Second, there are many kinds of problems that are best solved by means of the imperative programming model, under which a procedure carries out a computation by executing instructions and calling other procedures in a well-defined order.

In this chapter we turn to a form of abstraction shared by all programming languages that support the creation and use of procedures. Procedural abstraction presents a procedure as an abstract operation. What remains hidden by this abstraction is the procedure's implementation. Procedural abstraction focuses on what procedures do while ignoring how they do it.

In Section 2.1, we'll consider the primary benefit of procedural abstraction, that it permits procedures to be viewed as abstract operations. Section 2.2 introduces a notation for describing abstract operations, and Section 2.3 explores Java's exception mechanism (the exceptions that a procedure may throw is part of the procedure's specification). The remainder of this chapter covers two important methods made possible by procedural abstraction—a discipline for program development known as procedural decomposition (Section 2.4), and the programming technique of recursion (Section 2.5).

2.1 Abstract Operations and Procedures

A procedure can be viewed in two ways. First, a procedure represents an **abstract operation** that takes inputs and produces outputs and side effects. Second, a procedure describes a **computational process,** the steps by which the operation does whatever it does. These two views of a procedure are closely related: The computational process *implements* the abstract operation.

The definition of a procedure provides both views of the procedure at once. For example, consider the following definition of the procedure `square` for squaring positive integers:

```
static int square(int k) {
  return k * k;
}
```

On the one hand, this procedure definition describes an abstract operation. The operation takes a single input—a positive integer—and returns the square of its input value. On the other hand, the procedure definition describes a process for carrying out this operation: Given the input number k, multiply k by itself and return the result. In short, a procedure definition describes both what the procedure does (the abstract operation it promises) as well as how it does it (its implementation).

Procedural abstraction views a procedure as an abstract operation while hiding the computational process it describes. This is the appropriate view of a procedure from the perspective of clients that call it. What the procedure *does* is essential to the client for its own correctness, whereas *how* it does it is not relevant. Consider a simple example. The Pythagorean Theorem is well known: In a right triangle with legs of length a and b, the length c of the hypotenuse is given by the formula $c = \sqrt{a^2 + b^2}$. The following procedure uses this formula to compute the length of the hypotenuse of a right triangle with legs of integer length `a` and `b`:

```
static double hypotenuse(int a, int b) {
  int c2 = square(a) + square(b);
  return Math.sqrt(c2);    // returns the square root of c2
}
```

The implementation of the `hypotenuse` procedure depends on the operation promised by procedure `square`, but it does not depend on how `square` was implemented. Procedure `square` can be implemented as given earlier:

```
// version 1
static int square(int k) {
  return k * k;
}
```

Alternatively, the procedure can be implemented less efficiently but just as correctly like this:

```
// version 2
static int square(int k) {
  int res = 0;
  for (int i = 0; i < k; i++)
    res += k;
  return res;
}
```

The `square` procedure can also be implemented thus:

```
// version 3
static int square(int k) {
  float s = (float)Math.exp(2.0 * Math.log(k));
  return Math.round(s);
}
```

All three versions of `square` represent the same abstract operation—when called with a positive integer, each returns its input squared. Moreover, the correctness of any procedure that depends on `square` is unaffected by the version of `square` it uses; whichever version of `square` it uses, the procedure `hypotenuse` represents the same abstract operation.

Procedural abstraction offers two key advantages. First, by thinking of procedures as abstract operations, programmers may use them without knowing how the procedures are implemented. The procedures may be programmed at some other time or by some other person, or perhaps they belong to a library. In the case of procedure `hypotenuse`, the program could be written without knowledge of how the procedure `square` was implemented. This example might seem trite because procedure `square` admits a simple implementation. However, procedure hypotenuse also invokes the square-root-finding procedure `java.lang.Math.sqrt`. Here procedural abstraction comes in handy, sparing us the trouble of having to code our procedure for calculating square-roots or to understand how Java's version works.

A second advantage of procedural abstraction lies in the fact that the implementation of a procedure can be changed without affecting programs that use the procedure *as long as the abstract operation is held fixed*. Clients of the procedure depend on the operation it promises but not on its implementation. Consider procedure `hypotenuse`'s use of the procedure `square`. If we change the implementation of procedure `square` from (say) version 1 to version 2, `hypotenuse` remains correct. This is because both versions of procedure `square` represent the same abstract operation even though their implementations differ.

I have said that under procedural abstraction, a procedure is viewed as an abstract operation, a sort of "black box" that takes inputs and produces outputs and/or side effects. What is the best way to describe the abstract operation that a procedure represents?

One way is to supply the procedure's complete definition. After all, the implementation reveals what the procedure does. However, the implementation might be hard to understand—it might be complex and difficult, and it might rely on other procedures and objects that in turn must be understood. Moreover, the procedure definition might not be available. In any case, because one benefit of procedural abstraction is that the implementation remains hidden, one would expect there are ways of describing abstract operations that conceal implementation.

A better way to describe an abstract operation is to specify the range of inputs it takes and the output and side effects it produces in response to every possible input. Here is such a description for the procedure `square`:

```
static int square(int k)
  // input:  a positive integer k
  // output: an integer denoting k squared
```

The result of an operation might involve a side effect, such as reading from or writing to a stream, or modifying the state of some object. Here is an example of a procedure whose side effect is to write to the standard output stream:

```
static void printSquare(int k) {
  // input: a positive integer k
  // side effect: prints k squared
  //   to the standard output stream
  System.out.print(square(k));
}
```

And here is an example of a procedure whose side effect is to modify the state of the object it gets called with. The procedure `translate1` takes a point `p` and two integers `dx` and `dy`, and translates `p` by `dx` units along the x axis and `dy` units along the y axis:

```
static void translate1(Point p, int dx, int dy) {
  // input: a nonnull point p, and two integers dx and dy
  // side effect: translates point p by dx and dy
  p.setX(p.getX() + dx);
  p.setY(p.getY() + dy);
}
```

Procedure `translate1` has the side effect of changing the coordinates of its input point `p`, but returns no value. For example:

```
Point p = new Point(2, 3);
translate1(p, 4, 5);
System.out.println("p: " + p);     // p: (6,8)
```

It is important to be clear about the difference between return values and side effects. These are two different ways by which the action of a procedure is communicated to the rest of a program. In the case of a returned value, the using code receives a value back from the procedure it calls, often capturing this value in a variable. In the case of a side effect, the state of one or more objects is changed by the action of the procedure. In contrast to procedure `translate1`, the following procedure, `translate2`, is called with a point `p` and integers `dx` and `dy` and returns a new point that is equal to `p` translated by `dx` and `dy`. Point `p` is not affected by the operation:

```
static Point translate2(Point p, int dx, int dy) {
  // input: a nonnull point p, and two integers dx and dy
  // output: returns a new point equal
  //   to (p.getX()+dx, p.getY()+dy)
  int x = p.getX() + dx;
  int y = p.getY() + dy;
  Point q = new Point(x, y);
  return q;
}
```

Procedure `translate2` returns a value but produces no side effects. Although it constructs and returns a new point object, the procedure does not modify the state of any existing object; in particular, it does not change the state of its argument `p`. In contrast, procedure `translate1` has the side effect of changing the state of its argument `p` but returns no value. Here is a code fragment that demonstrates the two procedures:

```
Point p = new Point(2, 3);
Point q = translate2(p, 1, 2);
System.out.println("p: " + p);                    // p: (2,3)
System.out.println("q: " + q);                    // q: (3,5)
translate1(p, 4, 5);
System.out.println("p: " + p);                    // p: (6,8)
```

Exercises

2.1 It is certainly possible for a procedure to both return a value and cause side effects. Implement the following procedure:

```
static Point translate3(Point p,
                        int dx, int dy)
  // input: a nonnull point p, and
  //   integers dx and dy
  // side effect: translates p by dx and dy
  // output: point p after it is translated
```

2.2 Add the following two methods to the `Point` class of Chapter 1. The first method translates this point by its two inputs *dx* and *dy*. The second method computes the distance between this point and its input point:

```
// methods of Point class
public void translate(int dx, int dy)
  // side effect: translates this point by dx and dy

public double distance(Point p)
  // input: a nonnull point p
  // output: distance between this point and point p
```

You can test your methods using a short program such as this:

```
public class TryNewPointMethods {
  public static void main(String[] args) {
    Point p = new Point();
    Point q = new Point(p);
    q.translate(3, 4);
    System.out.println("q: " + q);
    System.out.println("dist: "+ p.distance(q));
  }
}
```

2.2 Specifying Procedures

The specification of a procedure describes the procedure's behavior, independent of its implementation. The specification spells out the terms of an agreement between the procedure and its clients. In the case of procedure `square`:

```
static int square(int k)
  // input:  a positive integer k
  // output: an integer denoting k squared
```

clients promise to call `square` with a positive value of type `int`. In response, the procedure `square` promises to return an integer equal to its input value squared.

The terms of this agreement are governed by a set of conditions known as the procedure's **preconditions** and **postconditions.** The preconditions are the requirements that any client invoking the procedure is expected to satisfy. The postconditions are the conditions that the procedure guarantees upon completion, provided that the client has satisfied the preconditions.

To indicate a procedure's preconditions and postconditions, we provide a specification comment following the procedure's header. The comment consists of up to three clauses:

- The **requires clause** states the procedure's preconditions, those conditions that using code is expected to satisfy.
- The **modifies clause** lists the names of objects that are modified by the procedure. These names are often inputs to the procedure, but more generally they include any element whose state the procedure may change.
- The **effects clause** describes the procedure's behavior on any input not ruled out by the requires clause. This clause relates the procedure's postconditions to its legal inputs, but says nothing about the procedure's behavior when the requires clause is not satisfied.

The requires clause is omitted if the procedure's preconditions are vacuously true (that is, when any input with which the procedure may be called is legal). The modifies clause is omitted whenever the procedure produces no side effects. Because every useful procedure effects some change, the effects clause should generally be present. Let's look at some examples that use this notation.

In the case of procedure `square`, the precondition is that the procedure is called with a positive value of type `int`, and the postcondition is that it returns an `int` equal to the input value squared. The input and return types are indicated by the procedure header, but the comments should at least convey the remaining aspects of the procedure's preconditions and postconditions:

```
static int square(int k)
  // REQUIRES: k is positive.
  // EFFECTS: Returns k squared.
```

As another example, here is the definition for procedure `translate1` presented near the end of the previous section:

```
static void translate1(Point p, int dx, int dy) {
  // REQUIRES: p is not null.
  // MODIFIES: p
  // EFFECTS: Translates p; that is,
  //    p_post==(p.getX()+dx, p.getY()+dy).
  p.setX(p.getX() + dx);
  p.setY(p.getY() + dy);
}
```

In the effects clause, `p_post` refers to the state of point `p` when the procedure returns, and `p` refers to its state when the procedure is called.

Here I repeat the definition of procedure `translate2` and include its specification comments:

```
static Point translate2(Point p, int dx, int dy) {
  // REQUIRES: p is not null.
  // EFFECTS: Returns a new point q
  //   where q==(p.getX()+dx, p.getY()+dy).
  int x = p.getX() + dx;
  int y = p.getY() + dy;
  Point q = new Point(x, y);
  return q;
}
```

Procedure `translate2` does not have a modifies clause because it doesn't modify the state of the input point p or any other object.

Procedure `translate3` is similar to `translate1` except that it also returns the now-translated point:

```
static Point translate3(Point p, int dx, int dy) {
  // REQUIRES: p is not null.
  // MODIFIES: p
  // EFFECTS: Returns p_post where p_post is
  //   p translated by dx and dy:
  //   p_post == (p.getX()+dx, p.getY()+dy).
  p.setX(p.getX() + dx);
  p.setY(p.getY() + dy);
  return p;
}
```

The specifications for `translate1`, `translate2`, and `translate3` should bear out that these procedures, although similar, exhibit distinct behaviors.

We'll see in the next chapter that procedural abstraction plays an important role in the object model. A client calls a procedure by sending a message to an object. The client uses the procedure as an abstract operation—a mapping of inputs to outputs and side effects. The operation is described by the procedure's requires, modifies, and effects clauses. Yet the client does not know *how* the operation is implemented. In fact, it is not even strictly correct to say that a client calls an object's procedures at all. When a client sends a message to an object, it does not in general know what method will be invoked in response.

Using procedural abstraction, the methods supplied by an object are viewed by the object's clients as abstract operations. By annotating each method with a requires, modifies, and effects clause, the method is described as an abstract operation. We will use this specification device throughout the book, including when we turn to the specification of a class' methods in the next chapter.

2.2.1 Making Assertions

Viewed as an abstract operation, a procedure represents a **contract** between the procedure and its callers. The preconditions and postconditions jointly spell out the terms of this contract. The preconditions, as specified by the requires clause, describe the callers' obligations. The postconditions describe the procedure's obligations assuming that the callers' obligations were satisfied. The effects clause describes these obligations as a function of all legal inputs. Postconditions often entail side effects, and the modifies clause lists the objects whose state may be modified by side effects.

Because the contractual view of a procedure call delineates responsibilities, it is possible to identify who is at fault when an error occurs. Consider what happens when a client calls a procedure. If the client violates any of the preconditions, it is at fault; however, if the client satisfies all the preconditions but the procedure fails to establish all of the postconditions, the procedure is at fault. For instance, a client that makes the procedure call

```
square(-2);
```

is at fault for passing a negative number, in violation of this procedure's precondition. However, if the call

```
square(4);
```

returns the value 7, the procedure `square` is at fault for not establishing its postcondition when its preconditions were met.

This observation leads to the debugging practice of **making assertions,** whereby a procedure's preconditions and postconditions are checked as part of its implementation. (More generally, an **assertion** is an expression that checks that a specific condition is satisfied.) Whenever an assertion is reached, the program in effect asserts that some condition should hold and produces an error if the condition does not hold. Here is a version of our `translate2` procedure that includes assertions for its preconditions and postconditions:

```
static Point translate2(Point p, int dx, int dy) {
  // REQUIRES: p is not null.
  // EFFECTS: Returns a new point q,
  //   where q==(p.getX()+dx,p.getY()+dy).
  Assert.pre(p != null, "argument p is null");
  int x = p.getX() + dx;
  int y = p.getY() + dy;
  Point q = new Point(x, y);
  Assert.post(q.getX() == p.getX()+dx,
             "result not translated by dx");
  Assert.post(q.getY() == p.getY()+dy,
             "result not translated by dy");
  return q;
}
```

If procedure `translate2` is called with a null first argument in violation of its requires clause, the `Assert.pre` method throws a new exception object (exceptions will be covered in the next section). The exception object contains an error message, a string describing the error. If the thrown exception is not caught, the Java interpreter prints the exception's error message and a trace of the call stack, and then exits. For example, the following instruction:

```
translate2(null, 2, 3);
```

produces the following message in my console window:

```
> java TryAssertions
Exception in thread "main" banana.FailedConditionException:
    precondition failed: argument p is not null
        at banana.Assert.pre(Assert.java:9)
        at TryAssertions.translate2(TryAssertions.java:12)
        at TryAssertions.main(TryAssertions.java:8)
```

The fact that the precondition failed tells us that the client is at fault.

Alternatively, suppose that our implementation of `translate2` were buggy; suppose, for example, that the statement declaring and initializing the variable `y` was mistakenly coded thus:

```
int y = p.getY() * dy;
```

Then, in response to the legal instruction

```
translate2(new Point(2, 3), 4, 5);
```

the interpreter produces an error message that includes the following line:

```
postcondition failed: result not translated by dy
```

Because the postcondition failed, we would know procedure `translate2` to be incorrect.

The `Assert` class assumed in this brief example defines the static methods `pre` and `post` for asserting preconditions and postconditions, respectively. The `pre` method is called with two arguments: a Boolean expression representing a precondition, and a string *msg*. If the Boolean expression evaluates to `true`, the method does nothing; however, if it evaluates to `false`, indicating that the precondition failed, the method throws an instance of the `FailedConditionException` class. This exception object includes a string describing the error. Similar remarks apply to the `Assert.post` method for checking postconditions. The `Assert` class also defines a `condition` method for checking generic conditions. Here is the class definition:

```
public class Assert {
  public static void pre(boolean test, String msg)
         throws FailedConditionException {
    // REQUIRES: msg is not null.
    // EFFECTS: If test is false
    //   throws FailedConditionException
    //   indicating the failed precondition.
```

```
      if (!test) {
        String s = "precondition failed: " + msg;
        throw new FailedConditionException(s);
      }
    }

    public static void post(boolean test, String msg)
          throws FailedConditionException {
      // REQUIRES: msg is not null.
      // EFFECTS: If test is false
      //    throws FailedConditionException
      //    indicating the failed postcondition.
      if (!test) {
        String s = "postcondition failed: " + msg;
        throw new FailedConditionException(s);
      }
    }

    public static void condition(boolean test, String msg)
          throws FailedConditionException {
      // EFFECTS: If test is false
      //    throws FailedConditionException
      //    indicating the failed condition.
      if (!test) {
        String s = "condition failed: " + msg;
        throw new FailedConditionException(s);
      }
    }
  }
```

Here is the definition of the `FailedConditionException` class:

```
public class FailedConditionException
     extends RuntimeException {
  public FailedConditionException(String msg) {
     super(msg); }
  public FailedConditionException() { }
}
```

Making assertions is quite helpful for debugging. However, their use results in more lines of code and slightly less efficient programs, although assertions can be removed when debugging is complete. Because formal assertions often explain (to the human reader) a procedure's behavior no more clearly than comments written in English and pseudo-code, we will not include assertions in the code presented in this book. Nonetheless, you may wish to use the `Assert` class while debugging your own programs.

2.3 Exceptions

Including assertions in the body of your procedures is a generic approach to detecting errors. When an asserted condition fails, the *type* of object that gets thrown is always the same—an instance of the `FailedConditionException` class. Although the string associated with the `FailedConditionException` object says something about the violation (such as whether it involved a precondition or a postcondition), the exception object's *type* says nothing about the specific error. Moreover, there may be information relevant to the failed condition, but the `FailedConditionException` class provides no fields for storing such information.

Java provides a much more general **exception mechanism** for handling errors and exceptions. An exception is a condition that is unusual yet is expected to arise in some situations. Examples of exceptions include trying to open a file that doesn't exist, reading past the end of a file, dividing by zero, or dereferencing a `null` reference. Java's exception mechanism allows code to both detect and handle exceptions, without cluttering the code for "normal" processing that occurs in the absence of any exceptions.

Exception handling is accomplished by **throwing** and **catching** exceptions. An exception is thrown whenever an unusual condition occurs. What gets thrown, in fact, is an object that encapsulates information describing the exception. The object's type is dictated by the nature of the exception. There are two ways in which exceptions are thrown: by a `throw` statement within some procedure, or by the Java interpreter when an illegal low-level operation is attempted.

When a procedure or operation throws an exception, the invoking code may catch the exception and handle it. Alternatively, the code may allow the exception to propagate up the procedure invocation stack, allowing other calling procedures the opportunity to handle the exception. If the exception is not caught at all, it is trapped by the Java interpreter which usually responds by halting execution and printing useful error information.

Throwing an exception is part of a procedure's specification, as much so as returning a value or causing a side effect. Just as a procedure's return type is declared by the procedure's header and explained by its effects clause, so must the types of exceptions that the procedure may throw. The exceptions that a procedure may throw are indicated in two places: in the `throws` clause of the procedure's header and in the effects clause of its specification comment. For example, here is the specification of a procedure for translating points:

```
static void translate4(Point p, int dx, int dy)
       throws NullPointerException
  // MODIFIES: p
  // EFFECTS: If p is null throws NullPointerException;
  //  else translates p by dx and dy:
  //   p_post==(p.getX()+dx,p.getY()+dy).
```

The procedure `translate4` throws a `NullPointerException` whenever it is called with a `null` first argument. Importantly, this behavior is described by its specification. Procedure `translate4` is similar to procedure `translate1` of the previous section in that both procedures translate the input point `p` by the input values `dx` and `dy`. However, they differ in that the precondition for `translate1`—that `p` is not `null`—does not apply to `translate4`. It is perfectly legal for code to call `translate4` with a `null` first argument. When this occurs, `translate4` responds by throwing an object of type `NullPointerException`. By catching this exception, the calling code can detect that this has occurred and can respond accordingly.

When a procedure may throw more than one type of exception, the procedure's effects clause should describe the conditions for which each type is thrown. Also, the header's `throws` clause should list the types of exceptions referred to in the effects clause. Here is the specification for a procedure that finds the position of some smallest integer in an array of integers:

```
static int min(int[] a)
       throws ZeroArraySizeException,
              NullPointerException
  // EFFECTS: If a is null throws NullPointerException;
  //    else if a has size zero throws
  //    ZeroArraySizeException; else returns the index
  //    of some smallest item in a.
```

2.3.1 Checked and Unchecked Exceptions

The `NullPointerException` is one of many exception classes predefined by Java, all of which belong to the class hierarchy pictured in Figure 2.1. At the root of this hierarchy lies the `java.lang.Throwable` class, which represents

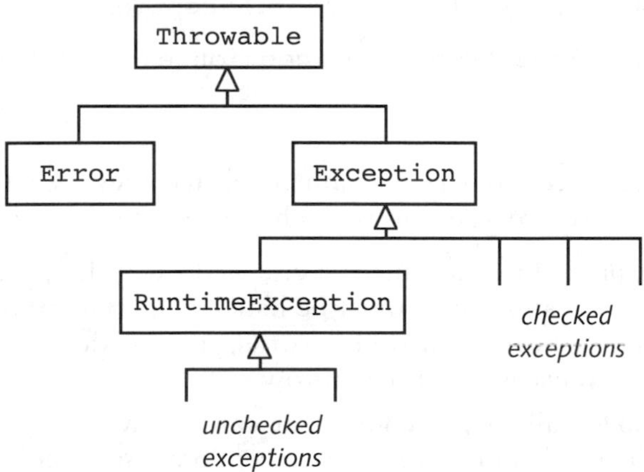

FIGURE 2.1 Subtypes of `RuntimeException` are unchecked; all other exceptions are checked.

the supertype of all objects—both errors and exceptions—capable of being thrown. Subclasses of the `Error` class represent errors involving the Java interpreter or resource insufficiencies; your programs should never need to throw these types of objects. Of the subtypes of the `Exception` class, Java distinguishes between **checked exceptions** and **unchecked exceptions.** Specifically, subtypes of `RuntimeException` are unchecked exceptions, whereas all other subtypes of `Exception` are checked exceptions.

Unchecked exceptions generally result from programming errors. Examples include arithmetic exceptions such as dividing by zero (`ArithmeticException`), attempting to index an array out of bounds (`ArrayIndexOutOfBounds`), attempting to parse a badly formed string as a number (`NumberFormatException`), and using `null` when a valid object reference is expected (`NullPointerException`). To define a class representing a new unchecked exception, you extend the `RuntimeException` class. Recall how we defined the `FailedConditionException` class, instances of which are thrown by the static methods of the `Assert` class (Section 2.2.1):

```
public class FailedConditionException
       extends RuntimeException {
  public FailedConditionException (String msg) {
    super(msg); }
  public FailedConditionException () { }
}
```

Checked exceptions represent situations that are due in part to the environment and are therefore beyond your program's control, but to which your program can respond intelligently. Examples include reading past the end of a file (`EOFException`), trying to open a file that can't be found (`FileNotFoundException`), and trying to open a badly formed URL (`MalformedURLException`). To define a class representing a new checked exception, you extend the `java.lang.Exception` class:

```
public class MyCheckedException extends Exception {
  ...
}
```

Checked exceptions are so named because they are checked by the compiler. There are two rules for using checked exceptions:

- If a procedure can throw a checked exception, the exception's type (or some supertype) must be listed in the `throws` clause of the procedure's header. In other words, a procedure must declare every checked exception it may throw.
- If code calls a procedure that can throw a checked exception, the calling code must handle the exception: it must either catch the exception, or declare its type as one that it may itself throw.

The compiler reports an error if these rules are not followed. However, these rules are relaxed in the case of unchecked exceptions: A procedure may *optionally* declare any unchecked exceptions it throws, and code may *optionally* handle any unchecked exceptions it produces.

My policy will be to declare every exception—whether checked or unchecked—that has a role in a procedure's specification. In other words, if the exception is mentioned in a procedure's effects clause, I will declare it in the procedure's `throws` clause.

2.3.2 Throwing Exceptions

To throw an exception, you use a `throw` statement where the argument is an instance of some subtype of the Exception class. For example:

```
throw new FileNotFoundException();
```

Exceptions are often created with an error message, a string that describes the exception:

```
throw new FileNotFoundException("cannot find file "+file);
```

where the string `file` is the file's name. To obtain an exception object's error message, you send it the *getMessage* message.

The static methods of the `Assert` class are examples of procedures that throw exceptions. The following implementation of the `translate4` procedure is another example:

```
static void translate4(Point p, int dx, int dy)
       throws NullPointerException {
  // MODIFIES: p
  // EFFECTS: If p is null throws NullPointerException;
  //    else translates p:
  //    p_post==(p.getX()+dx, p.getY()+dy).
  if (p == null) throw new NullPointerException();
  p.setX(p.getX() + dx);
  p.setY(p.getY() + dy);
}
```

2.3.3 Catching Exceptions

Exceptions are caught and handled using `try` blocks and `catch` blocks. Code that may result in exceptions is enclosed by a `try` block. Code for handling each type of possible exception is enclosed in any number of `catch` blocks that follow the `try` block. For example, the following code fragment attempts to parse the string `s` as an integer:

```
// string s is expected to denote a signed decimal integer
try {
  int i = Integer.parseInt(s);
} catch (NumberFormatException e) {
```

```
    // handle number format exception here
    ...
  }
```

If the string `s` is badly formed, the call to procedure `Integer.parseInt` throws a `NumberFormatException`. The thrown exception object is trapped by the `catch` block and bound to the `catch` block's parameter `e`, and then the `catch` block executes. Within the `catch` block, the thrown exception can be referenced through the parameter `e`.

Any number of `catch` blocks can follow a `try` block. When an exception is thrown, the catch blocks are examined from first to last, and the first one whose parameter can receive the exception is executed. Specifically, the rules of polymorphic assignment are assumed—if the `catch` block's parameter is of the same type or a supertype of the thrown exception, it executes. Here is an example involving two `catch` clauses, using the `min` procedure specified near the start of Section 2.3:

```
// a is an array of ints
try {
  int indx = min(a);
} catch (NullPointerException e) {
  // handle case where a is null
  ...
} catch (ZeroArraySizeException e) {
  // handle case where a has length zero
  ...
}
```

Only the first `catch` clause able to receive an exception executes; later `catch` clauses do not execute even if they too are able to receive the exception. If no `catch` clause can receive the thrown exception, the exception passes to the calling method to check whether *it* provides a suitable `catch` clause. In general, the exception propagates up the **call stack,** the sequence of method activations ordered from the current method to the first method invocation. Each method in turn is given an opportunity to catch the exception until one does so; if no method catches the exception, it passes to the Java virtual machine.

2.3.4 Handling Exceptions

When an exception occurs, the calling procedure can handle the exception in either of two ways. The first is to allow the exception to propagate. In this case, the exception must be declared as one that the calling procedure itself may throw (at least in the case of checked exceptions). The following procedure has the same specification as procedure `translate4` but a slightly different implementation: the `throw` statement that appears in `translate4` is omitted from the following implementation:

```
static void translate5(Point p, int dx, int dy)
      throws NullPointerException {
  // MODIFIES: p
  // EFFECTS: If p is null throws NullPointerException;
  //   else translates p:
  //   p_post==(p.getX()+dx, p.getY()+dy).
  p.setX(p.getX() + dx);
  p.setY(p.getY() + dy);
}
```

When procedure `translate5` is called with a `null` first argument, the first instruction causes the variable `p`, whose value is `null`, to be dereferenced illegally. In response, the Java interpreter throws a `NullPointerException`. Because `translate5` does not catch this exception, the exception propagates to *its* caller. Note that `translate5` declares `NullPointerException` in its `throws` clause and explains it in its effects clause.

The second way for code to handle an exception is to catch it using Java's `try` and `catch` block mechanism. In this case, the code that may throw the exception is enclosed in a `try` block, and the exception-handling code is placed in one of the `catch` blocks that follow. The exception-handling code can respond in either of two ways. First, after taking possible actions, it throws an exception object of its own, which may be either the same one it caught or a new exception object it constructs. Second, the exception-handling code may take actions that fully resolve the problem, making it unnecessary for it to throw an exception of its own.

Here is an example of the first sort, that of a procedure that catches an exception and responds by throwing an exception of its own. The following procedure translates every point in an array of points:

```
static void translatePoints1(Point[] points, int dx, int dy)
  throws NullPointerException, IllegalArgumentException {
  // MODIFIES: points
  // EFFECTS: If points is null throws
  //   NullPointerException; else if
  //   points[i] is null for some i throws
  //   IllegalArgumentException; else translates each
  //   points[i] by dx and dy.
  if (points == null) throw new NullPointerException();
  try {
    for (int i = 0; i < points.length; i++)
      translate5(points[i], dx, dy);
  } catch (NullPointerException e) {
    throw new IllegalArgumentException();
  }
}
```

The *for* loop that repeatedly calls `translate5` appears within a try block. Whenever `translate5` is called with the value `null`, it throws a `NullPointerException`. This causes execution to exit the enclosing `try` block and to resume in the sole `catch` block, where the parameter `e` is bound to the thrown exception object. The body of this `catch` block constructs and throws a new exception of type `IllegalArgumentException`.

The second way a procedure can handle an exception is by taking a rectifying action. The following procedure translates every point in an array of points by `dx` and `dy`. However, unlike the previous example, each `points[i]` that is `null` is set to a new point (`dx,dy`). Here is the procedure:

```
static void translatePoints2(Point[] points, int dx, int dy)
  throws NullPointerException {
  // MODIFIES: points
  // EFFECTS: If points is null throws
  //   NullPointerException; else for
  //   each i, if points[i] is null sets
  //   points[i] to new Point(dx,dy), else translates
  //   points[i] by dx and dy.
  if (points == null) throw new NullPointerException();
  for (int i = 0; i < points.length; i++) {
    try {
      translate5(points[i], dx, dy);
    } catch (NullPointerException e) {
      pcints[i] = new Point(dx, dy);
    }
  }
}
```

2.3.5 Using Exceptions

Besides throwing and catching exceptions, there are two other ways for code to identify and handle problems. First, a procedure can return a special value to indicate that an exception has occurred and use different special values to indicate the nature of the exception. Second, a procedure can set a flag that is visible to its clients. Indeed, both approaches have been used for decades and are even necessary when programming in languages that lack a specific exception mechanism. Yet Java's exception mechanism has several advantages, not least being that it allows us to describe a procedure's "normal" processing separate from its "exceptional" processing. Enclosing the code for normal processing in a `try` block distinguishes it from the exception-handling code that appears in the `catch` blocks that follow.

Two schools of thought exist on the use of exceptions in error checking. The practice of defensive programming recommends that methods check that they are used correctly, wherever practical. Specifically, when a method is called, it tests whether its requires clause is satisfied and, if not, throws an appropriate exception. This approach helps in debugging for it detects errors close to the point of their occurrence. It also provides a safety net for clients that may use a method incorrectly.

A second school of thought counsels programming strictly to the specification. In this view, a method throws exceptions only according to its specification, but takes no specific action if its requires clause is violated. This places the burden of satisfying requirements squarely on the client. There are several arguments for this approach. First, error checking takes time and, in cases where the client guarantees the preconditions (as will be the case if the program is correct), this extra time is wasted. Second, defensive programming may encourage laziness in the clients' authors if they believe that whenever they use a procedure in error, the procedure will, in a sense, catch the problem. Perhaps most importantly, throwing exceptions when a method detects that its preconditions have not been satisfied violates the spirit of the method's specifications. Throwing exceptions is part of a procedure's repertoire of actions it may take when its requires clause is satisfied. For debugging, it is fine to include assertions to test preconditions, but ultimately a procedure guarantees certain behaviors only when its preconditions are met.

This might suggest that it is best to design procedures whose requires clauses are vacuously true, to minimize the burden on clients and to maximize error-checking performed by the procedure. To the contrary, it is often useful to require strict preconditions. This is the case, for instance, when a procedure is designed for use in a context known to guarantee the preconditions. It also often happens that by requiring certain preconditions, it is possible to improve a procedure's performance. The key point is that exception throwing is part of the behavior guaranteed by a procedure, and such behavior is meaningful only when the procedure's requires clause is satisfied.

Exercises

2.3 Supply specification comments—requires, modifies, and effects clauses—for the following Java procedures. Each of the classes whose methods follow belongs to the `java.lang` package, except for the `java.util.Arrays` class. In the case of instance methods (those not declared `static`), your comments may include the term *this* to refer to the current object whose method is invoked (class methods, which are declared `static`, have no current object).

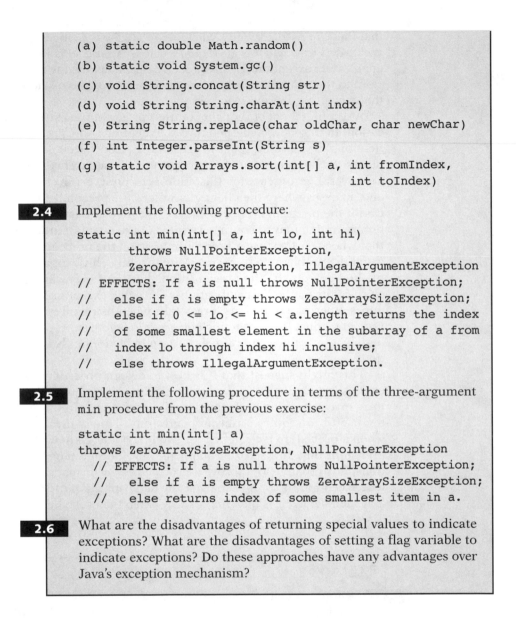

```
(a) static double Math.random()
(b) static void System.gc()
(c) void String.concat(String str)
(d) void String String.charAt(int indx)
(e) String String.replace(char oldChar, char newChar)
(f) int Integer.parseInt(String s)
(g) static void Arrays.sort(int[] a, int fromIndex,
                                     int toIndex)
```

2.4 Implement the following procedure:

```
static int min(int[] a, int lo, int hi)
        throws NullPointerException,
        ZeroArraySizeException, IllegalArgumentException
// EFFECTS: If a is null throws NullPointerException;
//   else if a is empty throws ZeroArraySizeException;
//   else if 0 <= lo <= hi < a.length returns the index
//   of some smallest element in the subarray of a from
//   index lo through index hi inclusive;
//   else throws IllegalArgumentException.
```

2.5 Implement the following procedure in terms of the three-argument `min` procedure from the previous exercise:

```
static int min(int[] a)
throws ZeroArraySizeException, NullPointerException
  // EFFECTS: If a is null throws NullPointerException;
  //   else if a is empty throws ZeroArraySizeException;
  //   else returns index of some smallest item in a.
```

2.6 What are the disadvantages of returning special values to indicate exceptions? What are the disadvantages of setting a flag variable to indicate exceptions? Do these approaches have any advantages over Java's exception mechanism?

2.4 Procedural Decomposition

Procedural decomposition, also known as **top-down structured design** and **stepwise refinement,** is a time-honored discipline for designing computer programs. It is the foremost design method for imperative programming languages such as C and Pascal. Because object-oriented languages such as Java also rely on procedures, procedural decomposition also plays an important role in object-oriented programming.

Given a problem to be solved, the idea is to subdivide the problem into subproblems that can be solved separately, and then combine the solutions to these subproblems into a solution to the original problem. The subproblems are themselves subject to the same process: they too are subdivided into subproblems, resulting in a hierarchy of subproblems. The subdivision process continues to the level of subproblems that are simple enough to be solved directly.

Mirroring this hierarchy of problems is a hierarchy of procedures. The main procedure where execution begins solves the original problem for which the program was designed. To do so, the main procedure calls other procedures that solve subproblems, the solutions to which, when combined, yield a solution to the original problem. The procedures called by the main program, in turn, call additional procedures that solve smaller problems. Each level of the hierarchy uses procedures at the next lower level as abstract operations. Procedural abstraction provides a view of what operations each level supports, while hiding how these operations are implemented in terms of operations supplied by even lower levels.

The rest of this section is devoted to an extended example. We will use procedural decomposition to develop a program named `SortIntegerArgs` that is called with integer program arguments and prints these arguments in nondecreasing sorted order. Here is the program in action, where user input is in bold:

```
> java SortIntegerArgs 6 4 2 3 9 34 8 26 4 1 7
1 2 3 4 4 6 7 8 9 26 34
```

The procedural decomposition of a program can be illustrated with a hierarchical diagram like the one in Figure 2.2. Each procedure is represented by a named box; the operations on which the procedure depends appear in the boxes to which it is linked one level lower. In general, each level of the diagram shows the set of operations required by the procedures one level higher, and the top level shows the operation that solves the problem as a whole. Figure 2.2 suggests that the top-level procedure in our program (`main`) works in three steps:

1. converts the program arguments to an array `a` of integers,
2. sorts array `a`, and
3. prints array `a`.

Here is the definition for procedure `main`:

```
// method of SortIntegerArgs class
public static void main(String[] args) {
  // EFFECTS: If args[i] is a badly formed integer for
  //   some i, prints an error message; else prints the
  //   ints denoted by args in nondecreasing order.
```

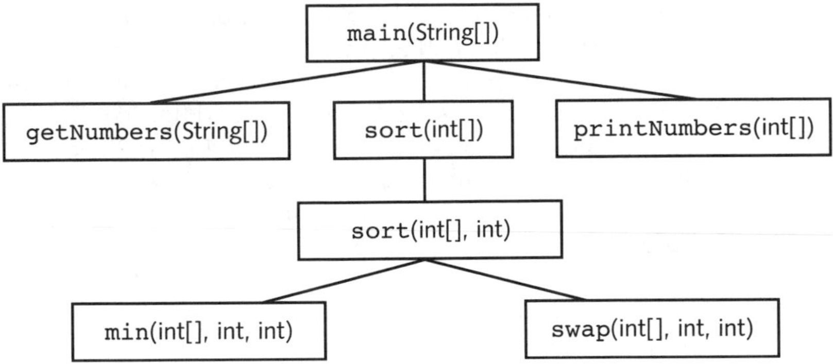

FIGURE 2.2 Structure of the *SortIntegerArgs* program.

```
    try {
      int[] a = getNumbers(args);
      sort(a);
      printNumbers(a);
    } catch (NumberFormatException e) {
      String msg = "Error: argument " + e.getMessage();
      msg += " is badly formed.";
      System.out.println(msg);
      System.exit(0);
    }
  }
```

The effects clause for procedure `main` explains that `main` solves the original problem. Because `main` is invoked through the command line, the program's client is the user. If the user calls the program with one or more badly formed arguments, the program prints an error message and exits. Here is a sample transcript showing this behavior:

```
> java SortIntegerArgs 4 pear 32 tomato
Error: argument pear is badly formed.
```

Procedure `main` depends on three procedures, to which we now turn. Here is the definition of the `getNumbers` procedure:

```
// method of SortIntegerArgs class
static int[] getNumbers(String[] args)
       throws NumberFormatException {
  // REQUIRES: args is not null.
  // EFFECTS: If some args[i] is badly formed throws
```

```
    //   NumberFormatException; else returns an int array
    //   containing the integers denoted by args.
    int[] a = new int[args.length];
    for (int i = 0; i < args.length; i++)
      a[i] = Integer.parseInt(args[i]);
    return a;
  }
```

If `getNumbers` is passed a badly formed argument, the `NumberFormatException` is generated by the `Integer.parseInt` method, and then propagated by the `getNumbers` method. Also, note that the integers in the array returned by procedure `getNumbers` appear in the same order as they do in the input array `args`. However, this is an artifact of the implementation and is not guaranteed by `getNumber`'s specification.

The `printNumbers` procedure is also called by `main`. Its definition is straightforward:

```
  // method of SortIntegerArgs class
  static void printNumbers(int[] a) {
    // REQUIRES: a is not null.
    // MODIFIES: System.out
    // EFFECTS: prints the items in array a
    //   in the order a[0], a[1], .., a[a.length-1]
    for (int i = 0; i < a.length; i++)
      System.out.print(a[i] + " ");
    System.out.println();
  }
```

The most interesting task performed by procedure `main` is sorting, the process of ordering items drawn from a universe of comparable items. In the case of our `SortIntegerArgs` program, we are sorting integers. Our one-argument procedure `sort` defers the real work of sorting to a more general, two-argument version of `sort`:

```
  // method of SortIntegerArgs class
  static void sort(int[] a) {
    // REQUIRES: a is not null.
    // MODIFIES: a
    // EFFECTS: Sorts array a in nondecreasing order.
    sort(a, a.length);
  }
```

Note that our `sort` procedure requires that it is called with a valid array reference. This is reasonable because we are developing `sort` for use in a context that guarantees this precondition: Whenever `sort` is called by procedure `SortIntegerArgs.main`, the argument it gets called with is known to be a valid array reference. It is, of course, possible to specify a more general version of `sort` appropriate for any context (see Exercises 2.9 and 2.10). Similar remarks apply to our `getNumbers` and `printNumbers` procedures.

Here is the specification for the two-argument version of procedure `sort`:

```
// method of SortIntegerArgs class
static void sort(int[] a, int n)
  // REQUIRES: a is not null, and 0 <= n <= a.length.
  // MODIFIES: a
  // EFFECTS: sorts a[0..n-1] in nondecreasing order.
```

The effects clause uses the notation $a[0..n-1]$ to denote the first n elements of array a. More generally, the expression $a[i..j]$ denotes the subarray of length $j-i+1$ comprising the elements $a[i]$, $a[i+1]$, ..., $a[j]$, where $0 \leq i \leq j < a.length$.

There are numerous methods for sorting. For our implementation of the two-argument procedure `sort`, we will use the algorithm known as **selection sort.** This method is less efficient than some other sorting methods, but it is easy to implement. Selection sort first scans the array $a[0..n-1]$ in search of some smallest item. When it is found, we swap it with the item in $a[0]$. Now $a[0]$ contains some smallest item, and $a[1..n-1]$ contains the remaining items. In the next iteration, we find the smallest integer from among the items in $a[1..n-1]$, and then swap it with item $a[1]$. Now $a[0..1]$ contains two smallest items in sorted order, and $a[2..n-1]$ contains the remaining items in arbitrary order. We continue in the same manner through a total of n iterations. In general, at the completion of i iterations, $a[0..i-1]$ contains the i smallest integers in sorted order, and $a[\mathrm{i}..n-1]$ contains the remaining integers in arbitrary order. After n iterations, $a[0..n-1]$ contains the n smallest integers in sorted order and we are done.

To implement selection sort, we need to be able to find some smallest item in a subarray. We could use the `min` procedure specified in Section 2.3. Alternatively, let us assume the following version of `min` with stronger preconditions as reflected by its requires clause:

```
// method of SortIntegerArgs class
static int min(int[] a, int lo, int hi) {
  // REQUIRES: Array a is not null,
  //   and 0 <= lo <= hi < a.length.
  // EFFECTS: Returns the index of some smallest
  //   element in a[lo..hi].
  int indx = lo;
  for (int i = lo+1; i <= hi; i++)
    if (a[i] < a[indx])
      indx = i;
  return indx;
}
```

Our selection sort procedure also requires a procedure for exchanging two items within an integer array:

```
// method of SortIntegerArgs class
static void swap(int[] a, int i, int j)
  // REQUIRES: 0 <= i,j < a.length.
  // MODIFIES: a
  // EFFECTS: Swaps the contents of a[i] and a[j]
```

Having described the operations `min` and `swap`, we are in a position to define the procedure `sort`, which implements selection sort:

```
// method of SortIntegerArgs class
static void sort(int[] a, int n) {
  // REQUIRES: Array a is not null and 0 <= n <= a.length.
  // MODIFIES: a
  // EFFECTS: Sorts a[0..n-1] in nondecreasing order.
  for (int i = 0; i < n; i++) {
    int indx = min(a, i, n-1);
    swap(a, i, indx);
  }
}
```

To summarize what was achieved in this extended example, we specified the problem of printing a list of integer program arguments in sorted order. We then decomposed this problem into three tasks: (1) converting the program arguments to an array of integers, (2) sorting an array of integers, and (3) printing an array of integers from left to right. The first and third tasks are solved directly by the procedures `getNumbers` and `printNumbers`, respectively. The task of sorting an integer array was decomposed into the more general task of sorting an integer subarray, achieved by our two-argument sort procedure. This in turn was decomposed into the task of finding the position of some smallest item in a subarray, which we implemented as the procedure `min`, and that of swapping two items in an array, implemented as the procedure `swap`.

Exercises

2.7 Implement the procedure `swap` described in the previous discussion.

2.8 To explore procedural decomposition in Java, it is convenient to declare related procedures to be class methods (by including the keyword `static` in each procedure's header) and placing the procedures in the same class. For example, the following program prints the side lengths of right triangles, all of whose sides have integer length:

```
public class RightTriangle {

  public static void main(String[] args) {
    if (args.length < 1) {
```

```
      String msg = "Usage: java RightTriangle n";
      System.out.println(msg);
      System.exit(0);
    }
    int n = Integer.parseInt(args[0]);
    printTable(n);
  }

  public static void printTable(int n) {
    for (int i = 1; i <= n; i++)
      for (int j = i+1; j <= n; j++) {
        double hyp = hypotenuse(i, j);
        if (hyp == Math.floor(hyp)) {
          System.out.print(i + "\t" + j + "\t");
          System.out.println((int)hyp);
        }
      }
  }

  public static double hypotenuse(int a, int b) {
    int c2 = square(a) + square(b);
    return Math.sqrt(c2);
  }

  public static int square(int k) {
    return k * k;
  }
}
```

The `RightTriangle` program is called with a program argument that specifies the length of the longest leg. For example:

```
> java RightTriangle 20
3       4       5
5       12      13
6       8       10
8       15      17
9       12      15
12      16      20
15      20      25
```

Implement the class `SortIntegerArgs` using the class methods described in this section. Make sure that your program works.

ESSENTIAL 2.9 Write a version of procedure sort with the following specification:

```
static void sort(int[] a, int n) throws
        NullPointerException, IllegalArgumentException {
  // MODIFIES: a
  // EFFECTS: If a is null throws NullPointerException;
  //    else if 0 <= n <= a.length sorts a[0..n-1]
  //    in nondecreasing order;
  //    else throws IllegalArgumentException.
```

In contrast, the version of procedure sort used in our SortIntegerArgs example does not throw exceptions—its requires clause prohibits its being called with a null reference or an illegal argument. Why was that nonexception-throwing version of sort sufficient in the context of the SortIntegerArgs program?

ESSENTIAL 2.10 Write a version of procedure sort with this specification:

```
static void sort(int[] a) throws
        NullPointerException {
  // MODIFIES: a
  // EFFECTS: If a is null throws NullPointerException;
  //    else sorts a in nondecreasing order.
```

2.11 Our implementation of procedure min actually satisfies a slightly stronger postcondition than what was stated in the text. This procedure could have been specified using the stronger postcondition like this:

```
static int min(int[] a, int lo, int hi)
  // REQUIRES: 0 <= lo <= hi < a.length.
  // EFFECTS: Returns the index of the smallest
  //    item in a[lo..hi] of least index.
```

However, the weaker postcondition as given in the text, requiring only that min return the index of *any* smallest item, was all that procedure sort required of procedure min for its own correctness. Similarly, as noted in the text, our implementation of the getNumbers procedure satisfies a slightly stronger postcondition than required by the procedure that calls it (procedure main). From the standpoint of correctness, is it ever a problem for a client to call a procedure that achieves a stronger postcondition than the client requires? From the standpoint of correctness, is it ever a problem for a client to call a procedure that requires a weaker precondition than the client satisfies? (We will explore such questions further when we treat polymorphism and the substitution principle in Section 5.5.)

2.12 Implement a program called `SortStringArgs` that does for strings what the `SortIntegerArgs` program does for integers. Here is a sample interaction:

```
> java SortStringArgs twas brillig and the slithy toves
and brillig slithy the toves twas
```

2.5 Recursion

Procedural decomposition is possible because we can implement abstract operations in terms of other, lower-level abstract operations. But it is also sometimes possible to implement an abstract operation in terms of the very same abstract operation, that is, in terms of itself. This technique is known as **recursion.** A procedure that calls itself one or more times is said to be **recursive.**

An example will show how this is possible. We'll develop a *recursive* implementation for the abstract operation realized by procedure `min`—that of finding the position of some smallest item in the subarray *a*[*lo*..*hi*]. Here is our strategy in pseudo-code:

```
if (lo==hi) then return lo;
else {
  best ⟵  index of some smallest item in a[lo+1..hi];
  if (a[lo]<a[best]) then return lo;
  else return best;
}
```

In the general case—when *lo* is strictly less than *hi*—the above pseudocode describes this process: Find some smallest item in the rest of the subarray (that is, in *a*[*lo*+1..*hi*]), and then return the index of either this item or of the item *a*[*lo*] based on whichever item is smaller. The task of finding the index of some smallest item in *a*[*lo*+1..*hi*] can be carried out by the procedure `min` as defined for our `SortIntegerArgs` program of Section 2.4. This observation leads to the following implementation for our new procedure, which we shall name `min2`:

```
static int min2(int[] a, int lo, int hi) {
  // REQUIRES: Array a is not null, and
  //   0 <= lo <= hi < a.length.
  // EFFECTS: Returns the index of some smallest
  //   element in a[lo..hi].
```

```
    if (lo == hi)
      return lo;
    else {
      int best = min(a, lo+1, hi);
      if (a[lo] < a[best]) return lo;
      else return best;
    }
  }
```

Because procedure `min2` does not call itself, it is not yet recursive. Here is the key observation that enables us to modify our definition of `min2` to make it recursive: *The procedures `min` and `min2` implement precisely the same abstract operation*. It follows that the first statement in the `else` block can be changed to this:

```
  int best = min2(a, lo+1, hi);
```

Here is the resulting *recursive* version of procedure `min2`:

```
  static int min2(int[] a, int lo, int hi) {
    // REQUIRES: Array a is not null, and
    //    0 <= lo <= hi < a.length.
    // EFFECTS: Returns the index of some smallest
    //    element in a[lo..hi].
    if (lo == hi)
      return lo;
    else {
      int best = min2(a, lo+1, hi);
      if (a[lo] < a[best]) return lo;
      else return best;
    }
  }
```

Recursion is possible when a problem can be decomposed into a *smaller* subproblem *of the same type*. The two key phrases are italicized. First, the subproblem must be smaller than the original problem in the sense that it is closer to a problem that can be solved directly. When a procedure calls itself, it must make progress toward a direct solution. Second, the subproblem must be of the same type as the original problem. Because both problems are solved by the same abstract operation, the same procedure used to solve the original problem can be used to solve the smaller subproblem.

To determine whether a problem is simple enough to be solved directly, the procedure tests whether certain **stopping conditions** are satisfied. Once some stopping condition is satisfied, the problem is simple enough to be solved directly and no further recursive calls are necessary. Applying these ideas to our recursive procedure `min2`, we find that:

- The *stopping condition* occurs when $lo{=}{=}hi$. The problem is of size one and can be solved directly.
- The *recursive condition* occurs when $lo<hi$. When $lo<hi$, the problem is of size $hi-lo+1$, the length of the subarray to be processed. The recursive call solves a strictly smaller problem, of size only $hi-lo$. Progress is made toward a problem that satisfies the stopping condition.

The use of recursion is suggested when an abstract operation is defined in terms of itself. Such as definition is called a **recursive definition** or an **inductive definition.** Consider the well-known factorial function defined by the nonnegative integers:

$$n! = n(n-1)(n-2)\cdots 3\cdot 2\cdot 1\cdot 1$$

The factorial function can also be cast as a recursive definition as follows:

$$n! = \begin{cases} 1 & \text{if } n=0 \\ n \cdot (n-1)! & \text{if } n > 0 \end{cases}$$

Note that under this definition, we have $0!=1$. This recursive definition leads to the following derivation of 4!:

$$\begin{aligned} 4! &= 4 \cdot 3! \\ &= 4 \cdot 3 \cdot 2! \\ &= 4 \cdot 3 \cdot 2 \cdot 1! \\ &= 4 \cdot 3 \cdot 2 \cdot 1 \cdot 0! \\ &= 4 \cdot 3 \cdot 2 \cdot 1 \cdot 1 \\ &= 24 \end{aligned}$$

The recursive definition of factorial suggests a recursive implementation for $n!$ in which the stopping condition is $n{=}{=}0$ and the recursive condition is $n>0$. The following recursive procedure results:

```
static int factorial(int n) {
  // REQUIRES: n is nonnegative.
  // EFFECTS: Returns the factorial of n.
  if (n == 0)
    return 1;
  else
    return n * factorial(n-1);
}
```

Our `factorial` procedure requires its argument to be nonnegative. It is certainly possible to revise the specification such that this precondition is dropped, while adding the postcondition that an `IllegalArgumentException` is thrown whenever `factorial` is called with a negative argument.

The most efficient way to do this is to define a new procedure with these revised specifications:

```
static int fact(int n) throws IllegalArgumentException {
  // EFFECTS: If n<0 then throws IllegalArgumentException;
  //   else returns the factorial of n.
  if (n < 0) throw new IllegalArgumentException();
  return factorial(n);
}
```

Procedure `fact` is not recursive, but the procedure it calls (`factorial`) is recursive. It is not possible for `fact` to call `factorial` with a negative argument because `fact` first throws an exception if its input `n` is negative. Thus whenever `fact` calls `factorial`, it guarantees that `factorial`'s requires clause is satisfied. A nonrecursive procedure such as `fact`, which provides proper inputs to a recursive procedure, is called a **nonrecursive shell.**

It sometimes happens that you must implement an abstract operation for which you're not given a recursive definition, yet you're able to formulate one. Consider the following abstract operation for counting the number of times that the integer x occurs in the integer subarray $a[lo..hi]$:

```
static int count(int x, int[] a, int lo, int hi)
// REQUIRES: Array a is not null, and
//   either 0 <= lo <= hi < a.length, or lo > hi.
// EFFECTS: If lo <= hi returns the number of times
//   that x occurs in a[lo..hi]; else returns 0.
```

An implementation based on iteration traverses the subarray $a[lo..hi]$ while keeping track of the number of times that x appears. It might go something like this:

```
static int count(int x, int[] a, int lo, int hi) {
  int count = 0;
  for (int i = lo; i <= hi; i++)
    if (a[i] == x)
      count++;
  return count;
}
```

In contrast, a recursive implementation could be based on the following recursive definition. Let $C_{i,j}$ denote the number of times that x appears in the subarray $a[i..j]$. We then have:

$$C_{i,j} = \begin{cases} 0 & \text{if } i > j \\ C_{i+1,j} & \text{if } i \le j \text{ and } x \ne a[i] \\ 1 + C_{i+1,j} & \text{if } i \le j \text{ and } x \ne a[i] \end{cases}$$

This definition covers three cases, from top to bottom. In the first case, the subarray $a[i..j]$ is empty, so x does not appear in it at all. In the second case, $a[i..j]$ is not empty, but because x is not equal to $a[i]$, the number of times that x appears in $a[i..j]$ is equal to the number of times that x appears in $a[i+1..j]$. In the third case, x is equal to $a[i]$, so the number of times that x appears in $a[i..j]$ is equal to one plus the number of times that x appears in $a[i+1..j]$. This recursive definition leads to the following recursive implementation of the procedure `count`:

```
static int count (int x, int[] a, int lo, int hi) {
  if (lo > hi)
    return 0;
  else if (x != a[lo])
    return count(x, a, lo+1, hi);
  else
    return 1 + count(x, a, lo+1, hi);
}
```

Recursion is a powerful idea which we will use later in this book. In later chapters, we will also explore **recursive structures,** data that is defined in terms of itself.

Exercises

2.13 In the two-argument procedure `sort` of Section 2.4, replace the call to procedure `min` by a call to `min2`, and then recompile and run your `SortIntegerArgs` program. Is your program still correct? It should be, because the procedures `min` and `min2` realize the same abstract operation.

2.14 The **power function** is defined recursively as follows, where b is a nonnegative integer:

$$a^b = \begin{cases} 1 & \text{if } b = 0 \\ a \cdot a^{b-1} & \text{if } b > 0 \end{cases}$$

For instance, here is the derivation of 2^3:

$$\begin{aligned} 2^3 &= 2 \cdot 2^2 \\ &= 2 \cdot 2 \cdot 2^1 \\ &= 2 \cdot 2 \cdot 2 \cdot 2^0 \\ &= 2 \cdot 2 \cdot 2 \cdot 1 \\ &= 8 \end{aligned}$$

Based on this recursive definition of a^b, write a recursive implementation for the procedure power:

```
static int power(int a, int b)
  // REQUIRES: b is nonnegative.
  // EFFECTS: Returns a raised to the power b.
```

2.15 If a recursive procedure runs and none of the stopping conditions is ever satisfied, the series of recursive calls goes on forever and the procedure never halts. Indeed, a recursive procedure is not correct (in the sense of implementing an algorithm) if there are legal inputs that result in an infinite regression of recursive calls. Write a recursive procedure in Java that never halts on any input. Also, write a recursive procedure that halts on some inputs but not on all inputs.

2.16 The **Fibonacci sequence** begins like this:

0, 1, 1, 2, 3, 5, 8, 13, 21, 34, 55, 89, ...

The first two elements are 0 and 1, and each remaining element is equal to the sum of the previous two elements. Here is its recursive definition:

$$fib(n) = \begin{cases} n & \text{if } n = 0 \text{ or } n = 1 \\ fib(n-1) + fib(n-2) & \text{if } n > 1 \end{cases}$$

Define a recursive procedure for computing elements in the Fibonacci sequence based on the inductive definition just given:

```
static long fib(int n)
  // REQUIRES: n is nonnegative.
  // EFFECTS: Returns element n in the Fib sequence.
```

Use your procedure in a Java program that takes a nonnegative integer program argument n and prints element n of the Fibonacci sequence:

```
> java Fib 6
Fib(6) = 8
```

You will find that your recursive version of procedure `fib` is grossly inefficient if it strictly follows the inductive definition given earlier. The problem is that many costly computations are being carried out redundantly. For instance, the procedure call `fib(40)` results in the calls `fib(39)` and `fib(38)`; the call `fib(39)` results in the calls `fib(38)` and `fib(37)`. Observe that the call `fib(38)` occurs twice. This same sort of redundancy recurs many times as the computation proceeds. This recursive version of procedure `fib` runs in time that is exponential in the input value *n*, so the time-cost is quite large even for relatively small values of *n*.

We cannot conclude from this experiment that recursion is intrinsically inefficient, only that the way we have used it here is inefficient. Here is a second recursive approach to the Fibonacci function that rivals the best iterative approach in efficiency (both run in time proportional to the input *n*):

```
static long fib(int n) {
  // REQUIRES: n >= 0.
  // EFFECTS: Returns element n in
  //   the Fibonacci sequence.
  return fibHelp(n, 0, 1);
}

static long fibHelp(int n, long a, long b) {
  // REQUIRES: a and b are successive elements in the
  //   Fibonacci sequence.
  // EFFECTS: Returns nth successor to a in the
  //   Fibonacci sequence.
  if (n == 0)
    return a;
  else
    return fibHelp(n-1, b, a+b);
   }
```

In this implementation, the nonrecursive shell `fib` calls the recursive procedure `fibHelp`. Code the preceding version of procedure `fib` and use it to compute element 100 of the Fibonocci sequence. Also, use your recursive version of `fib` to compute `fib(100)`. Which version is faster?

2.17 Write a recursive procedure implementing each of the following abstract operations:

(a) Sum the values in an integer subarray *a*[*lo*..*hi*]:

```
static int sumOver(int[] a, int lo, int hi)
  // REQUIRES: Array a is not null, and
  //   0 <= lo <= hi < a.length.
  // EFFECTS: Returns the sum a[lo]+..+a[hi].
```

(b) Replace each value in an integer subarray *a*[*lo*..*hi*] by its square:

```
static void squareMap(int[] a, int lo, int hi)
  // REQUIRES: Array a is not null, and
  //   0 <= lo <= hi < a.length.
  // MODIFIES: a
  // EFFECTS: Replaces each item x in a[lo..hi] by x².
```

(c) Compute the sum of all positive integers from 1 through n:

```
static int summation(int n)
  // REQUIRES: n is nonnegative.
  // EFFECTS: Returns 0+1+..+(n-1)+n
```

(See if you can devise a formula for computing the sum $1+2+...+n$ in constant time.)

(d) Report the index of the first occurrence of x in $a[lo..hi]$, or –1 if x does not occur in this subarray:

```
static int find(int x, int[] a, int lo, int hi)
  // REQUIRES: Array a is not null, and
  //   0 <= lo <= hi < a.length.
  // EFFECTS: Returns the position of first x in
  //   a[lo..hi];
  //   returns -1 if x does not occur in a[lo..hi].
```

2.18 **Merge sort** is another algorithm for sorting an array of integers. The abstract operation is as follows:

```
static void msort(int[] a, int lo, int hi)
  // REQUIRES: a is not null, and
  //   0 <= lo <= hi < a.length.
  // MODIFIES: a
  // EFFECTS: Sorts a[lo..hi] in nondecreasing order.
```

Sorting an array can be readily implemented in terms of procedure `msort`. For example, the one-argument procedure `sort` of Section 2.4 can be implemented using merge sort like this:

```
static void sort(int[] a) {
  // REQUIRES: a is not null.
  // MODIFIES: a
  // EFFECTS: Sorts array a in nondecreasing order.
  msort(a, 0, a.length-1);
}
```

To complete our work, we must implement procedure `msort`. Here is a pseudo-code description of how this procedure works:

```
if (lo==hi) then return;
else {
  mid ←— (lo + hi) / 2;
  sort a[lo..mid] in nondecreasing order;
  sort a[mid+1..hi] in nondecreasing order;
  merge(a, lo, mid, hi);
}
```

In the general case, when *lo*<*hi*, the idea is to split the subarray *a*[*lo*..*hi*] into two halves of roughly equal size, and then independently (and recursively) sort each of the two halves, and then combine the two now-sorted halves. The two halves are combined using the `merge` operation:

```
static void merge(int[] a, int lo, int mid, int hi)
  // REQUIRES: a is not null;
  //   0 <= lo <= mid < hi < a.length;
  //   a[lo..mid] and a[mid+1..hi] are both sorted in
  //   nondecreasing order.
  // MODIFIES: a
  // EFFECTS: Sorts a[lo..hi] in nondecreasing order.
```

The procedure `merge` combines two sorted subarrays *a*[*lo*..*mid*] and *a*[*mid*+1..*hi*] into the sorted subarray *a*[*lo*..*hi*]. It works by maintaining an index into each of the two sorted subarrays. The indexes start out at the leftmost position of each subarray. In each iteration, the two items currently being indexed are compared, and then the smaller of the two items is copied into a temporary array `b` and its index is advanced. Once one of the indexes passes beyond the rightmost element of its subarray, the remainder of the other subarray is copied into array `b`. Here is a pseudo-code implementation of procedure `merge`:

```
static void merge(int[] a, int lo, int mid, int hi) {
  int[] b = new int[hi-lo+1];
  int i = lo,      // index into a[lo..mid]
      j = mid+1,   // index into a[mid+1..hi]
      k = 0;       // index into b
  while (i < mid+1 and j < hi+1) {
    if (a[i] < a[j])
```

```
      b[k++] = a[i++];   // copy a[i] into b
    else
      b[k++] = a[j++];   // copy a[j] into b
  }
  if (i==mid+1) then copy a[j..hi] into b[k..hi-lo];
  else copy a[i..mid] into b[k..hi-lo];
  copy b into a[lo..hi];
}
```

Implement the procedures `msort` and `merge`. Then write a Java program that exercises your new sorting routine (you may want to revise the implementation of your `SortIntegerArgs` program so that it uses merge sort). To implement the procedure `merge`, you can use the `java.lang.System.arraycopy` method for copying subarrays.

Summary

A procedure can be viewed in two different ways: (1) as an abstract operation that maps inputs to outputs and side effects, and (2) as the description of a process that implements the operation. Procedural abstraction views a procedure as an abstract operation. This is the view that is best suited to clients of the procedure, and to authors of such clients. The primary benefit of procedural abstraction is that clients can treat a procedure as an operation while ignoring implementation details.

A procedure's preconditions are those conditions that must be satisfied by any client calling the procedure. A procedure's postconditions are those conditions that the procedure promises to satisfy upon completion, assuming that the client has satisfied the preconditions. In other words, preconditions are obligations placed on the procedure's clients, whereas postconditions are guarantees made by the procedure.

To specify the operation implemented by a procedure, we describe the procedure's preconditions through a requires clause and its postconditions through an effects clause, both of which appear as specification comments following the header. In addition, a modifies clause lists those objects (if any) whose state may be changed by the procedure. A procedure can use assertions to ensure that its requires clause and effects clause are satisfied. Java also provides an exception mechanism for throwing, catching, and handling exceptions.

The power of procedural abstraction can be appreciated when we build programs using procedural decomposition. The solution to a problem takes the form of a hierarchy of procedures in which each layer supplies the operations needed by the next-higher layer. The procedure at the top of the hierarchy represents the operation that solves the original problem as a whole. We also rely on procedural abstraction when we define recursive procedures, which are procedures that call themselves. A recursive procedure represents the very operation that it requires. By viewing a recursive procedure as an abstract operation, we can make sense of a procedure that calls itself.

Associated with every object is a set of procedures known as the object's methods. The methods represent the object's set of defined behaviors. By treating these methods as abstract operations, we are able to view the object in terms of its behavior while ignoring its implementation. Thus procedural abstraction serves as the key building block for data abstraction, the subject of the next chapter.

CHAPTER

3

Data Abstraction

In the previous chapter we examined procedural abstraction, whereby a procedure is viewed abstractly as an operation. Clients that call a procedure treat it as an operation whose implementation need not be known. In this chapter we explore a different kind of abstraction, one that is central to the object model. Under **data abstraction,** a data value, such as an object, is viewed not only as a chunk of data but also as a collection of closely related operations, together with a protocol for using those operations in meaningful ways. Clients interact with an abstract data value by calling its operations, without knowing how the underlying data is structured or how the operations are implemented. An abstract data value provides its clients with a public interface—a set of operations—while hiding its implementation.

Section 3.1 presents the basic idea behind data abstraction as well as its key benefits. Section 3.2 places data abstraction in a concrete setting by developing two new classes for representing points and rectangles in the plane. Section 3.3 discusses encapsulation and information hiding. Section 3.4 provides an overview of how to produce computer graphics using Java 2D, and Section 3.5 puts the material to use in an application for painting rectangles onto a frame (window) on the screen. Although this application is hardly remarkable for the graphics it produces, it serves as a template for other computer graphics applications that arise later in this book.

3.1 Abstract Data Types

A **concrete data type** is a collection of **data values** possessing a specific representation and set of operations. Java provides a number of *primitive* concrete data types: the numeric types, the `char` type, and the `boolean` type. For example, Java's `int` data type is the collection of integer values in the range from -2^{31} (–2147483648) through $2^{31}-1$ (2147483647). Integers in Java are stored using the four-byte signed two's complement representation, and they provide such operations as addition, subtraction, multiplication, integer assignment, and quite a few others.

As it happens, you can *use* integers without being familiar with four-byte signed two's complement representation, or with any other representation scheme for signed integers. You also do not need to know how integer operations are implemented. To use integers, you need knowledge only of *how to use* the operations for their manipulation. You can, for example, add two integers and assign the result to an integer variable using integer assignment and addition:

```
int i;
i = 6 + 7;
```

Yet, how integers are stored, and the processes by which they are added and otherwise manipulated, are irrelevant to their use as integers. (Nonetheless, Java provides several bitwise operators for manipulating integers as bit strings.)

Strings are another familiar data type. Like integers, you probably already know how to use strings, even if you don't know how strings are represented internally, or how string operations are implemented. Consider a short Java program that uses strings. The following program concatenates its program arguments in reverse order and converts the resulting string to uppercase:

```
public class SillyEcho {
  public static void main(String[] args) {
    String s = "";
    for (int i = 0; i < args.length; i++)
      s = args[i] + " " + s;
    System.out.println(s.toUpperCase());
  }
}
```

Here is an example of the program's use, where the user's command-line input is in bold and the computer's response in plain text:

```
> java SillyEcho Hello Goobly World
WORLD GOOBLY HELLO
```

To write the `SillyEcho` program, you must understand how to use certain `String` operations. You concatenate two strings using the binary +

operator, construct a string literal by enclosing a sequence of characters in double-quotes as in `"apple"`, and produce an uppercase string using the `toUpperCase` method of the `String` class. Each of these operations can be used without the need to know about how strings are represented. In fact, strings may be represented differently across different implementations of Java, but our program (and our thinking) is insulated from such issues.

In general, a concrete data type categorizes data values by their structure and behavior. However, when you use data values you are less concerned with their structure—how they are represented internally—than with their behavior—how they can be used. We may want to add or multiply two integers, but we do not care how those integers are stored in the computer. Similarly, we can concatenate two strings without knowing the internal structure of strings. This concern with the operations that can be applied to the values of a data type is addressed by the notion of abstract data types. An **abstract data type** (or more simply **data type**) is a collection of data values together with a set of operations for their manipulation. The adjective *abstract* emphasizes that the data values are known not by how they are represented or implemented but by how they can be used. **Data abstraction**—as realized through the use of abstract data types—presents the operations for using a data value while ignoring its representation and implementation.

Through data abstraction, a data value is presented as a chunk of data and a set of public operations. The operations make up the data value's **interface,** which clients use to interact with the data value. In contrast, a data value's implementation consists of its internal representation and the implementation of its operations based on this representation. Data abstraction presents clients with a data value's interface while insulating them from its implementation.

A number of benefits follow from the use of data abstraction. First, it spares the clients' authors from having to understand the details of the implementation. Thus we can use integers and strings without knowing how these data types are implemented. Second, because data abstraction insulates clients from the data type's representation, clients are not affected by changes to the data type's implementation as long as the data type's interface is held fixed. Lastly, because a data type's interface specifies all possible interactions between clients and data values, we are able to think of a data type as a module that exhibits well-defined behaviors. Thus, our thinking is lifted to the level of abstraction provided by the interface. We will explore these and other benefits of data abstraction in greater detail throughout this chapter.

In addition to the numeric, `char`, and `boolean` primitive data types, Java provides a wide range of predefined **compound data types**: the standard classes that come with the language. Compound data types are also sometimes called **reference types** because objects in Java are handled through references. When a data value is an instance of some class, we usually refer to it as an **instance** or an **object.** We refer to `"hello"` as an instance of the `String` class, or a `String` object, or more simply as a string.

Strings and integers are provided by Java. The language also provides the means for building new compound data types. This is done using Java's array, interface, and class constructs. Interfaces are used to define new data types without implementing them, whereas classes are used to both define and implement new data types. We'll postpone discussion of interfaces until later in this book, and focus on classes for the time being.

3.2 Specifying and Implementing Data Abstractions

This section explores data abstraction by developing two new classes for representing points and rectangles in the plane. To specify a class' behavior, we'll use the sort of specification comments discussed in the previous chapter; specifically, we'll annotate each method with its requires, modifies, and effects clauses.

3.2.1 Points

The Cartesian plane has two perpendicular axes that meet at the origin. The *x* axis extends to the right, and the *y* axis extends down. Each point is given by a pair (*x*,*y*) of integers that tell how to reach the point from the origin: Starting at the origin, travel *x* units along the *x* axis, and then *y* units parallel to the *y* axis. If *x* is positive, you travel along the positive *x* axis (to the right), and if *x* is negative you travel along the negative *x* axis (to the left). Similar remarks apply to the sign of the *y* component. The point (*0*,*0*) is called the **origin**. See Figure 3.1. (You may be familiar with the more common configuration in which the *x* axis points to the right and the *y* axis points up; however, the configuration I'm describing here, as portrayed in Figure 3.1, is consistent with Java's default system for painting. I'll say more about this later in this chapter.)

We'll develop a class for handling points in the plane, to be called the `PointGeometry` class. Where should we start? One should understand a data type before giving thought to implementing it; that is, one should first appreciate the type as an abstract data type. What operations does the type

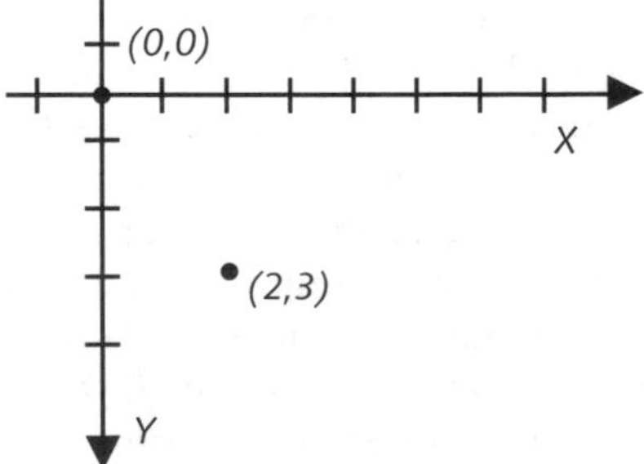

FIGURE 3.1 Cartesian plane and the point (2,3).

support? How are these operations used together? To understand our data type for points in the plane, it is helpful to study a **class skeleton** for our `PointGeometry` class:

```
public class PointGeometry {

  public PointGeometry(int x, int y)
    // EFFECTS: Initializes this to the point (x,y).

  public PointGeometry(PointGeometry p)
         throws NullPointerException
    // EFFECTS: If p is null throws NullPointerException;
    //   else initializes this to (p.getX(),p.getY()).

  public PointGeometry()
    // EFFECTS: Initializes this to the origin (0,0).

  // x coordinate property
  public int getX()
    // EFFECTS: Returns x coordinate.

  public void setX(int newX)
    // MODIFIES: this
    // EFFECTS: Changes x coordinate to newX.

  // y coordinate property
  public int getY()
    // EFFECTS: Returns y coordinate.

  public void setY(int newY)
    // MODIFIES: this
    // EFFECTS: Changes y coordinate to newY.

  // other methods
  public double distance(PointGeometry p)
         throws NullPointerException
    // EFFECTS: If p is null throws NullPointerException;
    //   else returns the distance between p
    //   and this point.

  public java.awt.Shape shape()
    // EFFECTS: Returns this point's shape.

  public void translate(int dx, int dy)
    // MODIFIES: this
```

```
    // EFFECTS: Translates this point by dx along x
    //   and dy along y:
    //   this_post.getX() == this.getX()+dx and
    //   this_post.getY() == this.getY()+dy.

  public boolean equals(Object obj)
    // EFFECTS: Returns true if obj is a PointGeometry
    //   and obj.getX()==getX() and obj.getY()==getY();
    //   else returns false.

  public String toString()
    // EFFECTS: Returns the string "(x,y)".
}
```

Although a class skeleton looks like Java code, it is not a formal construct of the language; for instance, class skeletons will not compile. I present class skeletons using a Java-like syntax only to help them better serve their purpose, which is to explain a class' methods without actually implementing them. You might think of the class skeleton as a home-grown construct for describing new data types.

A class skeleton explains how to use a class. We can usually gain an even fuller understanding by studying programs that use the class. The `TryPoint` class presented next is an application that uses the `PointGeometry` class. This program gets called with four program arguments: The first two integer arguments are the *x* and *y* coordinates of a point *p1*, and the second pair of integer arguments are the *x* and *y* coordinates of a second point *p2*. The program prints the points *p1* and *p2*, the distance between them, and the point *p1* after it's been translated by the coordinates of *p2*. If the second pair of program arguments is omitted, point *p2* is taken to be the origin (0,0). Here is a sample transcript:

```
> java TryPoint 3 4 -5 8
point 1: (3,4)
point 2: (-5,8)
distance: 8.94427190999916
point 1 translated: (-2,12)

> java TryPoint 3 4
point 1: (3,4)
point 2: (0,0)
distance: 5.0
point 1 translated: (3,4)
```

Here is my definition of the `TryPoint` class:

```
public class TryPoint {
  public static void main(String[] args) {
    if ((args.length != 2) && (args.length != 4)) {
```

```
      System msg = "USAGE: java TryPoint x1 y1 [x2 y2]";
      System.out.println(msg);
      System.exit(0);
    }
    int x1 = Integer.parseInt(args[0]);
    int y1 = Integer.parseInt(args[1]);
    PointGeometry p1 = new PointGeometry(x1, y1);
    PointGeometry p2 = new PointGeometry();
    if (args.length == 4) {
      int x2 = Integer.parseInt(args[2]);
      int y2 = Integer.parseInt(args[3]);
      p2.setX(x2);
      p2.setY(y2);
    }
    System.out.println("point 1: " + p1);
    System.out.println("point 2: " + p2);
    System.out.println("distance: " + p1.distance(p2));
    p1.translate(p2.getX(), p2.getY());
    System.out.println("point 1 translated: " + p1);
  }
}
```

When you call the `TryPoint` program from the command line as in

```
> java TryPoint 3 4 -5 8
```

execution begins at the static method `TryPoint.main`. Recall that when you run a Java program, you must provide the name of a class (in this case `TryPoint`). The system then locates and runs the class method named `main` for that class. The `main` method declares a parameter of type `String[]`. The system passes the program arguments to `main` through an array bound to this parameter (in this case the parameter is named `args`). Because these program arguments are strings, they must be converted to integers before they can be used to build points. The instruction

```
int x1 = Integer.parseInt(args[0]);
```

performs a string-to-integer conversion for the first program argument, and assigns the resulting integer to the variable `x1`. Observe that when the point `p2` is constructed, it represents the origin (0,0). However, if a second pair of program arguments is supplied, point `p2` is made to represent that point with this pair of instructions:

```
p2.setX(x2);
p2.setY(y2);
```

Now that we understand how the point data type is used, we turn our attention to implementing it. This requires that we do two things. First, we must decide on a representation for our `PointGeometry` class. We'll choose to represent a point by the values of its *x* and *y* coordinates and store these values in instance fields of the same name:

```
// fields of PointGeometry class
protected int x, y;
```

Second, we must implement the class' methods in terms of our chosen storage structure. We'll work on `PointGeometry`'s constructors first. The first constructor takes two integers and assigns their values to the fields:

```
public PointGeometry(int x, int y) {
  this.x = x;
  this.y = y;
}
```

In the preceding constructor, the keyword `this` refers to the object under construction and is used to access the object's fields. The expression `this.x` refers to the instance field `x` of this object, whereas the expression `x` (not qualified by `this`) refers to the method's parameter `x`.

The second constructor is called with a point and constructs a new point equal to its argument:

```
public PointGeometry(PointGeometry p)
          throws NullPointerException {
  this(p.getX(), p.getY());
}
```

In the preceding constructor, the keyword `this` is used to invoke the first constructor. The particular constructor that gets called through `this` is determined by the number and type of arguments. In this case, `this` is called with two integers, so the first constructor is invoked because it takes two integers. As an aside, the syntax wherein `this` is used as a method call may appear only as the first statement of a constructor.

The third and final constructor takes no arguments and constructs a new point representing the origin:

```
public PointGeometry() {
  this(0, 0);
}
```

Let us turn to the methods used to access and modify a point's *x* coordinate. A method that returns the value of a property is called a **getter.** The getter `getX` returns the value of a point's *x* coordinate property, which is stored in the point's field named `x`:

```
// method of PointGeometry class
public int getX() { return x; }
```

A method that modifies the value of a property is called a **setter.** The setter `setX` is used to change the value of a point's *x* coordinate:

```
// method of PointGeometry class
public void setX(int newX) { x = newX; }
```

A named feature for which a class provides both a setter and a getter is called a **property** of the class. By convention, the names of these methods are formed by prepending the strings *get* and *set* to the property name, where the property name's initial character is made uppercase. This is how we formed the method names `getX` and `setX` for this class' *x* property. A property's setter and getter methods are collectively known as **accessors.**

Setter methods belong to a broader category of methods known as mutator methods, or simply **mutators.** A mutator is any method that changes the values of its object's instance fields; that is, any method that can change the state of its object. Likewise, getter methods belong to a broader category of methods known as **selectors.** A selector is any method that accesses its object's instance fields without changing their values. It follows that setters are mutators used to change the value of specific properties, and getters are selectors used to access the value of specific properties.

It is important to observe that a class' properties need not coincide with its fields. In the case of the `PointGeometry` class, the value of a point's *x* coordinate is indeed stored in a field of the same name. However, in the next section we will see an example of a class whose properties are not stored in fields but rather are *derived* by computation. The value of a property does not have to be stored in a field of the class, and properties generally do not have to be implemented in any particular way. The properties of a class are part of the class' abstraction as viewed by its clients and pertain to the class' interface, not its implementation.

The `PointGeometry` class also defines the property *y*. The method definitions for the *y* property parallel those for the *x* property:

```
// methods of PointGeometry class
public int getY() { return y; }
public void setY(int newY) { y = newY; }
```

Having defined `PointGeometry`'s constructors and the accessors for its *x* and *y* properties, let's turn to its remaining methods. The `distance` method takes an input point *p* and returns the distance between *p* and this point. The Euclidean distance between two points is computed according to the Pythagorean theorem. The line segment connecting the two points serves as the hypotenuse of a right triangle whose sides are parallel to the *x* and *y* axes. The length of the hypotenuse is equal to the square root of the sum of the length of the sides squared. Here is the definition of `distance`:

```
// method of PointGeometry class
public double distance(PointGeometry p)
      throws NullPointerException {
  long dx = this.getX() - p.getX();
  long dy = this.getY() - p.getY();
  double d2 = dx * dx + dy * dy;
```

```
  return Math.sqrt(d2);
}
```

The shape method returns an object of type `java.awt.Shape`. We use the shapes of geometries to render them, as we'll see in Section 3.4. Here is this method's implementation:

```
// method of PointGeometry class
public java.awt.Shape shape() {
  return new Ellipse2D.Float(getX()-2, getY()-2, 4, 4);
}
```

The `translate` method translates this point by `dx` units parallel to the *x* axis and by `dy` units parallel to the *y* axis. Translation occurs to the right (parallel to the *positive x* axis) if `dx` is positive and to the left if `dx` is negative; similarly worded remarks apply to the sign of the parameter `dy` and the *y* axis. Here is the implementation:

```
// method of PointGeometry class
public void translate(int dx, int dy) {
  setX(getX() + dx);
  setY(getY() + dy);
}
```

Two points are considered equal if their respective *x* and *y* properties are of equal value. The `equals` method is used to compare two points for equality:

```
// method of PointGeometry class
public boolean equals(Object obj) {
  if (obj instanceof PointGeometry) {
    PointGeometry p = (PointGeometry)obj;
    return (p.getX() == getX()) && (p.getY() == getY());
  }
  return false;
}
```

Because the `equals` method can be called with an object of any type, the method first uses Java's built-in `instanceof` operator to test whether the argument is in fact a `PointGeometry` object. If it is, the method casts the argument down the class hierarchy:

```
PointGeometry p = (PointGeometry)obj;
```

Because the test using `instanceof` has first established that `obj` references a `PointGeometry` object, this type cast is valid. Next, point p's *x* and *y* properties are compared to those of the current point. Of course, if argument `obj` is not a `PointGeometry` object, the `equals` method returns `false`—the current point cannot equal any object that is not a point.

The `toString` method returns a string that represents a point using the familiar ordered-pair notation; for example, the point (5,7) is represented by the string `"(5,7)"`.

```
// method of PointGeometry class
public String toString() {
  return "(" + getX() + "," + getY() + ")";
}
```

The `toString` method gets invoked automatically whenever a point-to-string conversion is required. For example, where the variable `p1` references a point object, the expression

```
"point 1: " + p1
```

has mixed types: the + operator's left operand is a string and its right operand is a point. The left operand's type (`String`) informs the compiler that the + operator denotes string concatenation in this context. Because the right operand is a point and not a string, its `toString` method is called to obtain a string, and the expression as a whole evaluates to the string `"point 1: (5,7)"`.

Exercises

ESSENTIAL 3.1 Consider the implementation of the `distance`, `equals`, `shape`, `translate`, and `toString` methods just given. Each of these implementations avoids directly referencing the `x` and `y` fields of the `PointGeometry` class, and instead uses the `getX` and `getY` *methods* to obtain a point's coordinates. For example, the `toString` method might have been implemented like this:

```
public String toString() {
  return "(" + x + "," + y + ")";
}
```

What are the advantages and disadvantages of implementing methods in such a way that direct references to a class' fields are avoided?

ESSENTIAL 3.2 `Range` objects are used to represent intervals along the real number line. A range is determined by two integer properties: a *minimum value* (or *min*) property, and a *maximum value* (or *max*) property, where the min is no greater than the max. The range of real numbers x such that $2 \leq x \leq 6$ can be written as [2..6]. Here 2 is the min, and 6 is the max. The *length* of this range is the difference between its max and min values (6−2=4), and the *size* of this range is the number of integers it contains (5). Here is a skeleton of the `Range` class:

```
public class Range {

  public Range(int min, int max)
        throws IllegalArgumentException
    // EFFECTS: If max < min throws
```

```
  //   IllegalArgumentException; else initializes
  //   this range to [min..max].

public Range(Range r) throws NullPointerException
  // EFFECTS: If r is null throws
  //   NullPointerException; else initializes this
  //   to the range [r.getMin()..r.getMax()].

public Range()
  // EFFECTS: Initializes this range to [0..0].

public int getMin()
  // EFFECTS: Returns this range's min.

public void setMin(int newMin)
       throws IllegalArgumentException
  // MODIFIES: this
  // EFFECTS: If getMax() < newMin throws
  //   IllegalArgumentException; else sets min
  //   to newMin: this_post.getMin() == newMin.

public int getMax()
  // EFFECTS: Returns this range's max.

public void setMax(int newMax)
       throws IllegalArgumentException
  // EFFECTS: If newMax < getMin() throws
  //   IllegalArgumentException; else sets max
  //   to newMax: this_post.getMax() == newMax.

public void setMinMax(int newMin, int newMax)
       throws IllegalArgumentException
  // MODIFIES: this
  // EFFECTS: If newMax < newMin throws
  //   IllegalArgumentException; else updates
  //   min and max: this_post.getMin()==newMin
  //   and this_post.getMax()==newMax.

public int length()
  // EFFECTS: Returns this range's length: max-min

public int size()
  // EFFECTS: Returns this range's size: length() +1.
```

```
public boolean contains(int a)
  // EFFECTS: Returns true if getMin()<=a<=getMax();
  //   else returns false.

public boolean equals(Object obj)
  // EFFECTS: Returns true if obj is a Range and
  //   obj.getMin()==getMin() and
  //   obj.getMax()==getMax(); else returns false.

public String toString()
  // EFFECTS: Returns the string "[min..max]".
}
```

Define the Range class that implements the specification given above—your class should define a storage structure for representing ranges, and implement the methods declared by the class skeleton in terms of the chosen storage structure. Test your class using the following program. This program asks you to think of a number between 0 and 100, and then asks a series of questions to pin down the number. It uses a Range object to keep track of the current range of candidates. Initially, the range [0..100] is assumed (although the max value can be other than 100 if the program is called with an integer program argument). The response to each question is used to reduce the size of the range by half, until the range consists of only a single number, the number you are thinking of. This process of iteratively reducing the size of a candidate set by a factor of two is known as **binary search.**

```
public class GuessNumber {
  public static void main(String[] args) {
    int n = 100;
    if (args.length > 1) {
      System msg = "USAGE: java GuessNumber [n]";
      System.out.println(msg);
      System.exit(1);
    } else if (args.length == 1)
      n = Integer.parseInt(args[0]);
    Range rng = new Range(0, n);
    ScanInput in = new ScanInput();
    System.out.print("think of a number ");
    System.out.println("between 0 and " + n);
    String response;
    try {
```

```
        while (rng.size() > 1) {
          System.out.println("current range: " + rng);
          int mid = (rng.getMin() + rng.getMax()) / 2;
          System.out.print("is your number greater ");
          System.out.println("than " + mid + "?");
          response = in.readString();
          if (response.charAt(0) == 'y')
            rng.setMin(mid + 1);
          else
            rng.setMax(mid);
        }
        System.out.print("you're thinking of ");
        System.out.println(rng.getMin() + "!");
      } catch (IOException e) {
        System.out.println("i/o exception... bye!");
        System.exit(1);
      }
    }
  }
```

The `GuessNumber` program uses a `ScanInput` object to read and parse input from the terminal. The `ScanInput` class is described in Appendix A.

A straight line segment in the plane is represented by a `LineSegmentGeometry` object. A line segment has two properties corresponding to its two endpoints: the *p0* property corresponds to one of its endpoints, and the *p1* property to the other. In some contexts, we consider a line segment as being directed from its *p0* endpoint (called the line segment's **origin**) to its *p1* endpoint (its **destination**). Define the `LineSegmentGeometry` class having the following skeleton:

```
public class LineSegmentGeometry {

  public LineSegmentGeometry(PointGeometry p0,
                             PointGeometry p1)
        throws NullPointerException
    // EFFECTS: If p0 or p1 is null throws
    //    NullPointerException; else initializes this
    //    with endpoints equal to p0 and p1.

  public LineSegmentGeometry(int x0, int y0,
                             int x1, int y1)
```

```
    // EFFECTS: Initializes this with the endpoints
    //   (x0,y0) and (x1,y1).

  public PointGeometry getP0()
    // EFFECTS: Returns a copy of endpoint p0.

  public void setP0(PointGeometry newP0)
        throws NullPointerException
    // MODIFIES: this
    // EFFECTS: If newP0 is null throws
    //   NullPointerException; else updates the p0
    //   endpoint to a copy of newP0.

  public PointGeometry getP1()
    // EFFECTS: Returns a copy of endpoint p1.

  public void setP1(PointGeometry newP1)
        throws NullPointerException
    // MODIFIES: this
    // EFFECTS: If newP1 is null throws
    //   NullPointerException; else updates the p1
    //   endpoint to a copy of newP1.

  public double length()
    // EFFECTS: Returns the length of this segment.

  public java.awt.Shape shape()
    // EFFECTS: Returns the shape of this segment.

  public void translate(int dx, int dy)
    // MODIFIES: this
    // EFFECTS: Translates this segment by dx and dy:
    //   this_post.getP0().equals(getP0()+(dx,dy)),
    //   this_post.getP1().equals(getP1()+(dx,dy)).

  public String toString()
    // EFFECTS: Returns the string "p0-p1".
}
```

Here is a short program that exercises the `LineSegmentGeometry` class. Strings printed by this program appear as italicized comments:

```
public class TryLineSegment {
  public static void main(String[] args) {
```

```
    LineSegmentGeometry a =
      new LineSegmentGeometry(1, 2, 3, 4);
    PointGeometry p = a.getP0();
    p.setX(88);    // endpoint p0 of a not affected
    System.out.println("a: " + a);// a: (1,2)-(3,4)
    System.out.println("length: " + a.length());
                   // length: 2.8284271247461903
    PointGeometry q = new PointGeometry(7, 8);
    a.setP0(q);
    q.setX(34);    // endpoint p0 of a not affected
    System.out.println("a: " + a);// a: (7,8)-(3,4)
    a.translate(2, 3);
    System.out.println("a: " + a);// a: (9,11)-(5,7)
  }
}
```

Observe that the point p obtained from the expression `a.getP0()` cannot be used to modify the endpoint *p0* of line a. The object referenced by the expression `a.getP0()` is a *copy* of the point stored in line segment a's p0 field, and this object is not a part of point a's state. Similarly, the state of a is not affected by changes to point q, even after q was used to modify the value of a's *p0* endpoint. Generally, a line segment maintains its own protected endpoints (in the form of `PointGeometry` objects), and never allows clients direct access to its endpoints. I will give you the implementation of the `shape` method:

```
// method of LineSegmentGeometry class
public Shape shape() {
  return new Line2D.Float(p0.getX(), p0.getY(),
                          p1.getX(), p1.getY());
}
```

ESSENTIAL 3.4

An **attribute** is a name-value pair, where the name is a `String` and the value is an object of any type. Attributes can be used to indicate properties of an object. For instance, a polygon might have the attributes *"color" : Color.red* and *"number of sides" : 3* to indicate that it is a red triangle. Attributes are also used as entries in dictionaries, where each entry associates a unique name with a value. Here is a skeleton for the `Attribute` class:

```
public class Attribute {

  public Attribute(String name)
        throws NullPointerException
```

```
    // EFFECTS: If name is null throws
    //   NullPointerException; else initializes
    //   this to name:null.

  public Attribute(String name, Object value)
        throws NullPointerException
    // EFFECTS: If name is null throws
    //   NullPointerException; else initializes
    //   this to name:value.

  public Object getValue()
    // EFFECTS: Returns this attribute's value.

  public void setValue(Object newValue)
    // MODIFIES: this
    // EFFECTS: Changes this attribute's value
    //   to newValue.

  public String name()
    // EFFECTS: Returns this attribute's name.

  public boolean equals(Object obj)
    // EFFECTS: Returns true if obj is an Attribute
    //   and obj's name is equal to this attribute's
    //   name; else returns false.

  public String toString()
    // EFFECTS: Returns the string "name:value".
}
```

Note that *value* is a property of this class, but that *name* is not (there is no method for changing an attribute's name). Also, two attributes are considered equal if their names are equal, regardless of whether their values are equal. Here is a short program that exercises this class:

```
public class TryAttribute {
  public static void main(String[] args) {
    Attribute apple1 = new Attribute("apple", "red");
    Attribute apple2 = new Attribute("apple");
    if (apple1.equals(apple2))
      System.out.println("this should print");
    System.out.println("apple1: " + apple1.name() +
      ":" + apple1.getValue()); // apple1: apple:red
```

```
        apple2.setValue("green");
        System.out.println("apple2: " + apple2);
                                        // apple2: apple:green
    }
}
```

Implement the `Attribute` class and test it using `TryAttribute` or some similar test program.

3.2.2 Rectangles

A rectangle is a four-sided plane figure with four right angles. We will assume our rectangles to be in **standard orientation,** meaning that their sides are parallel to the *x* or *y* axes. We further assume that a rectangle's width and height are nonnegative integer values. We define a *rectangle's position* to be the position of its upper-left corner. Because of the orientation of our coordinate axes (with *x* increasing to the right and *y* increasing down), a rectangle's position is its corner of minimum *x* and *y* coordinates. A rectangle's *width* is the length of its horizontal sides, and its *height* is the length of its vertical sides (Figure 3.2). We will refer to a rectangle's position, width, and height properties jointly as the **rectangle's dimensions.**

Here is a class skeleton for our rectangle data type:

```
public class RectangleGeometry {

  public RectangleGeometry(int x, int y,
                            int width, int height)
        throws IllegalArgumentException
    // EFFECTS: If width or height is negative throws
    //   IllegalArgumentException; else initializes
    //   this to a rectangle at position (x,y) and of
```

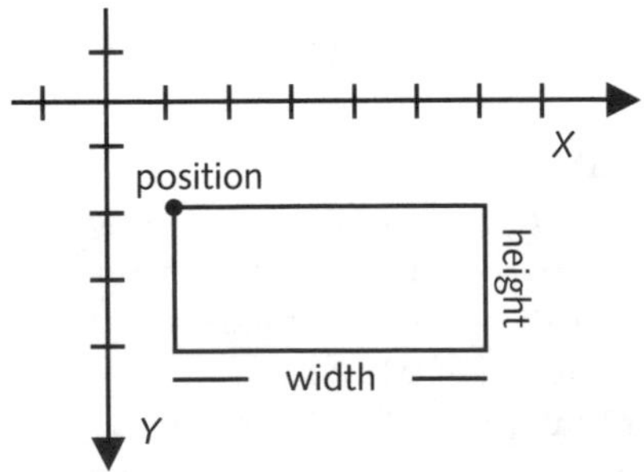

FIGURE 3.2 Cartesian plane with a rectangle shown.

```
  //   given width and height.

public RectangleGeometry(PointGeometry pos,
                         int width, int height)
       throws NullPointerException,
              IllegalArgumentException
  // EFFECTS: If pos is null throws
  //   NullPointerException; else if width or height
  //   is negative throws IllegalArgumentException;
  //   else initializes this to a rectangle at
  //   position (pos.getX(),pos.getY()) and of
  //   given width and height.

public RectangleGeometry(Range xRange, Range yRange)
       throws NullPointerException
  //EFFECTS: If xRange or yRange is null throws
  //   NullPointerException; else initializes this to
  //   a rectangle of specified x and y extents.

public RectangleGeometry(RectangleGeometry r)
       throws NullPointerException
  // EFFECTS: If r is null throws
  //   NullPointerException; else initializes this to
  //   a rectangle with the same dimensions as r.

public PointGeometry getPosition()
  // EFFECTS: Returns this rectangle's position.

public void setPosition(PointGeometry p)
       throws NullPointerException
  // MODIFIES: this
  // EFFECTS: If p is null throws
  //   NullPointerException; else sets this
  //   rectangle's position to (p.getX(),p.getY()).

public int getWidth()
  // EFFECTS: Returns this rectangle's width.

public void setWidth(int newWidth)
       throws IllegalArgumentException
  // MODIFIES: this
  // EFFECTS: If newWidth is negative throws
  //   IllegalArgumentException; else sets this
  //   rectangle's width to newWidth.

public int getHeight()
  // EFFECTS: Returns this rectangle's height.
```

```
  public void setHeight(int newHeight)
        throws IllegalArgumentException
    // MODIFIES: this
    //EFFECTS: If newHeight is negative throws
    //   IllegalArgumentException; else sets this
    //   rectangle's height to newHeight.

  public Range xRange()
    // EFFECTS: Returns the range spanned by
    //   this rectangle's x coordinates.

  public Range yRange()
    // EFFECTS: Returns the range spanned by
    //   this rectangle's y coordinates.

  public boolean contains(int x, int y)
    // EFFECTS: Returns true if the point (x,y) is
    //   contained in this rectangle; else returns false.

  public boolean contains(PointGeometry p)
        throws NullPointerException
    // EFFECTS: If p is null throws
    //   NullPointerException; else returns true if p is
    //   contained in this rectangle; else returns false.

  public java.awt.Shape shape()
    // EFFECTS: Returns the shape of this rectangle.

  public void translate(int dx, int dy)
    // MODIFIES: this
    // EFFECTS: Translates this rectangle by dx and dy:
    //   this_post.getPosition() is equal to
    //   this.getPosition()+(dx,dy).

  public String toString()
    // EFFECTS: Returns the string
    //   "Rectangle: (x,y),width,height".
}
```

Let's consider the behavior of the `RectangleGeometry` class before implementing it. We'll write an application named `TryRectangle` that gets called with four program arguments that describe the dimensions of a rectangle *r* (these program arguments match those of `RectangleGeometry`'s four-argument constructor). Our program first prints the string-descriptor for the rectangle *r*. Then the program issues a prompt, to which the user responds by entering the *x* and *y* coordinates of some point. The program then echoes the point entered by the user and reports whether this point lies inside or outside the rectangle *r*. In response to further prompts, the user inputs additional points and the program prints each point and reports whether it is contained in the rectangle *r*. The user inputs the point (0,0) to quit the program. In the following sample interaction, the program arguments describe a rectangle with upper–left corner at (10,10), and of width 30 and height 20:

```
> java TryRectangle 10 10 30 20
Rectangle: (10,10),30,20
? 20 15
(20,15): inside
? 40 30
(40,30): inside
? 41 30
(41,30): outside
? 10 16
(10,16): inside
? 0 0
(0,0): outside
>
```

The application is implemented by the `TryRectangle` class. The static method `main` first parses the program arguments and uses them to construct the rectangle *r*. Next it opens an input stream, and then iteratively issues the prompt '?', reads the coordinates of the next point from the input stream, constructs the point, and tests and reports whether the point is contained in the rectangle *r*. Here is the implementation:

```
public class TryRectangle {
  public static void main(String[] args) {
    if (args.length != 4) {
      String msg = "USAGE: java TryRectangle x y ";
      msg += "width height";
      System.out.println(msg);
      System.exit(1);
    }
    int x = Integer.parseInt(args[0]);
    int y = Integer.parseInt(args[1]);
    int width = Integer.parseInt(args[2]);
    int height = Integer.parseInt(args[3]);
    RectangleGeometry r =
      new RectangleGeometry(x, y, width, height);
    System.out.println(r);
    ScanInput in = new ScanInput();
    PointGeometry origin = new PointGeometry();
    while (true) {
      try {
        System.out.print("? ");
        x = in.readInt();
```

```
                y = in.readInt();
                PointGeometry p = new PointGeometry(x, y);
                System.out.print(p + ": ");
                if (r.contains(p)) System.out.println("inside");
                else System.out.println("outside");
                if (p.equals(origin)) break;
              } catch (NumberFormatException e) {
                System.out.println("please enter two numbers");
              } catch (IOException e) {
                System.out.println("i/o exception... bye!");
                System.exit(1);
              }
            }
          }
        }
```

Let us turn to an implementation for the `RectangleGeometry` class. Our class defines two fields of type `Range` (see Exercise 3.2):

```
// fields of RectangleGeometry class
protected Range xRange, yRange;
```

These two ranges jointly define a rectangle. Field `xRange` stores the range of x coordinates spanned by the rectangle's horizontal sides, and `yRange` stores the range of y coordinates spanned by its vertical sides. For example, the rectangle

```
new Rectangle(new PointGeometry(1,2), 3, 6)
```

is represented by the following two ranges:

```
xRange: new Range(1, 4)
yRange: new Range(2, 8)
```

This is by no means the only storage structure suitable for representing rectangles, but it is the one we will adopt here. The exercises explore other possibilities.

Here are class `RectangleGeometry's` four constructors:

```
public RectangleGeometry(int x, int y,
                         int width, int height)
      throws IllegalArgumentException {
  if ((width < 0) || (height < 0))
    throw new IllegalArgumentException();
  xRange = new Range(x, x + width);
  yRange = new Range(y, y + height);
}

public RectangleGeometry(PointGeometry pos,
                         int width, int height)
```

```
        throws NullPointerException,
               IllegalArgumentException {
    this(pos.getX(), pos.getY(), width, height);
  }

  public RectangleGeometry(Range xRange, Range yRange)
        throws NullPointerException {
    this(xRange.getMin(), yRange.getMin(),
        xRange.length(), yRange.length());
  }

  public RectangleGeometry(RectangleGeometry r)
        throws NullPointerException {
    this(r.getPosition(), r.getWidth(), r.getHeight());
  }
```

Observe that the second and third constructors directly call the first (four-argument) constructor, and that the fourth constructor indirectly calls the first constructor. Note also that of these four constructors, only the first directly accesses the instance fields `xRange` and `yRange`.

To obtain a rectangle's position, we extract the minimum values from its `xRange` and `yRange` fields:

```
  // method of RectangleGeometry class
  public PointGeometry getPosition() {
    return new PointGeometry(xRange.getMin(),
                             yRange.getMin());
  }
```

When you update a rectangle's position, you update the minimum values of its two ranges while ensuring that the rectangle's width and height are not affected:

```
  // method of RectangleGeometry class
  public void setPosition(PointGeometry p)
        throws NullPointerException {
    xRange.setMinMax(p.getX(), p.getX() + getWidth());
    yRange.setMinMax(p.getY(), p.getY() + getHeight());
  }
```

The width of a rectangle is equal to the length of its x range. Here is the width property's getter and setter procedures:

```
  // methods of RectangleGeometry class
  public int getWidth() {
    return xRange.length();
  }

  public void setWidth(int newWidth)
        throws IllegalArgumentException {
```

```
    if (newWidth < 0) throw new IllegalArgumentException();
    xRange.setMax(xRange.getMin() + newWidth);
  }
```

The shape method returns this rectangle's shape:

```
// method of RectangleGeometry class
public java.awt.Shape shape() {
  PointGeometry p = getPosition();
  return new Rectangle2D.Float(p.getX(), p.getY(),
                               getWidth(), getHeight());
}
```

The two contains methods report whether the input point is contained inside this rectangle. The point (*x*,*y*) lies inside this rectangle if and only if *x* lies within the rectangle's *x* range and *y* lies within its *y* range:

```
// methods of RectangleGeometry class
public boolean contains(int x, int y) {
  return xRange().contains(x) && yRange().contains(y);
}

public boolean contains(PointGeometry p)
      throws NullPointerException {
  return contains(p.getX(), p.getY());
}
```

Exercises

ESSENTIAL 3.5 Complete the implementation of class RectangleGeometry. This requires that you define its getHeight, setHeight, xRange, yRange, translate, and toString methods. To ensure that clients cannot directly access a rectangle's storage structure, the xRange method should return a copy of the object referenced by the xRange field (a similar remark applies to the yRange method). The following code fragment illustrates the behavior of the translate and toString methods:

```
RectangleGeometry r =
  new RectangleGeometry(new PointGeometry(2, 3),4,5);
System.out.println(r);  // Rectangle: (2,3),4,5
r.translate(10, 20);
System.out.println(r);  // Rectangle: (12,23),4,5
```

Try to make the implementation of your methods independent of the storage structure, the fields xRange and yRange.

3.3 Encapsulation

Encapsulation is the practice of grouping related software elements together. Java provides packages for encapsulating a set of related classes. In this section we focus on a more fundamental form of encapsulation that occurs at the level of objects: An object encapsulates a set of related data and methods. Moreover, the elements that make up an object are themselves encapsulated based on their accessibility to clients.

We can view an object as a set of data and methods enclosed by an outer membrane. In turn, some of the object's elements are placed within additional membranes nested within this outer membrane. At its simplest, we imagine those elements that contribute to the object's public interface residing within the outer membrane, and those elements contributing to its private implementation enclosed by a second, inner membrane (Figure 3.3). Clients live in the rest of the plane, beyond the outer membrane. The object's outer membrane is fully permeable, meaning that clients can send messages through it to the elements it encloses. However, the inner membrane is only semipermeable—it conveys only those messages that originate from privileged clients. Thus, all clients have access to the elements that reside between the two membranes, whereas only privileged clients have access to the elements enclosed by the inner membrane.

The use of encapsulation to conceal those elements that do not belong to an object's public interface is known as **information hiding.** Information hiding serves both an object and its clients. Because clients cannot access an object's private implementation, they are unable to bypass its intended interface. Thus the object mediates all interactions through its methods and so can ensure the consistency of its own state. Clients also benefit from information hiding—because clients rely only on an object's public interface, they are not affected by changes to the object's implementation that hold its interface fixed.

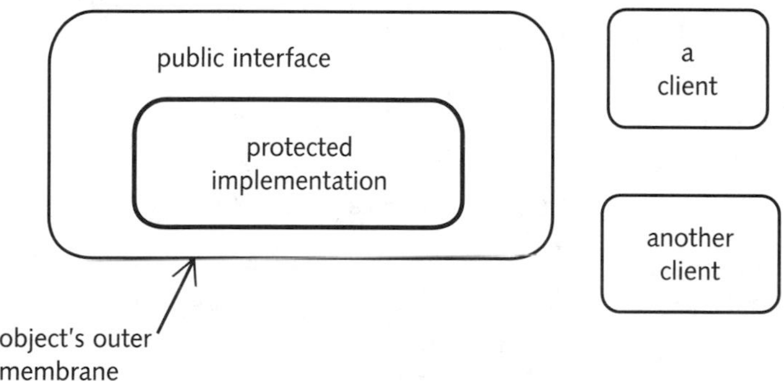

FIGURE 3.3 An object encapsulates a set of interfaces.

3.3.1 Encapsulation and Class Definitions

A class definition describes the methods and structure of objects belonging to the class. The class definition brings the objects' elements together in one place, thereby simplifying the task of those who must author, understand, or modify the class. The elements of a class are highly cohesive: The class' operations are implemented by its methods, and these methods access and modify an object's instance fields. The implementation may be grasped as a whole only by consideration of all its elements. Presenting the implementation in the same place is a convenience for programmers.

Nonetheless, class definitions do an imperfect job of localizing the elements of a class. There are two problems, the first of which is due to inheritance. When a new class extends an existing class (as is always the case in Java), the new subclass inherits its superclass' implementation and interface. The new class' implementation potentially depends on that of its superclass, and the superclass' implementation potentially depends on that of *its* superclass, and so forth, up the chain of inheritance to the root class `Object`. Thus, the implementation of a new class may depend on the implementation of any number of other classes (its supertypes). This leads to the so-called **yo-yo problem,** which requires the programmer to flip back and forth between several classes within an inheritance chain to understand just one of the classes. To help, integrated development environments are equipped with browsers for traversing the inheritance hierarchy, which programmers can use to readily locate and examine superclasses.

The second problem is that the elements that compose an object's interface and those that compose its implementation intermingle within a class definition. Although the client's author needs to understand only the interface to use the object, the class definition presents both the interface *and* the implementation. Consider the following class for counting. An `UpCounter` object maintains an integer value which is initialized to zero and is incremented by one each time the `inc` method is called. The class also provides a `value` method that returns the current value. Here is the class definition:

```
public class UpCounter {

  private int value;

  public UpCounter() {
    // EFFECTS: Initializes this counter to zero.
    this.value = 0;
  }

  public void inc() {
    // MODIFIES: this
    // EFFECTS: Increments this counter by one.
```

```
    this.value++;
  }

  public int value() {
    // EFFECTS: Returns this counter's current value.
    return this.value;
  }
}
```

The client's author is interested only in `UpCounter`'s interface, but the class definition presents so much more. It provides the very implementation details that information hiding is designed to conceal. Referring to Figure 3.3, a class definition lifts the reader *above* the page, providing a view of an object's structure and implementation whether or not the reader wants or requires such information.

Java's interface structure is useful for separating interface from implementation. An interface declares a set of operations while deferring their implementation to those classes that implement the interface. However, it is impractical to define an interface to parallel every class. In practice, to use a class it is often necessary to read its class definition.

3.3.2 Information Hiding

Information hiding is used to conceal those elements of an object that do not belong to its public interface. Such elements typically include all data fields, any nonpublic methods designed for use only by objects of the same class or closely related classes, and the implementation of all methods.

Information hiding can be approached with this question: From whom is an object's implementation hidden? There are two answers. First, an object's implementation is hidden from the programmer. This is a curious assertion in light of the fact that a class definition displays its implementation for all to see. Yet, programmers routinely rely on classes belonging to packages not of their own design, and they often don't have access to the package's source code. But what about when the programmer *does* have access to the source code, such as when she writes the code herself? Even in such cases that an object's implementation is at hand, it is expected to be hidden from the programmer's *thought*. Information hiding helps one to distinguish between different levels of abstraction. When writing code or developing a system that requires the services of some object, the object's implementation—the details of how it does what it does—should be kept out of mind. The distinction between an object's public interface and its protected implementation is one enforced not only by the compiler, but also by the programmer's thought processes.

Secondly, an object's implementation is hidden from its clients. A client may access a hidden member only if it has the requisite privileges. For example, the `xRange` and `yRange` fields of the `RectangleGeometry` class are declared `protected`. This means that only those clients that belong to the same package as `RectangleGeometry`, or to subtypes of `RectangleGeometry`, may access these fields.

Java provides the means to build interfaces at four different levels of accessibility. Within a class definition, information hiding is achieved by declaring members to be `public`, `protected`, or `private`, or through the omission of an access-control keyword (which implies that the member has package-level accessibility). The public interface, the most accessible, is available to all objects. The private interface, the least accessible, is accessible only to objects of the same type. Here are Java's levels of accessibility in order of increasing restriction:

- *public*: accessible to all objects,
- *protected*: accessible only to objects whose class belongs to the same package and to instances of any subtype,
- *package*: accessible only to objects whose class belongs to the same package,
- *private*: accessible only to objects of the same class.

As we move along the spectrum from public to private accessibility, the interface becomes less accessible but more capable. Imagine a refinement of Figure 3.3 in which the object is encapsulated by a series of four nested membranes instead of just two. The outermost membrane is fully permeable—it lets every message pass through—whereas each of the remaining (nested) membranes is less permeable than the membrane that encloses it. The services enclosed by each membrane are available only to those clients whose messages are conveyed by the membrane, as determined by the client's relationship to the object. Clients with greater privileges can reach deeper into the object and therefore can access a greater number of services.

As a simple demonstration, consider a Java program that takes a sequence of integer program arguments and prints separate counts of the number of even arguments and the number of odd arguments. The program uses two instances of the `UpCounter` class (Section 3.3.1) for the separate counts:

```
public class EvenOddCount {
  public static void main(String[] args) {
    UpCounter even = new UpCounter();
    UpCounter odd = new UpCounter();
    for (int i = 0; i < args.length; i++) {
      int k = Integer.parseInt(args[i]);
      if (k%2 == 0) even.inc();
      else odd.inc();
    }
    System.out.println("number of evens: "+even.value());
    System.out.println("number of odds: "+odd.value());
  }
}
```

For example, we have the following interaction:

```
> java EvenOddCount 0 2 4 6 9
number of evens: 4
number of odds: 1
```

In the `EvenOddCount` program, the procedure `main` uses the services of two counters—instances of the `UpCounter` class—but it cannot directly access the counters' hidden implementation. A compile-time error would result if `main` attempted to modify a counter's current value directly through its private field:

```
odd.value++;
```

rather than through the operation designed for this purpose:

```
odd.inc();
```

Information hiding prevents clients from bypassing an object's interface, and so helps to ensure that the object's state is not corrupted by its clients. Each client's interaction with the object is mediated by the elements of the interface to which the client has access.

Information hiding protects not only the server object but also its clients. This is because the client relies directly on the interface it has access to, but not on the parts of the implementation that are hidden from it. Clients are not affected by changes to the object's implementation as long as the object's interface is held fixed. By way of example, suppose that we were to revise the implementation of the `UpCounter` class without changing its interface. In the following implementation, a counter's current value is equal to the difference between the value stored in its `value` field and the smallest possible `int`:

```
// class UpCounter: version 2
public class UpCounter {

  private int value;

  public UpCounter() {
    this.value = Integer.MIN_VALUE;
  }

  public void inc() {
    this.value++;
  }

  public int value() {
    return this.value - Integer.MIN_VALUE;
  }
}
```

This second version of the `UpCounter` class presents precisely the same public interface as the original version. Because our `EvenOddCount` program depends only on this interface and not on the underlying implementation, it remains correct. It is not affected by this change in implementation. In contrast, suppose that our `EvenOddCount` program had violated information hiding by accessing its counters' `value` fields directly. For concreteness, suppose that the program were to print its results using the following two instructions:

```
System.out.println("number of evens: " + even.value);
System.out.println("number of odds: " + odd.value);
```

In this case, the program's behavior would be very much affected by the change in implementation to the `UpCounter` class. Indeed, the sample interaction given earlier would now be wrong:

```
> java EvenOddCount 0 2 4 6 9
number of evens: -2147483644
number of odds: -2147483647
```

By requiring clients to use an object through the object's public interface, information hiding helps guarantee the clients' own correctness.

Exercises

3.6 The fields of the `RectangleGeometry` class do not directly correspond to its properties. Although a rectangle has a *position* property, it does not define a field that stores its position. Rather, it extracts the value of its position property from its fields `xRange` and `yRange`. For this exercise, reimplement the `RectangleGeometry` class (while keeping its specification fixed) so that its storage structure directly corresponds to its properties:

```
// fields of RectangleGeometry class
//   (for this exercise)
PointGeometry pos;
int width, height;
```

For example, the rectangle

```
new RectangleGeometry(new PointGeometry(1,2),3,6)
```

would be represented as follows:

```
pos: (1,2)
width: 3
height: 6
```

Which methods of our original implementation of class `RectangleGeometry` must change? Must we change any of the original methods whose implementations do not directly access the original fields `xRange` and `yRange`? Run the `TryRectangle` application (Section 3.2.2) using your new version of the `RectangleGeometry` class (it should work because both versions of this class realize the same interface).

3.4 Java Graphics: Some Background

Up to now we've worked with several kinds of graphical objects such as rectangles and points, but we have yet to paint a thing. We'll remedy this in the next two sections. In this section I'll provide the background needed to produce computer graphics in Java. Then, in Section 3.5, we'll develop a Java program for painting a green rectangle into a window. While hardly remarkable in itself, this program will serve as a template for many of the graphics programs that you'll encounter (and write yourself) later in this book. The simplicity of this program's graphics will help us focus on what is common to all these programs, without distracting us by details that more complex graphics would require.

3.4.1 The Java 2D API Rendering Model

Rendering is the process of drawing graphics to an output device. In Java 2D, rendering centers on an object known variously as a **rendering context** or a **graphics context.** This is an instance of the `java.awt.Graphics2D` class. A rendering context serves three purposes:

- It represents the drawing surface, which can correspond to three kinds of output: the screen, a printer, or an off-screen buffer,
- It maintains the state of a set of rendering attributes. These include a font for drawing text strings, a paint (such as a solid color) for drawing and filling, and a stroke which specifies how the outline of figures are drawn,
- It presents a set of methods for rendering graphical objects—shapes, text, and images—into the drawing surface.

At its most basic, rendering in Java is a four-step process:

1. Acquire a `Graphics2D` object for the intended drawing surface.
2. Construct the graphical object or objects to be rendered.
3. Set the attributes of the `Graphics2D` object as desired.
4. Invoke a rendering method of the `Graphics2D` object. The appropriate rendering method depends on both the kind of graphical object being rendered and the desired effect.

The rest of this section explains each of these four steps in greater detail, while emphasizing those aspects that we will make use of in this book (e.g., rendering to the screen, rather than to a printer or an off-screen buffer).

3.4.2 Acquiring a Rendering Context

A top-level window with a title bar and border is called a **frame** in Java. Frames are the main application windows that populate your screen. A frame serves as a container of other components such as buttons, text fields, labels, and panels. These components occupy what is known as the frame's **content pane,** the rectangular area enclosed by the frame's border and title bar.

Some of the components in a frame are **atomic components,** meaning that they do not contain other components. Examples of atomic components include buttons, labels, and text fields. Other components are **containers,** meaning that they may contain other components. One example of a container is a **panel,** a generic container that often serves as a canvas into which graphics are drawn. (We will do all our drawing in a top-level panel contained in a frame.) In general, a frame contains top-level components, some of which are containers that contain still other components, some of which in turn may be containers holding still more components, and so forth, through any number of levels. The result is a **containment hierarchy** of components, whose root is the frame. Visually, each component appears on top of and enclosed by its parent container, with the frame lying behind and enclosing everything.

Figure 3.4 shows a Java application for maintaining name-value pairs. The frame's content pane—the portion of the frame to which we add components—contains three panels: the field panel holds the fields (and associated labels) that the user uses to enter new name-value pairs, remove existing pairs, and pose queries; the button panel holds the buttons by which the user issues commands; and the message panel presents the results of queries. Figure 3.4 also depicts the application's containment hierarchy as a tree. Note that the tree's internal nodes correspond to containers, whereas the tree's leaf nodes correspond to atomic components (text fields, buttons, and labels).

A frame repaints itself and its contents often throughout its lifetime. This occurs, for instance, whenever the frame is uncovered on your screen by the disappearance or movement of a frame above it, or when it is resized, or when it is displayed for the first time. The system detects such events and notifies the frame to repaint itself as necessary. A frame is also repainted whenever the content it displays changes in a significant way. Whenever this occurs, your program—which manages the frame's content—tells the frame to paint itself again by sending the frame a *repaint* message. The *repaint* message does not cause the frame to paint itself immediately; rather, it schedules the frame for painting at the next opportunity.

When the frame paints itself, it paints all the components it contains—the entire containment hierarchy of which it is the root. The frame first paints the background of its content pane, which is a filled gray rectangle.

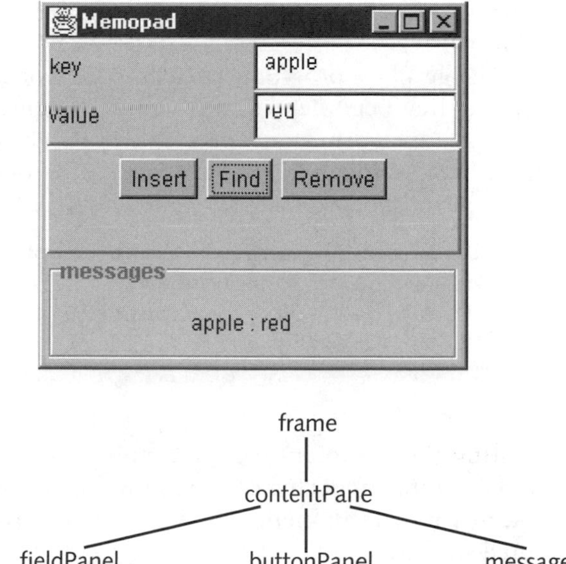

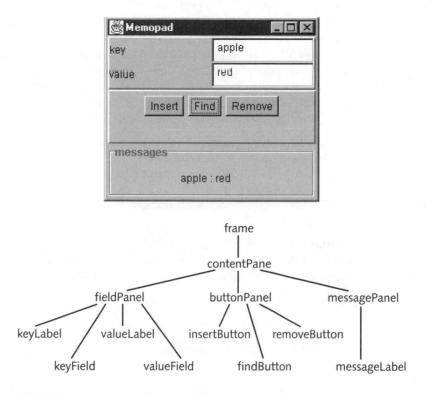

FIGURE 3.4 A Java application and its containment hierarchy.

Then it tells its top-level components to paint themselves. The atomic components, such as buttons and labels, paint themselves directly. A button, for instance, paints its background rectangle and then its label text on top. Container components are painted differently. Each container (such as a panel) first paints its background and any adornments such as borders, then tells each of the components it contains to paint itself. In this manner, the painting process propagates from the frame toward the leaves of the containment hierarchy. To summarize, every container paints itself, then paints its components; every atomic component paints itself directly.

Whenever a component is told to paint itself, it executes its `paintComponent` method. This method is called with a rendering context (an instance of the `Graphics2D` class). Here is the method's signature:

```
// method of javax.swing.JComponent class
public void paintComponent(Graphics g)
```

Although the parameter of method `JComponent.paintComponent` is declared as type `Graphics`, the actual argument that gets passed is of type `Graphics2D`. This is possible because `Graphics2D` is a subtype of `Graphics`.

Things were arranged this way to maintain compatibility with earlier versions of Java.

The graphics programs we will write render to the screen; specifically, to a panel that occupies a frame's content pane. The panel serves as the program's drawing surface. The graphics program describes its own rendering logic by overriding the `paintComponent` method it inherits. Your `paintComponent` method takes the following form:

```
public void paintComponent(Graphics g) {
  super.paintComponent(g);
  Graphics2D g2 = (Graphics2D)g;
  // program-specific rendering using g2
  ...
}
```

Casting the argument `g` as a `Graphics2D` ensures that your method has access to the rendering context's full functionality. The process of writing a `paintComponent` method and a graphics program generally will be elaborated shortly.

3.4.3 Constructing a Graphical Object

Three kinds of graphical objects can be rendered into a rendering context:

- **shapes,** which are geometrical forms such as rectangles, ellipses, lines, and curves. Every shape implements the `java.awt.Shape` interface.
- **text,** which can be rendered in different fonts, styles, and colors.
- **images,** which are typically instances of the `java.awt.image.BufferedImage` class.

Our focus in this book will be on rendering shapes. What little text rendering we do will be accomplished by reducing text to shapes known as **glyphs.**

Graphical objects are positioned and sized relative to a coordinate system known as **user space.** By default, the origin occurs in the upper-left corner of the drawing surface, and x coordinates increase to the right and y coordinates increase downward. When drawing to a screen, x and y coordinates are measured in pixels. The coordinates supplied to shapes are always given in terms of user space. (We shall see shortly that it is possible to transform user space; that is, to change its position, scale, and orientation relative to the drawing surface.)

The `java.awt.geom` package defines a number of classes that implement the `java.awt.Shape` interface. Examples include the `Rectangle2D.Float`, `Ellipse2D.Float`, and `Line2D.Float` classes. We have used some of these classes already. For example, recall that our implementation of the `PointGeometry.shape` method creates and returns a new `Ellipse2D.Float` object:

```
// method of PointGeometry class
public Shape shape() {
  return new Ellipse2D.Float(getX()-2, getY()-2, 4, 4);
}
```

This produces a circle with center (*x,y*) and diameter 4. The first two arguments to the `Ellipse2D.Float` constructor position the upper-left corner of a rectangle that tightly bounds the ellipse, and the last two arguments specify this rectangle's width and height. Note that method shape's return type of `Shape` is legal because the `Ellipse2D.Float` class implements the `Shape` interface.

Java 2D provides classes for many different kinds of shapes: ellipses, rectangles, rounded rectangles, arcs, lines, curves, general paths, and areas (areas provide methods for combining shapes by union, intersection, and difference). Rather than detail each kind of shape that Java 2D supports, I will introduce them as the need arises throughout the book.

3.4.4 Setting the Attributes of a Rendering Context

A `Graphics2D` object encapsulates state information needed for rendering. It provides methods for setting and getting the values of the following seven attributes:

- *paint*—the pixel pattern used to fill or stroke shapes.
- *stroke*—controls the appearance of a shape when its outline is drawn.
- *transform*—specifies the user space relative to the drawing surface.
- *font*—the font in which text is rendered.
- *composite*—describes how a rendering operation blends with the existing background.
- *clip*—a shape, known as the **clip area,** to which the rendering is restricted (the rendering operation has no effect outside of the clip area).
- *rendering hints*—provides some control over the quality and speed of the rendering process.

The `Graphics2D` class provides a setter and getter method for each of these attributes. For instance, where `g2` is a `Graphics2D` object, you can set `g2`'s current paint to green with this call:

```
g2.setPaint(Color.green);
```

And the following call obtains the rendering context's current stroke:

```
Stroke stroke = g2.getStroke();
```

In this book we will mainly use a rendering context's *paint, stroke,* and *transform* attributes.

A `Shape` can be painted in two different ways: its interior can be **filled** or its outline can be **stroked.** To fill the interior of a shape, you send a *fill* message to a `Graphics2D` object, passing the shape as an argument. To stroke the outline of a shape, you send the `Graphics2D` object a *draw* message, again passing the shape as an argument.

The `Graphic2D` object's *paint* attribute determines the color pattern used to fill and stroke shapes. The value of this attribute is any object that implements the `java.awt.Paint` interface. The simplest kind of paint is a `Color` object, which represents a solid color. Java also provides two other classes that implement `Paint`. The `GradientPaint` class defines a linear color gradient between two fixed colors. And the `TexturePaint` class enables you to paint with an image.

An attribute's value has effect until it is changed. For instance, you can fill a rectangle with solid blue like this:

```
g2.setPaint(Color.blue);
g2.fill(new Rectangle2D.Float(10, 20, 80, 40));
```

Subsequent shapes sent to `g2` are painted blue, until `g2`'s *paint* attribute is changed by another call to `setPaint`.

The *stroke* attribute of a `Graphics2D` object determines the shape of the marks made by an imaginary pen as the outline of a shape is drawn (that is, as the shape is stroked). Java provides the `java.awt.BasicStroke` class for representing strokes. With this class, you can specify the width of a stroke, how open stroke segments end (*end caps*), how two stroke segments are joined (*line joins*), and a stroke's dash pattern. The properties of a `BasicStroke` object are established when the object is constructed through the arguments passed to the constructor. The `BasicStroke` provides five different constructors for this purpose. You set a `Graphic2D`'s *stroke* attribute by sending it a `setStroke` message with a `BasicStroke` object as argument. For example, the following code draws a four-pixel-wide line from (20,30) to (50,80):

```
g2.setStroke(new BasicStroke(4));
g2.draw(Line2D.Float(20, 30, 50, 80));
```

The `Graphic2D` class' *transform* attribute is used to specify the user space, the coordinate system in which drawing occurs. By default, user space coincides with **device space**—the origin occurs at the drawing surface's upper-left corner, x coordinates increase to the right, y coordinates increase downward, and units are in pixels (assuming output is to the screen). One problem with using this default user space is that graphics centered at the origin appear off-center. For instance, the instruction:

```
g2.fill(new Ellipse2D.Float(-50, -50, 100, 100));
```

paints a circle centered at the origin. However, because the origin coincides with the drawing surface's upper-left corner, the circle appears in the upper-left corner, and in fact only one quadrant is visible. To solve this problem, we first *translate* the user space such that its origin coincides with the center of the drawing surface. Where the drawing surface's width and height are given by the variables `width` and `height`, this is achieved by the following code fragment:

```
g2.translate(width/2, height/2);  // translate q2
g2.fill(new Ellipse2D.Float(-50, -50, 100, 100));
```

Now when the circle is painted, it appears centered in the drawing surface. Subsequent rendering to `g2` assume this same translated user space, until `g2`'s user space is transformed by further commands.

Many of the graphics programs we will write include a `paintComponent` method whose definition begins thus:

```
public void paintComponent(Graphics g) {
  super.paintComponent(g);
  Graphics2D g2 = (Graphics2D)g;
  // translate the origin of g2's user space to
  //  the frame's center
  Dimension d = getFrame().getContentSize();
  g2.translate((int)(d.width/2), (int)(d.height/2));
  // program-specific rendering using g2
  ...
}
```

This translates the origin of `g2`'s user space to the center of the drawing surface prior to actual rendering. In Figure 3.5, the coordinate axes of the device space are shown in black, and those of the translated coordinate space in gray.

The `translate` method is only one of a number of methods provided for modifying the user space associated with a `Graphics2D` object. The `Graphics2D` class also provides `rotation`, `scale`, and `shear` methods, which

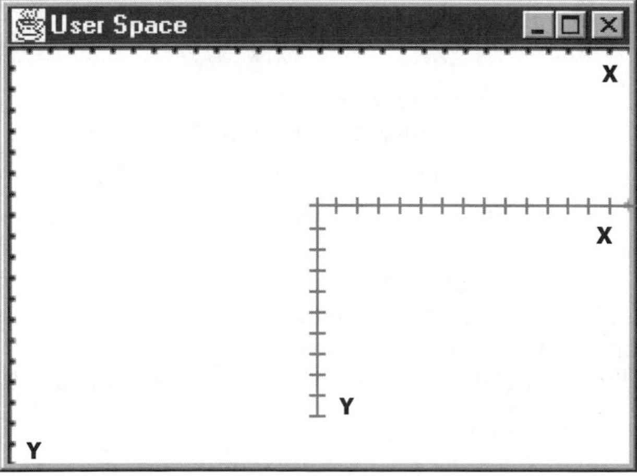

FIGURE 3.5 Device space in black; translated user space in gray.

together with `translate` comprise what are known as **elementary transforms.** Rotation is used to rotate the user space around an arbitrary point. Scale is used to shrink or enlarge user space by changing the units in which *x* coordinates and *y* coordinates are specified. Shear is used to skew the user space, which involves a scaled translation (for example, a rectangle becomes a parallelogram when sheared). The `Graphics2D` class also provides `setTransform` and `getTransform` methods for manipulating the user space directly in terms of an object known as a **transform** (an instance of the `AffineTransform` class). Generally, the user space associated with a rendering context has uses that go well beyond that of centering graphics in a drawing surface. We will return to this in Chapter 6.

3.4.5 Rendering

As I've noted, `Graphics2D` objects can render three kinds of graphical objects: shapes, text, and images. The emphasis in this book is on shapes—objects that implement the `java.awt.Shape` interface. Shapes can be painted in two ways: you can paint the interior of a shape (using the `fill` method) or stroke the outline of a shape (using the `draw` method). Both methods take the shape to be rendered as an argument:

```
// methods of Graphics2D class
public void fill(Shape s) throws NullPointerException
  // EFFECTS: If s is null throws NullPointerException;
  //   else fills the interior of s based on this
  //   rendering context's attributes.
public void draw(Shape s) throws NullPointerException
  // EFFECTS: If s is null throws NullPointerException;
  //   else strokes the outline of s based on this
  //   rendering context's attributes.
```

For example, the following code fragment fills with green a circle of diameter 100:

```
g2.setPaint(Color.green);
Shape circle = new Ellipse2D.Float(50, 50, 100, 100);
g2.fill(circle);
```

The circle appears in the drawing surface associated with the rendering context `g2`.

To stroke the outline of a shape, you send a *draw* message to a `Graphics2D` object, passing the shape as an argument. For example, the following code draws the perimeter of a rectangle with upper-left corner at (10,20), width 80, and height 40. The outline is red and four pixels wide:

```
g2.setPaint(Color.red);
g2.setStroke(new BasicStroke(4));
Shape rectangle = new Rectangle2D.Float(10, 20, 80, 40);
g2.draw(rectangle);
```

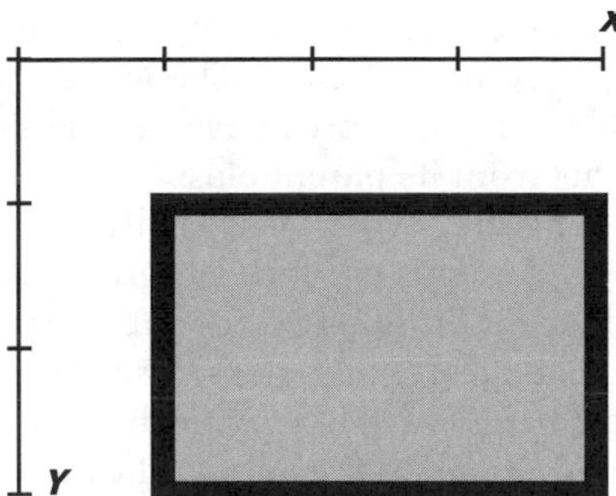

FIGURE 3.6 A rectangle filled and then stroked.

The rectangle's interior is not painted, only its outline.

Of course, it is possible to both draw and stroke the same shape. To do this, it is common to interleave commands for setting the rendering context's attributes with commands that perform the actual rendering. The following code fragment assumes that the `Graphics2D` object `g2` has already been acquired:

```
// construct a graphical object
Shape shape = new Rectangle2D.Float(50, 50, 150, 100);

// set rendering context's attributes and fill
g2.setPaint(Color.lightGray);
g2.fill(shape);

// set rendering context's attributes and draw outline
g2.setPaint(Color.darkGray);
g2.setStroke(new BasicStroke(8));
g2.draw(shape);
```

Figure 3.6 shows the picture produced by this code, where the axes' tick marks appear at 50 unit increments.

3.5 Making Graphics

In this section, we'll develop a program that paints a green rectangle onto the black background of a frame. In the process, we'll develop a program template to serve as a pattern for other graphics programs we'll write.

3.5.1 Painting a Rectangle

Until we reach Chapter 7, all of our graphics programs will run in a frame whose content pane contains only a single component: a panel. The panel occupies the full extent of the frame's content pane and serves as the canvas on which we draw our graphics. To write a graphics program, you define a child class of the `ApplicationPanel` class. The `ApplicationPanel` class, defined in Appendix B, is a panel that provides a few additional behaviors in addition to those it inherits from its parent class `javax.swing.JPanel`. As a subclass of `ApplicationPanel`, your class is also a panel. The fields and methods that your class implements produce the graphics.

Your panel is contained in an `ApplicationFrame` object, which is a kind of frame. The `ApplicationFrame` class, also defined in Appendix B, supplements the standard frame with a few new behaviors. Specifically, an `ApplicationFrame` can be closed in the standard ways (such as by clicking in the frame's close box) and appears centered in your screen.

Our green-rectangle-painting program will be named `PaintOneRectangle`. The program is called by a command line of this form:

```
> java PaintOneRectangle x y width height
```

The program creates a new frame in which is displayed a green rectangle at position (*x*,*y*) and of specified width and height. Here is the program in its entirety:

```
public class PaintOneRectangle extends ApplicationPanel {

  public PaintOneRectangle() {
    setBackground(Color.black);
  }

  public static void main(String[] args) {
    parseArgs(args);
    ApplicationPanel panel = new PaintOneRectangle();
    ApplicationFrame frame =
      new ApplicationFrame("A Green Rectangle");
    frame.setPanel(panel);
    panel.makeContent();
    frame.show();
  }

  // static fields storing parsed program arguments
  protected static int x, y, width, height;

  // parses the program arguments
  public static void parseArgs (String[] args) {
    if (args.length != 4) {
      String s = "USAGE: java PaintOneRectangle x y w h";
      System.out.println(s);
      System.exit(0);
    }
    x = Integer.parseInt(args[0]);
```

```
    y = Integer.parseInt(args[1]);
    width = Integer.parseInt(args[2]);
    height = Integer.parseInt(args[3]);
  }

  // instance field representing
  //   the contents of this panel
  protected RectangleGeometry rectangle;

  // creates the graphical contents of this panel
  public void makeContent() {
    rectangle =
      new RectangleGeometry(x, y, width, height);
  }

  // paints the contents of this panel
  public void paintComponent(Graphics g) {
    super.paintComponent(g);
    Graphics2D g2 = (Graphics2D)g;
    g2.setRenderingHint(RenderingHints.KEY_ANTIALIASING,
                        RenderingHints.VALUE_ANTIALIAS_ON);
    g2.setPaint(Color.green);
    g2.fill(rectangle.shape());
  }
}
```

Let's consider the elements of the `PaintOneRectangle` class one at a time. The constructor for `PaintOneRectangle` sets the panel's background color to black. If we did not define this constructor, the program would produce a green rectangle on a gray background, gray being a component's default background color.

Execution of the `PaintOneRectangle` program begins at the static `main` method, which gets called with four program arguments. Procedure `main` performs the following sequence of actions:

1. parses the program arguments by calling the `parseArgs` procedure,
2. constructs a new `PaintOneRectangle` object (stored in the local variable `panel`),
3. constructs a new frame (stored in the local variable `frame`),
4. adds the panel to the frame,
5. builds the graphics by sending a `makeContent` message to the panel, and
6. makes the frame visible by sending it a *show* message.

The `parseArgs` method converts the program arguments to a form that is usable by the program. Specifically, it converts the program arguments *x, y, width,* and *height* to integers and stores them in static fields of the same name.

The green rectangle that appears in the window is managed by the instance of the PaintOneRectangle class created by main (a reference to this instance is stored in the local variable panel). This instance is a kind of panel that defines two new instance methods: The makeContent method *creates* the panel's graphics, and the paintComponent *paints* the panel's graphics. To elaborate, the makeContent method creates the graphical content, in this case a green rectangle that is represented by a Rectangle-Geometry object. A reference to this rectangle is stored in the instance field rectangle. The paintComponent method paints this rectangle into this panel. To do so, it gives the superclass an opportunity to paint, and then casts its argument g to a Graphics2D object, named g2. Then it sends g2 a hint to use anti-aliasing while rendering, which improves the quality of the resulting graphics. The method then sends g2 the *setPaint* message to set the current color to green. Lastly, it sends g2 the *fill* message with an argument that describes that shape of the rectangle being painted.

3.5.2 A Graphics Program Template

The main purpose of our PaintOneRectangle program is to present a pattern that we can base other graphics programs on. Toward that end, let us extract the pattern that this program follows. Here is the form that this program takes:

```
public class MyGraphicsProgram extends ApplicationPanel {

  // constructor
  public MyGraphicsProgram() {
    ...
  }

  public static void main(String[] args) {
    parseArgs(args);
    ApplicationPanel panel = new MyGraphicsProgram();
    ApplicationFrame frame =
      new ApplicationFrame("My Program");
    frame.setPanel(panel);
    panel.makeContent();
    frame.show();
  }

  // static fields storing parsed program arguments
  ...

  // parses program arguments
  public static void parseArgs(String[] args) {
    ...
  }
```

```
  // primary storage structure
  // instance fields representing the contents of this
  //   panel go here:
  ...

  // make the contents of this panel
  public void makeContent() {
    ...
  }

  // paint the contents of this panel
  public void paintComponent(Graphics g) {
    super.paintComponent(g);
    Graphics2D g2 = (Graphics2D)g;
    g2.setRenderingHint(RenderingHints.KEY_ANTIALIASING,
                        RenderingHints.VALUE_ANTIALIAS_ON);
    ...
  }
}
```

To base your own graphics program on this template, replace all three occurrences of `MyGraphicsProgram` by the name of your program. In addition, define the fields and methods that are specific to your program. This requires you to replace the ellipses (...) by the code responsible for managing your program's graphics.

The only method that the compiler *requires* you to define is the static `main` method. The remaining methods are defined as do-nothing procedures in the parent class `ApplicationPanel`; when you implement these methods in your program, you override these do-nothing methods. In practice, it is sometimes not necessary to define a constructor for your program, and it is necessary to define the `parseArgs` procedure only if your program takes program arguments. However, if your program produces any graphics whatsoever, it *is* necessary to define a storage structure and to implement the `makeContent` and `paintComponent` methods that use this storage structure. If you fail to do so, your program will do no more than create a blank window (a feat even less arresting than that performed by our green-rectangle-painting program).

Exercises

3.7 Modify the PaintOneRectangle program so that it takes three additional program arguments that specify the rectangle's fill color:

`> java PaintOneRectangle` ***`x y width height`*** **`[`*****`red green blue`*****`]`**

If your program is called with only four program arguments instead of seven, the rectangle is filled with green.

3.8 Modify the program of the previous exercise so that it takes an optional eighth program argument, an integer:

```
> java PaintOneRectangle x y width height [red green blue [s-width]]
```

Your program fills the rectangle with the color indicated by the *red, green,* and *blue* program arguments, and then strokes the rectangle's outline in white using a stroke of width *s-width*. If the program argument *s-width* is not supplied, the program behaves like that of the previous exercise (it fills the rectangle without stroking it).

Summary

Data abstraction presents a data value as a chunk of data and a set of operations. The operations compose the data value's public interface, which clients use to interact with the data value. Information hiding conceals the object's internal structure and the implementation of its operations. Thus the object is protected from having its state corrupted by its clients, and its clients are protected from relying on implementation details that may change over time. Moreover, clients' authors need be familiar only with the object's public interface to use the object, without having to understand *how* the object works. The behaviors of an object can be specified by annotating each of its operations with requires, modifies, and effects clauses along the lines discussed in Chapter 2.

Encapsulation is the practice of grouping together related software elements. Packages encapsulate related classes, and objects encapsulate related data and methods. The elements that make up an object are also encapsulated: An object is divided into a public compartment—its public interface—and additional compartments of decreasing accessibility and increasing capability. The most restricted compartment—the object's private interface—is accessible only to objects of the same type, yet is the most capable of the object's several interfaces. The practice of concealing those elements of an object that comprise its implementation is known as information hiding.

Abstraction and information hiding are complementary concepts. Abstraction emphasizes what a client needs to know about an object to use it, whereas information hiding emphasizes what a client must not know about an object to prevent its misuse. Used together, abstraction and information hiding disclose the services that an object provides while concealing and protecting its implementation.

CHAPTER

4

Composition

One key advantage of object-oriented programming is that it supports reuse of software elements. In this chapter we study a primary mechanism for reuse known as **composition**. Composition is used to build new objects that contain other objects, thereby reusing the contained objects. The containing object is known as a **composite** and the object or objects that it contains are its **components.** A composite and its components share in a *whole–part relationship*: The composite is the whole and its components are its parts. Examples of composites abound, both in the natural world and in the artificial world. A personal computer is a composite made up of a central processing unit, dynamic memory, auxiliary electronics, and peripherals. A book is composed of a number of chapters. A plant is composed of roots, stems, and leaves.

Section 4.1 provides an overview of both composition and a related association between classes known as aggregation. Section 4.2 develops a number of composite classes for generating various types of random values. These classes will be used later to produce some interesting graphics. Section 4.3 develops a composite class for representing polylines, which are planar curves composed of straight-line edges. The component of the polyline class is a *collection* of vertices whose size is not known in advance. Section 4.4 presents the concept of *representation invariants*, which are conditions used to describe what it means for an object to be in a consistent state. We will use representation invariants to develop a class for representing ellipses and a class for representing rational numbers. Section 4.5 presents a template for *interactive* graphical programs that the user can control while the programs run.

4.1 Composition and Aggregation

Recall from Chapter 1 that there exists an association between two classes if instances of the two classes are linked. Composition and aggregation are two kinds of associations that model the whole-part relationship. In both cases, an object of one class (the whole) owns objects of the other class (its parts). Composition and aggregation differ with respect to the conditions each places on the whole-part relationship.

Composition is used to build complex objects that take the form of hierarchies. A composite object contains one or more simpler objects; in turn, each of these simpler objects contains even simpler objects, until eventually objects considered primitive (noncomposite) are reached. For example, consider the structure of a plant. Each of a plant's components—roots, stems, and leaves—is itself a composite. Consider just one of these components, a plant's leaves. A leaf is made of a leaf blade, a leaf stalk, and a leaf base that attaches the leaf to the branch. In turn, the leaf blade contains three kinds of tissue (epidermis, mesophyll, and veins). The cells that make up these different tissues are formed of chloroplasts and nuclei; the former is made up of chlorophyll and enzymes, whereas the latter is made up of DNA, mitochondria, and other nucleic structures. The other two top-level components of a plant—roots and stems—can be analyzed similarly into components and subcomponents.

A composite object is said to *strongly own* its components. Specifically, an object *B* is a component of object *A* if two conditions hold: (i) *B* belongs to *A* but to no other object besides *A*, and (ii) object *B* is created and disposed of by *A*. To put this sense of *strong ownership* in terms of Java programming, object *B* is a component of object *A* if:

1. *B* is referenced by *A* but by no other object besides *A*, and
2. the lifetime of *B* is controlled by *A*.

We can apply these conditions to the `RectangleGeometry` class of Section 3.2. Every instance of this class contains the fields `xRange` and `yRange`. I claim that the `Range` objects to which these fields refer are the rectangle's components. Condition 1 is satisfied because neither of these ranges is referenced by any objects besides the rectangle that owns them. Even when a client calls a rectangle's `xRange` method, the range that gets returned is a *copy* of the `Range` object referenced by field `xRange`, not the object itself. Condition 2 is satisfied because the two `Range` objects referenced by these fields are created by the rectangle's constructor and destroyed when the rectangle is destroyed. Their lifetimes are controlled by the rectangle that owns them. It follows that every `RectangleGeometry` object is a composite, and the two Range objects referenced by its fields are its components.

Figure 4.1 shows the UML class diagram for the `Range` and `RectangleGeometry` classes. The presence of the filled diamond indicates that the `RectangleGeometry` class is composed of `Range` objects (the multiplicity

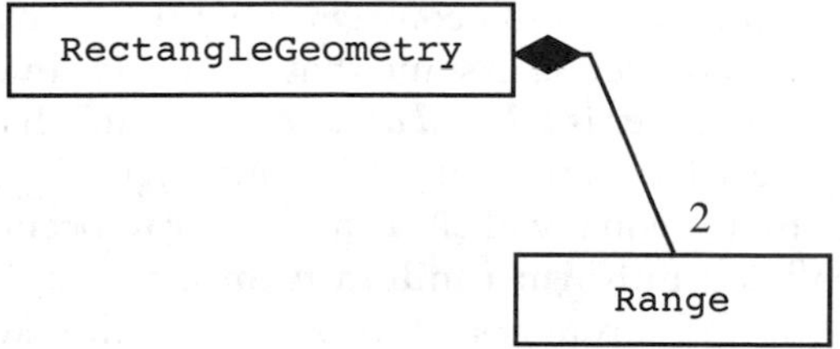

FIGURE 4.1 A class diagram showing that a rectangle is composed of two `Range` objects.

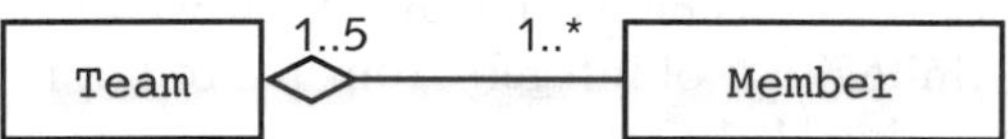

FIGURE 4.2 A class diagram showing that a team is an aggregate of one or more members, and a member belongs to between one and five teams.

value indicates that a rectangle is composed of exactly two `Range` objects). In general, a class diagram shows composition by joining two related classes by a line with a filled diamond at the composite's end.

Aggregation is a second kind of association between classes that partake in a whole-part relationship. Under aggregation, an object contains other objects as its parts, but conditions 1 and 2 noted above need not be satisfied. For example, a sports team is made up of its members, but some of the members may also belong to other teams; moreover, the life span of its members is not determined by the team (notwithstanding what sometimes happens in campy horror flicks). Hence a sports team is an aggregate whole whose parts are its members. A class diagram shows aggregation by connecting the two classes by a line with a hollow diamond at the end of the whole element (see Figure 4.2).

Aggregation is often used when composition does not apply, such as when a part may be shared by more than one whole. However, beyond the fact that aggregation is a kind of association, the semantics of aggregation are not specified. Although UML provides a notation for aggregation, its precise meaning may vary from one project to the next. This stands in contrast to composition, whose meaning is fully specified by UML. The present chapter focuses on composition.

4.2 Random-Value Generators

In this section we develop a number of classes for generating various kinds of random values: integers, points, rectangles, and colors. These different random-value-generating classes will be related by composition, forming a network of associations whose class diagram appears in Figure 4.3.

Before proceeding, we should consider what the term *random* means. To simplify the discussion, let us assume that the values in question are numbers. To say that a number is *selected at random* means that it is no more and no less likely to be selected than any other number. We speak of a **random number** as one that is equally likely as any other to occur. Technically, such a number is called a **uniform random number,** meaning that it obeys a uniform distribution. Throughout this book we will take *random* to mean *uniform random*.

In practice, random numbers are drawn from a range that is finite or at least bounded. For example, we might draw random fractions from the bounded range of fractions between 0 and 1. Or we might draw random integers from the finite range of integers from 1 through 1000, a range that we denote by the notation [1..1000].

Often, a *sequence* of random numbers is required. For example, a program may reach a point where it may proceed in different directions that appear equally promising, and a random number is used to determine which direction to take. If the program frequently reaches such branching points, the random numbers it requires are drawn from a sequence. (Such a program implements what is called a **randomized algorithm.**) Random number sequences are also used to construct sets of objects useful in computer graphics, such as a set of random points lying inside a given rectangle, a set of random colors, or a set of random triangles comprising a mesh. Randomly generated objects are especially fun to work with in computer graphics because their use gives rise to images that follow known principles, yet are nonetheless often unexpected and surprising.

Random number sequences are produced by programs called **random number generators.** The random number generators with which we'll work are **deterministic.** This means that the random number sequences they produce are obtained through a well-defined and reproducible sequence of steps. The numbers produced by deterministic random number generators are known as **pseudo-random numbers.** Because pseudo-random number sequences possess many of the same properties as true random number sequences, they serve as good approximations. One of the benefits of working with deterministic random number generators is that they can be initialized with a number known as a **seed.** This seed puts the random number generator into a specific state, thereby ensuring that it produces a well-defined sequence of random numbers until it is seeded again at a later time. Different seed values generally give rise to different random sequences, or at least different starting points within the same very long random sequence. Yet the same seed always produces the same random sequence. Knowing the seed and the random number generator, it is possible to reproduce the same random sequence again and again.

4.2.1 Java's Random Class

Java provides the class `java.util.Random` for generating random numbers. The following class skeleton includes only those methods that we will use in this book:

```
public class java.util.Random {

  public Random()
    // EFFECTS: Seeds this new object with the system time.

  public Random(long seed)
    // EFFECTS: Seeds this new object with the value seed.

  public void setSeed(long seed)
    // MODIFIES: this
    // EFFECTS: Reseeds this with seed: places this in
    //   the same state as the object new Random(seed).

  public int nextInt()
    // MODIFIES: this
    // EFFECTS: Returns the next random int, and changes
    //   the state of this to reflect the return
    //   of this new value.
}
```

The no-argument constructor seeds a new `Random` object using the current time. The constructor might be defined like this:

```
public Random() {
  this(System.currentTimeMillis());
}
```

The no-argument constructor invokes the one-argument constructor, which takes a seed.

Note the postcondition on the `setSeed` operation. Initializing an existing `Random` object with a given seed puts it into the same state as a new `Random` object constructed with the same seed: both produce the same sequence of numbers assuming neither is later reseeded. For example, the following code fragment never prints *this should not print:*

```
long anyPositiveInteger = 10000;
long anySeed = 1234597;
Random rnd1 = new Random(anySeed);
Random rnd2 = new Random();
rnd2.setSeed(anySeed);
for (int i = 0; i < anyPositiveInteger; i++)
  if (rnd1.nextInt() != rnd2.nextInt())
    System.out.println("this should not print");
```

Here is a short program that uses the `Random` class. The program simulates repeatedly flipping a fair coin while keeping track of the number of heads and tails, and then prints the results. If called with an optional program argument *n*, the program performs *n* coin flips; otherwise it performs 1000 coin flips:

```
public class CoinFlip {
  public static final int HEAD = 0, TAIL = 1;

  public static void main(String[] args) {
    long nbrFlips = 1000;
    if (args.length > 1) {
      System.out.println("USAGE: java CoinFlip [nbrFlips]");
      System.exit(1);
    } else if (args.length == 1)
      nbrFlips = Long.parseLong(args[0]);
    long nbrHeads = 0, nbrTails = 0;
    java.util.Random rnd = new java.util.Random();
    for (long i = 0; i < nbrFlips; i++) {
      int side = Math.abs(rnd.nextInt()) % 2;
      if (side == HEAD) ++nbrHeads;
      else ++nbrTails;
    }
    String msg1 = "Number of heads = " + nbrHeads;
    msg1 += "(" + ((float)nbrHeads/nbrFlips * 100) + "%)\n";
    String msg2 = "Number of tails = " + nbrTails;
    msg2 += "(" + ((float)nbrTails/nbrFlips * 100) + "%)";
    System.out.println(msg1 + msg2);
  }
}
```

In the rest of this section we'll develop classes for generating random values of various types: integers, points, rectangles, and colors. We'll refer to any instance of such a class as a **random-value generator,** whether it generates objects (in Java's sense of the word) or values of some primitive type such as integers. Each of our random-value generators will, for the most part, assume the same form as Java's `Random` class. With some variation, each will provide:

- a no-argument constructor that uses a seed derived from the system, generally the current time,
- a one-argument constructor that takes a seed provided by the client,
- a method for initializing the random value generator from a new seed, and
- one or more methods for obtaining the next random value.

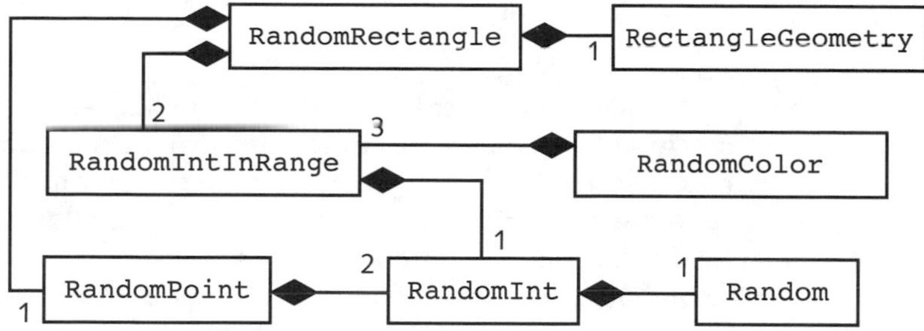

FIGURE 4.3 Some random-value generator classes defined by composition.

Because quite a few classes will be introduced in this section, I am including their class diagram at the outset (Figure 4.3). Refer to this diagram as new classes are introduced. Also, the exercises ask you to define several additional classes related to the ones in this class diagram. You may want to add these additional classes to the class diagram of Figure 4.3.

Exercises

4.1 The **law of large numbers** implies that as the number of coin flips *n* increases, the percentage of heads and the percentage of tails both converge to 50%. Test this by running the `CoinFlip` program with increasingly large values of *n*.

4.2 Write a program `DieRoll` that does for a single die what `CoinFlip` does for coins. The program simulates rolling a six-sided die *n* times, and then reports the number of times that each of the numbers 1 through 6 came up. Here *n* is given by an optional program argument, or *n* is equal to 1000 if the program argument is not supplied. [Hint: Use an integer array of length six to store the number of times each number is rolled.]

4.3 Write a program `DiceRoll` that simulates rolling two six-sided dice, and records the sum of the faces that appear (a number between 2 and 12). After *n* rolls, the program prints the number of times that each of the sums from 2 through 12 appeared. Again, *n* is an optional program argument which, if not supplied, defaults to 1000.

4.2.2 Random Integers

The random integers returned by the `Random.nextInt` method are drawn from the range of Java's `int` type: -2^{31} through $2^{31}-1$. However, sometimes you may wish to further restrict the range from which random integers are drawn. Rather than assigning a fixed range to the random number generator, the `RandomInt` class, to which we now turn, allows the range to vary each time a new random number is sought.

The `RandomInt` class, like Java's `Random` class, defines a `nextInt` method for obtaining the next random number. However, in the `RandomInt` class, this method is overloaded. The particular argument list with which `nextInt` gets called determines the range from which the next random number is drawn. Here is the class skeleton:

```
public class RandomInt {

  public RandomInt()
    // EFFECTS: Seeds this new object with
    //   the system time.

  public RandomInt(long seed)
    // EFFECTS: Seeds this new object with seed.

  public void setSeed(long seed)
    // MODIFIES: this
    // EFFECTS: Reseeds this with seed: places this
    //   in the same state as new RandomInt(seed).

  public int nextUnsigned()
    // MODIFIES: this
    // EFFECTS: Returns the next nonnegative random
    //   int, and updates the state of this to reflect
    //   the return of this new value.

  public int nextInt()
    // MODIFIES: this
    // EFFECTS: Returns the next random int and
    //   updates the state of this.

  public int nextInt(int n)
        throws IllegalArgumentException
    // MODIFIES: this
    // EFFECTS: If n <= 0 throws IllegalArgumentException;
    //   else returns the next random int in the range
    //   [0..n-1] and updates the state of this.
```

```
  public int nextInt(int m, int n)
        throws IllegalArgumentException
    // MODIFIES: this
    // EFFECTS: If n<m throws IllegalArgumentException;
    //   else returns the next random int in the range
    //   [m..n] and updates the state of this.

  public int nextInt(Range rng)
        throws NullPointerException
    // MODIFIES: this
    // EFFECTS: If rng is null throws
    //   NullPointerException; else returns the next
    //   random int in rng and updates the state of this.
}
```

We will implement `RandomInt` as a composite class whose sole component, a `Random` object, is stored in the instance field `rnd`:

```
// field of RandomInt class
protected Random rnd;
```

The constructors build a new object that is seeded by the current time or by a given seed:

```
public RandomInt() {
  rnd = new Random();
}

public RandomInt(long seed) {
  rnd = new Random(seed);
}
```

A `RandomInt` object can be reseeded through its `setSeed` method:

```
// method of RandomInt class
public void setSeed(long seed) {
  rnd.setSeed(seed);
}
```

The method `nextUnsigned` returns a random nonnegative integer.

```
// method of RandomInt class
public int nextUnsigned() {
  int i = rnd.nextInt();
  if (i < 0) i = -(i + 1);
  return i;
}
```

The `nextInt` method is overloaded. The no-argument version of this function simply forwards the request to the `Random` object referenced by the field `rnd`:

```
// method of RandomInt class
public int nextInt() {
  return rnd.nextInt();
}
```

The technique whereby a composite object forwards a message to one of its components is known as **delegation.** In the no-argument version of method `nextInt` just given, the `nextInt` message is delegated to the component `rnd`. Our implementation of the `setSeed` method, given above, also uses delegation.

When the `nextInt` method is called with a single integer argument n, it returns a new random number in the range $[0..n-1]$:

```
// method of RandomInt class
public int nextInt(int n)
       throws IllegalArgumentException {
  if (n <= 0) throw new IllegalArgumentException();
  int i = nextUnsigned();
  if (i >= (n * (Integer.MAX_VALUE / n)))
    return nextInt(n);
  else
    return i % n;
}
```

When the `nextInt` method is called with two integer values m and n, it returns a random number in the range $[m..n]$. Our implementation of this method works by first generating a random number in the range $[0..n-m]$, and then offsetting this random number by `m`:

```
// method of RandomInt class
public int nextInt(int m, int n)
        throws IllegalArgumentException  {
  int rangeSize = n - m + 1; // nbr of integers in [m..n]
  return nextInt(rangeSize) + m;
}
```

The class' remaining version of method `nextInt` gets called with a range and produces a random integer that lies within this range. Here is the implementation:

```
// method of RandomInt class
public int nextInt(Range rng)
       throws NullPointerException {
  return nextInt(rng.getMin(), rng.getMax());
}
```

Exercises

4.4 Consider the following alternate version of class RandomInt's nextUnsigned method, which returns the absolute value of the integer obtained from rnd:

```
// method of RandomInt class: version2 (faulty)
public int nextUnsigned() {
  int i = rnd.nextInt();
  return (i >= 0) ? i : -i;
}
```

Why is version 2 of method nextUnsigned faulty? [Hint: There are two problems. To discover the first, think of a negative int whose negation is not a positive int. For the second problem, consider whether every integer in the range [0..2^{31}–1] is equally likely to be selected.]

4.5 Here is yet another version of the nextUnsigned method. This version repeatedly gets a random integer from rnd until obtaining a nonnegative value, which it then returns:

```
// method of RandomInt class: version 3
public int nextUnsigned() {
  int i = rnd.nextInt();
  while (i < 0)
    i = rnd.nextInt();
  return i;
}
```

Compare this implementation of method nextUnsigned to that given in the text (version 1). Is version 3 as efficient as version 1? If not, describe in a sentence or two how much less so.

4.6 Here is an alternate implementation class RandomInt's one-argument nextInt method:

```
// method of RandomInt class: version 2
public int nextInt(int n)
       throws IllegalArgumentException {
  if (n <= 0)
    throw new IllegalArgumentException();
  return nextUnsigned() % n;
}
```

Although version 2 is simpler than the implementation given in the text, the latter version is preferable. Why?

4.7 Revise the implementation of the `CoinFlip` program of Section 4.2.1 so that it uses a `RandomInt` object instead of a `Random` object.

4.2.3 Random Integers in a Fixed Range

Using the `RandomInt` class that we've just defined, you can vary the range from which each random integer is drawn each time you call the `nextInt` method. However, in many applications, a random number generator's range is fixed throughout its lifetime. This is true, as we have seen, of the `java.util.Random` class: its range is precisely the range of the `int` data type. Yet suppose we require a class that, like Java's `Random` class, has a fixed range, yet unlike this class, allows the client to specify that range. The `RandomIntInRange` class, to which we now turn, provides this behavior. Whenever this class' `nextInt` method is called, it returns a new random integer from its fixed range. There are no arguments to be passed to `nextInt`.

When you make a new `RandomIntInRange` object, you provide arguments to the constructor specifying the desired range. Because the range is a property of the class, it is possible to both query and modify the object's range throughout its lifetime.

For conciseness, I will present the class in its entirety without first presenting its specification. First, consider the storage structure. A `RandomIntInRange` is a composite object; its sole component is a `RandomInt` object, a reference to which is stored in the instance field named `rnd`. In addition, a `RandomIntInRange` object defines integer fields `min` and `max` to hold the extreme values of its range. Here is the class definition:

```
public class RandomIntInRange {

  protected RandomInt rnd;
  protected int min, max;

  public RandomIntInRange(int min, int max)
         throws IllegalArgumentException {
    // EFFECTS: If max < min throws
    //    IllegalArgumentException; else initializes this
    //    to the range [min..max] and seeds this
    //    with the system time.
    if (max < min) throw new IllegalArgumentException();
    rnd = new RandomInt();
    setRange(min, max);
  }
```

```
public RandomIntInRange(Range range)
       throws NullPointerException {
  // EFFECTS: If range is null throws
  //   NullPointerException; else initializes this to
  //   range and seeds with the system time.
  this(range.getMin(), range.getMax());
}

public RandomIntInRange(int n)
       throw IllegalArgumentException {
  // EFFECTS: If n<=0 throws IllegalArgumentException;
  //   else initializes this to the range [0..n-1]
  //   and seeds this with the system time.
  this(0, n-1);
}

public void setSeed(long seed) {
  // MODIFIES: this
  // EFFECTS: Reseeds this with seed.
  rnd.setSeed(seed);
}

public int nextInt() {
  // MODIFIES: this
  // EFFECTS: Returns the next random int in the
  //   current range and updates the state of this
  //   to reflect the return of this new value.
  return rnd.nextInt(min, max);
}

public void setRange(int min, int max)
       throws IllegalArgumentException {
  // MODIFIES: this
  // EFFECTS: If max < min throws
  //   IllegalArgumentException; else changes the
  //   current range to [min..max].
  this.min = min;
  this.max = max;
}

public void setRange(Range range)
       throws NullPointerException {
  // MODIFIES: this
  // EFFECTS: If range is null throws
  //   NullPointerException; else sets the current
  //   range to [range.getMin()..range.getMax()].
  setRange(range.getMin(), range.getMax());
}
```

```
  public Range getRange() {
    // EFFECTS: Returns the current range.
    return new Range(min, max);
  }
}
```

Exercises

4.8 Generalize program `CoinFlip` of Section 4.2.1 and program `DieRoll` of Exercise 4.2 in the following way: Write a program `NumberToss` that takes two program arguments *n* and *m*. The program generates *n* random numbers in the range [1..*m*] while keeping a count of the number of times each number is selected. The program finishes by printing the number and percentage of times that each of the numbers from 1 through *m* appears. Your program should use the `RandomIntInRange` class.

4.9 Code a different implementation of the `RandomIntInRange` class based on the following storage structure:

```
// random-integer generator
protected RandomInt rnd;

// the current range
protected Range rng;
```

Be sure not to change the class' abstraction: Your version should provide precisely the same behaviors as the version of `RandomIntInRange` presented in this section. Test your new version using your `NumberToss` program of Exercise 4.8.

4.2.4 Random Points

In this section we develop a random point generator. The `RandomPoint` class does for points what the `RandomInt` class does for integers. Both are variable-range random-value generators for which you specify the range each time you request a new random value. In the case of the `RandomPoint` class, when you request a new random point, you call the `nextPoint` method with arguments that define a rectangle. The new random point returned by the call is guaranteed to lie inside the rectangle supplied as input. Here is the class skeleton:

```
public class RandomPoint {

  public RandomPoint()
    // EFFECTS: Seeds this new object with values
```

```
  //   based on system time.

public void setSeedX(long seed)
  // MODIFIES: this
  // EFFECTS: Reseeds the x coordinate generator.

public void setSeedY(long seed)
  // MODIFIES: this
  // EFFECTS: Reseeds the y coordinate generator.

public PointGeometry nextPoint()
  // MODIFIES: this
  // EFFECTS: Returns the next random point and
  //   updates the state of this to reflect the
  //   return of this new value.

public PointGeometry nextPoint(int m, int n)
      throws IllegalArgumentException
  // MODIFIES: this
  // EFFECTS: If m or n are nonpositive throws
  //   IllegalArgumentException; else returns the next
  //   random point in the rectangle [0..m-1]x[0..n-1]
  //   and updates the state of this.

public PointGeometry nextPoint(Range xRange,
                               Range yRange)
      throws NullPointerException
  // MODIFIES: this
  // EFFECTS: If xRange or yRange is null throws
  //   NullPointerException; else returns the next
  //   random point in the rectangle xRange x yRange
  //   and updates the state of this.

public PointGeometry nextPoint(RectangleGeometry bnds)
      throws NullPointerException
  // MODIFIES: this
  // EFFECTS: If bnds is null throws
  //   NullPointerException; else returns the next
  //   random point in the rectangle bnds and
  //   updates the state of this.
}
```

We'll implement the RandomPoint class as a composite that owns two components, both of type RandomInt. One of the components generates random *x* coordinates and the other generates random *y* coordinates:

```
// fields of RandomPoint class
protected RandomInt xRnd, yRnd;
```

The no-argument constructor seeds the random number generators bound to fields `xRnd` and `yRnd`. Their respective seeds should differ, or else they will generate the same sequence of integers and the resulting points will not be random. To ensure different seeds, `xRnd` is seeded with the current time, and `yRnd` with a number strictly larger than the seed used for `xRnd`:

```
// class field of RandomPoint class
final static int SeedOffset = 123; // any positive int

public RandomPoint() {
  xRnd = new RandomInt();
  yRnd = new RandomInt();
  yRnd.setSeed(System.currentTimeMillis() + SeedOffset);
}
```

The class provides methods for seeding the *x* and *y* coordinate generators independently:

```
// methods of RandomPoint class
public void setSeedX(long seed) {
  xRnd.setSeed(seed);
}

public void setSeedY(long seed) {
  yRnd.setSeed(seed);
}
```

The `nextPoint` method is used to obtain the next random point. If `nextPoint` is called with no arguments, the coordinates of the point may range over the integers:

```
// method of RandomPoint class
public PointGeometry nextPoint() {
  int x = xRnd.nextInt();
  int y = yRnd.nextInt();
  return new PointGeometry(x, y);
}
```

Method `nextPoint` may also be called with argument lists that define a rectangle. In each case, the new random point returned by the method is guaranteed to lie inside the rectangle. The rectangle may be described in three different ways, as exhibited by the three versions of `nextPoint` that follow:

```
// methods of RandomPoint class
public PointGeometry nextPoint(int m, int n)
       throws IllegalArgumentException {
  int x = xRnd.nextInt(m);
  int y = yRnd.nextInt(n);
```

```
  return new PointGeometry(x, y);
}

public PointGeometry nextPoint(Range xRange, Range yRange)
       throws NullPointerException {
  int x = xRnd.nextInt(xRange);
  int y = yRnd.nextInt(yRange);
  return new PointGeometry(x, y);
}

public PointGeometry nextPoint(RectangleGeometry bounds)
       throws NullPointerException {
  return nextPoint(bounds.xRange(), bounds.yRange());
}
```

Exercises

4.10 Write a (nongraphical) Java program `SomeRandomPoints` that takes a single program argument n, then generates and prints n random points contained in the rectangle [0..100]×[0..100].

4.11 Write a graphical Java program `PaintManyPoints` that takes a single program argument n, and then fills n blue random points inside the frame. Pattern your program after the *MyGraphicsProgram* template of Section 3.5. Your program can define a field to store the n random points like this:

```
protected PointGeometry[] points;
```

To ensure that the random points lie inside the frame, method `nextPoint` should be called (repeatedly) with a bounding rectangle of the same dimensions of the frame's content area. You can use the following code to construct the bounding rectangle `bounds` (where `nbrPoints` holds the number of points to be generated). The rest of the implementation for `makeContent`, which you must write, generates `nbrPoints` many new random point and stores them in the array `points`:

```
// method of PaintManyPoints class
public void makeContent() {
  points = new PointGeometry[nbrPoints];
  Dimension d = getFrame().getContentSize();
  RectangleGeometry bounds =
```

```
      new RectangleGeometry(0, 0, d.width, d.height);
    ...
  }
```

Of course, your `PaintManyPoints` program also requires you to implement the other elements of the *MyGraphicsProgram* template as well. If you have difficulty with this program, return to it after you have worked through Section 4.2.6.

4.12 Revise the implementation of class `RandomPoint's` constructor so that the random number generator `yRnd` is not seeded, as follows:

```
// constructor: version 2 (faulty)
public RandomPoint() {
  xRnd = new RandomInt();
  yRnd = new RandomInt();
}
```

Using this version, recompile and run your `PaintManyPoints` program of Exercise 4.11. Are the resulting points still distributed randomly within the frame? If not, why not? (If you did not solve Exercise 4.11, try this faulty version of the constructor using your program from Exercise 4.10.)

ESSENTIAL 4.13 Implement the class `RandomPointInRectangle` which does for points what the `RandomIntInRange` class does for integers. The random points are drawn from a bounding rectangle that is specified by arguments to the constructor. The bounding rectangle is a property of the class, enabling clients to query and modify it during the random-point generator's lifetime. Here is the class skeleton:

```
public class RandomPointInRectangle {

  public RandomPointInRectangle(Range xRange,
                                Range yRange)
         throws NullPointerException
    // EFFECTS: If xRange or yRange is null throws
    //   NullPointerException; else initializes this
    //   to the bounding rectangle xRange x yRange
    //   and seeds this with values based on
    //   the system time.

  public RandomPointInRectangle(RectangleGeometry bnds)
         throws NullPointerException
    // EFFECTS: If bnds is null throws
    //   NullPointerException; else initializes this
```

```
    //   to the bounding rectangle bnds and seeds
    //   this with values based on the system time.

  public void setSeedX(long seed)
    // MODIFIES: this
    // EFFECTS: Reseeds the x component generator.

  public void setSeedY(long seed)
    // MODIFIES: this
    // EFFECTS: Reseeds the y component generator.

  public PointGeometry nextPoint()
    // MODIFIES: this
    // EFFECTS: Returns the next random point in the
    //   current bounding rectangle and updates the
    //   state of this to reflect the return of this
    //   new value.

  public void setBounds(RectangleGeometry bnds)
        throws NullPointerException
    // MODIFIES: this
    // EFFECTS: If bnds is null throws
    //   NullPointerException; else sets the bounding
    //   rectangle to bnds.

  public void setBounds(Range xRange, Range yRange)
        throws NullPointerException
    // MODIFIES: this
    // EFFECTS: If xRange or yRange is null throws
    //   NullPointerException; else sets the bounding
    //   rectangle to xRange x yRange.

  public RectangleGeometry getBounds()
    // EFFECTS: Returns the current bounding rectangle.
}
```

Revise the program you wrote for Exercise 4.11 so that it uses the `RandomPointInRectangle` class instead of the `RandomPoint` class.

ESSENTIAL 4.14 Java provides the class `java.awt.Color` for representing colors. Here is the header for one of the class' constructors:

```
public Color(int red, int green, int blue)
```

To construct a new color, call `Color`'s constructor with three integer values in the range 0 through 255 to indicate the brightness level for that color component. For example,

```
new Color(255, 0, 0)       // red
new Color(0, 0, 255)       // blue
new Color(255, 255, 0)     // magenta
new Color(0, 255, 255)     // cyan
new Color(255, 255, 0)     // yellow
new Color(0, 0, 0)         // black
new Color(127, 127, 127)   // medium gray
new Color(255, 255, 255)   // white
new Color(255, 214, 0)     // gold
new Color(255, 191, 204)   // pink
new Color(64, 105, 207)    // royal blue
```

Develop the class `RandomColor` for generating random colors. Your class should use three random integer generators for producing integers in the range [0..255], one for each of the colors red, green, and blue. Here is the class skeleton:

```
public class RandomColor {

  public RandomColor()
    //EFFECTS: Initializes this with seeds
    //  based on the system time.

  public void setSeeds(long redSeed, long greenSeed,
    long blueSeed)
    // MODIFIES: this
    // EFFECTS: Reseeds the red, green, and blue
    //   random color-component generators.

  public Color nextColor()
    // MODIFIES: this
    // EFFECTS: Returns the next random color and
    //   updates the state of this to reflect the
    //   return of this new value.
}
```

Using your `RandomColor` class, revise your random-point-painting program of Exercise 4.11 so that each point is painted with a random color. It is not necessary to store the color with each point. Rather, you can let your program's `paintComponent` method generate random colors anew each time it is called. Alternatively, you may want to generate the random colors only once when the points are generated, and save the colors in an array that parallels the array in which the points are stored (that is, `color[i]` stores the color of the random point `points[i]`).

Incidentally (and not pertaining to the solution to this exercise), certain basic colors are constructed automatically when the `Color` class loads, and can be accessed through appropriately named static fields of the `Color` class. For instance, the `Color` class defines the static field:

```
public static final Color green;
```

allowing the color green to be obtained with the expression `Color.green`. The basic colors provided by the `Color` class in this way are black, blue, cyan, darkGray, gray, green, lightGray, magenta, orange, pink, red, white, and yellow.

4.2.5 Random Rectangles

This section presents a `RandomRectangle` class for generating random rectangles. Just as the position of random points are constrained to lie inside a bounding rectangle, we will constrain the position and size of random rectangles. To do so, we associate with every random-rectangle generator a bounding rectangle. The random rectangles produced by a generator are guaranteed to be entirely enclosed within the generator's bounding rectangle.

In addition to its bounding rectangle, a random-rectangle generator possesses a *width range* property and a *height range* property to constrain the dimensions of the random rectangles it produces. The width of random rectangles are guaranteed to lie between the minimum and maximum values of the generator's width range. The generator's height range functions similarly to constrain the height of random rectangles. The default width range extends from 1 through the width of the bounding rectangle; likewise, the default height range extends from 1 through the height of the bounding rectangle. This means that by default, the dimensions of random rectangles are unconstrained (as long as they are fully enclosed by the bounding rectangle). Being properties, a random-rectangle generator's *width range* and *height range* can be queried and changed.

Here is the specification for the `RandomRectangle` class:

```
public class RandomRectangle {

  public RandomRectangle(Range xRange, Range yRange)
        throws NullPointerException
    //EFFECTS: If xRange or yRange are null throws
    //   NullPointerException; else initializes this with
    //   the default width range and height range,
    //   sets the bounding rectangle to xRange x yRange
    //   and seeds this with values based on system time.

  public RandomRectangle(RectangleGeometry bnds)
        throws NullPointerException
    // EFFECTS: If bnds is null throws
    //   NullPointerException; else initializes this with
    //   the default width range and height range,
    //   sets the bounding rectangle to bnds, and seeds
    //   this with values based on the system time.

  public void setSeeds(long sdW, long sdH,
                       long sdX, long sdY)
    // MODIFIES: this
    // EFFECTS: Reseeds the generators for width, height,
    //   and x and y coordinates of position.

  public void setWidthRange(Range newRange)
   throws NullPointerException, IllegalArgumentException
    // MODIFIES: this
    // EFFECTS: If newRange is null throws
    //   NullPointerException; else if newRange.getMin()
    //   is nonpositive or newRange.getMax() exceeds the
    //   bounding rectangle's width throws
    //   IllegalArgumentException; else sets the
    //   width range property to newRange.

  public Range getWidthRange()
    // EFFECTS: Returns the current width range.

  public void setHeightRange(Range newRange)
    // MODIFIES: this
    // EFFECTS: If newRange is null throws
    //   NullPointerException; else if newRange.getMin()
    //   is nonpositive or newRange.getMax() exceeds the
    //   bounding rectangle's height throws
    //   IllegalArgumentException; else sets the
    //   height range property to newRange.
```

```
  public Range getHeightRange()
    // EFFECTS: Returns the current height range.

  public RectangleGeometry bounds()
    // EFFECTS: Returns the bounding rectangle.

  public RectangleGeometry nextRectangle()
    // MODIFIES: this
    // EFFECTS: Returns the next random rectangle
    //   enclosed by the bounding rectangle whose width
    //   and height constrained by the current width
    //   range and height range, and updates the state of
    //   this to reflect the return of this new value.
}
```

The class skeleton indicates that the bounding rectangle associated with a `RandomRectangle` object is set when the object is constructed and cannot be changed during its lifetime. In contrast, the object's *width range* and *height range* are properties that can be queried and modified. Note also that the class provides the `bounds` method for obtaining the bounding rectangle. Clients might need to know the bounding rectangle to ensure that they don't make the width range too wide or the height range too high. In other words, the `bounds` method is provided so that clients can call the `setWidthRange` and `setHeightRange` methods with reasonable arguments.

Shortly we'll use the `RandomRectangle` class in a graphics application that paints rectangles of random position, dimension, and color into a window. For now, we'll consider a simple code fragment that exercises this class. The following code fragment prints 10 random rectangles. Each of the rectangles is contained within the bounding rectangle [0..100]×[0..200]; moreover, their widths range between 20 and 40, and their heights between 30 and 60:

```
RectangleGeometry bounds =
  new RectangleGeometry(new Point(0, 0), 100, 200);
RandomRectangle rndRect = new RandomRectangle(bounds);
rndRect.setWidthRange(new Range(20, 40));
rndRect.setHeightRange(new Range(30, 60));
for (int i = 0; i < 10; i++)
  System.out.println(rndRect.nextRectangle());
```

Let's implement the `RandomRectangle` class. We'll store a `RandomRectangle`'s bounding rectangle in an instance field named `bounds`, and we'll represent the values of its *width range* and *height range* properties implicitly, as random integer generators used to produce the width and height of random rectangles. In addition, we'll maintain a random-point generator for producing the position of each random rectangle's upper-left corner:

```
// fields of RandomRectangle class
  // bounding rectangle
protected RectangleGeometry bounds;
  // generator for random rectangle positions
protected RandomPoint rndPnt;
  // generators for random widths and heights
protected RandomIntInRange rndWidth, rndHeight;
```

The various random-value generators used by this class are seeded by the constructors. Each of the following values is added to the system time to produce a seed. These seed values are in increasing order to ensure distinct seeds, but otherwise they are arbitrary values:

```
// class fields of RandomRectangle class
final static int SeedOffset1 = 4567, SeedOffset2 = 5678,
                 SeedOffset3 = 6789;
```

The first constructor is called with two `Range` objects that jointly determine the generator's bounding rectangle. It initializes the fields that comprise the storage structures and seeds the random-object generators with default seed values:

```
public RandomRectangle(Range xRange, Range yRange)
       throws NullPointerException {
  bounds =   new RectangleGeometry(xRange, yRange);
  rndWidth =
    new RandomIntInRange(new Range(1, xRange.length()));
  rndHeight =
    new RandomIntInRange(new Range(1, yRange.length()));
  rndPnt = new RandomPoint();
  long time = System.currentTimeMillis();
  rndHeight.setSeed(time + SeedOffset1);
  rndPnt.setSeedX(time + SeedOffset2);
  rndPnt.setSeedY(time + SeedOffset3);
}
```

The second constructor is defined in terms of the constructor just defined:

```
public RandomRectangle(RectangleGeometry bounds)
       throws NullPointerException {
  this(bounds.xRange(), bounds.yRange());
}
```

The `setSeeds` method enables clients to seed all the random-value generating components with a single call. It is defined like this:

```
// method of RandomRectangle class
public void setSeeds(long seedW, long seedH,
                     long seedX, long seedY) {
```

```
    rndWidth.setSeed(seedW);
    rndHeight.setSeed(seedH);
    rndPnt.setSeedX(seedX);
    rndPnt.setSeedY(seedY);
  }
```

The following five methods are easy to implement. The first method, `bounds`, returns the bounding rectangle. The next four methods are the accessors for the *width range* and *height range* properties. Each delegates its work to the appropriate component:

```
  // methods of RandomRectangle class
  public RectangleGeometry bounds() {
    return new RectangleGeometry(this.bounds);
  }

  public void setWidthRange(Range newRange)
        throws NullPointerException,
               IllegalArgumentException {
    if ((newRange.getMin() <= 0) ||
        (newRange.getMax() > bounds().xRange().length()))
      throw new IllegalArgumentException();
    rndWidth.setRange(newRange);
  }

  public Range getWidthRange() {
    return rndWidth.getRange();
  }

  public void setHeightRange(Range newRange)
         throws NullPointerException,
                IllegalArgumentException {
    if ((newRange.getMin() <= 0) ||
        (newRange.getMax() > bounds().yRange().length()))
      throw new IllegalArgumentException();
    rndHeight.setRange(newRange);
  }

  public Range getHeightRange() {
    return rndHeight.getRange();
  }
```

Lastly, we turn to the `nextRectangle` method which returns a new random rectangle. Our implementation for this method first generates the random rectangle's width w and height h. It then uses these two values to compute the dimensions of an **inset rectangle.** The inset rectangle, which is enclosed by the generator's bounding rectangle, is the region where a rectangle of width w and height h may be safely positioned to ensure that it does not extend beyond the sides of the bounding rectangle. In other words, if the upper-left corner of a $w \times h$ rectangle occurs inside the inset rectangle, the rectangle is guaranteed to be fully enclosed by the bounding rectangle. A random point *pos* is then generated within the inset rectangle. Lastly, the method constructs and returns a new $w \times h$ rectangle at position *pos*. Here is the code:

```
// method of RandomRectangle class
public RectangleGeometry nextRectangle() {
  int w = rndWidth.nextInt();
  int h = rndHeight.nextInt();
  int dw = bounds.getWidth() - w;
  int dh = bounds.getHeight() - h;
  RectangleGeometry insetRectangle =
    new RectangleGeometry(bounds.getPosition(), dw, dh);
  PointGeometry pos = rndPnt.nextPoint(insetRectangle);
  return new RectangleGeometry(pos, w, h);
}
```

Exercise

4.15 Here is a simpler, although incorrect, implementation of the `nextRectangle` method, based on the same storage structure described earlier:

```
// method of RandomRectangle class: version 2 (faulty)
public RectangleGeometry nextRectangle() {
  PointGeometry pos = rndPnt.nextPoint(bounds);
  int w = rndWidth.nextInt();
  int h = rndHeight.nextInt();
  return new RectangleGeometry(pos, w, h);
}
```

Explain the approach taken by this faulty version of the `nextRectangle` method. Why is this version faulty?

4.2.6 Painting Many Rectangles

In this section we'll use the *MyGraphicsProgram* template of Section 3.5 in a program that paints n rectangles of random position, size, and color into a window. Rather than present this program all at once, I'll supply the pieces one at a time.

Our program constrains the dimensions of the random rectangles it creates. Specifically, each rectangle's width and height is given by a random value in the range [*minLen..maxLen*] for integers $minLen \leq maxLen$. The command line for calling our program takes this form:

```
> java PaintManyRectangles [n [minLen maxLen]]
```

If called with no program arguments, default values are used; if called with a single program argument *n*, *n* random rectangles are generated of default dimensions; or if three program arguments are supplied, the last two arguments specify the constraints on the rectangles' dimensions. The values of *n*, *minLen*, and *maxLen* are stored in the following class fields:

```
// class fields of PaintManyRectangles class
protected static int nbrRectangles = 100;
protected static int minLength = 100, maxLength = 200;
```

The `parseArgs` method overrides these fields' default values if the program is called with program arguments. The method is defined thus:

```
// class method of PaintManyRectangles class
public static void parseArgs(String[] args) {
  if ((args.length == 2) || (args.length > 3)) {
    String s="USAGE: java PaintManyRectangles [n [min max]]");
    System.out.println(s);
    System.exit(0);
  }
  if (args.length > 0)
    nbrRectangles = Integer.parseInt(args[0]);
  if (args.length > 2) {
    minLength = Integer.parseInt(args[1]);
    maxLength = Integer.parseInt(args[2]);
  }
}
```

We turn now to the program elements that manage the graphics. We shall store the collection of random rectangles in the following array:

```
// field of PaintManyRectangles class
protected RectangleGeometry[] rectangles;
```

The makeContent method creates the random rectangles and stores them in the array `rectangles`:

```
// method of PaintManyRectangles class
public void makeContent() {
  // step 1: construct a random rectangle generator
  Dimension d = getFrame().getContentSize();
  Range frameWidth = new Range(0, d.width);
  Range frameHeight = new Range(0, d.height);
  RandomRectangle rndRect =
    new RandomRectangle(frameWidth, frameHeight);
  // step 2: set width and height range properties
  Range minMaxLengths = new Range(minLength, maxLength);
  rndRect.setWidthRange(minMaxLengths);
```

```
    rndRect.setHeightRange(minMaxLengths);
    // step 3: generate and save random rectangles
    rectangles = new RectangleGeometry[nbrRectangles];
    for (int i = 0; i < nbrRectangles; i++)
      rectangles[i] = rndRect.nextRectangle();
  }
```

The `makeContent` method works in three steps. First, it constructs a new random-rectangle generator `rndRect`, initialized with the dimensions of this frame's content area to ensure that every random rectangle fits inside the frame. In the second step, the `makeContent` method sets the random-rectangle generator's *width range* and *height range* properties. Recall that these properties place constraints on the dimensions of the rectangles produced by the generator. In the third step, the method constructs a new `RectangleGeometry` array and saves a reference to this array in the `rectangles` field. Then it creates the new random rectangles and stores references to them in this array.

Lastly, we implement the `paintComponent` method, which works by painting the rectangles stored in the array `rectangles`:

```
  // method of PaintManyRectangles class
  public void paintComponent(Graphics g) {
    super.paintComponent(g);
    Graphics2D g2 = (Graphics2D)g;
    RandomColor rndClr = new RandomColor();
    for (int i = 0; i < rectangles.length; i++) {
      // use the next random color for rendering
      g2.setPaint(rndClr.nextColor());
      // paint rectangle r in the current color
      RectangleGeometry r = rectangles[i];
      g2.fill(r.shape());
    }
  }
```

Exercises

4.16 Implement and run the `PaintManyRectangles` program.

4.17 As things stand, the `PaintManyRectangles` program generates new random colors each time the `paintComponents` method is called. This is reflected in the fact that whenever the frame is minimized then maximized, thereby requiring repainting, the random rectangles change color (try it). Modify the implementation of this program such that the random colors are generated and assigned to rectangles only once, by the `makeContent` method. To do so, you might want to define an array of colors

```
protected Color[] colors
```

to parallel the array of rectangles: `colors[i]` stores the color of `rectangle[i]`.

4.18 The colors produced by your `RandomColor` class (Exercise 4.14) are opaque—when you fill a shape with an opaque color, the shape completely paints over whatever graphics had appeared below it. It is also possible to work with colors that are translucent, or semitransparent. Java's `java.awt.Color` class provides the following constructor for creating translucent colors:

```
public Color(int red, int green, int blue, int alpha)
```

The argument `alpha` assumes values in the range [0..255], where an alpha value of 0 corresponds to full transparency and 255 to full opacity, and values inbetween to translucency. For instance, this expression

```
new Color(255, 0, 255, 220)
```

produces a slightly transparent magenta.

For this exercise, define a class for generating random translucent colors. This class defines an *alpha range* property—the random colors have an alpha value (opacity) that lies within the generator's alpha range. The red, green, and blue components of the random color may be generated randomly as in the `RandomColor` class. Here is a class skeleton:

```
public class RandomColorInAlphaRange {

  public RandomColorInAlphaRange(int minAlpha,
                                 int maxAlpha)
       throws IllegalArgumentException
    // EFFECTS: If 0 <= minAlpha <= maxAlpha <= 255
    //   initializes this with the alpha range
    //   [minAlpha..maxAlpha] and seeds this based
    //   on system time; else
    //   throws IllegalArgumentException.

  public RandomColorInAlphaRange(Range aRng)
       throws NullPointerException,
              IllegalArgumentException
    // EFFECTS: If aRng is null throws
    //   NullPointerException; else if
    //   0 <= aRng.getMin() and aRng.getMax() <= 255
```

```
      //   initializes this with aRng and seeds this
      //   based on the system time; else
      //   throws IllegalArgumentException.

   public RandomColorInAlphaRange()
      // EFFECTS: Initializes this with the alpha
      //   range [0..255] and seeds this based on
      //   the system time.

   public void setSeeds(long redSeed, long greenSeed,
                        long blueSeed, long alphaSeed)
      // MODIFIES: this
      // EFFECTS: Reseeds the red, green, blue, and
      //   alpha random color-component generators.

   public void setAlphaRange(int minAlpha,
                             int maxAlpha)
         throws IllegalArgumentException
      // MODIFIES: this
      // EFFECTS: If 0 <= minAlpha <= maxAlpha <= 255
      //   sets alpha range to [minAlpha..maxAlpha];
      //   else throws IllegalArgumentException.

   public void setAlphaRange(Range newARng)
         throws NullPointerException,
                IllegalArgumentException
      // MODIFIES: this
      // EFFECTS: If newARng is null throws
      //   NullPointerException; else if
      //   0 <= newARng.getMin() <= newARng.getMax()
      //   <= 255 sets alpha range to newARng;
      //   else throws IllegalArgumentException.

   public Range getAlphaRange()
      // EFFECTS: Returns current alpha range.

   public Color nextColor()
      // MODIFIES: this
      // EFFECTS: Returns new random color whose
      //   alpha component lies in the alpha range
      //   and updates the state of this to
      //   reflect the return of this new value.
}
```

4.19 Revise the `PaintManyRectangles` program of this section so that the random rectangles it produces are filled with random translucent colors. The command line takes this form:

```
> java PaintManyRectangles [n [minLen maxLen [minAlpha maxAlpha]]]
```

The fourth and fifth program arguments specify the alpha range for the random colors; if these arguments are not supplied, use the alpha range [0..255].

4.3 Composition of Many Parts

Each of the composite classes that we've seen so far share this in common: The number of components is small and known in advance. However, it sometimes happens that the number of parts contained in a composite, though fixed, is quite large and of a common type. In such cases it is more sensible to store the components in a collection object that is owned by the composite, rather than to declare a separate field for each distinct component. The game of monopoly includes 28 different properties (in the sense of real estate), but we would sensibly resist defining a `Monopoly` class that declares 28 fields with names such as `atlanticAvenue`, `shortlineRailroad`, and `parkPlace`.

In other situations, the number of components that a composite owns is not known prior to runtime or can change over the composite's lifetime, so there is no correct number of fields to declare. A menu has a variable number of items, a picture is composed of a variable number of figures, and a fire station controls a variable number of fire engines. Composite objects such as these should store their components in a collection object.

The benefits of storing components in collection objects goes well beyond convenience. The composite can use the collection's services to manipulate its components. Collections typically provide operations for accessing elements by various criteria, for inserting new elements, for removing elements, and others. By using these services, the implementation of the composite object is made simpler. Moreover, the composite object can include some of these same services as part of its own interface and implement them by delegating requests to its collection.

Let's take a look at the `Vector` class, one of Java's standard classes for manipulating collections. Then we'll put this class to work in an implementation of a class for representing polylines—paths composed of straight line segments.

4.3.1 Java's `Vector` Class

The `java.util.Vector` class implements a list of objects that can grow as necessary to accommodate new items. Like an array, a vector maintains objects in list order and allows objects to be accessed by zero-based index. Unlike an array, a vector allows new items to be inserted at any position; the items to the right of the new item are each shifted one position to the right to make space. If a new item is inserted at position 5, the item at position 5 moves to position 6, the item at position 6 moves to position 7, and so forth. Similarly, when an item is removed from a vector, the items to the right of the deleted item are each shifted one position to the left to fill the vacated space. Note that this behavior is not an implementation detail. Rather, it has to do with how items are indexed and hence how they are accessed by clients; in short, it concerns the vector's interface.

The following class skeleton specifies only those operations that we will make use of. You can refer to Java documentation for a more complete treatment.

```
public class java.util.Vector {

  public Vector()
    // EFFECTS: Initializes this to a new empty vector.

  public int size()
    // EFFECTS: Returns the number of items stored in
    //   this vector.

  public Object get(int i)
         throws ArrayIndexOutOfBoundsException
    // EFFECTS: If 0 <= i < size() returns the item
    //   stored at index i; else throws
    //   ArrayIndexOutOfBoundsException.

  public void set(int i, Object newObj)
         throws ArrayIndexOutOfBoundsException
    // MODIFIES: this
    // EFFECTS: If 0 <= i < size() replaces the item
    //   at index i with newObj; else throws
    //   ArrayIndexOutOfBoundsException.

  public void add(Object newObj)
    // MODIFIES: this
    // EFFECTS: Adds newObj to the end of this vector
    //   (at the index size()), increasing the size of
    //   this vector by one.

  public void add(int i, Object newObj)
         throws ArrayIndexOutOfBoundsException
    // MODIFIES: this
    // EFFECTS: If 0 <= i <= size(), inserts newObj at
    //   index i and increases by one the index of every
```

```
    //   item whose index had been equal to or greater
    //   than i, and increases the size of this vector by
    //   one; else throws ArrayIndexOutOfBoundsException.

  public boolean remove(Object obj)
    // MODIFIES: this
    // EFFECTS: If some element in this is equal to obj,
    //   removes such an element of least index i and
    //   returns true, while decreasing by one the index
    //   of every item whose index had been greater than
    //   i and decreasing the size of this vector by one;
    //   else returns false.

  public Object remove(int i)
        throws ArrayIndexOutOfBoundsException
    // MODIFIES: this
    // EFFECTS: If 0 <= i < size(), removes and returns
    //   the item at index i and decreasing by one the
    //   index of every item whose index had been greater
    //   than i and decreases the size of this vector by
    //   one; else throws ArrayIndexOutOfBoundsException.

  public void clear()
    // MODIFIES: this
    // EFFECTS: Removes all of the elements from this
    //   vector.

  public int indexOf(Object obj)
    // EFFECTS: Returns the index of the first occurrence
    //   of some item in this vector that is equal to
    //   obj; else if obj does not occur in this vector
    //   returns -1.
}
```

Objects of any type can be stored in vectors. This is because the items managed by vectors are declared as type `java.lang.Object`, and `Object` serves as a supertype for every reference type. In practice, it is common to use a vector to store objects of the same type or of some common supertype other than `Object`. A common idiom when accessing the elements of a vector is to immediately cast a returned object to its actual type or to a useful supertype, as in:

```
SomeType myObject = (SomeType)vector.get(someGoodIndex);
```

Vectors cannot be used to store primitive-type objects such as integers or floats. However, for each primitive type, Java provides a *wrapper class* for converting values to equivalent objects. For example, the following code fragment wraps the integer 7 and stores it in the vector `v` at position `indx`:

```
Integer iObj = new Integer(7);
v.add(indx, iObj);
```

The value 7 can then be obtained from the vector with a single instruction that accesses the `Integer` object stored at position `indx`, and then extracts the object's value:

```
int i = ((Integer)v.get(indx)).intValue();    // now i==7
```

Vectors are often used by composite objects to store a collection of components. As an example, we'll develop the `PolylineGeometry` class. In our implementation, a polyline object defines a vector that stores the polyline's vertices in order.

4.3.2 Polylines

A **polyline** is a path in the plane composed of straight line segments. The line segments are called the **edges** of the polyline, and the endpoints of the line segments are the polyline's **vertices.** The first and last vertex of the polyline are each met by one edge, and the other vertices are met by exactly two edges. A polyline with n vertices has $n-1$ edges. In the extreme case, a polyline consists of a single vertex and no edges. Polylines are permitted to self-intersect, meaning that it is permissible for edges to cross. Moreover, if two vertices happen to occupy the same position, they are still regarded as two distinct vertices.

Figure 4.4 shows our scheme for indexing the elements of a polyline. The n vertices are indexed in order from 0 through $n-1$; we label these vertices v_0 through v_{n-1}. The edges are indexed from 0 through $n-2$, where edge e_i connects the vertices v_i and v_{i+1}. Our class for representing polylines assumes this indexing scheme for accessing vertices and edges.

Here is the skeleton for our polyline class:

```
public class PolylineGeometry {

  public PolylineGeometry(PointGeometry[] vs)
    throws NullPointerException, ZeroArraySizeException
    // EFFECTS: If vs is null or vs[i] is null for some
    //    legal i throws NullPointerException; else if
    //    vs.length==0 throws ZeroArraySizeException;
```

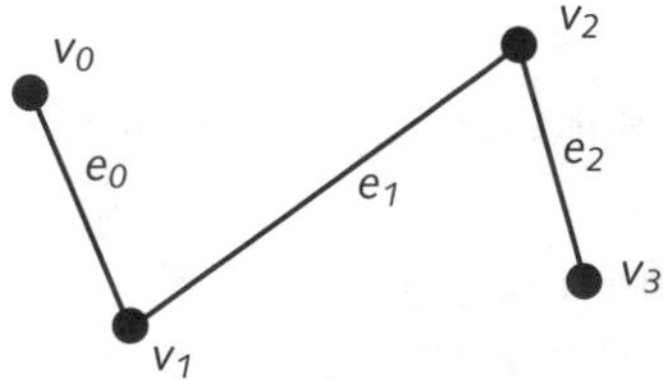

FIGURE 4.4 A polyline.

```
    //   else initializes this to the vertex sequence
    //   given by vs.

  public PolylineGeometry(PolylineGeometry poly)
         throws NullPointerException
    // EFFECTS: If poly is null throws
    //   NullPointerException; else initializes this
    //   to be a copy of poly.

  public PointGeometry getVertex(int i)
         throws IndexOutOfBoundsException
    // EFFECTS: If 0 <= i < nbrVertices() returns the
    //   position of the vertex at index i;
    //   else throws IndexOutOfBoundsException.

  public void setVertex(int i, PointGeometry v)
    throws NullPointerException, IndexOutOfBoundsException
    // MODIFIES: this
    // EFFECTS: If v is null throws NullPointerException;
    //   else if 0<=i<nbrVertices() changes the position
    //   of the vertex at index i to v;
    //   else throws IndexOutOfBoundsException.

  public LineSegmentGeometry edge(int i)
    throws IndexOutOfBoundsException
    // EFFECTS: If 0<=i<nbrEdges() returns the edge at
    //   index i; else throws IndexOutOfBoundsException.

  public int nbrVertices()
    // EFFECTS: Returns the number of vertices in this.

  public int nbrEdges()
    // EFFECTS: Returns the number of edges in this.

  public java.awt.Shape shape()
    // EFFECTS: Returns the shape of this polyline.

  public void translate(int dx, int dy)
    // MODIFIES: this
    // EFFECTS: Translates this polyline by dx along x
    //   and by dy along y.

  public String toString()
    // EFFECTS: Returns "Polyline: v0,v1,...,vn-1"
    //   where each vi describes vertex i.
}
```

Observe that the edges returned by a polygon are represented by `LineSegmentGeometry` objects (described in Exercise 3.3). The number of vertices in a `PolylineGeometry` object is fixed when the object is created. The class provides a method for moving an existing vertex to a new location in the plane (the `setVertex` method), but does not provide methods for inserting new vertices or deleting existing vertices. Here is a simple nongraphical program that illustrates the behavior of our `PolylineGeometry` class:

```
public class TryPolylineGeometry {
  public static void main(String[] args) {
    PointGeometry[] vs = new PointGeometry[] {
      new PointGeometry(0, 0),
      new PointGeometry(10, 0),
      new PointGeometry(10, 10)
    };
    PolylineGeometry poly1 = new PolylineGeometry(vs);
    System.out.println(poly1);
                // Polyline: (0,0),(10,0),(10,10)
    PolylineGeometry poly2 = new PolylineGeometry(poly1);
    poly2.setVertex(0, new PointGeometry(40, 50));
    System.out.println(poly2);
                // Polyline: (40,50),(10,0),(10,10)
    poly2.translate(100, 200);
    System.out.println(poly2);
                // Polyline: (140,250),(110,200),(110,210)
  }
}
```

Our implementation of the `PolylineGeometry` class stores a polyline's vertices in a `Vector`. The vertices are ordered by index: vertex v_i occurs at position i of the vector, which is declared thus:

```
// field of PolylineGeometry class
protected Vector vertices;
```

A new polyline is constructed from a nonempty array of points (its vertices), or from an existing polyline. In the latter case, the new polyline is a copy of the input polyline:

```
public PolylineGeometry(PointGeometry[] vs)
  throws NullPointerException, ZeroArraySizeException {
  if (vs.length == 0) throw new ZeroArraySizeException();
  vertices = new Vector();
  for (int i = 0; i < vs.length; i++)
    vertices.add(new PointGeometry(vs[i]));
}

public PolylineGeometry(PolylineGeometry poly)
      throws NullPointerException {
```

```
  vertices = new Vector();
  for (int i = 0; i < poly.nbrVertices(); i++)
    vertices.add(new PointGeometry(poly.getVertex(i)));
}
```

The getVertex method returns the position of the vertex at index i:

```
// methods of PolylineGeometry class
public PointGeometry getVertex(int i)
       throws IndexOutOfBoundsException {
  return new PointGeometry((PointGeometry)vertices.get(i));
}
```

If the getVertex method is called with an out-of-bounds index, it throws an exception by propagating the ArrayIndexOutOfBoundsException thrown by its call to vertices.get. The throws clause for method getVertex is legal because the type it declares (IndexOutOfBoundsException) is a supertype of the ArrayIndexOutOfBoundsException type.

The setVertex method is used to move the vertex at index i to a different location in the plane:

```
// method of PolylineGeometry class
public void setVertex(int i, PointGeometry v)
  throws NullPointerException, IndexOutOfBoundsException {
  vertices.set(i, new PointGeometry(v));
}
```

The edge method returns edge e_i, which connects vertices v_i and v_{i+1}. Because edges are not maintained by the storage structure, the desired edge is constructed on the fly:

```
// method of PolylineGeometry class
public LineSegmentGeometry edge(int i)
  throws IndexOutOfBoundsException {
  return new LineSegmentGeometry(getVertex(i),
                                 getVertex(i+1));
}
```

The methods for obtaining the number of vertices and number of edges are quite simple:

```
// methods of PolylineGeometry class
public int nbrVertices() {
  return vertices.size();
}

public int nbrEdges() {
  return nbrVertices() - 1;
}
```

You can translate a polyline by translating each of its vertices. The `translate` method translates this polyline by `dx` units along *x* and `dy` units along *y*:

```
// method of PolylineGeometry class
public void translate(int dx, int dy) {
  for (int i = 0; i < nbrVertices(); i++) {
    PointGeometry p = (PointGeometry)vertices.get(i);
    p.translate(dx, dy);
  }
}
```

The shape described by a polyline is created using Java's `GeneralPath` class, a member of the `java.awt.geom` package. This class represents paths composed of both curved and straight line segments. To describe a general path, you construct a new empty `GeneralPath` object, and then add an initial point using its `moveTo` method. To connect a new straight line segment to the last vertex of the current path, you call the `lineTo` method with the coordinates of the new line segment's second endpoint. You can grow a path segment by segment by calling the `lineTo` method repeatedly. Here is the implementation of the `shape` method:

```
// method of the PolylineGeometry class
public Shape shape() {
  GeneralPath path = new GeneralPath();
  PointGeometry v = getVertex(0);
  path.moveTo(v.getX(), v.getY());
  for (int i = 1; i < nbrVertices(); i++) {
    v = getVertex(i);
    path.lineTo(v.getX(), v.getY());
  }
  return path;
}
```

The string-descriptor for a polyline prints the word *Polyline* describing the type, followed by the sequence of vertices belonging to the polyline. The sequence of vertices is converted to `String` by the protected helper method `verticesToString`. Here is the implementation:

```
// methods of PolylineGeometry class
public String toString() {
  return "Polyline: " + verticesToString();
}

protected String verticesToString() {
  String res = "";
  for (int i = 0; i < nbrVertices() - 1; i++)
```

```
    res += getVertex(i) + ",";
  res += getVertex(nbrVertices()-1);
  return res;
}
```

Exercises

4.20 Using our *MyGraphicsProgram* template, write a graphical application that draws a yellow polyline. The application's program arguments consist of an even number of integers, no fewer than four in number:

```
> java PaintPolyline x0 y0 x1 y1 ...
```

The x and y coordinates of vertex v_i appear in positions $2i$ and $2i+1$ of the program arguments.

ESSENTIAL 4.21 A **dictionary** is a dynamic collection of *name-value pairs* in which each *name* appears at most once. Each *name* is a `String`, and each value is a nonnull object of any type. The value associated with any name can be looked up by name, new name-value pairs can be inserted, and existing pairs can be removed. Name-value pairs can also be accessed by index where the indexes range from zero up to one less than the current size of the dictionary. The pairs are stored in any order; stepping through the indexes in order yields the pairs in arbitrary order. Here is the class skeleton:

```
public class Dictionary {

  public Dictionary()
    // EFFECTS: Initializes this to an empty
    //   dictionary.

  public Object insert(String name, Object value)
         throws NullPointerException
    // MODIFIES: this
    // EFFECTS:If name or value is null throws
    //   NullPointerException; else if some pair
    //   named by name exists replaces its value
    //   by value; else inserts the new pair
    //   name-value into this dictionary.

  public Object remove(String name)
         throws NullPointerException
    // MODIFIES: this
```

```
    // EFFECTS: If name is null throws
    //   NullPointerException; else if some pair
    //   named by name exists removes it from this
    //   dictionary and returns its value;
    //   else returns null.

  public Object find(String name)
        throws NullPointerException
    // EFFECTS: If name is null throws
    //   NullPointerException; else if some pair
    //   named by name exists returns its value;
    //   else returns null.

  public int size()
    // EFFECTS: Returns the number of pairs
    //   stored in this dictionary.

  public boolean isFull()
    // EFFECTS: Returns true if no more pairs can
    //   be inserted into this dictionary;
    //   else returns false.

  public String name(int i)
        throws IndexOutOfBoundsException
    // EFFECTS: If 0 <= i < size() returns the name
    //   of the pair at index i; else throws
    //   IndexOutOfBoundsException.

  public Object value(int i)
        throws IndexOutOfBoundsException
    // EFFECTS: If 0<=i<size() returns the value
    //   of the pair at index i; else throws
    //   IndexOutOfBoundsException.

  public Object value(String name)
        throws NullPointerException
    // EFFECTS: If name is null throws
    //   NullPointerException; else if some pair
    //   named by name exists returns its value;
    //   else returns null.
}
```

Implement the `Dictionary` class.

[Hint: `Dictionary` is a composite class whose component is a collection of `Attribute` objects (the `Attribute` class is specified in

Exercise 3.4). Each attribute in the collection represents one of the name-value pairs in the dictionary. Be sure to use the operations supported by the `Attribute` class, as well as the operations supported by your collection (which may be a `Vector`, if you so choose). However, *clients* of your `Dictionary` class should not know anything about `Attributes`.

You may want to define a protected helper method for finding the index of the name-value pair having a given name. If you choose to store pairs in a vector, your helper method might be specified thus:

```
protected int findAttribute(String name)
  // EFFECTS: If a pair named by name exists
  //   returns its index; else returns -1.
```

The `findAttribute` method is helpful in implementing the class' public methods. For instance, to implement the `remove` method, use `findAttribute` to obtain the index of the attribute to be removed, and then call the vector's `remove` method with this index.]

4.22 This exercise describes a text-based application named `TryDictionary` that tests your `Dictionary` class with user input. The application allows the user to interactively manage name-value pairs whose values are strings. Here are the commands that the user may enter at the terminal:

- insert *name value*—inserts the pair *name-value* into the dictionary; if a pair so named already exists, updates its value to *value*.
- remove *name*—deletes the pair *name* from the dictionary; if no such pairs exists, does nothing.
- find *name*—prints the value of the pair *name*; if no such pair exists, prints a message to that effect.
- size—prints the size of the dictionary.
- print—prints the pairs in the dictionary in any order.
- quit—quits the application.

Here is a sample interaction, where user input is in bold:

```
> java TryDictionary
? insert banana yellow
? insert apple red
? find banana
```

```
yellow
? find artichoke
*** artichoke not found ***
? insert banana blue
? size
2
? print
banana:blue
apple:red
? remove apple
? find apple
*** apple not found ***
? print
banana:blue
? quit
```

4.4 Representation Invariants

A concrete class provides an implementation for its type—it provides a representation scheme for objects and implements its methods in terms of the chosen representation. The representation scheme describes how to represent values belonging to the type. Instances of the `PointGeometry` class represent points in the plane: The values of an instance's `x` and `y` fields indicate the point's x and y coordinates. Instances of the `RectangleGeometry` class represent rectangles in the plane: The values of a `RectangleGeometry`'s fields indicate the rectangle's position, width, and height.

Depending on the representation scheme, it is possible to imagine objects that are invalid in the sense that they fail to represent anything. A `RectangleGeometry` object whose fields indicate a rectangle of negative width is an example, because the width of a rectangle must be nonnegative. Another example of an invalid representation is a `PolylineGeometry` object whose `vertices` vector contains no points at all. Such an object would correspond to a polyline possessing no vertices, which by definition cannot exist.

This section focuses on representation invariants, which describe what it means for a representation to be valid. After presenting an overview, I'll describe two classes possessing nontrivial representation invariants: a class for ellipses in the plane and a class for rational numbers.

4.4.1 Overview

An object's behavior is influenced by its history. The reason that behavior depends on past events is that objects have a form of memory known as

state. Such remarks apply not only to Java objects but also to many real-life things. As a human being, you are influenced by the sum of experiences you've endured over the course of your life. Each experience leaves its mark on you—in your memory, on your body, in your temperament and thoughts. The sum of your experiences gives rise to your current state of being, which *influences*—some would go so far as say *determines*—your behavior. As a more mundane example, consider a radio. When you turn on a radio, it plays the station to which it was last tuned. Station tuning is part of the radio's state. If you tune to a different station, the radio's behavior changes (it plays a new station) because its state changes (it stores the new station's frequency).

In Java, the state of an object corresponds to the values stored in its fields. As the object responds to messages it receives, these values may change over time. Such changes are known as **state transitions.** We can observe the influence of history on a Java object by examining its fields during the course of a number of messages. In the following code fragment, we assume the implementation of the `RectangleGeometry` class that was given in Section 3.2.2, in which a rectangle possesses two `Range` fields named `xRange` and `yRange`:

```
RectangleGeometry r = new RectangleGeometry(2, 2, 4, 5);
                      // xRange: [2..6],  yRange: [2..7]
r.setPosition(new PointGeometry(8, 9));
                      // xRange: [8..12],  yRange: [9..14]
r.setWidth(7);        // xRange: [8..15],  yRange: [9..14]
r.getHeight();        // xRange: [8..15],  yRange: [9..14]
```

Some kinds of messages result in state changes (such as `setWidth`), whereas other kinds of messages don't (`getHeight`). As noted in Section 3.2, those methods that are capable of causing state transitions are known as *mutators*, and those methods that access state without causing state transitions are known as *selectors*.

An object's state captures only what is significant with respect to the object's abstraction. It is usually not necessary for an object to store its complete history. A radio stores its current station tuning, but not a history of all the tunings it has assumed in the past. As another example, observe that the code fragment in the previous paragraph leaves the `RectangleGeometry` object `r` in precisely the same state as the following object `s`:

```
RectangleGeometry s = new RectangleGeometry(8, 9, 7, 5);
                      // xRange: [8..15],  yRange: [9..14]
```

Although the objects `r` and `s` have very different histories, you cannot establish this fact by examining only their states.

Every object's state is distinct from that of all other objects, including objects of the same type. In the code fragments just given, `RectangleGeometry` objects `r` and `s` happen to be in the same state. But if we were to send a state-changing message to either object, its state would change without affecting the other object's state. The instruction

```
s.setPosition(new PointGeometry(12, 14));
```

changes the state of rectangle s without changing the state of `r`.

For many types of objects, the set of states they can legally assume is limited by **consistency constraints.** An FM radio can be tuned only to a frequency within the standard FM band. Similarly, the width and height of a `RectangleGeometry` object must be nonnegative. Each object's methods are defined such that they ensure that the object's consistency constraints are honored. A radio's tuner control limits the range of frequencies that the radio can be set to receive. Similarly, clients of a `RectangleGeometry` object `s` cannot use the `setWidth` method to set its width property to a negative number. The instruction

```
s.setWidth(-18);
```

does not change the width of rectangle `s` to −18; rather, it throws an illegal argument exception.

Likewise, information hiding prevents clients from corrupting an object's state by directly accessing its fields. Objects enforce their own consistency constraints by forcing clients to use their public interfaces. Radios boast hard plastic covers which, among other things, prevent users from directly manipulating the radio's internal electronics. Along the same lines, clients of a `PolylineGeometry` object `p` cannot set its `vertices` vector to an empty vector:

```
p.vertices = new Vector();
```

because the `vertices` field is protected. The compiler flags this assignment as an access error, at least for those clients not permitted access to `PolylineGeometry's` protected fields.

Consistency constraints are expressed as **representation invariants.** Whereas preconditions and postconditions describe the behavior of a procedure, representation invariants describe the representation properties of class instances. Representation invariants describe what it means for class instances to be in a consistent state. Our `PolylineGeometry` class includes the following representation invariant:

> *The instance field* `vertices` *is a vector that contains one or more points, and only points.*

In contrast, the representation invariant for the `PointGeometry` class is vacuously satisfied because *any* pair of values for the fields `x` and `y` corresponds to a point in the plane.

An object's representation invariants should be established when the object is created. This is the responsibility of the class' constructors. Moreover, public methods should ensure that the representation invariants are satisfied whenever the method is exited. Thus the representation invariants of a class place an obligation on its public methods. However, public methods benefit insofar as they can assume that the representation invariants are satisfied whenever they are called.

Representation invariants need not be satisfied *while* a method of the class is executing. Methods work toward certain goals. One of a method's goals is establishing the postconditions that it promises. Another goal is establishing the representation invariants. In the process of carrying out its work, the method may violate one or more representation invariants, just as it may violate its own postconditions. However, the method should restore its representation invariants and establish its own postconditions by the time it completes its work.

The role of representation invariants underscores the importance of information hiding. If information hiding is used properly, only those clients requiring direct access to an object's fields will have such access, whereas all other clients interact with the object only through its public methods. If the methods are implemented correctly, the object's representation invariants will be preserved. In contrast, if information hiding is broken and clients have unwarranted access to the object's fields, they may change the fields' values and thereby corrupt the object's state. Once clients are able to bypass an object's public interface, the object can no longer guarantee the validity of its representation.

4.4.2 Ellipses

In this section we will develop a class for ellipses. Our implementation explores the idea of representation invariants discussed in the previous section.

An **ellipse** is the set of points p in the plane such that the sum of the distances from p to two fixed points is some constant number D. Each of the two fixed points is called a **focus** of the ellipse; jointly, they are the ellipse's **foci.** The **major axis** of the ellipse is the line segment that contains the two foci and connects opposite points of the ellipse. It is not hard to show that the length of the major axis is equal to D. See Figure 4.5.

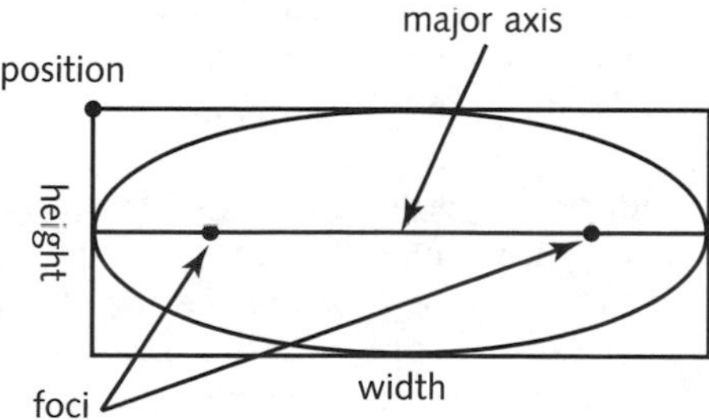

FIGURE 4.5 An ellipse and its bounding box.

Picture the plane to be the face of a sheet of wood, with a nail protruding from each of the two foci. A string of length *D* is attached at either end to the two nails. Imagine pulling a pencil against the string so that the string is taut, and then placing the point of the pencil against the wood plane. Now, trace the pencil around the foci while keeping the string taut at all times. The pencil traces an ellipse.

The ellipses with which we will work are in standard orientation, meaning that each ellipse's major axis is oriented either vertically or horizontally. The **bounding box** of an ellipse is the smallest axis-parallel rectangle that encloses the ellipse. We can define an ellipse's position and size in terms of its bounding box. The **position** of an ellipse is taken to be its bounding box's upper-left corner. The **width** and **height** of an ellipse is defined as the width and height of its bounding box, respectively (see Figure 4.5). As with rectangles, we will refer to an ellipse's position, width, and height as its *dimensions*.

Our ellipse type is similar to our rectangle type presented in Chapter 3. The main difference is that an ellipse provides a method for obtaining its bounding box, but does not provide `xRange` or `yRange` methods (the ranges that an ellipse spans can be extracted from its bounding box). Here is the specification for the `EllipseGeometry` class:

```
public class EllipseGeometry {

  public EllipseGeometry(int x, int y,
                         int width, int height)
        throws IllegalArgumentException
    // EFFECTS: If width or height is negative throws
    //    IllegalArgumentException; else initializes this
    //    ellipse to position (x,y) and specified
    //    width and height.

  public EllipseGeometry(PointGeometry pos,
                         int width, int height)
    throws NullPointerException, IllegalArgumentException
    // EFFECTS: If pos is null throws
    //    NullPointerException; else if width or height
    //    is negative throws IllegalArgumentException;
    //    else initializes this to position pos and
    //    specified width and height.

  public EllipseGeometry(Range xRange, Range yRange)
        throws NullPointerException
    // EFFECTS: If xRange or yRange is null throws
    //    NullPointerException; else initializes this
    //    to the dimensions of xRange x yRange.
```

```
public EllipseGeometry(EllipseGeometry r)
       throws NullPointerException
  // EFFECTS: If r is null throws NullPointerException;
  //   else initializes this to an ellipse with the
  //   same dimensions as r.

public PointGeometry getPosition()
  // EFFECTS: Returns this ellipse's position.

public void setPosition(PointGeometry p)
       throws NullPointerException
  // MODIFIES: this
  // EFFECTS: If p is null throws NullPointerException;
  //   else changes this ellipse's position to
  //   (p.getX(),p.getY()).

public int getWidth()
  // EFFECTS: Returns this ellipse's width.

public void setWidth(int newWidth)
       throws IllegalArgumentException
  // MODIFIES: this
  // EFFECTS: If newWidth is negative throws
  //   IllegalArgumentException; else changes this
  //   ellipse's width to newWidth.

public int getHeight()
  // EFFECTS: Returns this ellipse's height.

public void setHeight(int newHeight)
       throws IllegalArgumentException
  // MODIFIES: this
  // EFFECTS: If newHeight is negative throws
  //   IllegalArgumentException; else changes this
  //   ellipse's height to newHeight.

public RectangleGeometry boundingBox()
  // EFFECTS: Returns this ellipse's bounding box.

public boolean contains(int x, int y)
  // EFFECTS: Returns true if the point (x,y) is
  //   contained in this ellipse; else returns false.

public boolean contains(PointGeometry p)
       throws NullPointerException
```

```
    // EFFECTS: If p is null throws NullPointerException;
    //   else returns true if p is contained in this
    //   ellipse; else returns false.

  public java.awt.Shape shape()
    // EFFECTS: Returns the shape of this ellipse.

  public void translate(int dx, int dy)
    // MODIFIES: this
    // EFFECTS: Translates this ellipse by dx along x
    //   and by dy along y.

  public String toString()
    // EFFECTS: Returns "Ellipse: (x,y),width,height".
}
```

Let's turn to the implementation. The representation for ellipses is more complicated than for rectangles. We'll store an ellipse's `position`, `width`, and `height` in fields of the same name:

```
// fields of EllipseGeometry class
protected PointGeometry position;
protected int width, height;
```

And we'll store the positions of an ellipse's two foci in fields of type `PointGeometry`, and the length of its major axis in an integer field:

```
// fields of EllipseGeometry class
  // positions of the two foci
protected PointGeometry focus1, focus2;
  // length of the major axis
protected int majorAxis;
```

These last three fields are required by the two-argument `contains` method, which is handed the *x* and *y* coordinates of a point *p* and reports whether this ellipse contains *p*. The implementation relies on the definition of *ellipse* given at the outset of this section: The method returns `true` if and only if the sum of the distances from point *p* to the two foci is no greater than the length of this ellipse's major axis:

```
// method of EllipseGeometry class
public boolean contains(int x, int y) {
  PointGeometry p = new PointGeometry(x, y);
  return
(focus1.distance(p)+focus2.distance(p))<=majorAxis;
}
```

Correctness of the `contains` method depends on the correctness of the values stored in the fields `focus1`, `focus2`, and `majorAxis`. In turn, these values depend on the ellipse's current dimensions. When the ellipse is constructed and its dimensions initialized, these three fields (`focus1`, `focus2`, and `majorAxis`) are initialized. Similarly, whenever any of the ellipse's dimensions changes, these three fields are updated accordingly. This, then, is the representation invariant:

> *The values stored in the* `focus1`, `focus2`, *and* `majorAxis` *fields represent this ellipse's foci and major axis length, where the values stored in the* `position`, `width`, *and* `height` *fields represent this ellipse's dimensions.*

This representation invariant should be established when an ellipse is constructed and maintained throughout its lifetime. Consider construction first. The four-argument constructor initializes the `position`, `width`, and `height` fields, and then invokes the protected `computeFoci` method to initialize the remaining three fields:

```
public EllipseGeometry(int x, int y, int width, int height)
       throws IllegalArgumentException {
  if ((width < 0) || (height < 0))
     throw new IllegalArgumentException();
  this.position = new PointGeometry(x, y);
  this.width = width;
  this.height = height;
  computeFoci();
}
```

The `computeFoci` method sets the fields that store the two foci and the length of the major axis, based on the ellipse's current dimensions. The method works by computing the center *(x,y)* of the ellipse under construction, and then uses trigonometry to compute the position of the two foci. The length of its major axis is equal to the ellipse's width or height, whichever is greater:

```
// method of EllipseGeometry class
protected void computeFoci() {
  // REQUIRES: Position is not null, and height
  //   and width are not negative.
  // EFFECTS: Sets the fields focus1 and focus2
  //   to this ellipse's foci, and majorAxis to the
  //   length of its major axis.
  double a = getWidth() / 2.0;
  double b = getHeight() / 2.0;
  PointGeometry pos = getPosition();
  int x = (int)(pos.getX() + a);
  int y = (int)(pos.getY() + b);
  int c;
  if (a > b) {  // ellipse has horizontal major axis
    c = (int)Math.round(Math.sqrt(a*a - b*b));
```

```
      focus1 = new PointGeometry(x + c, y);
      focus2 = new PointGeometry(x - c, y);
      majorAxis = getWidth();
    } else {   // ellipse has vertical major axis
      c = (int)Math.round(Math.sqrt(b*b - a*a));
      focus1 = new PointGeometry(x, y + c);
      focus2 = new PointGeometry(x, y - c);
      majorAxis = getHeight();
    }
  }
```

`ComputeFoci` is a helper method that other methods use to establish the representation invariant. Because this method is not part of `EllipseGeometry`'s public interface, it is not declared by the class skeleton given earlier.

The remaining constructors need not call `computeFoci` directly because they are defined in terms of the four-argument constructor just defined:

```
public EllipseGeometry(PointGeometry pos,
                       int width, int height)
 throws NullPointerException, IllegalArgumentException {
  this(pos.getX(), pos.getY(), width, height);
}

public EllipseGeometry(Range xRange, Range yRange)
       throws NullPointerException {
  this(xRange.getMin(), yRange.getMin(),
       xRange.length(), yRange.length());
}

public EllipseGeometry(EllipseGeometry e)
       throws NullPointerException {
  this(e.getPosition(), e.getWidth(), e.getHeight());
}
```

The representation invariant must be established not only when a new ellipse is constructed, but also maintained throughout its lifetime (between calls to public methods). There are only three operations that can potentially falsify the representation invariant—the operations `setPosition`, `setWidth`, and `setHeight`—which are used to change an ellipse's dimensions. We implement each of these operations so that it restores the representation invariant before returning. The general approach is to update the ellipse's position, width, or height as called for by the particular method, and then to call `computeFoci` to restore the representation invariant:

```
// methods of EllipseGeometry class
public void setPosition(PointGeometry p)
       throws NullPointerException {
  position.setX(p.getX());
```

```
    position.setY(p.getY());
    computeFoci();
  }

  public void setWidth(int newWidth)
         throws IllegalArgumentException {
    if (newWidth < 0) throw new IllegalArgumentException();
    width = newWidth;
    computeFoci();
  }

  public void setHeight(int newHeight)
         throws IllegalArgumentException {
    if (newHeight < 0) throw new IllegalArgumentException();
    height = newHeight;
    computeFoci();
  }
```

The shape method, which returns the shape of this ellipse, can be defined thus:

```
// method of EllipseGeometry class
public java.awt.Shape shape() {
  PointGeometry pos = getPosition();
  return new Ellipse2D.Float(pos.getX(), pos.getY(),
                             getWidth(), getHeight());
}
```

Exercises

ESSENTIAL **4.23** Implement the remaining methods of the EllipseGeometry class. The following code fragment illustrates the behavior of the toString and translate methods:

```
EllipseGeometry e = new EllipseGeometry(2, 3, 7, 8);
System.out.println(e);  // Ellipse: (2,3),7,8
e.translate(10, 20);
System.out.println(e);  // Ellipse: (12,23),7,8
```

4.24 Let me describe another way to implement the EllipseGeometry class. Eliminate the focus1, focus2, and majorAxis fields, as well as the representation invariant that refers to them. Also, change the implementation of the two-argument contains method as follows: Whenever this method is called, it computes the ellipse's foci and major axis length, and then uses these values to decide whether the input point it was called with lies inside the ellipse. The method definition might take the following form:

```
// method of EllipseGeometry class: version 2
public boolean contains(int x, int y) {
  PointGeometry focus1, focus2;
  int majorAxis;
  // initialize the local variables focus1,
  //   focus2, and majorAxis
  ...
  PointGeometry p = new PointGeometry(x, y);
  return (focus1.distance(p) + focus2.distance(p))
                                    <= majorAxis;
}
```

What are the advantages and disadvantages of this approach, compared to the implementation of `EllipseGeometry` presented in the body of this section?

4.25 You may have observed that the points stored in the `focus1` and `focus2` fields sometimes fail to accurately capture the ellipse's true foci. The problem is that the coordinates of the true foci are sometimes noninteger real numbers, yet the foci are represented by `PointGeometry` objects having integer coordinates. One solution is to represent the foci by points with floating-point coordinates using Java's `Point2D.Double` class, included in the `java.awt.geom` package. (`Point2D.Double` is a static nested class belonging to the `Point2D` class.) The expression:

```
new Point2D.Double(5.1, 6.2)
```

creates a new `Point2D` object representing the point (5.1,6.2). Based on this approach, `EllipseGeometry`'s `focus1` and `focus2` fields would then be declared like this:

```
Point2D.Double focus1, focus2;
```

Implement an `EllipseGeometryF` class that follows this approach. [Hint: This change in representation requires that you revise the implementation of the `computeFoci` and `contains` methods of the original `EllipseGeometry` class. You can obtain the *x* and *y* coordinates of a `Point2D.Double` object using its `getX` and `getY` methods. And the method

```
// method of Point2D.Double class
public double distance(Point2D p)
```

can be used to compute the distance between point `p` and this point.]

4.26 Write a graphical application that paints *n* randomly colored random points inside an ellipse. Your program takes five program arguments:

```
> java PaintPointsInEllipse n x y width height
```

The ellipse is positioned at (*x*,*y*) and has given *width* and *height*. [Hint: Generate random points inside the ellipse's bounding rectangle, but discard those points that lie outside the ellipse.]

4.27 For all circles, the ratio of a circle's circumference to its diameter is fixed, and this ratio is denoted by π, which is about 3.1415926535898. One strategy for computing π is to create a square and inscribe a circle inside the square. Where the circle has radius *r*, the length of each side of the square is equal to *2r*. Next, generate a large number *N* of random points inside the square, while keeping track of the number *M* of points that also lie inside the circle. Thus we obtain the fraction $P=\frac{M}{N}$, which yields the approximation to π that we seek: $\pi \approx 4P$.

This approach works because *P* approximates the ratio of the area A_c of the circle (πr^2) to the area A_s of the square ($(2r)^2$). It follows that $\pi \approx 4P$ by simple algebra:

$$P \approx \frac{A_c}{A_s} = \frac{\pi r^2}{(2r)^2} = \frac{\pi r^2}{4r^2} = \frac{\pi}{4}$$

Write the program `FindPi`, which is called with a `long` argument indicating the number of random points *N* to generate, and outputs the resulting approximation to π:

```
> java FindPi 100
rectangle: (0,0),10000,10000
ellipse: (0,0),10000,10000
pi = 3.16
> java FindPi 10000
rectangle: (0,0),10000,10000
ellipse: (0,0),10000,10000
pi = 3.1388
> java FindPi 1000000
rectangle: (0,0),10000,10000
ellipse: (0,0),10000,10000
pi = 3.141276
```

4.4.3 Rational Numbers

In this section we'll develop a class for representing rational numbers. The representation invariants are more complicated (and interesting) than those for our ellipse class. A rational number is formed by the ratio *a/b* where *a* and *b* are integers and *b* is nonzero. Here, *a* is called the **numerator** and *b* the **denominator.** Here is the skeleton for our `Rational` class:

```
public class Rational {

  public Rational(long num, long denom)
        throws IllegalArgumentException
    // EFFECTS: If denom equals zero throws
    //   IllegalArgumentException; else initializes
    //   this to num/denom.

  public Rational(long num)
    // EFFECTS: Initializes this to the rational num.

  public Rational()
    // EFFECTS: Initializes this to the rational 0.

  public Rational add(Rational a)
    // EFFECTS: Returns the rational equal to this + a.

  public Rational multiply(Rational a)
    // EFFECTS: Returns the rational equal to this * a.

  public Rational subtract(Rational a)
    // EFFECTS: Returns the rational equal to this - a.

  public Rational divide(Rational a)
        throws IllegalArgumentException
    // EFFECTS: If a equals zero throws
    //   IllegalArgumentException; else returns the
    //   rational equal to this / a.

  public boolean equals(Object a)
    // EFFECTS: Returns true if a is a Rational and
    //   a denotes the same rational number as this;
    //   else returns false.

  public int compareTo(Object obj)
        throws ClassCastException
    // EFFECTS: If this and obj are incomparable throws
    //   ClassCastException; else returns a negative
    //   integer, zero, or a positive integer if this
    //   is less than, equal to, or greater than obj,
    //   respectively.
```

```
  public boolean isInteger()
    // EFFECTS: Returns true if this denotes an
    //   integer; else returns false.

  public long numerator()
    // EFFECTS: Returns the numerator.

  public long denominator()
    // EFFECTS: Returns the denominator.

  public String toString()
    // EFFECTS: Returns the "num/denom".

  public double toDouble()
    // EFFECTS: Returns a double approximating this.
}
```

Study the class skeleton and you'll see that none of the methods changes the state of a `Rational` object—none of the methods' specifications includes a modifies clause. There is no method for changing a rational's numerator or denominator. Moreover, the `add` method does not change this rational; rather, it produces a new rational:

```
Rational a = new Rational(2, 4);
Rational b = new Rational(2, 8);
Rational c = a.add(b);
System.out.println("a: " + a);    // a: 1/2
System.out.println("b: " + b);    // b: 1/4
System.out.println("c: " + c);    // c: 3/4
```

Likewise, the `subtract`, `multiply`, and `divide` methods do not change the state of this rational. An object whose state cannot be changed by clients is said to be **immutable.** `Rational` objects are immutable because they provide no public mutators for changing their state. In contrast, `PointGeometry` objects are **mutable** because they provide public mutators (such as the `setX` and `setY` methods) for changing the state of points.

Immutable types such as `Rational` should define an `equals` method. This is because two immutable objects that represent the same value are identical, for all intents and purposes. There is no sequence of messages that can cause an immutable object to represent any value other than the value it represents upon its creation. Hence, any two immutable objects that are equal at any point in time must always be equal. In contrast, because mutable objects (such as `PointGeometry` objects) may be driven from state to state, the equivalence of two mutable objects is a transient condition, one that can change at any time.

Before implementing the `Rational` class, I'll demonstrate its behavior. The following program `FindPiLiebniz` is called with an integer program argument n, and computes and prints an approximation to π based on the first n terms of an infinite series. The series, which converges to $\pi/4$, is due to Leibniz:

$$1 - \tfrac{1}{3} + \tfrac{1}{5} - \tfrac{1}{7} + \tfrac{1}{9} \cdots$$

The following program implements this series. It is called with a program argument n that indicates the number of terms to compute:

```
public class FindPiLiebniz {
  public static void main(String[] args) {
    if (args.length != 1) {
      System.out.println("USAGE: FindPiLiebniz n");
      System.exit(0);
    }
    long n = Long.parseLong(args[0]);
    long sign = 1;
    long bottom = 1;
    Rational pi = new Rational(0);
    for (int i = 0; i < n; i++) {
      Rational term = new Rational(sign, bottom);
      pi = pi.add(term);
      sign = -sign;
      bottom += 2;
    }
    Rational answ = pi.multiply(new Rational(4));
    String msg = "pi = " + answ + " = " + answ.toDouble();
    System.out.println(msg);
  }
}
```

Unfortunately, Liebniz's series converges very slowly. When you experiment with the `FindPiLiebniz` program, you'll find that values of n exceeding 22 cause the variable `pi` to overflow.

Let's develop a storage structure for the `Rational` class. It is natural to store a rational number's numerator and denominator in two integer variables respectively:

```
// fields of Rational class
protected long num, denom;
```

The rational number that these two fields jointly represent is *num/denom*. But that is not the end of the story, for there are conditions that constrain the state of `Rational` objects. Describing these constraints requires a brief digression.

The **greatest common divisor (gcd)** of two positive integers a and b is the largest integer that evenly divides both numbers. In other words, gcd(a,b)=n if n divides both a and b without leaving a remainder, and there exists no integer larger than n that does the same. The gcd of 12 and 18 is 6, the gcd of 3 and 9 is 3, and the gcd of 4 and 7 is 1. Two positive integers whose gcd is equal to one are said to be **relatively prime.** Thus 4 and 7 are relatively prime, whereas 12 and 18 are not.

The notion of greatest common divisor is used in the representation invariants of the `Rational` class. These invariants are given in terms of the storage structure, the fields `num` and `denom`:

- *gcd condition*: the absolute values of `num` and `denom` are relatively prime if `num` is nonzero,
- *zero condition*: `denom` == 1 if `num` is zero, and
- *sign condition*: `denom` > 0 .

Any rational number may be expressed in infinitely many different ways; for example, 1/2 = 2/4 = 18/36 = (−200)/(−400). The purpose of the representation invariants is to provide a unique representation for every distinct rational number. By reducing every rational to a standard form, we ensure that any two `Rational` objects that represent the same rational number are in identical states. Here are some examples:

equivalent rational numbers		***object state***
1/2, 2/4, 18/36, (−200)/(−400)	⟶	`num: 1, denom: 2`
(−2)/3, 2/(−3), (−4)/6, 8/(−12)	⟶	`num: -2, denom: 3`
0/1, 0/18, 0/(−36)	⟶	`num: 0, denom: 1`

A number of benefits follows from adopting a unique representation for rational numbers. For one, it allows us to test for equivalence very easily: Two `Rational` objects are equal if and only if their numerators are equal and their denominators are equal. For another, it reduces the magnitudes of numerators and denominators, thereby minimizing the likelihood of overflow.

Having defined the storage structure, we'll implement the methods of the `Rational` class. Here are all three constructors:

```
public Rational(long num, long den)
       throws IllegalArgumentException {
  if (denom == 0) throw new IllegalArgumentException();
  this.num = num;
  this.denom = den;
  normalize();
}

public Rational(long num) {
  this(num, 1);
}

public Rational() {
  this(0, 1);
}
```

The two-argument constructor initializes the num and denom fields, and then calls the normalize method to establish the representation invariants. The remaining two constructors don't need to call normalize directly because they call the two-argument constructor. The normalize method is defined like this:

```
// method of Rational class
protected void normalize() {
  // MODIFIES: this
  // EFFECTS: Establishes the representation
  //   invariants such that this
  //   denotes the rational num/denom.
  long bigdivisor;
    // establish the sign condition
  if (denom < 0) {
    num = -num;
    denom = -denom;
  }
  // establish the zero condition
  if (num == 0)
    denom = 1;
    // establish the gcd condition
  else {
    long tempnum = (num < 0) ? -num : num;
    bigdivisor = gcd(tempnum, denom);
    if (bigdivisor > 1) {
      num /= bigdivisor;
      denom /= bigdivisor;
    }
  }
}
```

The procedure gcd computes the greatest common denominator of two integers and is defined thus:

```
// method of Rational class
protected long gcd(int a, int b) {
  // REQUIRES: a and b are positive.
  // EFFECTS: Returns the greatest common divisor
   //   of a and b.
  while (b > 0) {
    int rem = a % b;
    a = b;
    b = rem;
  }
  return a;
}
```

The add method takes a rational argument, adds the argument to this rational, and returns the result. Similarly, the multiply method takes a rational argument, multiplies it by this rational, and returns the result. Neither method changes the state of the argument or the receiver. Here is an example of their use:

```
Rational a = new Rational(2,4);
Rational b = new Rational(2,8);
Rational c = a.add(b);
System.out.println("a: " + a);  // a: 1/2
System.out.println("b: " + b);  // b: 1/4
System.out.println("c: " + c);  // c: 3/4
Rational d = c.multiply(a);
System.out.println("d: " + d);  // d: 3/8
```

These methods apply the following standard rules for adding and multiplying fractions:

$(a/b) + (c/d) = (ad + bc)/(bd)$

$(a/b)\ (c/d) = (ac)/(bd)$

The add and multiply procedures are defined thus:

```
// methods of Rational class
public Rational add(Rational a) {
  long top = numerator() * a.denominator() +
             denominator() * a.numerator();
  long bot = denominator() * a.denominator();
  return new Rational(top, bot);
}

public Rational multiply(Rational a) {
  long top = numerator() * a.numerator();
  long bot = denominator() * a.denominator();
  return new Rational(top, bot);
}
```

Notice that the Rational objects returned by add and multiply are guaranteed to be in a consistent state. This is because every such rational is constructed by invoking the constructor:

```
Rational a = new Rational(2,4);
Rational b = new Rational(2,8);
Rational c = a.add(b);
  // return new Rational(4*1 + 2*1, 2*4), same as
  // return new Rational(6, 8); constructs
  // a Rational with num==3 and denom==4
```

Because Rational objects are in standard form, we can compare two rationals for equivalence by comparing their respective numerators and denominators:

```
// method of Rational class
public boolean equals(Object obj) {
  if (obj instanceof Rational) {
    Rational a = (Rational)obj;
    return ((numerator() == a.numerator()) &&
            (denominator() == a.denominator()));
  }
  return false;
}
```

The compareTo method is called with a rational argument obj, and compares obj and this rational. It returns a negative integer (−1), zero, or a positive integer (1) if this rational is less than, equal to, or greater than the argument obj respectively:

```
// method of Rational class
public int compareTo(Object obj)
       throws ClassCastException {
  Rational a = (Rational)obj;
  long leftSide = numerator() * a.denominator();
  long rightSide = denominator() * a.numerator();
  if (leftSide < rightSide) return -1;
  else if (leftSide == rightSide) return 0;
  else return 1;
}
```

Observe that compareTo is consistent with the meaning of the equals method. Where r and s are rationals, the expression r.compareTo(s) returns zero if and only if the expression r.equals(s) returns true.

The isInteger method reports whether this rational represents some integer. The implementation takes advantage of the representation invariants, which ensure that the Rational representation of an integer has the value 1 in its denominator:

```
// method of Rational class
public boolean isInteger() {
  return denominator() == 1L;
}
```

In closing, observe that the representation invariants for a Rational object are established when the object is constructed, and that they are preserved throughout its lifetime because the object's state never changes. Indeed, the same holds for all immutable objects: The constructors establish the representation invariants, and the remaining methods necessarily preserve these invariants because they don't alter the object's state. In contrast,

Ellipse objects are mutable, so each of its mutator methods must take care to preserve the representation invariants. In the case of mutable objects, the representation invariants should be established by the constructors and preserved by each of its mutator methods.

Exercises

ESSENTIAL **4.28** Complete the implementation of the Rational class. A noninteger rational is expressed by a string of the form *num/denom*, and an integer rational by a string of the form *num*:

```
System.out.print("one-half: " + new Rational(3,6));
  // one-half: 1/2
System.out.print("five: " + new Rational(10, 2));
  // five: 5
```

4.29 Another approach to approximating π uses the following fact, due to Ernesto Cesaro and cited in *Structure and Interpretation of Computer Programs*: The probability that two random integers are relatively prime is equal to $6/\pi^2$. Write a program that uses this fact to approximate π. Use the gcd method presented in this section to iteratively test whether two random positive integers are relatively prime. (Recall that a and b are relatively prime if and only if gcd(a,b) equals one.) The long program argument n specifies the number of pairs of random integers to test:

```
> java FindPiCesaro 1000
pi = 3.133682700398331

> java FindPiCesaro 1000000
pi = 3.1409239115514453
```

4.5 Interacting with Pictures

Up to now, we've developed a number of graphics applications based on the *MyGraphicsProgram* template of Section 3.5. Using this program template, you can write programs that create and display custom graphics content, but that do not allow the user to manipulate the content while the program is running. This section presents a new program template, which I call the *MyInteractiveProgram* template, which lets you define a **controller** object that mediates interactions between the user and the program's graphical content. Programs based on this template are interactive—they respond to textual input that the user keys into the console window while the program runs. First I'll present an application based on the *MyInteractiveProgram* template. Then, I'll extract the pattern from this program and present the template more formally.

4.5.1 Splattering Points

The program `PlaySplatterPoints` is used to paint random points into the frame's content area. The user guides the process through the *current color* and the *current rectangle*, two values maintained by the program. Whenever new random points are generated, they are positioned inside the current rectangle and painted the current color. Initially, the current color is white and the current rectangle is a square positioned at (0,0) and of width and height equal to 100, but the user may change these values. The program provides the following commands for generating new random points and for updating the current rectangle and the current color:

- rectangle *x y width height*—updates the current rectangle to position (*x*,*y*) and specified *width* and *height*.
- show—shows the current rectangle as a white outline.
- hide—hides the current rectangle.
- new *n*—generates *n* random points inside current rectangle; the *n* points are filled with the current color.
- color *red green blue*—updates the current color to the specified integer color components, where 0 < *red, green, blue* ≤ 255.
- quit—quits the application.

The application comprises two classes. The first class, `PlaySplatterPoints`, is responsible for constructing a new frame and panel and for constructing and starting a new controller. This class also implements the `paintComponent` method. Here is the class definition in its entirety:

```
public class PlaySplatterPoints extends ApplicationPanel {

  public PlaySplatterPoints() {
    setBackground(Color.black);
  }

  static PlaySplatterPointsController controller;

  public static void main(String[] args) {
    ApplicationPanel panel = new PlaySplatterPoints();
    ApplicationFrame frame =
      new ApplicationFrame("PlaySplatterPoints");
    frame.setPanel(panel);
    controller = new PlaySplatterPointsController(frame);
    frame.show();
    controller.start();
  }
```

```
  public void paintComponent(Graphics g) {
    super.paintComponent(g);
    Graphics2D g2 = (Graphics2D)g;
    g2.setRenderingHint(RenderingHints.KEY_ANTIALIASING,
                        RenderingHints.VALUE_ANTIALIAS_ON);
    Vector points = controller.points();
    Vector colors = controller.colors();
    for (int i = 0; i < points.size(); i++) {
      PointGeometry point = (PointGeometry)points.get(i);
      Color color = (Color)colors.get(i);
      g2.setPaint(color);
      g2.fill(point.shape());
    }
    if (controller.isVisible()) {
      RectangleGeometry rectangle=controller.rectangle();
      g2.setPaint(Color.white);
      g2.draw(rectangle.shape());
    }
  }
}
```

The second class, named `PlaySplatterPointsController`, defines the controller. This class is defined such that it runs within its own thread of execution. This means that the controller and the static `main` method (of the `PlaySplatterPoints` class) run in separate threads, independent of one another. This allows the controller to continue running even after the `main` method exits. The frame also runs in its own thread.

To enable a `PlaySplatterPointsController` object to run in its own thread, we define the class to be an extension of Java's `Thread` class. The static `main` method of the `PlaySplatterPoints` class creates a new controller and starts it running within its own thread through the following two instructions:

```
controller = new PlaySplatterPointsController(frame);
controller.start();
```

Here is the implementation of the `PlaySplatterPointsController` class:

```
class PlaySplatterPointsController extends Thread {

  protected ApplicationFrame frame;
  protected Vector points;
  protected Vector colors;
  protected RectangleGeometry rectangle;
  protected boolean isVisible;
```

```
protected
  PlaySplatterPointsController(ApplicationFrame frame) {
  this.frame = frame;
  points = new Vector();
  colors = new Vector();
  isVisible = true;
  rectangle = new RectangleGeometry(0, 0, 100, 100);
}

protected Vector points() {
  return points;
}

protected Vector colors() {
  return colors;
}

protected RectangleGeometry rectangle() {
  return rectangle;
}

protected boolean isVisible() {
  return isVisible;
}

public void run() {
  ScanInput in = new ScanInput();
  Color currentColor = Color.white;
  RandomPoint rand = new RandomPoint();
  while (true) {
    try {
      System.out.print("? ");
      String s = in.readString();
      int x, y, w, h, r, g, b, n;
      switch (s.charAt(0)) {
        case 'r':  // rectangle x y width height
          x = in.readInt();
          y = in.readInt();
          w = in.readInt();
          h = in.readInt();
          rectangle.setPosition(new PointGeometry(x, y));
          rectangle.setWidth(w);
          rectangle.setHeight(h);
          break;
        case 's':  // show
          isVisible = true;
          break;
```

```
                case 'h':  // hide
                  isVisible = false;
                  break;
                case 'n':  // new n
                  n = in.readInt();
                  for (int i = 0; i < n; i++) {
                    points.add(rand.nextPoint(rectangle));
                    colors.add(currentColor);
                  }
                  break;
                case 'c':   // color r g b
                  r = in.readInt();
                  g = in.readInt();
                  b = in.readInt();
                  currentColor = new Color(r, g, b);
                  break;
                case 'q':
                  System.exit(0);
                  break;
                default:
                  System.out.println("bad command");
                  break;
              }
              frame.repaint();
            } catch (NumberFormatException e) {
              System.out.println("please enter numbers");
            } catch (IOException e) {
              System.out.println("i/o exception... bye!");
              System.exit(1);
            }
          }
        }
      }
```

The `PlaySplatterPointsController` class defines five fields:

```
// fields of PlaySplatterPointsController class
protected ApplicationFrame frame;
protected Vector points;
protected Vector colors;
protected RectangleGeometry rectangle;
protected boolean isVisible;
```

The `frame` field stores a reference to the frame being controlled. The controller needs this reference so that it can refresh the frame as needed. The `points` vector stores the random points that have been generated so far, and the `colors` vector stores their colors (specifically, `colors[i]` stores the color of `points[i]`). The `rectangle` field holds the current rectangle. And the `isVisible` field indicates whether the current rectangle is currently visible on the screen.

Class `PlaySplatterPointsController` defines the methods `points`, `colors`, `rectangle`, and `isVisible` to provide access to its graphics content (I will refer to these as **content selector methods**). The `paintComponent` method calls these content selector methods to find out what to paint. These four selector methods jointly define the controller's interface that the `PlaySplatterPoints` class uses for display.

Class `PlaySplatterPointsController's` run method defines the controller's principal behavior. The `run` method is invoked when the controller is started, and it runs in its own thread of control. The `run` method iteratively reads and processes the user's commands. At the end of each iteration, it sends a *repaint* message to the frame to ensure that the display is up-to-date.

One way to better understand a system design is to develop scenarios. A **scenario** models the sequence of messages that pass between external agents (such as the user) and key elements of a system in a typical interaction. With regard to our point-splattering program, one scenario occurs when the user issues the *new* command to create *n* new random points. Another scenario occurs when the user issues the *rectangle* command to change the current rectangle.

UML provides two kinds of interaction diagrams for depicting scenarios: **sequence diagrams** and **collaboration diagrams.** Both kinds of diagrams depict communications between objects, but they differ in their focus. Sequence diagrams emphasize the order in which messages are sent between objects, whereas collaboration diagrams emphasize the links between objects. We will use sequence diagrams in this book (see Appendix C for more information about sequence diagrams).

A sequence diagram consists of a series of columns, one for each object that participates in the scenario. From each object box there descends a vertical line, the object's lifeline. A message is shown by a horizontal arrow from the sending object's lifeline to the receiving object's lifeline. Time passes as you move from the top of the diagram to the bottom, so the messages are sequenced in time from top to bottom. It's best to consider an example. Figure 4.6 depicts the scenario when the user creates *n* new random points by issuing the command *new n*, where *n* is a positive integer. In this scenario, the key agents are the user, the controller object (which is an instance of `PaintSplatterPointsController`), the panel object (an instance of `PaintSplatterPoints`), and the frame object (an instance of `ApplicationFrame`). The user is an **external agent,** an element belonging to the environment with which the system interacts, whereas the other three objects belong to the system proper.

Two aspects of Figure 4.6 are noteworthy. First, to show an object sending a message to itself, you draw an arrow from the object's lifeline back to itself. Second, the diagram models the scenario at a certain level of abstraction,

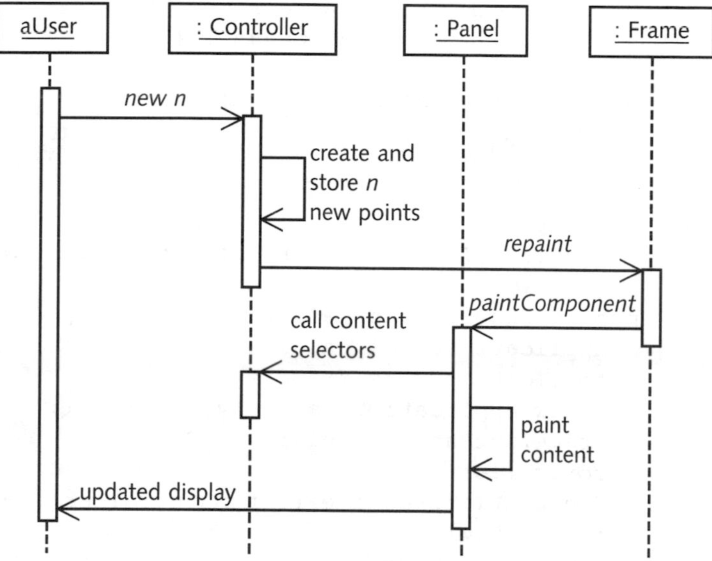

FIGURE 4.6 Sequence diagram for creating n new random points.

implying that interactions that are too detailed are not depicted. In the process of creating and storing new random points, the controller object repeatedly sends the *add* message to the vectors `points` and `colors` that store the points and colors. Yet this interaction is too low-level to be shown; in fact, the vectors `points` and `colors` do not even appear in this sequence diagram. Similarly, there are myriad interactions that result when the frame receives a *repaint* message, leading to the frame's `paintComponent` message to its panel. But these interactions are not specific to this scenario—they are generic display processes involving objects not shown here—and they too are omitted from this sequence diagram.

4.5.2 An Interactive Graphics Program Template

Let's extract from our `PlaySplatterPoints` program a template that you can base your interactive programs on. The template comprises the two classes: `MyInteractiveProgram` and `MyInteractiveProgramController`. In your program, replace all occurrences of these two names with the name of your program and the name of your controller, respectively. The `MyInteractiveProgram` class constructs the frame and panel, and constructs the controller and starts it. It is also responsible for painting the panel. The class can also define the static `parseArgs` method if your program takes program arguments, as occurs in the `MyGraphicsProgram` template. Here is the form of the first class:

```
public class MyInteractiveProgram
      extends ApplicationPanel {

  public MyInteractiveProgram() {
    ...
  }

  protected
    static MyInteractiveProgramController controller;

  public static void main(String[] args) {
    ApplicationPanel panel = new MyInteractiveProgram();
    ApplicationFrame frame =
      new ApplicationFrame("My Program");
    frame.setPanel(panel);
    controller =
      new MyInteractiveProgramController(frame);
    frame.show();
    controller.start();
  }

    // paints the contents of this panel
  public void paintComponent(Graphics g) {
    super.paintComponent(g);
    Graphics2D g2 = (Graphics2D)g;
    g2.setRenderingHint(RenderingHints.KEY_ANTIALIASING,
                        RenderingHints.VALUE_ANTIALIAS_ON);
    ...
  }
}
```

The second class, which defines the controller, maintains the graphical content in its storage structure. This class provides content selector methods that the `paintComponent` method uses to query the graphical content for display. This class also implements the `run` method, which gets called when the controller is started in its own thread. Here is the form of the class:

```
class MyInteractiveProgramController extends Thread {

  // storage structure
  protected ApplicationFrame frame;
    // other fields specific to this application
  ...

  // constructor
  protected
    MyInteractiveProgramController(ApplicationFrame f) {
    this.frame = f;
```

```
      ...
   }

   // content selector methods required by
   //   the paintComponent method
   ...

   public void run() {
      ...
   }
}
```

Exercises

4.30 In our `PlaySplatterPoints` program, draw the sequence diagram for the scenario in which the user issues the command *new n* where *n* is *not* a well-formed integer.

4.31 Add the following two commands to the `PlaySplatterPoints` application:

- clear—deletes all random points generated so far,
- recolor—assigns the current color to every random point that lies inside the current rectangle; random points that lie outside the current rectangle retain their old color.

4.32 Following the *MyInteractiveProgram* template, develop a program (named `PlayDrawLines`) for painting line segments into the frame's content area. Whenever the user issues a *line* command with the coordinates of the new line, the new line is drawn using the current color (which initially is white). Here are the commands supported by this program:

- line *x0 y0 x1 y1*—draws a new line from (*x0*,*y0*) to (*x1*,*y1*) in the current color,
- color *red green blue*—updates the current color to the specified integer color components, where $0 \leq$ *red, green, blue* ≤ 255, and
- quit—quits this application.

4.33 Enhance your `PlayDrawLines` program of the previous exercise so that it maintains a *stroke-width* property, which initially is 1. Whenever the user issues a line command, the current value of the *stroke-width* property determines the line's width:

- stroke *n*—updates the current stroke-width to the integer value *n*.

4.34 In the *MyInteractiveProgram* template, the controller class provides content selector methods that the panel class `MyInteractiveProgram` requires for rendering. These content selector methods are necessary because the controller maintains the graphics content. Another approach is to make the controller class an *inner class*, defined inside the panel class. The graphics content is then maintained in fields belonging to the panel class to which the controller class—as an inner class—has direct access. This eliminates the need for content selector methods. Revise the implementation of the `PlaySplatterPoints` class based on this approach. Subsequently, whenever the *MyInteractiveProgram* template is called for, you may prefer instead to define the controller to be an inner class in the manner described here.

Summary

One of the key benefits of object-oriented programming is that it supports reuse of software elements. Two of the principal mechanisms for reuse are composition and inheritance. Composition is a kind of association between classes which models the whole-part relationship in which an object of one class (the composite whole) owns instances of the other class (its components). Each component belongs only to its composite, and the component's lifetime is controlled by its composite. Complex objects constructed by composition take the form of hierarchies: A composite is composed of simpler objects that are themselves composites composed of still simpler objects, and so forth, until primitive (noncomposite) objects are reached. Aggregation is another kind of association between classes that partake in the whole-part relationship. Aggregation is often used to model situations in which a part can be shared by more than one whole, although the UML does not fully specify the semantics of aggregation.

The number of components belonging to a composite is sometimes quite large and may vary in number over time or across composites of the same type. In such cases, the components are often maintained in a collection object that the composite owns. Collections provide such services as finding elements, inserting new elements, and deleting existing elements. Examples of collection classes include arrays, vectors, and classes that implement the `java.util.Collection` interface. Composites use the services of collection objects to manage their components, and may include some of these services as part of their own public interfaces.

An object possesses a form of memory known as state, represented by the values stored in its fields. An object's state affects its behavior, and may change over time in the case of mutable objects. For an object to be in a self-consistent state, it must satisfy a set of representation invariants. These are conditions that the object must satisfy when it is constructed, and between calls to its public methods.

CHAPTER

5

Inheritance

The object model provides two primary mechanisms for defining new classes in terms of existing ones: composition and inheritance. We studied composition in Chapter 4, and in this chapter we'll look into inheritance. Using inheritance, a new class acquires the behaviors of an existing class. The new class then *modifies* acquired behaviors and *defines* new behaviors—it may modify some of the behaviors it acquires, and it may define new behaviors that are not present in the existing class, or that are specified but not implemented by the existing class. In this manner, the new class is made to represent an abstraction that is similar to, but not identical to, the abstraction represented by the existing class.

Section 5.1 introduces the uses of inheritance, sometimes referred to as **forms of inheritance.** Sections 5.2 through 5.4 cover these forms of inheritance. Section 5.5 discusses polymorphism, and Section 5.6 puts polymorphism to use in several new classes designed to bundle a geometry with an appearance.

5.1 The Uses of Inheritance

To use inheritance, we define a new class as an **extension** of an existing class. The new class is called a **subclass,** or **child class,** of the existing class. The existing class is called the **superclass,** or **parent class,** of the new class. A subclass may in turn serve as a superclass to any number of other classes. What results is an **inheritance hierarchy.** Figure 5.1 presents a class diagram for such a hierarchy. In this figure, `Boat` is a child class of the `Watercraft` class; in turn, `Boat` is the parent class of the `Motorboat`, `Paddleboat`, and `Sailboat` classes. The `Watercraft` class lies at the root of this inheritance hierarchy.

A class `B` is a **descendant** of some class `A` if either (i) `B` is a subclass of `A` or (ii) `B` is a descendant of some subclass of `A`. Intuitively, the descendants of a class `A` are those classes that belong to the inheritance hierarchy rooted at class `A`. Class `A` is called an **ancestor** of class `B` if `B` is a descendant of `A`. Every class appearing in the diagram of Figure 5.1 is a descendant of the `Watercraft` class, except for `Watercraft` itself. The ancestors of the `Kayak` class are the `Paddleboat`, `Boat`, and `Watercraft` classes. The ancestors of a class form a “chain” of classes that connects the class to the root class.

The root class of an inheritance hierarchy serves as a **supertype** for itself and all its descendants. The root class’ descendants, and the root class itself, are **subtypes** of the root class. All of the classes shown in Figure 5.1 are subtypes of the `Watercraft` class, whereas the subtypes of the `Paddleboat` class include only `Canoe`, `Kayak`, and the `Paddleboat` class itself. A supertype specifies an interface that each of its subtypes provides. Thus each subtype of `Watercraft` provides, at the very least, the behaviors specified by the `Watercraft` class. Families of types are also created using Java’s interface mechanism, which we’ll cover in Section 5.4.

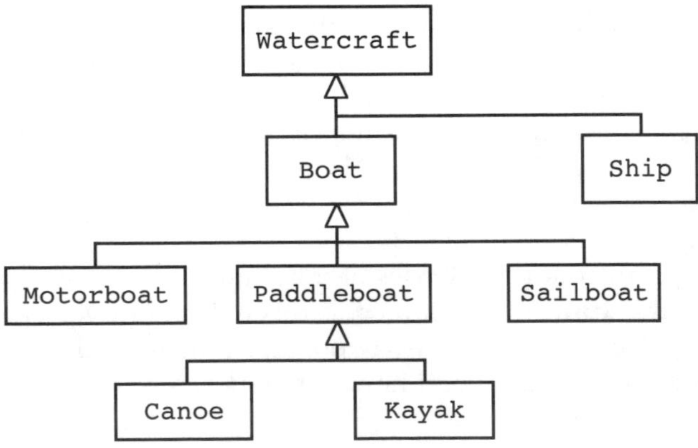

FIGURE 5.1 An inheritance hierarchy.

Figure 5.1 suggests—and it is indeed the case—that a class can have any number of subclasses. Moreover, every class has exactly one superclass, except for the `java.lang.Object` class, which has no superclass. This `Object` class lies at the root of a single global inheritance hierarchy to which all classes belong. However, because a class diagram presents only those classes relevant to the part of the system under consideration, the `Object` class, like other classes not relevant to the particular subsystem, is usually not depicted.

You are probably already familiar with the syntax for defining a new class through inheritance. Where `A` is a class, a new subclass `B` is defined by:

```
class B extends A {
  // fields and methods of B
  ...
}
```

If the `extends` clause is omitted, the new class becomes a subclass of the `Object` class. Here, class `C` extends the `Object` class:

```
class C {
  // fields and methods of C
  ...
}
```

Inheritance is a mechanism for reuse: A child class reuses its parent class. What gets reused are the fields and behaviors of the parent class; specifically, each child class acquires the nonprivate fields and methods defined in its parent class. In keeping with this analogy of familial relationships, the child class is said to *inherit* these elements from its parent class.

If a child class were to provide no definitions of its own, its structure and behavior would be no different from that of its parent class and little would be gained by its definition. Rather, inheritance is used to define a new class that extends, modifies, and defines the structure and behavior of the parent class. By defining new methods, overriding inherited methods, and implementing methods only specified but not implemented by the parent class, the new child class defines a new type that is similar to its parent class, but somewhat different. Consider a brief example, in which the `Waiter` class extends the `Employee` class. This is a natural use of inheritance because, in a restaurant setting, a waiter is a kind of employee:

```
public class Employee {
  public void greeting(String name) {
    System.out.println("Welcome to Eat and Run, "+name+".");
  }
  public void farewell(String name) {
    System.out.println("Please come back soon, "+name+"!");
  }
}
```

```
class Waiter extends Employee {
  public void greeting(String name) {
    System.out.println("Can I take your order, "+name+"?");
  }
  public void recommendation() {
    System.out.println("I'd stick to the pizza.");
  }
}
```

The `Employee` class defines two methods, `greeting` and `farewell`, which are inherited by its subclass `Waiter`. By defining a new method, `recommendation`, the `Waiter` class *adds a new behavior* to the two it inherits. (A waiter, unlike a generic employee, is in a position to recommend foods.) In addition, the `Waiter` class *overrides* the `greeting` method by providing an implementation of its own. This is a case of method overriding because `Waiter`'s version of the `greeting` method has the same signature as the `greeting` method of its superclass:

```
public void greeting(String name)
```

The `Waiter` class inherits the `farewell` method and leaves it unchanged; both employees in general and waiters in particular bid customers farewell in the same way. Because the `farewell` method does not appear in the `Waiter` class definition, `Waiter` objects inherit and leave unchanged the `farewell` method defined by the `Employee` superclass. Here is a short program that exercises these classes:

```
class TryEmployeeAndWaiter {
  public static void main(String[] args) {
    String name = "Elisa";
    if (args.length > 0)
      name = args[0];
    Employee e = new Employee();
    Waiter w = new Waiter();
    e.greeting(name);      // Welcome to Eat and Run, Elisa.
    w.greeting(name);      // Can I take your order, Elisa?
    w.recommendation();    // I'd stick to the pizza.
    w.farewell(name);      // Please come back soon, Elisa!
    e.farewell(name);      // Please come back soon, Elisa!
  }
}
```

Inheritance is generally used to define a class that represents a special type of its superclass. A subclass and its superclass partake in the *is-a* relationship: every instance of the subclass is an instance of the superclass. This holds true, for example, of the classes in Figure 5.1. The more specialized subclass provides all the behaviors of its superclass and may also provide additional behaviors of its own. Regarding the `Waiter` and `Employee` classes, every waiter is a kind of employee, and every waiter is capable of the same behaviors as a generic employee; in addition, unlike employees in general, waiters can make recommendations.

Unfortunately, using inheritance properly is not as simple as discovering whether two concepts are related by the is-a relationship. When two concepts share in the is-a relationship, it is not necessary, and sometimes not desirable or possible, for their corresponding classes to be related by inheritance. For example, a concept may specialize more than one concept, yet its class is permitted to extend no more than one other class (a teaching assistant is both a kind of university employee and a kind of student, yet a `TeachingAssistant` class can have only one parent class). Moreover, the is-a relationship is sometimes best captured by implementing an interface that represents a more general concept, rather than inheriting from a parent class. In light of this complexity, it is best to approach inheritance by considering the reasons for using it.

In Chapter 3, we examined how data abstraction and encapsulation are used to create a separation between *interface* and *implementation*. A data type is known by its public interface, whereas its implementation remains hidden as irrelevant to the needs of its clients. It's worthwhile to consider inheritance in light of this distinction between interface and implementation. Does a subclass extend its superclass in order to inherit the superclass' interface, or its implementation, or both? The answer depends on why inheritance is used. There are three main reasons for using inheritance, which are sometimes referred to as **forms of inheritance:**

- **Inheritance for extension:** A subclass extends an existing class in order to define new behaviors to supplement those it inherits. The subclass defines new methods and/or fields, but without overriding the methods it inherits. The new behaviors introduced by the subclass are neither present in nor applicable to its superclass. Here, the superclass' interface and implementation are both inherited.
- **Inheritance for specialization:** A subclass extends an existing class in order to modify some of the existing class' behavior while leaving unchanged the rest of the behavior it inherits. Here, the subclass inherits the superclass' interface and part of its implementation, while overriding the rest of the implementation it inherits.
- **Inheritance for specification:** Here, it is assumed that some methods of the superclass are abstract, meaning that they are declared, but not implemented, by the superclass. The abstract methods represent a specification of behavior. In the ideal form of inheritance for specification, the superclass is either an interface or an abstract class all of whose methods are abstract, so the subclass inherits an interface but no implementation. In the hybrid form of inheritance for specification, the

superclass is an abstract class that implements some but not all of the methods it declares, so the subclass inherits a full interface and a partial implementation. In both cases, by implementing the abstract methods it inherits, a subclass provides the behaviors promised by its superclass' specifications.

In practice, a subclass often extends its superclass for two or all three of the preceding reasons. In the earlier example in which the `Waiter` class extends the `Employee` class, the first two forms of inheritance apply. The `Waiter` class both adds a new behavior (the `recommendation` method) and overrides an inherited behavior (the `greeting` method).

To understand inheritance, we will approach each of these three forms separately. This is the goal of the three sections to follow.

5.2 Inheritance for Extension

When using inheritance for extension, a subclass defines new fields and methods that supplement those it inherits. In this section, we'll use this form of inheritance to develop a class for representing points that can be scaled and rotated. Transformable points will exhibit the full range of behaviors offered by its parent class, `PointGeometry`, without modifying these behaviors. In addition, they'll provide several new methods for transforming points. We'll also develop a class for representing lines that are unbounded in both directions, so-called infinite lines. But first we'll consider an example that illustrates inheritance for extension in a simpler setting.

5.2.1 N-Step Counters

An **n-step counter** is a counter whose value is incremented and decremented by a fixed integer, called its **step.** An `NStepCounter` object is initialized with its step when it is constructed. Its `inc` method increments the counter by its step, its `dec` method decrements the counter by its step, its `step` method reports its step, and its `value` method reports its current value. Here is the class definition:

```
public class NStepCounter {

  protected int step, value;

  public NStepCounter(int step) {
    // EFFECTS: Initializes this counter to
    //   value zero and given step.
    this.step = step;
    this.value = 0;
  }
```

```
  public NStepCounter() {
    // EFFECTS: Initializes this counter's value
    //   to zero and step to 1.
    this(1);
  }

  public void inc() {
    // MODIFIES: this
    // EFFECTS: Increments value by step.
    value += step;
  }

  public void dec() {
    // MODIFIES: this
    // EFFECTS: Decrements value by step.
    value -= step;
  }

  public int step() {
    // EFFECTS: Returns this counter's step.
    return step;
  }

  public int value() {
    // EFFECTS: Returns this counter's value.
    return value;
  }
}
```

We can use inheritance for extension to define a new `ClearableCounter` class that offers the same services as `NStepCounter`, but which also provides a `clear` method that resets the counter's value to zero. Here is the class definition:

```
public class ClearableCounter extends NStepCounter {

  public ClearableCounter(int step) {
    // EFFECTS: Initializes this counter
    //   to value zero and given step.
    super(step);
  }

  public ClearableCounter() {
    // EFFECTS: Initializes this counter's value
    //   to zero and step to 1.
    this(1);
  }
```

```
public void clear() {
    // MODIFIES: this
    // EFFECTS: Resets this counter's value to zero.
    value = 0;
  }
}
```

The `ClearableCounter` class adds a new method (`clear`) but redefines none of the methods it inherits. Note that the class also inherits its superclass' `value` field, to which it refers in the implementation of its `clear` method.

For both types of counter, the `value` method returns the running total resulting from calls to methods `inc` and `dec` since the last time the counter was cleared. The two classes differ in that `NStepCounters` are cleared only once, upon their construction, whereas `ClearableCounters` are cleared both when constructed and whenever the `clear` method is called.

Exercises

5.1 *Step* is not a property of the `ClearableCounter` class because this class does not provide accessor methods for getting and setting a counter's step. Using inheritance, define the class `VariableNStepCounter` for which *step* is a property. Your class should extend the `ClearableCounter` class and supply the following methods:

```
public void setStep(int newStep)
   // MODIFIES: this
   // EFFECTS: Changes this counter's step to newStep.

public int getStep()
   // EFFECTS: Returns this counter's step.
```

5.2 Write an application that tests the `NStepCounter` class. Your application is called with a command line of this form:

```
> java TryNStepCounter step n1 n2 ...
```

The program creates a new n-step counter `count` whose step is specified by the first program argument. It then processes the remaining integer program arguments as follows: It increments `count` n_1 many times and prints `count`'s state; then decrements `count` n_2 many times and prints `count`'s state, and so on. In general, it processes the program arguments left to right, incrementing the counter n_i times if i is odd, and decrementing the counter n_i times if i is even. Here is a sample transcript:

```
> java TryNStepCounter 2 6 3 9 1
step = 2
6 increments: value = 12
3 decrements: value = 6
9 increments: value = 24
1 decrements: value = 22
```

5.2.2 Transformable Points

Geometric transformations (or simply **transformations**) serve a number of purposes in computer graphics. Transformations are used in modeling, whereby graphical objects are constructed and combined to form scenes of arbitrary complexity. They are also used when generating views of 3-D scenes. Here, a virtual camera is situated in space and the view from the camera is obtained through a series of 3-D transformations, including projection from 3-D to 2-D. Transformations are also used in several aspects of animation, such as in specifying the motion of virtual cameras and the motion of scene elements such as geometries, lights, and textures. We'll consider how transformations can be used to modify the shape, position, and orientation of graphical objects. Although transformations make sense in any number of dimensions, we'll work with 2-D transformations and apply them to points in the plane.

The basic transformations are **translation, scaling,** and **rotation.** *Translation* repositions an object along a straight-line path from one position to another position without changing the object's orientation or shape. In Figure 5.2, the point $p=(4,0)$ is translated by $dx=1$ along the x axis and by $dy=4$ along the y axis. Its new position is $p'=(4,0)+(1,4)=(4+1,0+4)=(5,4)$.

Scaling changes both the size and position of an object. If the scale factors are the same in both x and y, we have **uniform scaling;** otherwise, we have **nonuniform** or **differential scaling**. Scaling occurs about some point in the plane, called the **anchor point.** The space around the anchor point is effectively stretched or shrunk by the scaling operation: The space is stretched if the positive scale factors are greater than one and shrunk if the positive scale factors are less than one. When the object being scaled is a point, the point's size (which is infinitesimal) is not affected, but its distance from the anchor point is. In Figure 5.2, the point $q=(3,1)$ is scaled about the origin by scale factor $sfx=2$ along the x axis and by $sfy=3$ along the y axis. Its new position is $q'=(3\cdot 2,\ 1\cdot 3)=(6,3)$.

Rotation repositions an object along a circular path whose center is some anchor point. The rotation operation takes a real number θ (theta) specifying the angle of rotation. In Java's default coordinate system, rotation assumes a clockwise sense if θ is positive and a counterclockwise sense if θ is negative. In Figure 5.2, the point r=(2,0) is rotated around the origin by θ=90° to the position r'=(0,2).

The `TransformablePointGeometry` class illustrates inheritance for extension in its pure sense—it defines new methods without overriding any inherited methods. The following skeleton specifies only those new methods that the class introduces:

```
public class TransformablePointGeometry
         extends PointGeometry {

  public TransformablePointGeometry (int x, int y)
    // EFFECTS: Constructs a new transformable point
    //   at (x,y).

  public TransformablePointGeometry (PointGeometry p)
         throws NullPointerException
    // EFFECTS: If p is null throws NullPointerException;
    //   else constructs a new transformable point
    //   at position p.

  public TransformablePointGeometry ()
    // EFFECTS: Constucts a new transformable point
    //   at (0,0).

  public void rotate(double theta)
    // MODIFIES: this
    // EFFECTS: Rotates this point by theta degrees
    //   around the origin.

  public void rotate(double theta, PointGeometry anchor)
         throws NullPointerException
    // MODIFIES: this
    // EFFECTS: If anchor is null throws
```

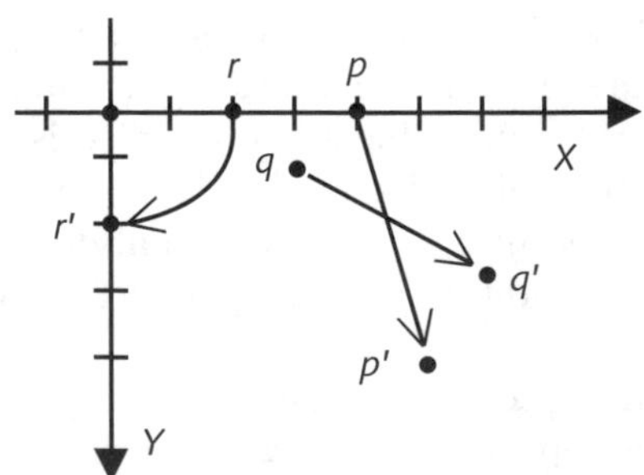

FIGURE 5.2 Transforming points.

```
    //   NullPointerException; else rotates this point
    //   by theta degrees around anchor.

  public void scale(double sfx, double sfy)
    // MODIFIES: this
    // EFFECTS: Scales this point by scale factor sfx
    //   along the x axis and by sfy along the y axis
    //   relative to the origin.

  public void scale(double sf)
    // MODIFIES: this
    // EFFECTS: Scales this point uniformly by scale
    //   factor sf, relative to the origin.

  public void scale(double sfx, double sfy,
                    PointGeometry anchor)
       throws NullPointerException
    // MODIFIES: this
    // EFFECTS: If anchor is null throws
    //   NullPointerException; else scales this point
    //   by scale factor sfx along the x axis and by
    //   sfy along the y axis, relative to anchor.

  public void scale(double sf, PointGeometry anchor)
       throws NullPointerException
    // MODIFIES: this
    // EFFECTS: If anchor is null throws
    //   NullPointerException; else scales this point
    //   by scale factor sf, relative to anchor.
}
```

The following program illustrates the class' behavior. Italicized comments indicate what gets printed as the program executes:

```
public class TryTransformablePointGeometry {
  public static void main(String[] args) {
    PointGeometry origin = new PointGeometry();
    TransformablePointGeometry p =
      new TransformablePointGeometry(3, 4);
    System.out.println("p: " + p);  // p: (3,4)
    System.out.println("distance: "+p.distance(origin));
                                    // distance: 5.0
    p.translate(1, -4);
    System.out.println("p: " + p);  // p: (4,0)
    p.rotate(90);
    System.out.println("p: " + p);  // p: (0,4)
    p.scale(2);
    System.out.println("p: " + p);  // p: (0,8)
```

```
    p.scale(0.25);
    System.out.println("p: " + p);   // p: (0,2)
    p.rotate(180, new PointGeometry(1, 2));
    System.out.println("p: " + p);   // p: (2,2)
  }
}
```

Observe that transformable points inherit the behavior of the parent class `PointGeometry`. For instance, the preceding test program calls a transformable point's `distance` method. Similarly, the `toString` method, called implicitly whenever `p` is converted to a string, is also inherited from the parent class. Having described how transformable points behave, we are in a position to define the class:

```
public class TransformablePointGeometry
      extends PointGeometry {

  public TransformablePointGeometry(int x, int y) {
    super(x, y);
  }

  public TransformablePointGeometry(PointGeometry p)
        throws NullPointerException {
    this(p.getX(), p.getY());
  }

  public TransformablePointGeometry() {
    this(0, 0);
  }

  public void rotate(double degrees) {
    double radians = Math.toRadians(degrees);
    double cos = Math.cos(radians);
    double sin = Math.sin(radians);
    int newX =
      (int)Math.round(cos * getX() - sin * getY());
    int newY =
      (int)Math.round(sin * getX() + cos * getY());
    setX(newX);
    setY(newY);
  }

  public void rotate(double degrees, PointGeometry anchor)
        throws NullPointerException {
    translate(-anchor.getX(), -anchor.getY());
    rotate(degrees);
    translate(anchor.getX(), anchor.getY());
  }
```

```
    public void scale(double sfx, double sfy) {
      setX((int)Math.round(sfx * getX()));
      setY((int)Math.round(sfy * getY()));
    }

    public void scale(double sf) {
      scale(sf, sf);
    }

    public void scale(double sfx, double sfy,
                      PointGeometry anchor)
          throws NullPointerException {
      translate(-anchor.getX(), -anchor.getY());
      scale(sfx, sfy);
      translate(anchor.getX(), anchor.getY());
    }

    public void scale(double sf, PointGeometry anchor)
          throws NullPointerException {
      scale(sf, sf, anchor);
    }
  }
```

Consider the one-argument version of `rotate`, which rotates this point around the origin. Trigonometry can be used to show that rotating the point $p=(x,y)$ by θ degrees around the origin yields the point $p'=(x',y')$, where

$$x' = x \cdot \cos\theta - y \cdot \sin\theta \qquad y' = x \cdot \sin\theta + y \cdot \cos\theta$$

The sense of rotation moves from the positive x axis toward the positive y axis, which is a clockwise sense of rotation under our coordinate system in which the x axis points to the right and the y axis points downward. The `Math.toRadians` method is needed to convert from degrees to radians because Java's trigonometry functions expect input in radians.

The two-argument version of `rotate` rotates this point around an input point `anchor`. The implementation reduces this to a rotation around the origin: first translate this point by `-anchor`, and then rotate around the origin, amd then translate back by `anchor`. (Here, I'm using `-anchor` as shorthand for the point `(-anchor.getX(), -anchor.getY())`). Scaling about an arbitrary anchor point is achieved similarly: first, translate by `-anchor`, and then scale about the origin, and then translate back by `anchor`.

Let's use the `TransformablePointGeometry` class in a graphics application, to be named `PaintCirclePoints`. This program places n points evenly along the circumference of an invisible circle of specified radius, centered in the frame. We'll refer to this invisible circle as the **guide circle.** The points are drawn as small circles of radius two, and each is filled with a random color.

Our application follows the *MyGraphicsProgram* template of Section 3.5, where the `PaintCirclePoints` class replaces the `MyGraphicsProgram` class of the template. This template requires us to define static fields and the static method `parseArgs` of the `PaintCirclePoints` class, as well as the `makeContent` and `paintComponent` methods.

The `PaintCirclePoints` class defines two static fields:

```
// static fields of PaintCirclePoints class
protected static int nbrPoints = 20, radius = 100;
```

`NbrPoints` many points are to be spaced evenly along the circumference of the guide circle of given `radius`. These fields are assigned the default values indicated earlier, but their values may be changed through program arguments. The generic command line for calling our program looks like this:

```
> java PaintCirclePoints [n [radius]]
```

If called with no program arguments, the default values are used; if called with one or two program arguments, the default argument values are replaced as evidenced by the following definition of the `parseArgs` method:

```
// static method of PaintCirclePoints class
public static void parseArgs(String[] args) {
  if (args.length > 2) {
    String s="USAGE: java PaintCirclePoints [n [radius]]";
    System.out.println(s);
    System.exit(0);
  }
  if (args.length > 0)
    nbrPoints = Integer.parseInt(args[0]);
  if (args.length > 1)
    radius = Integer.parseInt(args[1]);
}
```

Class `CirclePoint`'s only instance field stores an array of transformable points:

```
// field of PaintCirclePoints class
protected TransformablePointGeometry[] points;
```

The `makeContent` method assigns to the `points` field an array of transformable points located along the guide circle. Here is the method's implementation:

```
// method of PaintCirclePoints class
public void makeContent() {
  double deltaDegrees = 360.0 / nbrPoints;
  double curDegrees = 0.0;
  points = new TransformablePointGeometry[nbrPoints];
```

```
      // create point and position it at (radius, 0)
    TransformablePointGeometry eastPoint =
      new TransformablePointGeometry();
    eastPoint.translate(radius, 0);
      // fill array points with copies of eastPoint
      // positioned along the guide circle
    for (int i = 0; i < nbrPoints; i++) {
      TransformablePointGeometry p =
          new TransformablePointGeometry(eastPoint);
      p.rotate(curDegrees);
      points[i] = p;
      curDegrees += deltaDegrees;
    }
  }
```

The `makeContent` method works like this: It constructs a transformable point named `eastPoint`, and then translates this point to the position (*radius*,0), which is the "east" point of the guide circle. The method then iteratively locates `nbrPoints` many points along the guide circle's circumference. In each iteration, it constructs a new copy of `eastPoint`—this copy also initially occurs at position (*radius*,0)—and then rotates this copy through the angle `curDegrees` to its proper position along the guide circle and stores it in the array `points`.

The `paintComponent` method paints the points stored in the array `points` with random colors. The method is defined thus:

```
  // method of PaintCirclePoints class
  public void paintComponent(Graphics g) {
    super.paintComponent(g);
    Graphics2D g2 = (Graphics2D)g;
      // center the rendering context g2 in the frame
    Dimension d = getFrame().getContentSize();
    g2.translate((int)(d.width/2), (int)(d.height/2));
      // paint each point with a random color
    RandomColor rndClr = new RandomColor();
    for (int i = 0; i < points.length; i++) {
      g2.setColor(rndClr.nextColor());
      PointGeometry p = points[i];
      g2.fill(p.shape());
    }
  }
```

In the `paintComponent` method, the `Graphics2D` object `g2` is sent the *translate* message in order to center the guide circle, and hence the resulting circle of points, within the frame. Every rendering context (such as `g2`) defines a coordinate system that, by default, coincides with the drawing surface's coordinate system (the origin occurs at the upper-left corner, and the

x axis increases to the right and the y axis to the left). Yet we would like the guide circle to be centered at the frame's center, rather than at its upper-left corner. To achieve this, we translate the rendering context g2 using the instructions

```
Dimension d = getFrame().getContentSize();
g2.translate((int)(d.width/2), (int)(d.height/2));
```

Section 3.4 provides more details. To actually paint the points, method paintComponent traverses the array points. For each point p, it sets the rendering context g2 to a new random color, and then sends g2 a *fill* message with point p's shape. Note that a point's color may change each time the frame is repainted. Later in this chapter, we'll develop classes we can use to associate appearances (such as fill color) with geometries.

Exercises

5.3 The implementation of the TransformablePointGeometry class never refers to the fields x and y inherited from its superclass PointGeometry. Instead, the selector methods x and y are used to get the x and y coordinates, and the mutator methods setX and setY are used to change the coordinates. In other words, whereas the subclass uses the *methods* it inherits in its own implementation, it avoids relying on the *fields* it inherits. What are the advantages of this practice? What are the disadvantages?

5.4 Here is an alternate version of the PaintCirclePoints class' makeContent method:

```
// method of PaintCirclePoints class: version 2(faulty)
public void makeContent() {
  double deltaDegrees = 360.0 / nbrPoints;
  points = new TransformablePointGeometry[nbrPoints];
  TransformablePointGeometry point =
      new TransformablePointGeometry();
  point.translate(radius, 0);
  for (int i = 0; i < nbrPoints; i++) {
    points[i] = point;
    point = new TransformablePointGeometry(point);
    point.rotate(deltaDegrees);
  }
}
```

Explain the idea behind version 2 of the makeContent method. Why does this method often fail to produce a circle of points? Try it out.

5.5 Write an application `PaintPointGrid` that draws randomly colored points at the intersection points of an invisible grid. Your application takes two integer program arguments indicating the distance between successive vertical gridlines (*m*) and the distance between successive horizontal gridlines (*n*):

```
> java PaintGridPoints m n
```

Suppose that the frame's content area has width *w* and height *h*:

```
// method makeContent of PaintPointGrid class
// (code fragment)
Dimension d = getFrame().getContentSize();
int w = d.width;
int h = d.height;
```

Then a point should be placed at each position (x,y) where $x=i \cdot m$ and $y=j \cdot n$, where $0 \leq i < [w/m]$ and $0 \leq j < [h/n]$.

ESSENTIAL 5.6 Define the class `ComparableAttribute` as a subclass of the `Attribute` class (Exercise 3.4). The `ComparableAttribute` class defines a new method used to compare two attributes under the alphabetic (lexicographic) ordering of their respective names:

```
public int compareTo(Object obj)
     throws NullPointerException, ClassCastException
  // EFFECTS: If obj is null throws
  //    NullPointerException; else if obj is not
  //    comparable throws ClassCastException;
  //    else returns a negative integer, zero, or
  //    positive integer if this attribute is less
  //    than, equal to, or greater than obj,
  //    under lexicographic ordering on name.
```

Thus `ComparableAttributes` can be ordered linearly in the same way as integers under `<`, or strings under the `String` class' `compareTo` method. The following code fragment illustrates the behavior of the compareTo method:

```
ComparableAttribute apple, grape;
apple = new ComparableAttribute("apple", "red");
grape = new ComparableAttribute("grape", "green");
apple.compareTo(grape);     // returns -1
grape.compareTo(apple);     // returns 1
apple.compareTo(apple);     // returns 0
```

5.2.3 Lines

In this section, we develop a class for representing lines in the plane. Lines are unbounded in the sense that they extend to infinity in both directions. A line is constructed from any pair of distinct points p_0 and p_1 through which the line passes. The two points determine both the line and its direction—the line is directed from p_0 toward p_1. By attributing direction to lines, it is possible to classify points in the plane with respect to a line: Any point lies to the left of the line, to the right of the line, or on the line. In Figure 5.3, the line's direction is shown by the unfilled arrowhead.

Our `LineGeometry` class extends the `LineSegmentGeometry` class used to represent line segments (see Exercise 3.3). From the standpoint of behavior, lines introduce a new behavior that supplements those inherited from line segments—we can classify points with respect to a line—making this an example of inheritance for extension. The `LineGeometry` class provides a `classifyPoint` operation that takes a point as input and reports the point's classification with respect to the line. Here is a skeleton for this class. As usual, the skeleton specifies only those methods that the class introduces or overrides:

```
public class LineGeometry extends LineSegmentGeometry {

  public LineGeometry(int x0, int y0, int x1, int y1)
         throws IllegalArgumentException
    // EFFECTS: If (x0,y0) is equal to (x1,y1) throws
    //    IllegalArgumentException; else constructs the
    //    line (x0,y0)<-->(x1,y1).

  public LineGeometry(PointGeometry p0, PointGeometry p1)
    throws NullPointerException, IllegalArgumentException
    // EFFECTS: If p0 or p1 are null throws
    //    NullPointerException; else if p0 equals p1
    //    throws IllegalArgumentException;
    //    else constructs the line p0<-->p1.


  // values returned by point classification methods
  public static final int LEFT = 0, ON = 1, RIGHT = 2;
```

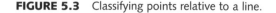

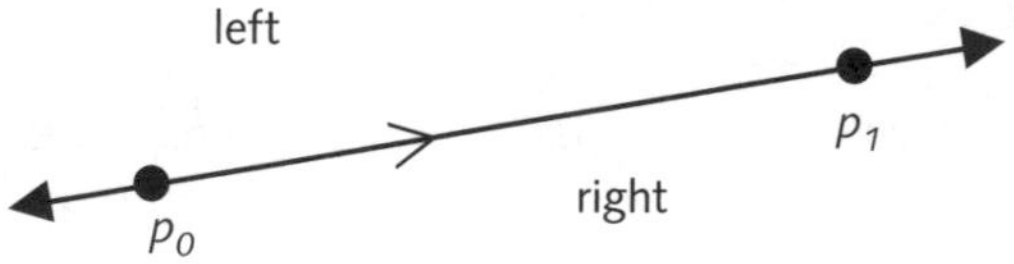

FIGURE 5.3 Classifying points relative to a line.

```
  public int classifyPoint(int x, int y)
    // EFFECTS: Returns LEFT, ON, or RIGHT if (x,y) lies
    //   to the left of, on, or to the right of this line

  public int classifyPoint(PointGeometry p)
        throws NullPointerException
    // EFFECTS: If p is null throws NullPointerException;
    //   else returns LEFT, ON, or RIGHT if (x,y) lies to
    //   the left of, on, or to the right of this line.

  public String toString()
    // EFFECTS: Returns "p0<-->p1" where p0 and p1
    //   determine this line.
}
```

Let us implement the LineGeometry class. There is no need to extend the storage structure it inherits—internally, we will represent a line by a line segment. The constructors are defined thus:

```
public LineGeometry(int x0, int y0, int x1, int y1)
      throws IllegalArgumentException {
  super(x0, y0, x1, y1);
  if (getP0().equals(getP1()))
    throw new IllegalArgumentException();
}

public LineGeometry(PointGeometry p0, PointGeometry p1)
 throws NullPointerException, IllegalArgumentException {
  this(p0.getX(), p0.getY(), p1.getX(), p1.getY());
}
```

The two-argument classifyPoint method is called with the *x* and *y* coordinates of a point *p,* and returns an integer that classifies point *p* with respect to the current line. Here is the implementation:

```
// static field of LineGeometry class
public static final int LEFT = 0, ON = 1, RIGHT = 2;

// method of LineGeometry class
public int classifyPoint(int x, int y) {
  int ax = getP1().getX() - getP0().getX(); // va=(ax,ay)
  int ay = getP1().getY() - getP0().getY();
  int bx = x - getP0().getX();              // vb=(bx,by)
  int by = y - getP0().getY();
  int res = ax * by - bx * ay;
  if (res < 0) return LEFT;
```

```
    else if (res > 0) return RIGHT;
    else return ON;

}
```

The implementation of `classifyPoint` uses linear algebra. The method builds two vectors $v_a=p_1-p_0$ and $v_b=p-p_0$ where $p=(x,y)$ is the input point. Then it computes and stores in the local variable `res` the determinant $|v_a v_b|$, which is equal to twice the signed area of the triangle with vertices p_0, p_1, and p. The sign of `res` indicates whether point p lies to the left of, to the right of, or on the current line.

The one-argument `classifyPoint` method is implemented in terms of the two-argument version:

```
// method of LineGeometry class
public int classifyPoint(PointGeometry p)
       throws NullPointerException {
  return classifyPoint(p.getX(), p.getY());
}
```

Our `LineGeometry` class overrides the `toString` method to ensure that line segments and infinite lines have different string descriptors:

```
// method of LineGeometry class
public String toString() {
  return getP0() + "<-->" + getP1();
}
```

Had we chosen not to override the `toString` method, the `LineGeometry` class would inherit solely for extension, specifically, to augment the behaviors of the `LineSegmentGeometry` class with its own new behaviors for classifying points.

Exercises

5.7 Write a graphics program that paints a line L and n random points. The color of each random point is determined by its classification with respect to the line. The program is invoked with five integer program arguments:

```
> java PaintClassifyPoints n x0 y0 x1 y1
```

The infinite line L is determined by the distinct points (x_0,y_0) and (x_1,y_1). Each of the n random points is painted red, green, or blue, depending on whether the point lies to the left of L, on L, or to the right of L, respectively.

5.8 Our representation for lines is *nonunique*: Any given line admits many different representations. For example, the positive x axis (directed toward increasing values of x) can be described by the pair of points p_0=(0,0) and p_1=(1,0), or by the pair of points p_0=(−12,0) and p_1=(6,0). In fact, any pair of points $p_0=(x_0,0)$ and $p_1=(x_1,0)$ where $x_0<x_1$ will do.

Let us say that two `LineGeometry` objects are equal if the lines they represent are collinear and have the same direction. Because our representation for lines is nonunique, equality testing for a pair of lines is nontrivial—it requires more than simply checking whether the lines' corresponding fields are equal.

Implement the method

```
// method of LineGeometry class
public boolean equals(Object a)
```

that returns `true` if and only if this line and the line `a` represent the same line with the same direction. Add your `equals` method to the `LineGeometry` class defined in this section.

Your `equals` method may proceed in three steps:

1. If `a` is not an instance of `LineGeometry`, return `false`.
2. Check whether the two lines are collinear. Choose two points p_0 and p_1 that lie on this line and classify them with respect to line `a`. If either p_0 or p_1 does not lie on the line `a`, `equals` returns `false`. Otherwise, we have established that the two lines are collinear.
3. Check whether the two lines (now known to be collinear) have the same direction. Generate a point q that does not lie on the line. If point q lies to the same side of both lines, `equals` returns `true`; otherwise it returns `false`.

Write a short program that tests your implementation of the `equals` procedure.

5.9 As things stand, the `LineGeometry` class inherits the `shape` method from its parent class. Thus, a line and a line segment whose *p0* and *p1* properties are equal will be rendered the same. We might prefer to depict a line by a straight line that extends beyond both p_0 and p_1 in both directions, clear across the screen. Implement the `shape` method in your `LineGeometry` class to do just this. To do so, your `shape` method defines points q_0 and q_1 that lie on the line, and then returns this shape:

```
new Line2D.Float(q0.getX(), q0.getY(),
                 q1.getX(), q1.getY());
```

Here point q_1 lies *well beyond* point p_1: The distance from p_0 to q_1 is (say) 100 times the distance from p_0 to p_1. Point q_1 might be obtained by a code fragment such as this:

```
public static final int LineScaleFactor = 100;

int dx = getP1().getX() - getP0().getX();
int dy = getP1().getY() - getP0().getY();
int x = getP0().getX() + LineScaleFactor * dx;
int y = getP0().getY() + LineScaleFactor * dy;
PointGeometry q1 = new PointGeometry(x, y);
```

Similarly, point q_0 lies well beyond point p_0 in the other direction. Try your `PaintClassifyPoints` program (Exercise 5.7) after you have implemented the `shape` method.

5.3 Inheritance for Specialization

When inheritance is used for specialization, a class extends its superclass in order to redefine some of the superclass' methods, while leaving unchanged the rest of the methods it inherits. The inherited methods that are redefined are said to be **overridden** by the subclass. By overriding certain methods, the subclass *specializes* the behavior of its superclass.

There are several reasons for a subclass to override methods, of which these are the most common:

- **To create a class, some of whose behaviors are more specialized than those of its parent class.** Here, the new class represents a concept that is a specialization of that of its parent class.
- **To create a class that is a variation of its parent class.** The subclass reuses the elements of its superclass to simplify its own implementation.
- **To create a class that is more efficient than its superclass.** The new subclass exhibits the same behaviors as its superclass but does so more efficiently, typically using less time or space.
- **To create a class that is more powerful than its superclass.** The new subclass is more powerful in the sense that it does more with less. Greater power is achieved in one or both of the following ways:

  (1) **Some of the subclass' methods override methods requiring stronger preconditions.** This means that the subclass accomplishes as much as its superclass but requires less of its clients, or

(2) **Some of the subclass' methods override methods promising weaker postconditions.** This means that the subclass accomplishes more than its superclass, but without placing additional requirements on its clients.

One common example of inheritance for specialization occurs when there is a generally correct behavior for a class of objects, but more specialized classes of objects override this behavior. A case in point is the `ApplicationPanel` class, which we use in applications that follow the *MyGraphicsProgram* template. This class' generally correct behavior for making graphical content is to do nothing; its `makeContent` method is implemented by a do-nothing body. When you define a child class of `ApplicationPanel`, your class overrides the `makeContent` method, thereby specializing the `ApplicationPanel` class. In like fashion, your class also overrides the `paintComponent` method so that it can paint the graphics. A subclass of `ApplicationPanel` that fails to override the `makeContent` and `paintComponent` methods produces a blank closeable frame; by overriding these two methods, your class acquires its distinct behavior (see Figure 5.4).

5.3.1 Polygons

One use for inheritance is to define a new class that represents an abstraction that is similar to, yet not identical to, an existing class. By inheriting from the existing class, the new class is implemented more easily than would be possible if it were implemented from scratch. The new class is a variation of its superclass. In this section, we'll define a class for representing polygons by extending the `PolylineGeometry` class (of Section 4.3.2) for polylines.

A **polygon** is a path in the plane composed of straight line segments, such that its first and last vertices are one and the same. Thus a polygon is similar to a polyline, except that a polygon forms a cycle whereas a polyline does not. (It may happen that a polyline's first and last vertices happen to coincide in the plane, but they are still considered two distinct vertices.) In a

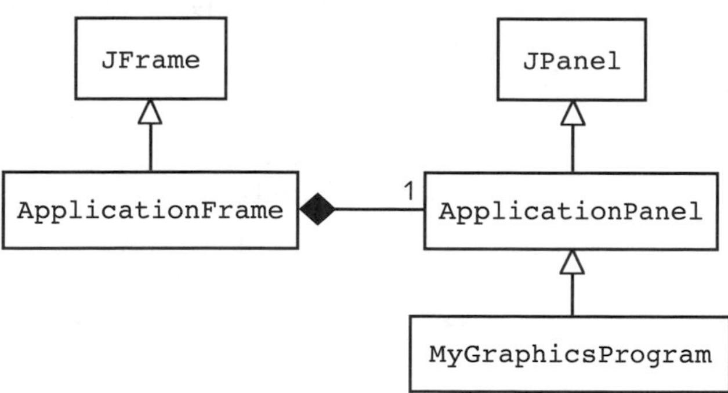

FIGURE 5.4 `MyGraphicsProgram` specializes `ApplicationPanel`.

polygon, every vertex is met by exactly two of the polygon's edges, so a polygon with n vertices has n edges. In the case of a one-vertex polygon, a single edge (called a **loop**) connects the vertex to itself. In the case of a two-vertex polygon, the two vertices are joined by *two* distinct edges. For brevity, we sometimes use the term *n-gon* to mean *n-vertex polygon*.

Figure 5.5 shows our indexing scheme. The n vertices of a polygon are indexed from 0 through $n-1$, and we label these vertices v_0 through v_{n-1}. The n edges are indexed from 0 through $n-1$, where the edge e_i joins the vertices v_i and v_{i+1} for $0 \leq i < n-1$, and the edge e_{n-1} joins the vertex v_{n-1} to the vertex v_0. Although a 1-gon contains a single edge of length zero, we may draw the edge as a loop that connects the vertex to itself. Figure 5.5 also shows a 2-gon whose two edges are drawn as distinct curves to distinguish them visually; conceptually, the two edges are straight line segments that coincide.

The drawing in Figure 5.5 shows that it is possible for a polygon to intersect itself. In contrast, a **simple polygon** is a polygon that does not self-intersect. A simple polygon with more than two distinct vertices separates the plane into two connected regions: the polygon's bounded interior and its unbounded exterior. In this book, we will not require our polygons to be simple.

Like rectangles and ellipses, polygons enclose area, known as the polygon's **interior.** Whenever we fill a polygon, or ask whether a given point lies inside a polygon, the operation in question refers to the polygon's interior. For simple polygons, the definition of *interior* is intuitive—it is the connected bounded area that the polygon encloses. However, in the case of self-intersecting polygons, the definition of *interior* is not so obvious. To clarify what *interior* means, we associate a **winding rule** with a polygon. A winding rule shows how to decide whether any point p is contained in a polygon's interior. Java provides support for two different winding rules: the even-odd winding rule and the nonzero winding rule.

Under the **even-odd winding rule,** we imagine drawing an infinite ray starting from point p. If this ray crosses the polygon an odd number of times, point p is inside the polygon; if not, point p is not inside the polygon. This winding rule is also called the **parity winding rule** to emphasize the concern with the parity (oddness or evenness) of the number of crossings. Remarkably, the parity depends only on point p and the polygon, but not on the direction of the ray.

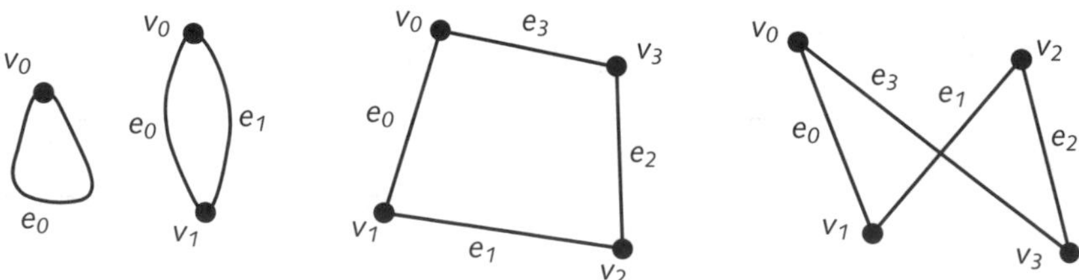

FIGURE 5.5 Four polygons.

To understand the **nonzero winding rule,** again imagine drawing a ray starting from point p. This time, we imagine starting at a vertex of the polygon and then tracing along the polygon's edges from vertex to vertex until returning to the starting vertex. While doing so, we count the number of times we cross the ray from left to right and the number of times we cross the ray from right to left. Point p lies inside the polygon if and only if these two numbers are not equal.

In the case of simple polygons, both winding rules coincide with the intuitive definition of *polygon interior*. However, for many nonsimple polygons, the even-odd and nonzero winding rules lead to different definitions of *polygon interior*. When we fill such a polygon, the resulting picture varies according to which winding rule is in force. Figure 5.6 shows the same nonsimple polygon filled according to the two different winding rules.

Besides defining different constructors, class `PolygonGeometry`'s interface differs from that of class `PolylineGeometry`'s in that the former provides `contains` methods for deciding whether a given point lies inside a polygon. (Point containment doesn't make sense for polylines because they don't enclose area.) In addition, the nonzero winding rule is assumed for all polygons (although Exercise 5.12 modifies the interface of `PolygonGeometry` so that clients can select the winding rule):

```
public class PolygonGeometry extends PolylineGeometry {

  public PolygonGeometry(PointGeometry[] vs)
    throws NullPointerException, ZeroArraySizeException
    // EFFECTS: If vs is null or vs[i] is null for some
    //   legal i throws NullPointerException; else if
    //   vs.length==0 throws ZeroArraySizeException;
    //   else constructs this polygon to have the
    //   vertex sequence given by vs.

  public PolygonGeometry(PolygonGeometry poly)
    throws NullPointerException
```

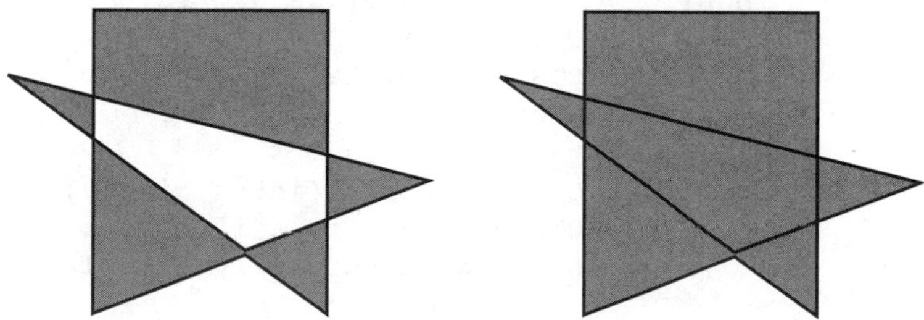

FIGURE 5.6 The same polygon filled using the even-odd winding rule (left) and the nonzero winding rule (right).

```
  // EFFECTS: If poly is null throws
  //   NullPointerException; else initializes this
  //   with the same vertex sequence as poly.

public PointGeometry getVertex(int i)
       throws IndexOutOfBoundsException
  // EFFECTS: If 0 <= i < nbrVertices() returns
  //   the position of the vertex at index i;
  //    else throws IndexOutOfBoundsException.

public void setVertex(int i, PointGeometry v)
  throws NullPointerException, IndexOutOfBoundsException
  // MODIFIES: this
  // EFFECTS: If v is null throws NullPointerException;
  //   else if 0 <= i < nbrVertices() moves the vertex
  //   at index i to position v in the plane;
  //   else throws IndexOutOfBoundsException.

public LineSegmentGeometry edge(int i)
       throws IndexOutOfBoundsException
  // EFFECTS: If 0 <= i < nbrEdges() returns the edge i;
  //   else throws IndexOutOfBoundsException.

public int nbrVertices()
  // EFFECTS: Returns the number of vertices
  //   in this polygon.

public int nbrEdges()
  // EFFECTS: Returns the number of edges
  //   in this polygon.

public java.awt.Shape shape()
  // EFFECTS: Returns the shape of this polygon.

public void translate(int dx, int dy)
  // MODIFIES: this
  // EFFECTS: Translates this polygon by dx along x
  //   and by dy along y.

public boolean contains(int x, int y)
  // EFFECTS: Returns true if the point (x,y) is
  //   contained in this polygon; else returns false.

public boolean contains(PointGeometry p)
       throws NullPointerException
  // EFFECTS: If p is null throws NullPointerException;
```

```
    //   else returns true if p is contained in this
    //   polygon; else returns false.

  public String toString()
    // EFFECTS: Returns "Polygon: v0,v1,...,vn-1"
    //   where each vi describes vertex i.
}
```

Our implementation of the `PolygonGeometry` class exploits the observation that we can convert a polyline into a polygon by inserting a new edge e_{n-1} that joins the polyline's last vertex v_{n-1} to its first vertex v_0. We will represent a polygon by the polyline that lacks this edge e_{n-1} but is otherwise identical. In this way, we represent polygons using the representation of polylines inherited from the parent class.

A polygon can be constructed from an array of one or more points locating the polygon's vertices. A polygon can also be constructed as a copy of a second polygon. Here are the constructors' definitions:

```
public PolygonGeometry(PointGeometry[] vs)
  throws NullPointerException, ZeroArraySizeException {
  super(vs);
}

public PolygonGeometry(PolygonGeometry poly)
       throws NullPointerException {
  super(poly);
}
```

We have chosen to represent a polygon by the polyline that lacks the edge e_{n-1} but is otherwise identical. This makes it necessary to override those methods that must account for this extra edge in the polygon. For one, it is necessary to override the `edge` method. (Recall that the `edge` method is called with an index and returns the edge so indexed.) When the `edge` method is called with the index $n-1$, it constructs the extra edge e_{n-1}; when called with any index strictly less than $n-1$, it calls the parent class' `edge` method to produce the edge being sought:

```
// method of PolygonGeometry class
public LineSegmentGeometry edge(int i)
       throws IndexOutOfBoundsException {
  if (i == nbrVertices() - 1)
    return new LineSegmentGeometry(getVertex(i),
                                   getVertex(0));
  else
    return super.edge(i);
}
```

The nbrEdges method must also be overridden to account for the polygon's extra edge e_{n-1}:

```
// method of PolygonGeometry class
public int nbrEdges() {
  return nbrVertices();
}
```

The string-descriptor for a polygon consists of the word *Polygon* followed by the sequence of the polygon's vertices ordered by index. PolygonGeometry's parent class defines the protected method verticesToString for converting the vertex-sequence to a string (in fact, PolylineGeometry uses this method in the implementation of its own toString method). Because protected methods are accessible to subclasses, we can also use this method in PolygonGeometry's version of the toString method:

```
// method of PolygonGeometry class
public String toString() {
  return "Polygon: " + verticesToString();
}
```

The implementation of the shape method is similar to that of class PolylineGeometry's shape method. In the case of polygons, we apply closePath to the general path to connect the last vertex to the first vertex with an edge:

```
// method of PolygonGeometry class
public Shape shape() {
  GeneralPath path = new GeneralPath();
  PointGeometry v = getVertex(0);
  path.moveTo(v.getX(), v.getY());
  for (int i = 1; i < nbrVertices(); i++) {
    v = getVertex(i);
    path.lineTo(v.getX(), v.getY());
  }
  path.closePath();
  return path;
}
```

In the cases of 1-gons and 2-gons, the shape method as just defined does not produce pictures like those of Figure 5.5. Rather, a 1-gon appears as a small dot positioned at the sole vertex, and a 2-gon appears as a line segment joining the two vertices. In Section 5.6.4, we'll develop a class that draws 1-gons as loops and 2-gons as distinct curves.

A point p=(x,y) is contained inside a polygon if it lies within the polygon's interior or along its boundary, where the nonzero winding rule determines the notion of polygon interior. In particular, this implies that a polygon contains its vertices because they lie along its boundary. We'll delegate the task of deciding point containment to the polygon's shape. To implement the `contains` methods, we'll use the `Shape.intersects` method. We'll center a small square on the input point `p` and report that point `p` is contained in this polygon if this square intersects the polygon's interior or boundary:

```
// methods of PolygonGeometry class
public boolean contains(int x, int y) {
  return shape().intersects(x-0.01, y-0.01, 0.02, 0.02);
}

public boolean contains(PointGeometry p) {
  return contains(p.getX(), p.getY());
}
```

It happens that the `Shape` interface specifies a `contains` method, but it does not meet our needs because `Shape`'s notion of point containment differs from ours. Specifically, `Shape.contains(p)` is `true` if and only if point `p` lies either in the shape's interior or along that portion of the boundary such that the shape's interior lies immediately to the right or below. For example, under this definition of containment, an axes-aligned square contains only those points that lie in its interior and along its top and left sides, but not along its bottom and right sides. Because our notion of containment differs from that of Java's `Shape` class, we use the `Shape.intersects` method instead of the `Shape.contains` method to test for point containment.

Exercises

5.10 A **1-step counter** is an n-step counter whose step is fixed at the value one. Define the class `OneStepCounter` by extending the `NStepCounter` class of Section 5.2.1.

5.11 Write a graphical application that paints a polygon that is filled in red and outlined in blue. The application's program arguments consist of an even number of integers, no fewer than four in number:

```
> java PaintPolygon x0 y0 x1 y1 ...
```

The x and y coordinates of vertex v_i appear in positions $2i$ and $2i+1$ of the program arguments.

5.12 Revise the definition of the `PolygonGeometry` class so that it defines a *winding rule* property whose value determines the winding rule in force. The default winding rule is the nonzero rule. Your revised `PolygonGeometry` class may define a field that stores the property's value:

```
// field of PolygonGeometry class:
//   winding rule property
protected int windingRule;
```

as well as a setter and getter method for the property. The `windingRule` field may assume either of the following two values:

```
// static fields of the PolygonGeometry class
static public int
  WIND_EVEN_ODD =
    java.awt.geom.GeneralPath.WIND_EVEN_ODD,
  WIND_NON_ZERO =
    java.awt.geom.GeneralPath.WIND_NON_ZERO;
```

To apply the winding rule, add the instruction

```
path.setWindingRule(windingRule);
```

to your `shape` method, just prior to returning the shape.

5.13 Write a graphical application like that of Exercise 5.11, but whose first program argument specifies the winding rule in force:

```
> java PaintWindPolygon winding-rule x0 y0 x1 y1 ...
```

where `winding-rule` is replaced by one of the strings *even-odd* or *nonzero*. This exercise depends on the previous exercise.

ESSENTIAL 5.14 Recall that our `Dictionary` class maintains its name–value pairs in arbitrary order (see Exercise 4.21). For this exercise, define a class `OrderedDictionary` that maintains its pairs ordered alphabetically by name: The names increase as you step through the ordered dictionary's indexes. Thus the postconditions of the `name` and `value` methods, for accessing the elements of a name-value pair by index, are strengthened:

```
// methods of OrderedDictionary
public String name(int i)
       throws IndexOutOfBoundsException
  // EFFECTS: If 0 <= i < size() returns the name
  //   of the pair at index i where the pairs are
  //   ordered lexicographically by name;
  //   else throws IndexOutOfBoundsException.

public String value(int i)
       throws IndexOutOfBoundsException
  // EFFECTS: If 0 <= i < size() returns the value
  //   of the pair at index i where the pairs are
```

```
//   ordered lexicographically by name;
//   else throws IndexOutOfBoundsException.
```

[Hint: Your class should extend the Dictionary class and override method(s) as needed to ensure that name-value pairs are maintained in order. You may want to represent pairs by ComparableAttribute objects, stored in the collection maintained by your class (see Exercise 5.6). When you compare two comparable attributes, be sure to cast them to the ComparableAttribute type.

To test your class, replace the Dictionary object by an OrderedDictionary object in the TryDictionary program you wrote in Exercise 4.22. Whenever the user enters the *print* command, the dictionary's pairs should be printed in order.

In this exercise, you use inheritance to define a new class that is more powerful than its superclass: Ordered dictionaries maintain name-value pairs in alphabetical order, whereas dictionaries maintain name-value pairs in arbitrary order.]

5.3.2 Tally Counters

A child class often inherits for both extension and specialization at once. We saw this in the simple example involving the Waiter and Employee classes at the start of Section 5.1. We also saw this in your version of the PolygonGeometry class that accommodates the winding rule (Exercise 5.12). Here we'll look at a short example involving counters.

A **tally counter** is an n-step counter that keeps track of the total number of times its increment and decrement methods are called. Its incTally method reports the number of times that the inc method is called since the counter was created, and its decTally method does the same for the dec method.

To illustrate a tally counter, consider the following variation of the program presented in Exercise 5.2. The TryTallyCounter program maintains a tally counter whose step is specified by the first program argument. The remaining programming arguments determine how this counter is manipulated: It is incremented n_1 many times, and then decremented n_2 many times, and then incremented n_3 many times, and so on. After every set of increments or decrements, the counter's value and current tallies are printed. Here is a sample interaction:

```
> java TryTallyCounter 2 6 3 9 1
step = 2
6 incs, 0 decs: value = 12
6 incs, 3 decs: value = 6
```

```
15 incs, 3 decs: value = 24
15 incs, 4 decs: value = 22
```

Each line of output (except for the first) is produced by these three instructions:

```
System.out.print(cnt.incTally() + " incs, ");
System.out.print(cnt.decTally() + "decs: ");
System.out.println("value = " + cnt.value());
```

where the variable `cnt` holds the program's `TallyCounter` object. Here is the class definition:

```
public class TallyCounter extends NStepCounter {

  protected int incTally, decTally;

  public TallyCounter(int step) {
    super(step);
    incTally = decTally = 0;
  }

  public TallyCounter() {
    this(1);
  }

  public void inc() {
    super.inc();
    incTally++;
  }

  public void dec() {
    super.dec();
    decTally++;
  }

  public int incTally() { return incTally; }

  public int decTally() { return decTally; }
}
```

The `TallyCounter` class uses inheritance for both specialization and extension. The class overrides the `inc` method so that the method both increments the counter's value and updates the increment tally. The `inc` method increments the value by calling the superclass' implementation of `inc`:

```
super.inc();
```

Here the `super` keyword acts as a reference to the current object, yet it treats the current object as an instance of its superclass. In this way, the `inc` method allows the superclass to carry out its *increment* behavior, and then augments this with a behavior of its own, specifically, the instruction

```
incTally++;
```

The `TallyCounter` class overrides the `dec` method similarly.

`TallyCounter` also uses inheritance for extension in that it defines two new methods, `incTally` and `decTally`. The methods it overrides (`inc` and `dec`) and the new methods it defines (`incTally` and `decTally`) work together to carry out a tally counter's specialized service of maintaining tallies.

Exercises

5.15 Implement the `TryTallyCounter` program demonstrated at the start of this section.

5.16 Define the class `ClearableTallyCounter` that represents a tally counter whose value can be cleared (set to zero by a `clear` method). The `incTally` method reports the number of times that the method `inc` is called since the most recent call to `clear`, or since the counter was constructed if `clear` has never been called. The `decTally` method behaves similarly for decrements. Should your class extend the `TallyCounter` class or the `Clearable-Counter` class? Are both approaches feasible?

5.4 Inheritance for Specification

Inheritance is used for specification when a child class implements abstract methods declared by its parent class or by an interface that it implements. Through its implementation, the class provides the behavior specified by the abstract methods. Indeed, the purpose of an abstract method is to specify behavior while deferring its implementation to subclasses.

5.4.1 Interfaces and Abstract Classes

Java provides two different mechanisms for supporting inheritance of specification:

- A class `A` may **implement an interface** or interfaces. Each interface declares a number of methods without implementing them. When class `A` implements a method declared by an interface, class `A` realizes the behavior specified by that method.
- A class `A` may **extend an abstract class.** The abstract class declares a number of methods some of which it implements, some not. Those methods that the class does not implement are its **abstract methods.**

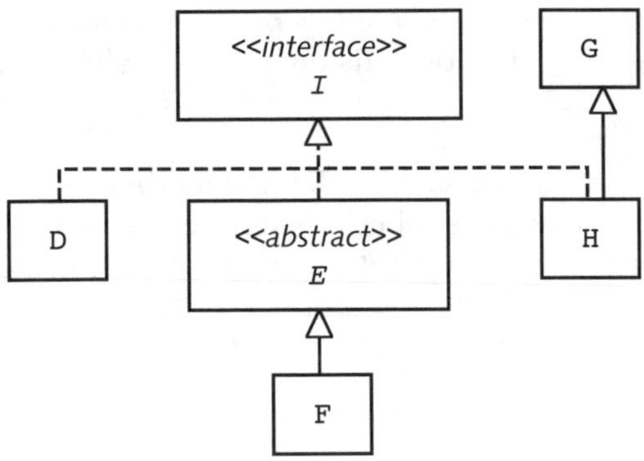

FIGURE 5.7 Inheritance for specification.

> When class A implements an abstract method declared by its abstract superclass, it realizes the behavior specified by that method.

When a class implements an interface, it promises to implement the methods declared by the interface. The class diagram for the following short example appears in Figure 5.7:

```
public interface I {
  public void f(int i);
  public void g(String s);
}

public class D implements I {
  public void f(int i) {
    System.out.println(i);
  }
  public void g(String s) {
    System.out.println(s);
  }
}
```

Here class D implements the interface I. The interface I declares the methods f and g but defers their implementation to those classes that implement the interface (in this example, class D). Because class D implements *every* method declared by interface I, class D is a **concrete class,** implying that it is possible to create instances of class D.

It is not required that a class implement every method (or even any method) declared by those interfaces it implements. Here the class E implements one of the methods declared by interface I without implementing the other method (method g):

```
abstract public class E implements I {
  public void f(int i) {
    System.out.println("arg = " + i);
  }
}
```

Class `E` provides only a partial implementation of the interface `I`. Because class `E` does not implement all of the methods declared by interface `I`, class `E` is an **abstract class.** Because class `E` is an abstract class, it cannot be instantiated. Any attempt to do so is flagged as an error by the Java compiler:

```
E e = new E();    // error: E is an abstract class
```

Inheritance for specification also occurs when a child class extends an abstract class. Abstract classes declare an interface but generally provide only a partial implementation. Just as interfaces are designed to be implemented, abstract classes are designed to be extended. The child classes of an abstract class inherit the abstract class' specification and partial implementation, and are free to complete the implementation by implementing the abstract methods of their abstract parent class. In the following, class `F` extends the abstract class `E` and implements class `E`'s sole abstract method:

```
public class F extends E {
  public void g(String s) {
    System.out.println(s);
  }
}
```

Here, class `F` inherits only the specification of the method `g` and supplies its own implementation. It also inherits the full implementation of the method `f`. Because class `F` is fully implemented, it is a concrete class.

A class may extend one class (its parent class) and implement any number of interfaces. Suppose that class `G` has been defined. We may then define a new class `H` that both extends class `G` and implements interface `I`:

```
public class H extends G implements I {
  public void f(int i) {
    System.out.println("arg: " + i);
  public void g(String s) {
    System.out.println("the string is " + s);
}
```

Java is said to support **multiple interface inheritance** because a class can implement any number of interfaces. A class inherits an interface and a partial implementation from the class it extends. It also inherits an interface from each of the interfaces it implements. In this example, the class `H` inherits an interface and partial implementation from its parent class `G` and an interface from the interface `I`.

In Figure 5.7, the annotations <<*interface*>> and <<*abstract*>> that appear in certain class boxes are examples of **stereotypes** in the Unified Modeling Language (UML). Note the use of a dashed edge connecting the classes `D, E`, and `H` to the interface `I`. This convention reminds the reader that `I` is not the parent class of these classes; rather, `I` is an interface that these classes implement.

The **supertypes** of a class consist of the class itself, the class it extends and the interfaces it implements, *and* the supertypes of its superclass and interfaces. A class is a **subtype** of each of its supertypes. In Figure 5.7, the supertypes of class `F` are `F, E,` and `I`, and the supertypes of class `H` are `H, I,` and `G`. The subtypes of the interface `I` include every class and interface that appears in the diagram, except for class `G`.

The notions of subtype and supertype are important because a class inherits the interface of each of its supertypes. We'll explore the implications of this when we look into polymorphism later in this chapter.

5.4.2 Rectangular Geometries

We often develop abstract classes by discovering behaviors that are common to a number of similar classes. The common behaviors are extracted from these classes and placed in a new abstract class that serves as their common parent class, a process known as **factorization.** In this subsection, we'll use factorization to define a new abstract class to serve as a common parent to the `RectangleGeometry` and `EllipseGeometry` classes. It is easy to see that these two geometry classes have several behaviors in common. Both classes have *position*, *width*, and *height* properties. Both classes define `contains` methods for deciding whether a given point lies inside the region defined by the geometry and a `translate` method for moving the geometry. And both classes define a `shape` method.

Yet, because there are also significant differences between rectangles and ellipses, it would not do to combine these two classes into a single class. Rectangles and ellipses have different shapes, different methods for deciding point containment, and different string descriptors.

To construct a common abstract superclass for these two classes, we factor out the behaviors common to both and locate these behaviors in a new parent class, to be named the `RectangularGeometry` class. This class represents the concept of **rectangular geometries,** geometries that are defined by an enclosing axes-parallel rectangle. The methods shared by its subclasses will be declared by the `RectangularGeometry` class. Moreover, we will move as much of the *implementation* as possible into this abstract parent class.

Which behaviors can we expect the `RectangularGeometry` class to implement, and which behaviors can it only specify but not implement? Rectangles and ellipses have *position*, *width*, and *height* properties by virtue of their being rectangular geometries. Because the behaviors for these properties—the properties' accessor methods—are standard across all rectangular geometries, they can be implemented in the RectangularGeometry class. The translate method can also be implemented because it is carried out by changing a geometry's position, a property shared by all rectangular geometries.

In contrast, the RectangularGeometry class declares two abstract methods:

```
// abstract methods of RectangularGeometry class
abstract public boolean contains(int x, int y);
abstract public Shape shape();
```

Implementation of these abstract methods is deferred to the subclasses. Because rectangular geometries come in different shapes (e.g., rectangles versus ellipses), the RectangularGeometry class cannot implement the shape method. Similarly, a rectangular geometry cannot decide point containment based solely on the geometry's dimensions. Given a rectangle and an ellipse having the same bounding box, there are points (such as the rectangle's corners) that are contained in the rectangle but not the ellipse.

As noted, the translate method can be implemented in terms of a rectangular geometry's *position* property:

```
// method of RectangularGeometry class
public void translate(int dx, int dy) {
  PointGeometry pos = getPosition();
  int x = pos.getX();
  int y = pos.getY();
  setPosition(new PointGeometry(x + dx, y + dy));
}
```

Although the RectangularGeometry class defers implementation of the two-argument contains method, it can implement the one-argument version:

```
// method of RectangularGeometry class
public boolean contains(PointGeometry p) {
  return contains(p.getX(), p.getY());
}
```

The two-argument version of contains that gets called is an abstract method of the RectangularGeometry class whose implementation is supplied by subclasses.

Let us complete the definition of the RectangularGeometry class. We'll represent a rectangular geometry by two Range objects. These two ranges jointly define the geometry's bounding box, a rectangle. This is the same storage structure used in our implementation of our RectangleGeometry class given in Section 3.2.2. Not surprisingly, the implementation of the RectangularGeometry closely follows that of the RectangleGeometry class. Here is the class definition:

```
public abstract class RectangularGeometry {

  protected Range xRange, yRange;

  public abstract boolean contains(int x, int y);
  public abstract Shape shape();

  protected RectangularGeometry(int x, int y,
                                int width, int height)
          throws IllegalArgumentException {
    if ((width < 0) || (height < 0))
      throw new IllegalArgumentException();
    xRange = new Range(x, x + width);
    yRange = new Range(y, y + height);
  }

  protected RectangularGeometry(PointGeometry pos,
                                int width, int height)
   throws NullPointerException,IllegalArgumentException {
    this(pos.getX(), pos.getY(), width, height);
  }

  protected RectangularGeometry(Range xRange,Range yRange)
          throws NullPointerException {
    this(xRange.getMin(), yRange.getMin(),
         xRange.length(), yRange.length());
  }

  protected RectangularGeometry(RectangularGeometry r)
          throws NullPointerException {
    this (r.getPosition(), r.getWidth(), r.getHeight());
  }

  public PointGeometry getPosition() {
    return new PointGeometry(xRange.getMin(),
                             yRange.getMin());
  }

  public void setPosition(PointGeometry p)
        throws NullPointerException {
    xRange.setMinMax(p.getX(), p.getX() + getWidth());
    yRange.setMinMax(p.getY(), p.getY() + getHeight());
  }

  public int getWidth() {
    return xRange.length();
  }
```

```
  public void setWidth(int newWidth)
         throws IllegalArgumentException {
    if (newWidth < 0) throw new IllegalArgumentException();
    xRange.setMax(xRange.getMin() + newWidth);
  }

  public int getHeight() {
    return yRange.length();
  }

  public void setHeight(int newHeight)
         throws IllegalArgumentException {
    if (newHeight < 0)
      throw new IllegalArgumentException();
    yRange.setMax(yRange.getMin() + newHeight);
  }

  public RectangleGeometry boundingBox() {
   return new RectangleGeometry(getPosition(),
                                getWidth(), getHeight());
  }

  public boolean contains(PointGeometry p)
         throws NullPointerException {
    return contains(p.getX(), p.getY());
  }

  public void translate(int dx, int dy) {
    PointGeometry pos = getPosition();
    int x = pos.getX();
    int y = pos.getY();
    setPosition(new PointGeometry(x + dx, y + dy));
  }

  protected String dimensionsToString() {
    return getPosition() + "," + getWidth() +
           "," + getHeight();
  }
}
```

The `RectangularGeometry` class provides a protected `dimensionsToString` method for use by its subclasses in their own `toString` methods. String-descriptors for specialized rectangular geometries (such as ellipses) are formed by the type name followed by the geometry's dimensions:

```
RectangularGeometry e = new EllipseGeometry(1, 2, 3, 4);
System.out.println(e);    // Ellipse: (1,2),3,4
```

The implementation of the ellipse's `toString` method calls upon the inherited `dimensionsToString` method to construct the string's dimensions component.

Having defined the `RectangularGeometry` class, we can revise the implementation of our `RectangleGeometry` class. Our new version of `RectangleGeometry` extends the `RectangularGeometry` class:

```
public class RectangleGeometry
       extends RectangularGeometry {

  public RectangleGeometry(int x, int y,
                           int width, int height)
        throws IllegalArgumentException{
    super(x, y, width, height);
  }

  public RectangleGeometry(PointGeometry position,
                           int width, int ht)
   throws NullPointerException,IllegalArgumentException{
    super(position, width, ht);
  }

  public RectangleGeometry(Range xRange, Range yRange)
         throws NullPointerException {
    super(xRange, yRange);
  }

  public RectangleGeometry(RectangularGeometry r)
         throws NullPointerException {
    super(r);
  }

  public boolean contains(int x, int y) {
    PointGeometry pos = getPosition();
    int minX = pos.getX();
    int minY = pos.getY();
    return (minX <= x) && (x <= minX + getWidth()) &&
           (minY <= y) && (y <= minY + getHeight());
  }

  public Shape shape() {
    PointGeometry pos = getPosition();
    return new Rectangle2D.Float(pos.getX(), pos.getY(),
                                 getWidth(), getHeight());
  }
```

```
  public Range xRange() {
    int x = getPosition().getX();
    return new Range(x, x + getWidth());
  }

  public Range yRange() {
    int y = getPosition().getY();
    return new Range(y, y + getHeight());
  }

  public String toString() {
    return "Rectangle: " + dimensionsToString();
  }
}
```

Note that the `RectangleGeometry` class implements the abstract methods `shape` and `contains` declared by its parent class.

Exercise

Revise the implementation of the `EllipseGeometry` class so that it extends the `RectangularGeometry` class.

5.4.3 Abstract Geometries

In this section, we continue the process of factorization begun with the definition of `RectangularGeometry` in the previous subsection. Our goal is to develop the inheritance hierarchy for geometries shown in the class diagram of Figure 5.8. This inheritance hierarchy will remain intact through the remainder of this book.

Figure 5.8 includes the `AreaGeometry` and `Geometry` interfaces, both of which are new. The `Geometry` interface declares two operations common to all geometries: for obtaining the geometry's shape and for translating the geometry. Here is the definition:

```
public interface Geometry {
  public abstract java.awt.Shape shape();
    // EFFECTS: Returns this geometry's shape.

  public abstract void translate(int dx, int dy);
    // MODIFIES: this
    // EFFECTS: Translates this geometry by dx
    //   along x and dy along y.
}
```

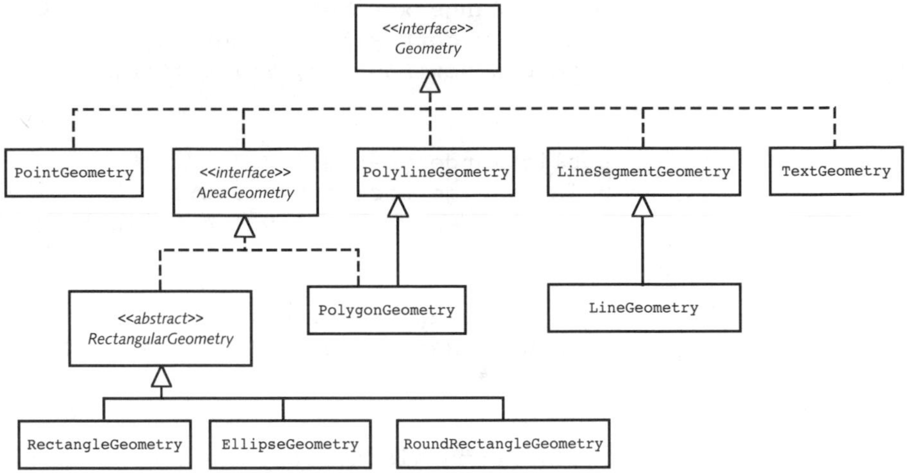

FIGURE 5.8 Class diagram for our `Geometry` subtypes.

The `AreaGeometry` interface represents geometries that enclose area. So far, we've seen three geometries of this type: rectangles, ellipses, and polygons. All three define `contains` methods for deciding point containment. The `AreaGeometry` interface is defined like this:

```
public interface AreaGeometry extends Geometry {
  public abstract boolean contains(int x, int y);
    // EFFECTS: If this geometry contains (x,y) -- that
    //   is, (x,y) lies in this geometry's interior or
    //   boundary -- returns true; else returns false.

  public abstract boolean contains(PointGeometry p)
        throws NullPointerException;
    // EFFECTS: If p is null throws NullPointerException;
    //   else if this geometry contains p returns true;
    //   else returns false.
}
```

Note that the `AreaGeometry` interface *extends* the `Geometry` interface. Interfaces cannot implement other interfaces; only classes can implement interfaces. An interface is extended using the `extends` keyword.

Deciding whether a general concept is best realized by an interface or by an abstract class involves a tradeoff. Java supports multiple inheritance of interfaces, meaning that a class may implement any number of interfaces. Defining interfaces takes advantage of this language feature. In contrast, abstract classes have the advantage that they can provide partial implementations that descendants inherit, leading to subclass implementations that are simpler and less prone to error. However, because a subclass can extend only one class, the subclasses of an abstract class cannot inherit implementation from any other source.

`Geometry` is clearly best realized as an interface. The `Geometry` interface represents a geometry that is too abstract to admit a particular shape or means of translation—it would not be possible for `Geometry` to implement either of its two methods. The matter is not so simple in the case of `AreaGeometry`. We might consider defining `AreaGeometry` as an abstract class because it can in fact provide a partial implementation: either of its two `contains` methods can be implemented in terms of the other. For instance, it is possible to define an abstract `AbstractAreaGeometry` class as follows:

```
public abstract class AbstractAreaGeometry
       implements Geometry {
  public abstract boolean contains(int x, int y);

  public boolean contains(PointGeometry p)
         throws NullPointerException {
    return contains(p.getX(), p.getY());
  }

}
```

Under this approach, descendants of the `AbstractAreaGeometry` class would implement the two-argument `contains` method while inheriting the already implemented one-argument `contains` method. (In fact, this is precisely the approach that the `RectangularGeometry` class takes with its `contains` methods.) Unfortunately, this approach proves troublesome whenever we want to define a new class that seeks to inherit the *interface* declared by `AbstractAreaGeometry` but its implementation from a different class. Figure 5.8 illustrates a similar example: The `PolygonGeometry` class inherits part of its interface from `AreaGeometry` but its implementation from the `PolylineGeometry` class. When the implementation supplied by an abstract class is slight, as occurs in the case of the `AbstractAreaGeometry` class, it is often best to define an interface instead.

The best of both worlds is also possible. One can define both an `AreaGeometry` interface and an abstract `AbstractAreaGeometry` class that implements the interface, as illustrated in Figure 5.9. New classes that do not require implementation from some other parent class are free to extend the `AbstractAreaGeometry` class, thereby benefiting from `AbstractAreaGeometry`'s implementation. This is what the `RectangularGeometry` class does this in Figure 5.9. Yet, those new classes that need to inherit implementation from a different parent class can still implement the `AreaGeometry` interface, as the `PolygonGeometry` class does.

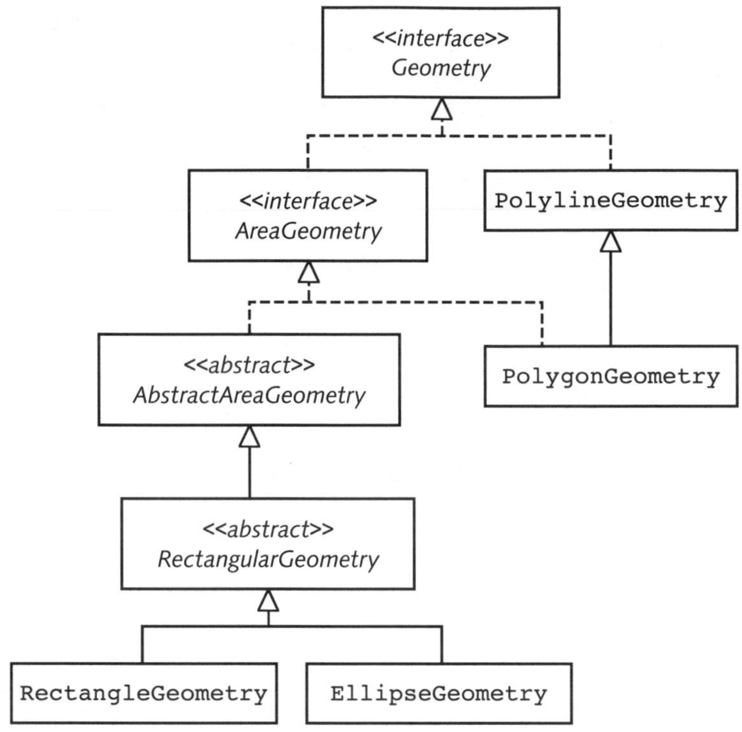

FIGURE 5.9 In this design, `AbstractAreaGeometry` provides a partial implementation of the `AreaGeometry` interface.

Exercises

Edit the geometry classes to realize the inheritance hierarchy shown in Figure 5.8. The headers of the `PointGeometry`, `LineSegmentGeometry`, and `PolylineGeometry` classes must be revised to reflect the fact that they now implement the `Geometry` interface, and the headers of the `RectangularGeometry` and `PolygonGeometry` classes must be revised to implement the `AreaGeometry` interface. In addition, the one-argument constructors for the `RectangleGeometry` and `EllipseGeometry` classes should be generalized so that they take a rectangular geometry; for example:

```
public EllipseGeometry(RectangularGeometry r)
       throws NullPointerException
    // EFFECTS: If r is null throws
    //   NullPointerException; else constructs an
    //   ellipse with the same dimensions as r.
```

Are any other modifications necessary? (Round rectangles and text geometries are treated in the next two exercises.)

ESSENTIAL 5.19

A **round rectangle** is a rectangle with rounded corners. The width and height of the ellipses used to round the corners are specified by two properties, *arcw* and *arch*, respectively (see Figure 5.10). Many of the operations presented by our round rectangle class are inherited from its superclass, `RectangularGeometry`. The following class skeleton shows only those methods that the class must implement:

```
public class RoundRectangleGeometry
       extends RectangularGeometry {

 public RoundRectangleGeometry(int x, int y,
                               int width, int height,
                               double arcw, double arch)
        throws IllegalArgumentException
    // EFFECTS: If width, height, arcw, or arch is
    //   negative throws IllegalArgumentException;
    //   else constructs a round rectangle at
    //   position (x,y) and with given width and
    //   height, and with corner-rounding ellipse
    //   of width arcw and height arch.

 public RoundRectangleGeometry(Position pos,
                               int width, int height,
                               double arcw, double arch)
         throws NullPointerException,
                IllegalArgumentException
    // EFFECTS: If pos is null throws
    //   NullPointerException; else if width,
    //   height, arcw, or arch are negative throws
    //   IllegalArgumentException; else constructs
```

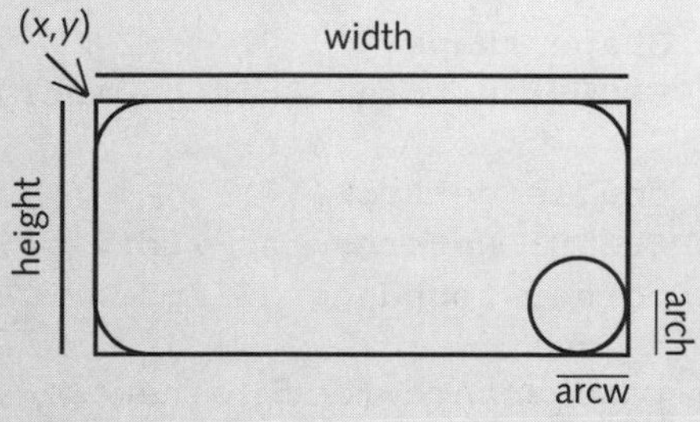

FIGURE 5.10 A round rectangle geometry.

```
  //   a round rectangle at position (x,y) and
  //   with given width and height, and with
  //   corner-rounding ellipse of width arcw
  //   and height arch.

public RoundRectangleGeometry(Range xRange,
       Range yRange, double arcw, double arch)
       throws NullPointerException,
              IllegalArgumentException
  // EFFECTS: If xRange or yRange is null
  //   throws NullPointerException; else if arcw
  //   or arch is negative throws
  //   IllegalArgumentException; else constructs
  //   a round rectangle of given x
  //   and y extents, and with corner-rounding
  //   ellipses of width arcw and height arch.

public RoundRectangleGeometry(
            RectangularGeometry r,
            double arcw, double arch)
       throws NullPointerException,
              IllegalArgumentException
  // EFFECTS: If r is null throws
  //   NullPointerException; else if arcw or arch
  //   is <0 throws IllegalArgumentException;
  //   else constructs a round rectangle with
  //   the same dimensions as r, and with  corner-
  //   roundingellipses of width arcw and
  //   height arch.

public boolean contains(int x, int y)
  // EFFECTS: If this geometry contains (x,y)
  //   returns true; else returns false.

public Shape shape()
  // EFFECTS: Returns this geometry's shape.

public double getArcw()
  // EFFECTS: Returns the width of the
  //   corner-rounding ellipse.

public void setArcw(double newArcw)
       throws IllegalArgumentException
```

```
    // MODIFIES: this
    // EFFECTS: If newArcw < 0 throws
    //   IllegalArgumentException; else sets the
    //   width of the corner-rounding ellipses
    //   to newArcw.

  public double getArch()
    // EFFECTS: Returns the height of the
    //   corner-rounding ellipse.

  public void setArch(double newArch)
         throws IllegalArgumentException
    // MODIFIES: this
    // EFFECTS: If newArch < 0 throws
    //   IllegalArgumentException; else sets the
    //   height of the corner-rounding ellipses
    //   to newArch.

  public String toString()
    // EFFECTS: Returns the string
    //   "Round-rectangle: (x,y),width,height,
    //   arcw,arch".
}
```

Implement the `RoundRectangleGeometry` class. A rounded rectangle shape can be constructed using the `java.awt.geom.RoundRectangle2D.Double` class:

```
// method of RoundRectangleGeometry class
public Shape shape() {
  PointGeometry pos = getPosition();
  return new RoundRectangle2D.Double(pos.getX(),
              pos.getY(), getWidth(), getHeight(),
              getArcw(), getArch());
}
```

To implement the two-argument `contains` method, you may want to delegate to the round rectangle's shape.

ESSENTIAL 5.20 Painting strings is quite simple in Java: You send the *drawString* message to a rendering context, passing it the string to be painted and the *x* and *y* coordinates of the string's starting point. For instance, the following instruction paints the string `"hello world"` into the rendering context `g2`:

```
g2.drawString("hello world", 50, 100);
```

Here, the baseline of the first character (*h*) occurs at the position (50,100) in user space. Other characteristics of the painted text, such as font and paint, are determined by g2's current attributes.

This exercise presents a class for strings that implements the Geometry interface. As an example of usage, the following code fragment paints the string "hello world" into the graphics context g2, starting at the point (50,100):

```
Geometry s = new TextGeometry("hello world");
s.translate(50, 100);
g2.fill(s.shape());
```

To implement the TextGeometry class, we are not able to use the Graphics2D.drawString method directly. This is because classes that implement the Geometry interface promise to provide a shape method, but drawString is too high-level—it draws the string but without providing access to the string's shape. Rather, our implementation of the TextGeometry class follows the basic process that the drawString method uses to carry out its work.

When a string is painted, it is first converted to a vector of shapes called **glyphs.** These glyphs, which represent the string's visual appearance, are a function not only of the string's character sequence, but also of such factors as the chosen font, font size, font style, and metrics determining character spacing. To create this glyph vector, you can send the *createGlyphVector* message to a Font object. It is the Font object that describes the type of font, its style (plain, bold, italic, or bold-italic), its size, and character layout. To construct this glyph vector, a Font object also requires what is known as a **font rendering context,** which stores information for measuring the size of the text as well as rendering hints. We will not cover text rendering in greater detail, except to note that the process described here is encapsulated by the following class definition:

```
public class TextGeometry implements Geometry {

  // default font if not supplied to constructor
  public static final Font DefaultFont =
    new Font("SansSerif", Font.BOLD, 12);

    // glyphs for this string
  protected GlyphVector glyphs;

    // position of text baseline of first character
  protected int x, y;
```

```
  public TextGeometry(Font font, String s)
         throws NullPointerException {
    // EFFECTS: If font or s is null throws
    //   NullPointerException; else constructs
    //   this for string s in the given font.
    FontRenderContext frc =
      new FontRenderContext(null,true,false);
    glyphs = font.createGlyphVector(frc, s);
    x = y = 0;
  }

  public TextGeometry(Graphics2D g, String s)
         throws NullPointerException {
    // EFFECTS: If g or s are null throws
    //   NullPointerException; else constucts this
    //   for s using the font and font rendering
    //   context in the graphics context g.
    FontRenderContext frc = g.getFontRenderContext();
    Font font = g.getFont();
    glyphs = font.createGlyphVector(frc, s);
    x = y = 0;
  }

  public TextGeometry(String s)
         throws NullPointerException {
    // EFFECTS: If s is null throws
    //   NullPointerException; else constructs
    //   this for string s using the default font.
    this(DefaultFont, s);
  }

  public Shape shape() {
    // EFFECTS: Returns the shape of this text.
    return glyphs.getOutline(x, y);
  }

  public void translate(int dx, int dy) {
    // MODIFIES: this
    // EFFECTS: Translates this text by dx and dy.
    this.x += dx;
    this.y += dy;
  }
}
```

The `GlyphVector` and `FontRenderContext` classes belong to the package `java.awt.font`. For this exercise, write a graphics program that exercises both the `RoundRectangleGeometry` and `TextGeometry` classes. For instance, your program might fill a red round rectangle whose position and dimensions are specified by the program arguments, and paint a silly message such as *See my curves!* beneath it. Where `s` is a `TextGeometry` object, explore the difference between filling `s`:

```
g2.fill(s.shape())
```

and stroking `s`:

```
g2.draw(s.shape())
```

5.5 Polymorphism

The term *polymorphism* is Greek in origin and means literally *many forms.* In the object model, polymorphism describes a situation in which a software element can assume any one of a number of forms. Specifically, through polymorphism—also known as **subtype polymorphism**—a type can take the form of any of its subtypes. A client using the interface promised by the type can work with instances of any of its subtypes.

5.5.1 Java's Mechanism for Polymorphism

To explain polymorphism, I'll make use of the `Employee` and `Waiter` classes presented at the start of Section 5.1 and repeated here:

```
public class Employee {
  public void greeting(String name) {
    // MODIFIES: System.out
    // EFFECTS: Prints a friendly greeting to name.
    System.out.println("Welcome to Eat and Run, "+name+".");
  }
  public void farewell(String name) {
    // MODIFIES: System.out
    // EFFECTS: Prints a farewell to name.
    System.out.println("Please come back soon, "+name+"!");
  }
}

class Waiter extends Employee {
  public void greeting(String name) {
```

```
    System.out.println("Can I take your order, "+name+"?");
  }
  public void recommendation() {
    // MODIFIES: System.out
    // EFFECTS: Prints a recommendation to name.
      System.out.println("I'd stick to the pizza.");
    }
  }
```

Whenever you use an object in Java, two types come into play: the object's actual type and its apparent type. The **actual type** of an object is the class to which it belongs. The **apparent type** of an object is the type of the expression that refers to (or uses) the object. For example, consider the following code fragment:

```
Employee e = new Waiter();  // line 1
e.greeting("David"); // line 2: Can I take your order, David?
```

The `Waiter` object created in line 1 is used in line 2. The type of expression `e` that references the `Waiter` object in line 2 is determined by the declaration of `e` as `Employee` in line 1. In line 2, the object referenced by the variable `e` has the apparent type `Employee` and the actual type `Waiter`.

Keep in mind that an object's actual type is established when the object is constructed and remains fixed throughout its lifetime. In contrast, an object's apparent type is relative to an expression and may vary from one expression to the next. Suppose we continue the preceding code fragment as follows:

```
Waiter w = (Waiter)e; // line 3
w.recommendation();   // line 4: I'd stick to the pizza.
```

In line 4, the object referred to by the expression `w` has the same apparent type and actual type: `Waiter`.

An object's apparent type can be deduced by the compiler. In line 2, the object's apparent type of `Employee` follows from the type declaration of the variable `e` in line 1. Similarly, the object's apparent type of `Waiter` in line 4 follows from the declaration of the variable `w` in line 3.

Objects are often used through reference variables, as in the preceding code fragments, but other ways of referring to objects are also possible. For example, we may create an object for immediate use without capturing a reference to the object:

```
int len = new String("hello").length();
```

In this example, the object referenced by the expression `new String("hello")` has the same apparent type and actual type, that of `String`. Expressions can also involve type casts. For example, with respect to the following expression:

```
(Employee)new Waiter()
```

the object has the actual type `Waiter` and, due to the type cast, the apparent type `Employee`.

The actual type of an object constrains its apparent type: *An object's apparent type is always a supertype of its actual type.* This is certainly true of the preceding code fragments. In line 2, the object's apparent type (`Employee`) is a supertype of its actual type (`Waiter`). And in line 4, the object's apparent type (`Waiter`) is a supertype of its actual type (`Waiter`), because a type includes itself as one of its supertypes. In contrast, the following initialization is flagged by the compiler as illegal:

```
Employee e2 = new PointGeometry(4, 5);  // illegal
```

The problem is that the expression `e2` cannot be used legally: The object's apparent type (`Employee`) is not a supertype of its actual type (`PointGeometry`).

When an object is used, its actual type and apparent type come into play based on two key rules. The first rule concerns the object's interface: *When an object is used, its interface is defined by its apparent type*. For example, because the `Employee` type includes the `greeting` method as part of its interface, line 6 of the following code segment is legal:

```
Employee e = new Waiter();   // line 5
e.greeting("David"); // line 6: Can I take your order, David?
e.recommendation(); // line 7: illegal
```

However, because the `Employee` type does *not* include the `recommendation` method as part of its interface, line 7 is illegal. This is the case even though the object's *actual* type includes the `recommendation` method as part of its interface.

The second rule concerns an object's behavior: *When an object is used, its behavior is defined by its actual type*. Consider the behavior exhibited when the `Waiter` object referenced by `e` is sent the *greeting* message in line 6. This behavior is clearly determined by the object's actual type (`Waiter`), not by its apparent type (`Employee`). Although both the `Employee` class and the `Waiter` class define a `greeting` method, it is the `Waiter`'s version of this method that gets executed. This is because the object's actual type is `Waiter`.

These two rules can be summarized as follows:

When an object is used, its interface is defined by its apparent type, and its behavior is defined by its actual type.

This principle forms the basis of polymorphism. Client code manipulates objects through a common supertype that defines the objects' common interface. Yet each object responds to messages according to its actual type. For example, consider the following procedure:

```
static void servileGreeting(Employee e, String name) {
  System.out.println(name + ", how lovely to see you.");
```

```
    e.greeting(name);
}
```

When procedure `servileGreeting` is called, its argument `e` is bound to an object belonging to some subtype of `Employee`. The procedure can legally send the *greeting* message to `e` because `e` implements the interface promised by the supertype `Employee`; in particular, it implements the `greeting` method. Moreover, the specific behavior evoked by the *greeting* message depends on the *actual* type of the object `e`. The procedure call:

```
servileGreeting(new Employee(), "Elisa");
```

produces the following output:

```
Elisa, how lovely to see you.
Welcome to Eat and Run, Elisa.
```

In contrast, the following procedure call:

```
servileGreeting(new Waiter(), "Phyllis");
```

produces this output:

```
Phyllis, how lovely to see you.
Can I take your order, Phyllis?
```

Here is a more useful example. When called with a rendering context `g2` and an array of geometries, the procedure `fillGeometries` paints each geometry into the rendering context:

```
static void fillGeometries(Graphics2D g2,
                           Geometry[] geoms) {
  for (int i = 0; i < geoms.length; i++) {
    Geometry geom = geoms[i];
    g2.fill(geom.shape());
  }
}
```

Within the body of the *for* loop, the assignment statement

```
Geometry geom = geoms[i];
```

is legal because the object stored in `geoms[i]` belongs to some subtype of the `Geometry` interface. Because the `Geometry` interface declares the method

```
public Shape shape();
```

it is legal to send the *shape* message to the object referenced by the variable `geom`:

```
geom.shape()
```

The `fillGeometries` procedure does not know the actual type of the geometries stored in its input array. Nor must it know, because each subtype of Geometry returns a shape appropriate to its actual type: An EllipseGeometry returns an ellipse shape, a PointGeometry a point shape, and so forth. The apparent type of each object (Geometry) provides the interface that fillGeometries expects, whereas the actual type of each object provides the behavior that fillGeometries expects.

5.5.2 Java's Comparable Interface and Sorting

In Section 2.4 we developed a program that takes a sequence of integer program arguments, then sorts and prints them. The program arguments are sorted as integers using the < operator. In fact, it is possible to sort values of any type for which a linear ordering (such as <) has been defined. Java provides the java.lang.Comparable interface for defining a linear ordering for data types:

```
public interface java.lang.Comparable {
  public int compareTo(Object obj)
         throws ClassCastException;
    // EFFECTS: If this object and obj cannot be
    //   compared throws ClassCastException; else
    //   returns a negative integer, zero, or positive
    //   integer if this object is less than, equal to,
    //   or greater than obj, respectively.
}
```

The compareTo method compares this object to the object obj, and returns a negative integer, zero, or a positive integer if this object is less than, equal to, or greater than obj, respectively. Any type that implements the Comparable interface can be linearly ordered. For instance, the String class implements the Comparable interface; its compareTo method compares two strings under the lexicographic (dictionary) ordering:

```
"apple".compareTo("banana")      // evaluates to -1
"banana".compareTo("apple")      // evaluates to 1
"apple".compareTo("apple")       // evaluates to 0
```

Our Rational class (Section 4.4.3) also defines a compareTo method with the signature and specification called for by the Comparable interface. Hence, to make this Rational class implement the Comparable interface, we need only revise the class definition's header in this way:

```
public class Rational implements Comparable {
```

We can develop a Sort class that provides a static sort method for sorting an array of Comparable objects. We will use the selection sort strategy described in Section 2.4. Here is the class:

```
public class Sort {

  public static void sort(Comparable[] a)
   throws NullPointerException, ClassCastException {
    // MODIFIES: a
    // EFFECTS: If a is null throws NullPointerException;
    //   else if some pair of elements in a cannot be
    //   compared throws ClassCastException;
    //   else sorts the elements of a.
    if (a == null) throw new NullPointerException();
    sort(a, a.length);
  }

  protected static void sort(Comparable[] a, int n)
            throws ClassCastException {
    // REQUIRES: 0 <= n <= a.length.
    // MODIFIES: a
    // EFFECTS: If some pair of elements in a cannot
    //   be compared throws ClassCastException;
    //   else sorts the elements of a[0..n-1].
    for (int i = 0; i < n; i++) {
      int indx = min(a, i, n-1);
      Comparable temp = a[i];
      a[i] = a[indx];
      a[indx] = temp;
    }
  }

  protected static int min(Comparable[] a,
                              int lo, int hi)
            throws ClassCastException {
    // REQUIRES:  0 <= lo <= hi < a.length.
    // EFFECTS: If some pair of elements in a cannot
    //   be compared throws ClassCastException; else
    //   returns the index of some smallest element
    //   in a[lo..hi].
    int indx = lo;
    for (int i = lo+1; i <= hi; i++)
      if (a[i].compareTo(a[indx]) < 0)
        indx = i;
    return indx;
  }
}
```

Our implementation of `Sort` differs from our integer sorting program of Section 2.4 in only one respect: `Sort` compares `Comparable` objects using their compareTo method, whereas in Section 2.4 we compared int values using the < operator. In fact, as evident in the preceding code, the compareTo method is used only in the min procedure for finding the position of some smallest object within a subarray.

The Sort.sort method cannot be used to sort primitive types, such as int values, because primitive types cannot implement the Comparable interface. Indeed, primitive values are not objects, and they cannot implement interfaces. Nonetheless, we can convert primitive values into objects using **wrapper classes.** A wrapper class adapts a value's interface to one expected by the client.

Java provides a wrapper class for each of its primitive types. Java's Integer class, for example, is used to convert an int value into an object. The expression

```
Integer iObj = new Integer(7);
```

constructs a new Integer object denoting the value 7. The Integer class implements the Comparable interface; the compareTo method realizes the less-than operation for comparing integers:

```
iObj.compareTo(new Integer(9))      // -1 since 7 < 9
iObj.compareTo(new Integer("-6"))   // 1 since 7 > -6
```

However, few of the operations provided by the int data type are supported by the Integer class. For example, Integer objects cannot be added or multiplied. Fortunately the intValue method is provided to extract the equivalent int value:

```
int i = iObj.intValue();
System.out.println("i = " + i);   // i = 7
```

The following program, named SortIntegerArguments, performs essentially the same task as the SortIntegerArgs program of Section 2.4: The program takes a sequence of program arguments denoting integers and prints them in nondecreasing sorted order. However, the following program uses the Sort.sort method to perform the sort. To do so, it converts the program arguments into equivalent Integer objects and stores them in an array, sorts this array using the Sort.sort method, and then prints the array from left to right. Here is the implementation:

```
public class SortIntegerArguments {
  public static void main(String[] args) {
    Integer[] a = getIntegers(args);
    Sort.sort(a);
    printIntegers(a);
  }

  static Integer[] getIntegers(String[] args) {
    Integer[] a = new Integer[args.length];
    for (int i = 0; i < a.length; i++)
```

```
      a[i] = new Integer(args[i]);
    return a;
  }

  static void printIntegers(Integer[] a) {
    for (int i = 0; i < a.length; i++)
      System.out.print(a[i] + " ");
    System.out.println();
  }
}
```

The `Sort` class owes its generality to polymorphism. Its methods use the input objects' `compareTo` method to compare pairs of objects. The objects are known to provide a `compareTo` operation because they implement the `Comparable` interface. Yet the actual type of objects being sorted is not known at compile time—they may be `Integer` objects, `Rational` objects, `String` objects, or objects of any other type that implements the `Comparable` interface.

Exercises

ESSENTIAL **5.21** Revise the header in class `Rational's` definition so that this class now implements the `Comparable` interface. Then, write the program `SortRationalArguments` that takes an even number of integer program arguments and treats each pair as a rational: The numerator and denominator of the *i*'th rational appear in positions $2i$ and $2i+1$ of the program arguments. The program sorts and prints the rational numbers in sorted order. Here is a sample transcript:

```
> java SortRationalArguments 1 2 3 4 1 3 1 4 1 9 1 8 2 5
1/9 1/8 1/4 1/3 2/5 1/2 3/4
```

5.22 Use the `Sort` class to implement a program that sorts its program arguments as strings:

```
> java SortStringArguments did gyre and gimble in the wabe
and did gimble gyre in the wabe
```

ESSENTIAL **5.23** We can impose a linear ordering on points in the plane as follows. Let $p=(x_p,y_p)$ and $q=(x_q,y_q)$. Under this ordering, point p is less than point q if and only if

(1) $x_p < x_q$, or

(2) $x_p = x_q$ and $y_p < y_q$

Revise the `PointGeometry` class so that it implements the `Comparable` interface. Its `compareTo` method should compare two points as just described. Write the following two programs to test your work.

(a) Write an application that takes an even number $2n$ of integer arguments and interprets them as n points:

```
> java SortPoints x1 y1 x2 y2 ... xn yn
```

The program prints the n points in sorted order. For example:

```
> java SortPoints 5 2 3 1 3 7 2 9 5 8
(2,9) (3,1) (3,7) (5,2) (5,8)
> java SortPoints 3 4 hi there
Error: argument hi is badly formed.
> java SortPoints 1 2 3
Error: requires an even number of arguments.
```

(b) Develop a graphical program `PaintSortedPoints` that takes an integer program argument n, and then generates n random points and sorts them. The color each point should be painted is determined by its rank (position) among the sorted points. Specifically, the i'th point is assigned the following color:

```
Color.getHSBColor(i / (float)n, 1, 1)
```

This color has maximum saturation and brightness, and its hue is specified by the floating-point value `i/(float)n`. What appears in the frame are n random points which, when viewed from left to right, assume the colors of the spectrum ranging from red, yellow, green, cyan, blue, magenta, and back to red.

5.5.3 The Substitution Principle

When an object is used, its interface is determined by its apparent type, that is, the type of the referring expression. Client code expects the object to behave in accordance with this interface. This expectation follows from the **substitution principle:**

> *Subtype objects can be used wherever the supertype is expected without affecting the correctness of client code. The client code relies on the specifications provided by the supertype.*

An inheritance hierarchy that satisfies the substitution principle allows client code to be written to the specification of supertypes. Unfortunately, the Java compiler does not (and could not) enforce the substitution principle, and it is easy enough to develop inheritance hierarchies that violate it. It is up to the programmer to ensure that new classes she authors conform to this principle.

By way of example, recall the following method which prints a fawning greeting:

```
static void servileGreeting(Employee e, String name) {
  // MODIFIES: System.out
  // EFFECTS: Prints a fawning, friendly greeting to name.
  System.out.println(name + ", how lovely to see you.");
  e.greeting(name);
}
```

The `servileGreeting` method can legally send the *greeting* message to `e` because the `greeting` method is specified by the `Employee` type's interface. Yet, `servileGreeting` doesn't know the *actual* type of object to which `e` refers—the object may belong to any subtype of `Employee`. The correctness of `servileGreeting` depends on the expectation that every subtype of `Employee` implements the `greeting` method in accordance with this method's specification. In this case, `servileGreeting` expects `e` to print a friendly greeting. When `servileGreeting` is called with a `Waiter` object, this indeed occurs:

```
servileGreeting(new Waiter(), "Karen");
  // Karen, how lovely to see you.
  // Can I take your order, Karen?
```

When you extend a class, your subclass inherits the interface of its supertypes. Any methods that your class overrides should conform to the specifications of these supertypes. This allows client code to rely on these specifications for its own correctness. When the `Waiter` class overrides the `greeting` method, it does so in a way that conforms to the method's specification in the `Employee` class: It prints a friendly greeting; indeed, a friendly greeting appropriate to a waiter. The `Waiter` class satisfies the substitution principle, relative to its supertype `Employee`.

It is worth considering an example that violates the substitution principle. Suppose we define a subclass `Cook` as follows:

```
class Cook extends Employee {
  public void greeting(String name) {
    System.out.println("Get the hell out of my kitchen!");
  }
}
```

When `servileGreeting` is called with a `Cook` object, Karen gets greeted in a decidedly unfriendly manner:

```
servileGreeting(new Cook(), "Karen");
  // Karen, how lovely to see you.
  // Get the hell out of my kitchen!
```

The problem is that the Cook class overrides the greeting method in a way that violates the method's specification. The specification calls for the printing of a *friendly* greeting, whereas Cook.greeting prints an unfriendly message. The Cook class violates the substitution principle. Consequently, the servileGreeting method, whose expectation of Employee objects is thwarted, is incorrect whenever it gets called with instances of the Cook class.

The specifications of a method are conveyed by its preconditions and postconditions. In our example involving waiters and cooks, the specification of the greeting method is imprecise due to the vagueness of the word *friendly*: the word means one thing in Kansas, another in New York. Let us consider an example involving a specification that is more precise. The containsInIntersection procedure takes as input a point p and two area geometries a and b implementing the AreaGeometry interface. The procedure reports whether point p is contained in the intersection a∩b of the two areas. The following implementation of this procedure returns true if and only if the point p is contained in both areas:

```
static boolean containsInIntersection(PointGeometry p,
                          AreaGeometry a, AreaGeometry b)
      throws NullPointerException {
   // EFFECTS: If p, a, or b is null throws
   //   NullPointerException; else if a∩b contains p
   //   returns true; else returns false.
   return a.contains(p) && b.contains(p);
}
```

The containsInIntersection procedure does not know the actual types of the objects a and b with which it's called. They may be instances of RectangleGeometry, EllipseGeometry, PolygonGeometry, or any other subtype of AreaGeometry. Yet the procedure's correctness does not depend on the actual type of a or b—its correctness depends only on the expectation that these input objects correctly implement the contains method specified by the AreaGeometry interface:

```
public abstract boolean contains(PointGeometry p)
      throws NullPointerException;
   // EFFECTS: If p is null throws NullPointerException;
   //   else if this geometry contains p returns true;
   //   else returns false.
```

Every kind of area geometry implements the contains method in its own way, but each is expected to conform to the effects clause indicated earlier. Correctness of the containsInIntersection procedure depends on the expectation that the AreaGeometry objects it gets called with implement the contains method in accordance with its specification.

A subtype's methods should satisfy their specifications in the supertype. But this does not mean that the specifications must be identical. Rather, it means that the preconditions for each of the subclass' methods should be no stronger than those specified by the supertype, and the postconditions for each method should be no weaker than those specified by the supertype. In other words, the subclass is permitted to achieve more than its supertype with less:

- If some method of the subclass has a weaker precondition than that required by the supertype, the method requires less of the client while accomplishing as much.
- If some method of the subclass has a stronger postcondition than that promised by the supertype, the method accomplishes more for its client while requiring no more from it.

The correctness of the client, which uses the subtype object through the supertype, is not affected by such differences in the subtype object. By satisfying the supertype's preconditions, the client satisfies the subtype object's possibly weaker preconditions. And by achieving its possibly stronger postconditions, the subtype object achieves the postconditions of the supertype and thus satisfies the client's expectations.

Consider an analogy based on banking. Suppose that you open a new checking account with a bank named *SuperBank*. Your checking account provides the following terms:

1 Precondition: You agree to maintain a minimum balance of $500.
2. Postcondition: The bank promises to pay you 5% interest annually.

Suppose that, unbeknownst to you, the bank subcontracts your account to a second bank named *SubBank*. (In this analogy, you are the client using the supertype *SuperBank*, and the actual type of object you're using is *SubBank*.) Without informing you, *SubBank* alters the terms of your contract as follows:

1'. Precondition: You agree to maintain a minimum balance of $250.
2'. Postcondition: The bank promises to pay you 6% interest annually.

Here, *SubBank* has weakened the precondition you must satisfy and strengthened the postcondition it guarantees. This change in terms will surely cause you no difficulty. In fact, if you never check your statements or account balance, you wouldn't be aware of the change at all. You would maintain a minimum balance of $500, which certainly satisfies precondition 1', and you would withdraw money based on the assumption that it was accruing interest at the rate of 5% annually, which is certainly satisfied by postcondition 2'. Your expectations are determined by the terms you agreed to with *SuperBank*, yet they are fulfilled by the work carried out by *SubBank* and you are none the wiser. Hence, *SubBank* satisfies the specifications of its supertype *SuperBank:* Its precondition 1' is no stronger than precondition 1 of *SuperBank*, and its postcondition 2' is no weaker than postcondition 2 of *SuperBank*.

The `OrderedDictionary` class (Exercise 5.14) is an example of a class that is more powerful than its parent class (`Dictionary`). An ordered dictionary orders its name-value pairs lexicographically by name, whereas an unordered dictionary imposes no ordering on its pairs. Consider a client that uses an `OrderedDictionary` through its `Dictionary` supertype. When the client accesses the dictionary's pairs by index, it obtains the pairs in lexicographic order even though it expects them in no particular order. The `OrderedDictionary`'s methods for accessing name-value pairs have stronger postconditions than their counterparts in the parent class, and they satisfy the specifications of the `Dictionary` class as well as the expectations of the client.

Whenever you define a new class, use the substitution principle to ensure that it conforms to its supertypes. When you define a new class `B` that implements some method `f` specified by the supertype `A`, you may replace the method's preconditions by weaker ones and/or its postconditions by stronger ones. In other words, the preconditions for `B.f` should be no stronger than those for `A.f`, and the postconditions for `B.f` should be no weaker than those for `A.f`.

Exercises

5.24 With respect to our banking analogy, we could imagine a disagreeable situation in which *SuperBank* subcontracts your account to a *SubGreedyBank* which, without informing you, alters the terms of your saving account thus:

1". Precondition: You agree to maintain a minimum balance of $1000.

2". Postcondition: The bank promises to pay you 4% interest annually.

Why would this violate the substitution principle? Would either condition 1" or 2" alone still violate this principle?

5.25 Draw the class diagram for the counter classes presented in this chapter. Does each of these counter classes satisfy the substitution principle?

5.26 Consider the following specification for a counter class that increments by one step value and decrements by a second step value:

```
public class DoubleStepCounter
      extends NStepCounter {
```

```
    public DoubleStepCounter(int incStep,
                             int decStep)
      // EFFECTS: Initializes this counter's value
      //   to zero, and initializes the increment
      //   step to incStep and the decrement step
      //   to decStep.

    public void inc()
      // MODIFIES: this
      // EFFECTS: Increments this counter's
      //   value by incStep.

    public void dec()
      // MODIFIES: this
      // EFFECTS: Decrements this counter's
      //   value by decStep.

    public int step()
      // EFFECTS: Returns incStep.

    public int value()
      // EFFECTS: Returns this counter's value.
}
```

Would the `DoubleStepCounter` class satisfy the substitution principle? Why or why not?

ESSENTIAL 5.27 The substitution principle sometimes prevents us from using inheritance in situations where its use otherwise looks promising. For example, because a square is a kind of rectangle, we might hope to define a `SquareGeometry` class as an extension of the `RectangleGeometry` class. Our `SquareGeometry` class would have to override the `setWidth` and `setHeight` methods to ensure that sides are always of equal length. These two methods might be declared thus:

```
// methods of SquareGeometry class
public void setWidth(int newSide)
      throws IllegalArgumentException
  // MODIFIES: this
  // EFFECTS: If newSide is negative throws
  //   IllegalArgumentException; else update's
  //   this square's width
  //   and height to newSide.
```

```
public void setHeight(int newSide)
      throws IllegalArgumentException
  // MODIFIES: this
  // EFFECTS: If newSide is negative throws
  //    IllegalArgumentException; else update's
  //    this square's width
  //    and height to newSide.
```

Now consider client code that expects a `RectangleGeometry` object. Specifically, consider the following procedure for scaling the size of a rectangle `r` by the scale factor `sf`:

```
static void scale(RectangleGeometry r, int sf) {
  r.setWidth(sf * r.getWidth());
  r.setHeight(sf * r.getHeight());
}
```

The `scale` procedure works as expected when called with a `RectangleGeometry` object, but works unexpectedly when called with a `SquareGeometry` object. To see why, suppose that the `scale` procedure is used in the following code fragment where the call to the constructor `SquareGeometry` produces a square with sides of length two:

```
RectangleGeometry s = new SquareGeometry(2);
scale(s, 2);
System.out.println("width of s: " + s.getWidth());
System.out.println("height of s: " + s.getHeight());
```

What does the code fragment print? Does the call to the `scale` procedure achieve what the client expects? What is the problem? Does the `SquareGeometry` class satisfy the substitution principle?

5.6 Figures and Painters

When you think of a tangible object such as a ball, you regard its appearance as an essential part of the object. Although a red ball has the attributes *sphereness* and *redness*, when you manipulate an actual ball you treat it and all its attributes as a single entity. When you throw a red ball, you hardly expect its sphereness to fly off in one direction and its redness in another.

In this section, we will develop a `Figure` class that combines a geometry with an appearance. This will enable us to represent, say, a rectangle filled with the color blue as a single `Figure` object. We've already developed a type for representing geometries: the `Geometry` interface. In this section, we develop the `Painter` type for representing appearances. The `Figure` type joins a `Painter` and a `Geometry` (see Figure 5.11).

The `Painter` interface is defined thus:

```
public interface Painter {
  public abstract void paint(Graphics2D g2,
                             Geometry geometry);
    // REQUIRES: g2 and geometry are not null.
    // EFFECTS: Paints geometry into rendering context g2.
}
```

Painters (objects that implement the `Painter` interface) implement the `paint` operation for painting a geometry into a rendering context. In other words, painters support expressions such as this:

```
aPainter.paint(g2, aGeometry);
```

where `g2` is a `Graphics2D` object. Here, the painter `aPainter` may fill `aGeometry` with a particular paint, or stroke the geometry, or fill-and-stroke the geometry, or paint `aGeometry` in some other manner depending on how its `paint` method is implemented.

5.6.1 Figures

We will shortly develop a hierarchy of painter classes rooted in the `Painter` interface. But first I want to present the `Figure` class, which the class diagram of Figure 5.11 shows to be an aggregate whole composed of at most one `Geometry` and `Painter`.

The services of a `Figure` object are quite simple. A figure defines a *geometry* property and a *painter* property, implying that it is possible for a figure's geometry and/or appearance to change over time. In addition, a figure provides `paint` method which takes a `Graphics2D` object as input. When a figure receives a *paint* message, it responds by sending a *paint* message to its painter, passing its geometry and the `Graphics2D` object as arguments. Here is the definition of the `Figure` class:

```
public class Figure {

  protected Painter painter;
  protected Geometry geometry;
```

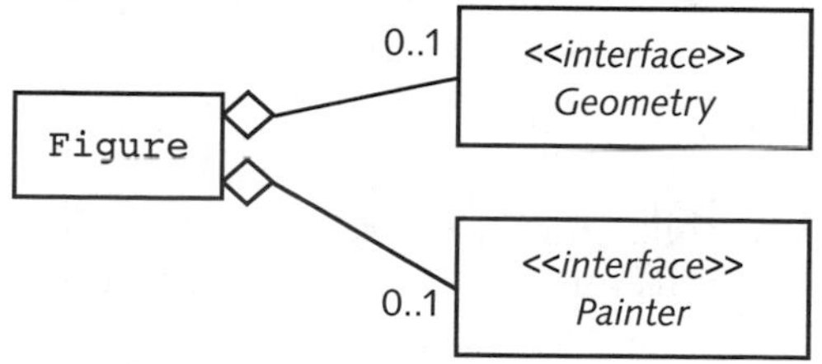

FIGURE 5.11 A figure combines a geometry and an appearance.

```
  public Figure(Geometry geometry, Painter painter) {
    this.geometry = geometry;
    this.painter = painter;
  }

  public Figure(Geometry geometry) {
    this(geometry, null);
  }

  public Figure(Painter painter) {
    this(null, painter);
  }

  public Figure() {
    this(null, null);
  }

    // painter property
  public Painter getPainter() { return painter; }

  public void setPainter(Painter painter) {
    this.painter = painter;
  }

    // geometry property
  public Geometry getGeometry() { return geometry; }

  public void setGeometry(Geometry geometry) {
    this.geometry = geometry;
  }

  public void paint(Graphics2D g2) {
    // REQUIRES: g2 is not null.
    // EFFECTS: Paints this figure's geometry into g2
    //   using this figure's painter if the geometry
    //   and painter are non-null;
    //   else does nothing.
    if ((painter != null) && (geometry != null))
      painter.paint(g2, geometry);
  }
}
```

You can paint a collection of figures by sending each figure the *paint* message in turn. For instance, the following procedure paints an array of `Figure` objects into the rendering context `g2`:

```
static void paintManyFigures(Graphics2D g2,
                             Figure[] figs) {
  for (int i = 0; i < figs.length; i++)
    figs[i].paint(g2);
}
```

Due to polymorphism, the `paintManyFigures` method works regardless of the actual type of geometry and painter each figure `figs[i]` refers to.

5.6.2 Painters for Filling and Drawing

Before we can create some figures, we need to define some concrete classes that implement the `Painter` interface, whose definition is repeated here:

```
public interface Painter {
  public abstract void paint(Graphics2D g2,
                             Geometry geometry);
   // REQUIRES: g2 and geometry are not null.
   // EFFECTS: Paints geometry into rendering context g2.
}
```

Figure 5.12 depicts the class diagram for the painter classes presented in the remainder of this chapter.

Whether a `Painter` draws an outline or fills an interior, it must first set the current `Paint`. (Recall from Section 3.4 that the `java.awt.Paint` interface describes the color pattern to be used for draw or fill operations. The `Color` class implements `Paint`.) The abstract `PaintPainter` class defines a *paint* property for use by its subclasses. Here is the class definition:

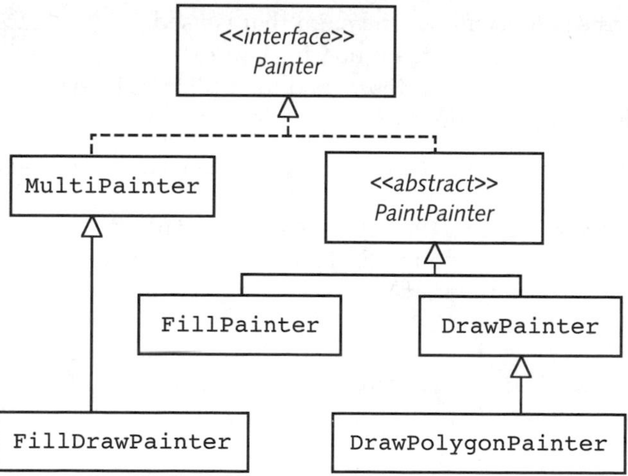

FIGURE 5.12 Subtypes of the `Painter` interface.

```
public abstract class PaintPainter implements Painter {

  protected Paint paint;

  protected static final Paint DefaultPaint = Color.white;

  protected PaintPainter(Paint paint)
            throws NullPointerException {
    setPaint(paint);
  }

  protected PaintPainter() {
    this(DefaultPaint);
  }

    // paint property
  public void setPaint(Paint newPaint)
         throws NullPointerException {
    if (newPaint == null)
      throw new NullPointerException();
    this.paint = newPaint;
  }

  public Paint getPaint() {
    return this.paint;
  }
}
```

The `FillPainter` class is used to fill the interior of a geometry. The current value of its *paint* property—inherited from the superclass `PaintPainter`—determines the paint that is used. When `FillPainter's paint` method is called with a rendering context and a geometry, it sets the rendering context's *paint* attribute, and then fills the interior of the geometry. Here is the class definition:

```
public class FillPainter extends PaintPainter {

  public FillPainter(Paint paint)
         throws NullPointerException {
    super(paint);
  }

  public FillPainter() {
    super();
  }
```

```
    public void paint(Graphics2D g2, Geometry geometry) {
      g2.setPaint(getPaint());
      g2.fill(geometry.shape());
    }
  }
```

Consider a short example of how a geometry and a painter combine to form a figure. The following procedure takes an array of point geometries and a paint. It returns a figure representing a filled polygon whose vertices are determined by the input points. The polygon is filled by the specified paint:

```
static Figure makePolygonFigure(PointGeometry[] vertices,
                                Paint paint) {
  PolygonGeometry geometry = new PolygonGeometry(vertices);
  FillPainter painter = new FillPainter(paint);
  return new Figure(geometry, painter);
}
```

Next, we'll define the `DrawPainter` class, which also extends the abstract `PaintPainter` class. The `DrawPainter` class is used to draw the outline of a geometry. The current value of its *paint* property—inherited from the superclass—determines the paint that is used. The `DrawPainter` class also has a *stroke* property whose value is the `Stroke` to be used when tracing the geometry's outline. When `DrawPainter's paint` method is called with a rendering context and a geometry, it sets the rendering context's *paint* and *stroke* attributes, and then strokes the outline of the geometry. Here is the specification for this class:

```
public class DrawPainter extends PaintPainter {

  public DrawPainter(Paint paint, Stroke stroke)
         throws NullPointerException
    // EFFECTS: If paint or stroke is null throws
    //   NullPointerException; else initializes this
    //   with the specified paint and stroke.

  public DrawPainter(Paint paint)
         throws NullPointerException
    // EFFECTS: If paint is null throws
    //   NullPointerException; else initializes this
    //   with the specified paint and default stroke
    //   (one-pixel wide).

  public DrawPainter()
    // EFFECTS: Initializes this with the default
    //   paint (white) and default stoke (1-pixel wide).
```

```
    // stroke property
  public void setStroke(Stroke newStroke)
         throws NullPointerException
    // MODIFIES: this
    // EFFECTS: If stroke is null throws
    //   NullPointerException; else sets stroke
    //   to newStroke.

  public Stroke getStroke()
    // EFFECTS: Returns the current stroke.

  public void paint(Graphics2D g2, Geometry geometry)
    // REQUIRES: g2 and geometry are not null.
    // EFFECTS: Paints geometry into rendering
    //   context g2 by drawing the outline using
    //   the current paint and stroke.
}
```

Exercises

ESSENTIAL **5.28** Implement the `DrawPainter` class.

5.29 Write a graphical application that fills a polygon in red. The program arguments fix the vertices of the polygon and are interpreted the same as those of the `PaintPolygon` program of Exercise 5.11. Here is the generic command line:

```
> java PaintPolygonWithFillPainter x0 y0 x1 y1 ...
```

Your program should represent a polygon by a `Figure` object whose geometry is a `PolygonGeometry` object and whose painter is a `FillPainter` object.

5.30 Write a graphical application that draws the outline of a polygon in blue. Your program is called like this:

```
> java PaintPolygonWithDrawPainter stroke x0 y0 x1 y1 ...
```

The first program argument is a positive integer indicating the stroke size and the remaining program arguments fix the polygon's vertices.

5.31 Revise the implementation of the `PaintManyRectangles` program (Section 4.2.6) so that it uses `Figure` objects. Specifically, instead of using an array of `RectangleGeometry` objects, the program defines an array or vector of `Figure` objects, each of which holds a rectangle geometry and a fill painter representing a random color.

5.6.3 Combining Painters

The two concrete painters presented so far, `FillPainter` and `DrawPainter`, are used to fill the interior of a geometry and to stroke the outline of a geometry, respectively. But suppose we want to both fill and stroke a given geometry? We can do this using the `MultiPainter` class. More generally, this class is used to apply *any* two painters in order.

The `MultiPainter` class has two properties, named *first painter* and *second painter*, both of which are `Painter`-valued. When a `MultiPainter` receives a *paint* message, it forwards a *paint* message first to its first painter, and then to its second painter. For example, the following procedure paints a rectangle filled with green and outlined by a blue stroke that is four pixels wide:

```
static void paintPrettyRectangle(Graphics2D g2) {
  Painter fill = new FillPainter(Color.green);
  Painter draw =
    new DrawPainter(Color.blue, new BasicStroke(4));
  Painter multiPainter = new MultiPainter(fill, draw);
  Geometry rectangle =
    new RectangleGeometry(0, 0, 100 100);
  Figure fig = new Figure(rectangle, multiPainter);
  fig.paint(g2);
}
```

The `MultiPainter` class is an aggregate class whose two components are painters (see Figure 5.13). Here is its definition:

```
public class MultiPainter implements Painter {

  protected Painter first, second;

  public MultiPainter(Painter first, Painter second)
        throws NullPointerException {
    // EFFECTS: If first or second is null throws
    //   NullPointerException; else sets the first
    //   painter and second painter.
    setFirstPainter(first);
    setSecondPainter(second);
  }
```

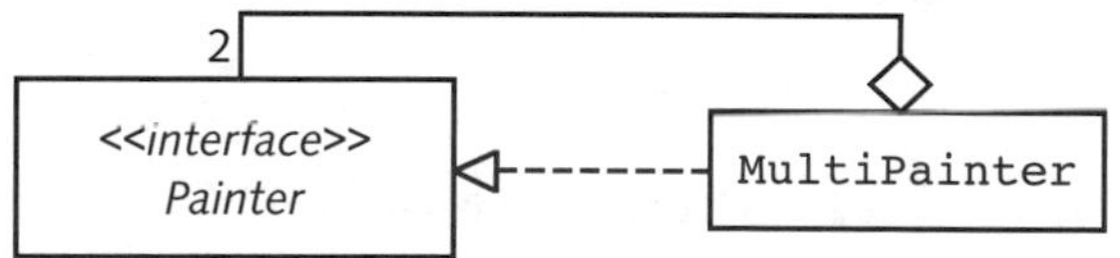

FIGURE 5.13 A `MultiPainter` is composed of two `Painters`.

```
  public void paint(Graphics2D g2, Geometry geometry) {
    // REQUIRES: g2 and geometry are not null.
    // EFFECTS: Paints geometry into rendering context
    //   g2 using the first painter followed by the
    //   second painter.
    first.paint(g2, geometry);
    second.paint(g2, geometry);
  }

  public void setFirstPainter(Painter painter)
         throws NullPointerException {
    // MODIFIES: this
    // EFFECTS: If painter is null throws
    //   NullPointerException; else sets the
    //   first painter to painter.
    if (painter == null)
      throw new NullPointerException();
    first = painter;
  }

  public Painter getFirstPainter() {
    // EFFECTS: Returns the first painter.
    return first;
  }

  public void setSecondPainter(Painter painter)
         throws NullPointerException {
    // MODIFIES: this
    // EFFECTS: If painter is null throws
    //   NullPointerException; else sets the
    //   second painter to painter.
    if (painter == null)
      throw new NullPointerException();
    second = painter;
  }

  public Painter getSecondPainter() {
    // EFFECTS: Returns the second painter.
    return second;
  }
}
```

You can use the `MultiPainter` class to combine any number of painters. To combine more than two painters, you set the second painter of a `MultiPainter` object `a` to another `MultiPainter` `b`. When object `a` receives a *paint* message, it responds by sending a *paint* message to its first painter, and then to its second painter `b`. In response, `b` sends a *paint* message to its own first painter, and then to its second painter which in turn may be yet another `MultiPainter`. In this way, you can construct a sequence of `MultiPainter` objects in which each object's second painter references the next `Multi-Painter` in the sequence. Whenever the initial `MultiPainter` is sent the *paint* message, *paint* messages cascade down the sequence of painters. For example, the following procedure fills a rectangle with green and outlines it with a 2-pixel-wide red stroke painted on top of a 4-pixel-wide blue stroke:

```
static void paintCoolRectangle(Graphics2D g2) {
  Painter fill = new FillPainter(Color.green);
  Painter drawBlue =
    new DrawPainter(Color.blue, new BasicStroke(4));
  Painter drawRed =
    new DrawPainter(Color.red, new BasicStroke(2));
  Painter multiDraw = new MultiPainter(drawBlue, drawRed);
  Painter multiPainter =
    new MultiPainter(fill, multiDraw);
  Geometry rectangle = new Rectangle(0, 0, 100 100);
  Figure fig = new Figure(rectangle, multiPainter);
  fig.paint(g2);
}
```

When the figure `fig` sends `multiPainter` a *paint* message in response to the last instruction, a *paint* message is sent first to the painter `fill` which fills the rectangle with green, and then to the painter `drawBlue` which strokes the rectangle with 4-pixel-wide blue, and lastly to the painter `drawRed` which strokes the rectangle with 2-pixel-wide red.

Exercises

5.32 In the `paintPrettyRectangle` procedure given in this subsection, suppose we were to replace the third instruction, which constructs a new `MultiPainter` object, by the following instruction:

```
Painter multiPainter = new MultiPainter(draw, fill);
```

How would this affect the resulting picture?

5.33 Write a graphical application that fills a polygon in red and outlines it in blue. Your program is called like this:

`> java PaintPolygonWithPainter` ***`stroke x0 y0 x1 y1 ...`***

where the program arguments are interpreted as in the program of Exercise 5.30. Your program should represent a polygon by a `Fig-ure` object whose geometry is a `PolygonGeometry` object and whose painter is a `MultiPainter` object.

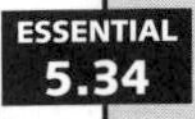

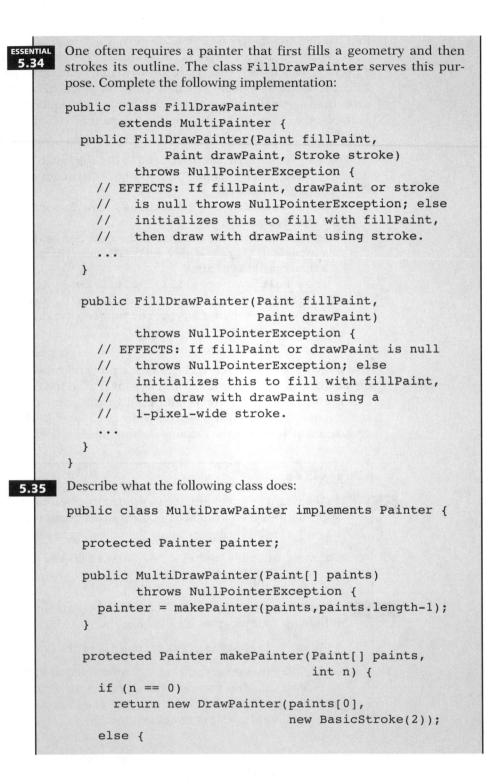

5.34 One often requires a painter that first fills a geometry and then strokes its outline. The class `FillDrawPainter` serves this purpose. Complete the following implementation:

```
public class FillDrawPainter
      extends MultiPainter {
  public FillDrawPainter(Paint fillPaint,
           Paint drawPaint, Stroke stroke)
        throws NullPointerException {
    // EFFECTS: If fillPaint, drawPaint or stroke
    //   is null throws NullPointerException; else
    //   initializes this to fill with fillPaint,
    //   then draw with drawPaint using stroke.
    ...
  }

  public FillDrawPainter(Paint fillPaint,
                         Paint drawPaint)
        throws NullPointerException {
    // EFFECTS: If fillPaint or drawPaint is null
    //   throws NullPointerException; else
    //   initializes this to fill with fillPaint,
    //   then draw with drawPaint using a
    //   1-pixel-wide stroke.
    ...
  }
}
```

5.35 Describe what the following class does:

```
public class MultiDrawPainter implements Painter {

  protected Painter painter;

  public MultiDrawPainter(Paint[] paints)
        throws NullPointerException {
    painter = makePainter(paints,paints.length-1);
  }

  protected Painter makePainter(Paint[] paints,
                                int n) {
    if (n == 0)
      return new DrawPainter(paints[0],
                             new BasicStroke(2));
    else {
```

```
      Painter second = makePainter(paints, n - 1);
      Painter first = new DrawPainter(paints[n],
                          new BasicStroke(2*(n + 1)));
      return new MultiPainter(first, second);
    }
  }

  public void paint(Graphics2D g2, Geometry geometry) {
    painter.paint(g2, geometry);
  }
}
```

Use the `MultiDrawPainter` class in an application that strokes a polygon whose vertices are given by the program arguments:

```
> java DrawPolygonWithColors x0 y0 x1 y1 ...
```

The polygon's outline should be drawn as a 2-pixel-wide yellow stroke on top of a 4-pixel-wide blue stroke on top of a 6-pixel-wide green stroke on top of an 8-pixel-wide red stroke.

5.6.4 Polygon Painters

To this point, the computer renderings of `PolygonGeometry` objects have been less than ideal in the case of one-vertex polygons (which are rendered as tiny dots) and two-vertex polygons (rendered as single line segments). We would prefer that such polygons were rendered as in the first two drawings of Figure 5.5, in which a 1-gon is drawn as a loop and a 2-gon as a pair of distinct curves corresponding to the 2-gon's two edges. The `DrawPolygonPainter` class is designed to draw polygons in this manner. The expression

```
aDrawPolygonPainter.paint(g2, aPolygonGeometry)
```

draws the polygon `aPolygonGeometry` into the rendering context `g2` in this preferred manner.

The `DrawPolygonPainter` class extends the `DrawPainter` class. Its constructors behave like those of `DrawPainter` and are defined as follows:

```
public DrawPolygonPainter(Paint paint, Stroke stroke)
       throws NullPointerException {
  super(paint, stroke);
}

public DrawPolygonPainter(Paint paint)
       throws NullPointerException {
  super(paint);
}
```

```
public DrawPolygonPainter() {
  super();
}
```

The implementation of `DrawPolygonPainter's` `paint` method is similar to that of its parent's `paint` method: both methods set the paint and the stroke, and then draw the geometry's shape. The only difference occurs when the geometry to be drawn is a `PolygonGeometry`. In this case, `DrawPolygonPainter's` `paint` method constructs its own shape for the polygon using its protected `polygonShape` method. The `paint` method is defined thus:

```
// method of DrawPolygonPainter class
public void paint(Graphics2D g2, Geometry geometry) {
  g2.setPaint(getPaint());
  g2.setStroke(getStroke());
  if (geometry instanceof PolygonGeometry)
    g2.draw(polygonShape((PolygonGeometry)geometry));
  else
    g2.draw(geometry.shape());
}
```

The task of producing a revised shape for the polygon falls to the `polygonShape` method. This method defines three constants that control the dimensions of the curves drawn in the cases of 1-gons and 2-gons:

```
// constants of DrawPolygonPainter class
  // 1-gon case: controls length of loop:
  //   larger values produce longer loops.
protected static final int LoopExtent = 40;
  // 1-gon case: ratio of the loop's width to height
protected static final float LoopScale = 0.5f;
  // 2-gon case: ratio of the loop's width to length
protected static final float TwoEdgeScale = 0.25f;
```

The `polygonShape` method's task is easy if the input polygon contains at least three vertices: it delegates the task of constructing a shape to the polygon itself. Alternatively, if the input polygon contains fewer than three vertices, the `polygonShape` method constructs the shape itself out of curves. Here is the method's definition:

```
// method of DrawPolygonPainter class
protected Shape polygonShape(PolygonGeometry poly) {
  if (poly.nbrVertices() > 2)
    return poly.shape();
  else {
    GeneralPath path = new GeneralPath();
    PointGeometry v = poly.getVertex(0);
    path.moveTo(v.getX(), v.getY());
```

```
    if (poly.nbrVertices() == 1) {  // poly is a 1-gon
      TransformablePointGeometry p =
        new TransformablePointGeometry(v);
      TransformablePointGeometry q =
        new TransformablePointGeometry(p);
      p.translate(LoopExtent,(int)(LoopExtent*LoopScale));
      q.translate(LoopExtent,(int)(-LoopExtent*LoopScale));
      path.curveTo(p.getX(), p.getY(), q.getX(), q.getY(),
                   v.getX(), v.getY());
    } else {  // poly is a 2-gon
      PointGeometry v0 = poly.getVertex(0);
      PointGeometry v1 = poly.getVertex(1);
      int mX = (v1.getX() + v0.getX()) / 2;
      int mY = (v1.getY() + v0.getY()) / 2;
      TransformablePointGeometry m =
        new TransformablePointGeometry(mX, mY);
      int nX = (int)(-m.getY() * TwoEdgeScale);
      int nY = (int)(m.getX() * TwoEdgeScale);
      PointGeometry normal = new PointGeometry(nX, nY);
      m.translate(normal.getX(), normal.getY());
      path.quadTo(m.getX(),m.getY(),v1.getX(),v1.getY());
      m.translate(-2*normal.getX(), -2*normal.getY());
      path.quadTo(m.getX(),m.getY(),v0.getX(),v0.getY());
    }
    return path;
  }
}
```

In the case of one-vertex polygons, the `polygonShape` method constructs a shape consisting of a single looping curve. The two control points `p` and `q` guide the curve. The `curveTo` method, which adds a cubic curve to the path, takes as input the coordinates of the two control points `p` and `q` followed by those of the curve's terminating endpoint. In this case, the last two arguments guide the curve back to the polygon's sole vertex, resulting in a loop.

In the case of two-vertex polygons, the `polygonShape` method constructs a shape consisting of two curves. To do so, it creates two control points, one on either side of the straight line segment that connects the polygon's two vertices. Each of the two calls to the `quadTo` method adds to the path a quadratic curve guided by one of the two control points.

Exercises

5.36 Revise the `PaintPolygonWithPainter` program of Exercise 5.33 so that it draws 1-gons and 2-gons using curves as described in this section (if the polygon contains more than two vertices, it's rendered as a filled and stroked polygon).

5.37 Revise your `DrawPolygonWithColors` program of Exercise 5.35 so that it draws 1-gons and 2-gons using curves as described in this section. [Hint: Define a subclass of the `MultiDrawPainter` class that constructs a `MultiPainter` representing a sequence of `DrawPolygonPainter` objects.]

5.38 This exercise asks you to develop a command-driven program for painting and editing rectangular figures (those with a rectangle or an ellipse geometry). The graphics in the frame depict the current set of figures. The user assigns each figure a unique name at the time of its construction and refers to figures by name. The program maintains three properties: the *current dimensions,* the *current color*, and the *current figure*. The user creates and names a new rectangle with a single command:

```
new name rectangle
```

where *name* becomes the figure's name. The new rectangle *name* is initialized with the current dimensions (position, width, and height) and filled with the current color. A new ellipse is created and named similarly:

```
new name ellipse
```

The properties of existing figures can be modified. To do so, you first set the program's current dimensions and current color properties to the desired values. For instance, the commands

```
color 0 255 255
dimensions 100 120 50 25
```

set the current color to cyan (green plus blue) and the current dimensions to the position (100,120), width 50, and height 25. Next, you select the figure to be modified by name:

```
select name
```

Lastly, you apply the current settings to the selected figure using the no-argument *apply* command:

```
apply
```

Initially, the current color is white, the current figure is null, and the current dimensions consist of the position (0,0), width 100, and height 100. The program supports the following commands:

- **dimensions *x y width height***—sets the current dimensions to the position (*x*,*y*) and specified *width* and *height*.

- **color *red green blue***—updates the current color to the specified integer color components, where 0 ≤ *red, green, blue* ≤ 255.
- **new *id* [rectangle | ellipse]**—creates a new figure with the current dimensions and color, and assigns it the name *id*. The second argument determines whether the figure is a rectangle or an ellipse. If a figure named by *id* already exists, that figure is replaced by the new figure. The new figure becomes the current figure.
- **select *id***—makes the figure named by *id* the current figure. If no figure is named by *id*, the current figure is null.
- **apply**—applies the current dimensions and color settings to the current figure, or does nothing if the current figure is null.
- **delete**—deletes the current figure and sets the current figure to null, or does nothing if the current figure is null.
- **print**—prints (a) the current dimensions, (b) the current color, (c) the name of the current figure (if any), and (d) the names of all figures.
- **quit**—quits the application.

In response to every command, the frame is updated to display the current set of figures. The current figure (if any) is highlighted: it is filled with its color, and its outline is drawn with a two-color stroke consisting of a 2-pixel-wide red stroke on top of a 4-pixel-wide white stroke. The remaining figures are simply filled with their respective colors.

In the following sample interaction, comments show the effects of each command:

```
> java PlayRectangularFigures
? color 255 0 0        // sets current color to red
? new a rectangle      // creates red rectangle a:(0,0),100,100
? dimensions 100 120 50 60  // sets dimensions to (100,120),50,60
? color 0 0 255        // sets current color to blue
? new b ellipse        // creates blue ellipse b:(100,120),50,60
? print
dimensions: (100,120),50,60
color: 0,0,255
current figure: b
figures: a b
? color 255 255 0      // sets current color to yellow
? dimensions 40 40 20 30  // sets dimensions to (40,40),20,30
? select a             // makes a the current figure
```

```
? apply                 // changes the color of a to yellow and
                        // the dimensions of a to (40,40),20,30
? quit
```

Summary

Like composition, inheritance is a key mechanism for software reuse. When a new class is defined using inheritance, it acquires the fields and methods of an existing class, known as its superclass or parent class. The new class is called a subclass or child class of its parent class. A child class may in turn serve as the parent class of any number of other classes (its subclasses), resulting in an inheritance hierarchy of classes. The root class of an inheritance hierarchy serves as a supertype for its descendants (its proper subtypes). Similarly, an interface serves as a supertype for the classes that implement it and the interfaces that extend it.

At its most basic, an instance of a class *is a kind of* whatever concept its parent class represents (for example, a waiter is a kind of employee). However, inheritance is a versatile mechanism which can serve several purposes:

- **Inheritance for extension:** A subclass defines new fields and methods that supplement those it inherits.
- **Inheritance for specialization:** A subclass overrides one or more of the methods belonging to its superclass.
- **Inheritance for specification:** A subclass implements one or more methods that are specified but not implemented by its (abstract) superclass. A class can also implement any number of methods specified by the interface(s) that the class implements.

A class is concrete if it implements every abstract method specified by its supertypes; otherwise the class is abstract. Concrete classes can be instantiated whereas abstract classes exist only to be subclassed. Both classes and interfaces specify an interface, but they differ with respect to implementation: A concrete class provides a full implementation, an abstract class provides a partial implementation, and an interface provides no implementation. A class extends exactly one class—its parent class—but can implement any number of interfaces.

Under polymorphism, an object can be used wherever one of its supertypes is expected. The supertype determines the interface, but the object's actual type determines its behavior. The substitution principle states that clients can use subtype objects wherever a supertype is expected without affecting their own correctness. A class satisfies this principle if it conforms to the specifications of its supertypes.

CHAPTER

6

Design Patterns

We've seen throughout this book that software reuse is one of the benefits of object orientation. So far we've focused on two key forms of reuse—composition and inheritance—which support the reuse of individual classes. In this chapter we explore a form of reuse that describes *arrangements* of classes and objects and the relationships and collaborations between them. Such arrangements are known as **design patterns.** In this chapter we consider why design patterns are useful, and examine in some detail three specific patterns—the iterator, template method, and composite design patterns. Lastly, we locate these three patterns, and several others, within an accepted scheme for classifying design patterns.

6.1 The Need for Design Patterns

Design patterns are useful for solving recurring software design problems. They address the recognition that problems that have been solved in the past should not need to be solved from scratch each time they reappear. Rather, it should be possible to reuse a solution that has worked before. A design pattern describes both a generic problem and a design solution to the problem. The solution is *flexible* in that it is reusable in different contexts and accommodates the various forms that the problem it solves may assume.

Design patterns serve several purposes. When a software developer encounters a problem, she can try to match the problem to a known design pattern; if she succeeds, she can apply the matching design pattern directly with an understanding of its use and ramifications. She can also use the design patterns to document her system so that others can more readily grasp her system's design and intent. Developers can study design patterns to enhance their design skills and to gain familiarity with proven solutions. Moreover, because design patterns and their main elements are named, they provide a shared terminology that developers can use to think about and discuss design issues.

The usefulness of a design pattern depends largely on how well it is described. Any description of a design pattern must be abstract enough to convey the full generality of the problem it solves. Yet, the description must also be concrete enough to instruct how to apply the design pattern in practice. A format for describing design patterns is advanced by *Design Patterns: Elements of Reusable Object-Oriented Software,* by Gamma, Helm, Johnson, and Vlissides, one of the first books to catalog design patterns systematically. This book identifies four essential elements of any design pattern description:

- The **pattern name** identifies the pattern. The name describes the design pattern and extends the pattern vocabulary.
- The **problem** describes when the pattern can be applied.
- The **solution** describes and names the elements—classes, interfaces, objects, and methods—that make up the design solution. It also describes each element's responsibilities and the relationships and collaborations among elements. The solution is described both in general terms and through concrete examples.
- The **consequences** present the results and tradeoffs of using the pattern, which helps you decide the best solution when there are several promising alternatives.

Sections 6.2 through 6.4 explore three design patterns chosen for both their general usefulness and their specific applicability to our graphics theme. The **iterator pattern** is used to access the elements of an aggregate—such as a vector, list, or polygon—without exposing the aggregate's interface or internal structure. The **template method pattern** is used to implement an algorithm, some of whose steps can vary from one use to the next. The **composite pattern** is used to create hierarchies of objects representing complex objects composed of simpler parts. Section 6.5 describes four additional design patterns. It should be understood that these are but a few of the scores of established design patterns (the book *Design Patterns* alone describes 23 fundamental patterns).

6.2 The Iterator Design Pattern

The iterator design pattern is used to access the elements of an aggregate—a structured group of elements such as a vector, list, dictionary, or polygon—without exposing the aggregate's interface or internal structure. An **iterator** object presents a set of operations for visiting an aggregate's elements in order (often referred to as **traversing** the aggregate). It also keeps track of its current position in the traversal, known as the iterator's **traversal state.** For example, an iterator for lists might provide access to the list's elements in first-to-last order while keeping track of the element visited most recently. A list iterator provides an operation for visiting the next element in the list if the last element has not yet been reached and an operation for testing whether the last element has been reached.

The iterator pattern takes the responsibility for access and traversal out of the aggregate object and places it into iterator objects. By using iterators, clients are freed from dealing with the complexity of the aggregate object's interface and instead use the simpler interface of an iterator whose purpose is limited to element access. Iterators support **control abstraction,** which abstracts the operations for controlling access to an aggregate's elements.

In this section, we first look at the example of this design pattern provided by Java's `Iterator` interface. Then, we'll develop our own version of an iterator for traversing and modifying polygons.

6.2.1 Java's `Iterator` Interface

Consider the following procedure for printing the elements of a vector:

```
static void printVector(Vector a) {
  for (int i = 0; i < a.size(); i++) {
    Object obj = a.get(i);
    System.out.print(obj + " ");
  }
}
```

A procedure for printing the elements of an array could employ the same control logic used by `printVector`. The two procedures would differ only in that arrays and vectors are accessed differently. We might implement a `printArray` procedure like this:

```
static void printArray(Object[] a) {
  for (int i = 0; i < a.length; i++) {
    Object obj = a[i];
    System.out.print(obj + " ");
  }
}
```

The `printVector` and `printArray` procedures differ with respect to the syntax used to access elements. Yet, the two procedures employ the same control logic: While the collection `a` contains a next element, obtain this next element from `a` and print it. Indeed, this same control logic could be used to print the elements of *any* type of collection object.

Control abstraction captures the control logic for iterating through the elements of a collection while hiding the details that vary from one type of collection to the next. Control abstraction is supported through the use of an object known as an **iterator**. The `java.util` package includes several interfaces for iterators, but we will presently concentrate on the `java.util.Iterator` interface:

```
public interface Iterator {
  public boolean hasNext();
    // EFFECTS: Returns true if this iterator has more
    //   elements; else returns false.

  public Object next() throws NoSuchElementException;
    // MODIFIES: this
    // EFFECTS: If the iterator has no more elements
    //   throws NoSuchElementException; else returns
    //   the next element.

  public void remove()
         throws UnsupportedOperationException,
                IllegalStateException;
    // MODIFIES: this, and the underlying collection
    // EFFECTS: If remove is not supported throws
    //   UnsupportedOperationException; else if next
    //   has not yet been called or remove has been
    //   called since the last call to next throws
    //   IllegalStateException; else removes the last
    //   element returned by this iterator.
}
```

An `Iterator` object is associated with an **underlying collection,** such as a vector, which it traverses. The `next` method visits and returns the next element in the underlying collection. The `hasNext` method returns `true` if the underlying collection contains more elements not yet visited by the `next` method. The `next` method is typically called only if there remain elements that have not yet been visited. Idiomatically, the `hasNext` and `next` methods are used together like this:

```
while (iter.hasNext())
  doSomething(iter.next());
```

where `iter` implements the `Iterator` interface.

You can obtain an `Iterator` object for a vector by calling the vector's `iterator` method. Where `v` is a `Vector` object, the expression

```
Iterator iter = v.iterator();
```

captures an iterator for `v`. This works because the `Vector` class implements the `java.util.Collection` interface whose specification includes an `iterator` method for acquiring an iterator. Indeed, where `aCollection` is any object that implements the `Collection` interface, the expression

```
aCollection.iterator()
```

returns an `Iterator` object for `aCollection`.

Because it is possible to obtain an iterator for any collection, we can devise a procedure that uses the control logic of the `printVector` procedure, yet which is capable of printing the elements of *any* object implementing the `Collection` interface (including `Vectors`). To print the elements in a collection, first acquire an iterator for the collection, and then use the iterator's `hasNext` and `next` methods to obtain and print each element in turn. Here is the resulting procedure:

```
static void printCollection(Collection c) {
  Iterator iter = c.iterator();
  while (iter.hasNext())
    System.out.print(iter.next() + " ");
}
```

You can use the `printCollection` procedure to print the elements in a `Vector` object `v` like this:

```
printCollection(v);
```

The situation is slightly more complicated for arrays because arrays do not implement the `Collection` interface. However, it is possible to view an array as a `List`, which *does* implement the `Collection` interface. Thus the following expression prints the elements of an array `a`:

```
printCollection(Arrays.asList(a));
```

As an aside, the `remove` method specified by the `Iterator` interface is used to remove from the underlying collection the last element visited by `next`. The `remove` operation is often not supported in practice, and when called in such cases it simply throws an exception.

Exercise

6.1 The printCollection procedure enables us to print the elements in any collection, but suppose that we want to apply some other operation to the elements. It would then be necessary to write a different procedure for applying this new operation. For instance, given a collection of Figures, we might want to paint every figure into a given rendering context. We could do this with the following procedure:

```
static void paintCollection(Graphics2D g2, Collection c) {
  Iterator iter = c.iterator();
  while (iter.hasNext()) {
    Figure fig = (Figure)iter.next();
    fig.paint(g2);
  }
}
```

It should be apparent that the paintCollection and printCollection procedures employ the same control logic and differ only with respect to the operation that gets applied to each element of the collection.

An elegant way to decouple control logic from the operation it applies is to represent the operation as an object. An object that represents an operation is known as a **functor**. A functor can be passed to the procedure that implements the control logic, which in turn applies the operation that the functor represents. By defining different functors, the control logic can be reused with different operations. In the following procedure, mapCollection, the first argument map takes a functor that defines a method f representing the desired operation:

```
static void mapCollection(Functor map, Collection c) {
  Iterator iter = c.iterator();
  while (iter.hasNext())
    map.f(iter.next());
}
```

The mapCollection procedure applies the operation map.f to each element in collection c. Here, Functor is an interface that promises an operation f that may perform any action on its input:

```
public interface Functor {
  public void f(Object obj);
    // MODIFIES: anything
    // EFFECTS: Any.
}
```

To use the `mapCollection` procedure, you first define a class that implements the `Functor` interface. Your class' implementation of the method `f` determines the operation that gets applied to the elements in a collection. For example, for printing the elements in a collection, we can define the following functor class:

```
public class PrintFunctor implements Functor {
  public void f(Object obj) {
    System.out.print(obj + " ");
  }
}
```

We can then print the elements in a `Collection` object `c` using the following instruction:

```
mapCollection(new PrintFunctor(), c);
```

As another example, we can define the following functor class for painting a collection of `Figure` objects into a given rendering context:

```
public class PaintFunctor implements Functor {
  protected Graphics2D g2;

  public PaintFunctor(Graphics2D g2) {
    this.g2 = g2;
  }

  public void f(Object obj) {
    Figure fig = (Figure)obj;
    fig.paint(g2);
  }
}
```

We can then use the following instruction to paint a collection `figs` of `Figure` objects into the rendering context `g2`:

```
mapCollection(new PaintFunctor(g2), figs);
```

(a) Revise the `paintComponent` method of the `PaintManyRectangles` class you wrote for Exercise 5.31 so that it uses a `PaintFunctor` to paint its collection of rectangle figures.

(b) Define a functor class `AttachPainterFunctor` for attaching a given `Painter` object to every element in a collection of `Figure` objects. The `AttachPainterFunctor` constructor is called with any object that implements the `Painter` interface. The following expression attaches the painter `aPainter` to every `Figure` in the collection `figs`:

```
mapCollection(new AttachPainterFunctor(aPainter),
              figs);
```

(c) Define a functor class `TranslateFunctor` for translating every `Geometry` in a collection by `dx` units along the *x* axis and `dy` units along the *y* axis. The `TranslateFunctor` constructor is called with the values of `dx` and `dy`. Here is an example in which the collection `geometries` initially contains the `PointGeometry` objects (1,2) and (4,5), which are then translated by *dx*=6 and *dy*=−2:

```
mapCollection(new PrintFunctor(), geometries);
  // (1,2) (4,5)
mapCollection(new TranslateFunctor(6,-2),geometries);
mapCollection(new PrintFunctor(), geometries);
  // (7,0) (10,3)
```

6.2.2 Dynamic Polygons

The polygons we've been working with up to now—instances of the `PolygonGeometry` class—are static in the sense that they are fixed at the time of construction. In contrast, *dynamic* polygons provide operations for inserting new vertices and deleting existing vertices, and for moving existing vertices to new positions. Under the design presented in the current section, dynamic polygons are accessed and modified through iterators. To use a dynamic polygon, a client acquires an iterator for the polygon, and then manipulates the polygon using the iterator's operations.

The `PolygonIterator` interface specifies the operations promised by a polygon iterator; clients use a polygon iterator through this interface. The `PolygonIterator` interface is implemented by the `DynamicPolygonIterator` class. We will define `PolygonIterator` and `DynamicPolygonIterator` later in this section. Figure 6.1 shows that a dynamic polygon iterator owns one dynamic polygon geometry—the iterator operates on its underlying polygon, much as a collection iterator operates on its underlying collection. Figure 6.1 also indicates that any number of polygon iterators may operate on the same underlying polygon.

Figure 6.1 also suggests the structure of a dynamic polygon. A dynamic polygon is composed of one or more `Vertex` objects, ordered as they occur along the polygon. In turn, a `Vertex` object defines a field for its position in the plane (a `PointGeometry` object) and two fields for its successor and predecessor within the polygon (`Vertex` objects). I'll elaborate on this design as we go.

We'll proceed by first describing the behavior of dynamic polygons. Next, we'll implement the `DynamicPolygonGeometry` class and the `Vertex` class on which it depends. Lastly, we'll consider the behavior and implementation of polygon iterators.

The Behavior of Dynamic Polygons

The interface presented by dynamic polygons is different from that presented by static polygons (of the `PolygonGeometry` class) in two key ways. First, whereas static polygons provide operations for accessing a polygon's vertices and edges by index, a dynamic polygon provides an operation for obtaining an iterator. A dynamic polygon is manipulated by its clients by means of iterators. Second, dynamic polygons provide a protected method for inserting new vertices (`insertAfterVertex`) and for deleting existing vertices (`removeVertex`). Both methods belong to the polygon's protected interface and are intended to facilitate implementation of `PolygonIterator` subtypes (clients in general cannot access these two methods). Here is the skeleton for the `DynamicPolygonGeometry` class:

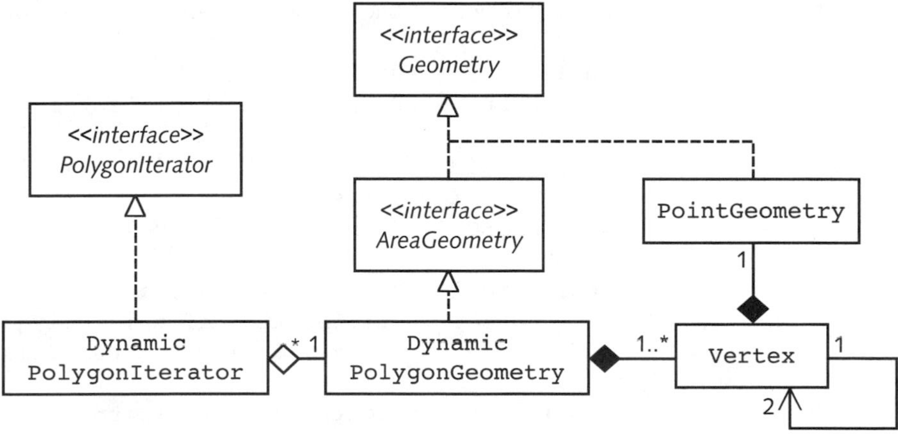

FIGURE 6.1 A dynamic polygon is composed of one or more vertices, and a vertex references a point (its position) and two vertices (its successor and predecessor).

```
public class DynamicPolygonGeometry
      implements AreaGeometry {

  public DynamicPolygonGeometry(PointGeometry p)
        throws NullPointerException
    // EFFECTS: If p is null throws NullPointerException;
    //   else constructs a one-vertex polygon positioned
    //   at p.

  public DynamicPolygonGeometry(PointGeometry[] points)
   throws NullPointerException, ZeroArraySizeException
    // EFFECTS: If points is null or points[i] is null
    //   for some legal i throws NullPointException;
    //   else if points has length zero throws
    //   ZeroArraySizeException; else creates a polygon
    //   whose vertex sequence is given by points.

  public int nbrVertices()
    // EFFECTS: Returns the number of vertices in
    //   this polygon.

  public PolygonIterator iterator()
    // EFFECTS: Returns a new iterator for this polygon.

  public String toString()
    // EFFECTS: Returns "Polygon: v0, v1, ... vn-1"
    //   where each vi describes vertex i.

  //
  // implements the Geometry and AreaGeometry interfaces
  //
  public Shape shape()
    // EFFECTS: Returns the shape of this polygon.

  public void translate(int dx, int dy)
    // MODIFIES: this
    // EFFECTS: Translates this polygon by dx and dy.

  public boolean contains(int x, int y)
    // EFFECTS: Returns true if this polygon contains
    //   the point (x,y); else returns false.

  public boolean contains(PointGeometry p)
        throws NullPointerException
    // EFFECTS: If p is null throws NullPointerException;
    //   else returns true if this polygon contains p;
    //   else returns false.
```

```
    protected Vertex vertex()
      // EFFECTS: Returns some vertex in this polygon.

    protected Vertex insertAfterVertex(Vertex v,
                                       PointGeometry p)
      // REQUIRES: v and p are not null, and v belongs
      //   to this polygon.
      // MODIFIES: this
      // EFFECTS: Inserts a new vertex w after v at
      //   position p, and returns the new vertex w.

    protected void removeVertex(Vertex v)
      // REQUIRES: v is not null, v belongs to this
      //   polygon, and this polygon contains at least one
      //   other vertex besides v.
      // MODIFIES: this
      // EFFECTS: Removes vertex v from this polygon.
  }
```

The most interesting part of the `DynamicPolygonGeometry` class is its protected interface, whose use will be discussed when we cover polygon iterators later in this section. For now, we'll content ourselves with a short procedure that uses the protected interface to build a polygon. The `buildPolygon` procedure is called with an array of n>0 points that position the vertices of a new n–gon that it builds and returns:

```
static DynamicPolygonGeometry
      buildPolygon(PointGeometry[] points) {
  DynamicPolygonGeometry poly =
    new DynamicPolygonGeometry(points[0]);
  Vertex v = poly.vertex();
  for (int i = 1; i < points.length; i++)
    v = poly.insertAfterVertex(v, points[i]);
  return poly;
}
```

For example, the code fragment:

```
PointGeometry[] points = { new PointGeometry(5, 5),
                           new PointGeometry(20, 5),
                           new PointGeometry(10, 15)
                         };
DynamicPolygonGeometry poly = buildPolygon(points);
```

produces a polygon with vertices at (5,5), (20,5), and (10,15) in the forward sense of rotation (that is, (5,5) precedes (20,5), and (20,5) precedes (10,15)). Note that the `buildPolygon` procedure could be implemented more directly using `DynamicPolygonGeometry`'s second constructor, but the purpose of this brief example is to illustrate the behavior of the class' protected interface.

Exercise

6.2 Rewrite the implementation of the `buildPolygon` procedure using `DynamicPolygonGeometry`'s second constructor.

The Vertex Class

Let's proceed with the next step in our implementation: understanding how a dynamic polygon is represented. In our chosen storage structure, a polygon is composed of `Vertex` objects, one for each of the polygon's vertices. The `Vertex` objects are linked by references as they appear along the polygon—each `Vertex` links to the next vertex (its successor) and to the previous vertex (its predecessor), making it possible to traverse a polygon's chain of vertices in both forward and backward senses of rotation. A `Vertex` also stores a `PointGeometry` object that locates the vertex in the plane.

The `DynamicPolygonGeometry` class defines two fields: its `vertex` field refers to any one of the polygon's vertices, and its integer `nbrVertices` field indicates the total number of vertices in the polygon. It is helpful to picture the storage structure used to represent a nontrivial dynamic polygon. Figure 6.2 shows the storage structure for the polygon `poly`, constructed thus:

```
PointsGeometry[] points = { new PointGeometry(5, 5),
                            new PointGeometry(20, 5),
                            new PointGeometry(10, 15)
                          };
DynamicPolygonGeometry poly = buildPolygon(points);
```

In Figure 6.2, arrows stand for references—an arrow originates in the field where the reference is stored and points to the object it references. It is noteworthy that the storage structure does not specify *which* vertex a `DynamicPolygonGeometry` object references; it may reference any one of

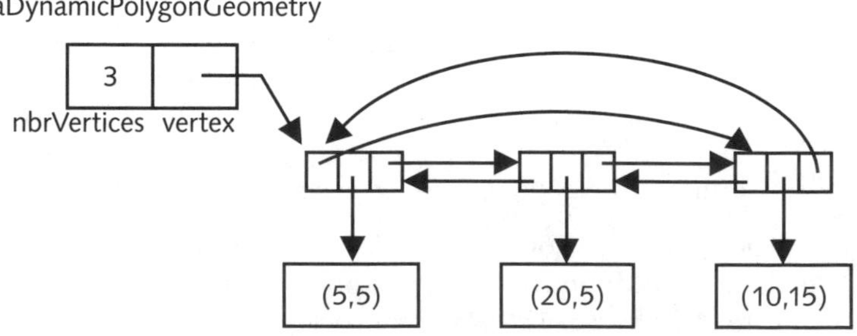

FIGURE 6.2 The representation for a dynamic polygon.

its vertices. Also of note is the fact that in the storage structure for a one-vertex polygon, a single `Vertex` object is linked twice to itself—the vertex both follows and precedes itself in the polygon. Here is the specification for the `Vertex` class:

```
class Vertex {
  protected Vertex(PointGeometry p)
    // REQUIRES: p is not null.
    // EFFECTS: Initializes this vertex at location p,
    //   and makes it its own successor and predecessor.

  protected PointGeometry point()
    // EFFECTS: Returns a reference
    //   to this vertex's position.

  protected Vertex next()
    // EFFECTS: Returns a reference to
    //   this vertex's successor.

  protected Vertex prev()
    // EFFECTS: Returns a reference
    //   to this vertex's predecessor.

  protected Vertex insertAfter(PointGeometry p)
    // REQUIRES: p is not null.
    // MODIFIES: this
    // EFFECTS: Constructs a new vertex v at position p,
    //   makes v this vertex's successor and returns v.

  protected void remove()
    // MODIFIES: this
    // EFFECTS: Removes this vertex, and makes this
    //   vertex's successor the successor of this
    //   vertex's predecessor.

  public String toString()
    // EFFECTS: Returns a string-descriptor for this
    //   vertex, indicating its position.
}
```

Our implementation of the `Vertex` class represents a vertex by these three fields:

```
// fields of Vertex class
 // position of this vertex
protected PointGeometry point;
 // next and previous vertices
protected Vertex next, prev;
```

The `Vertex` class provides a one-argument constructor which makes the new vertex its own successor and predecessor:

```
protected Vertex(PointGeometry point) {
  this.point = point;
  this.next = this;
  this.prev = this;
}
```

A vertex provides access to its position (a point), and to its successor and predecessor:

```
// methods of Vertex class
protected PointGeometry point() {
  return this.point;
}

protected Vertex next() {
  return this.next;
}

protected Vertex prev() {
  return this.prev;
}
```

The string-descriptor for a vertex is the same as the string-descriptor for its position:

```
// method of Vertex class
public String toString() {
  return point.toString();
}
```

Figure 6.3 illustrates the effects of calling the `insertAfter` and `remove` methods on a chain of vertices. Where the variable `a` references a vertex, the instruction

```
Vertex b = a.insertAfter(anyPoint);
```

transforms configuration *L* to configuration *R*. The variable `b` references the new vertex positioned at `anyPoint`. If we were then to execute the instruction

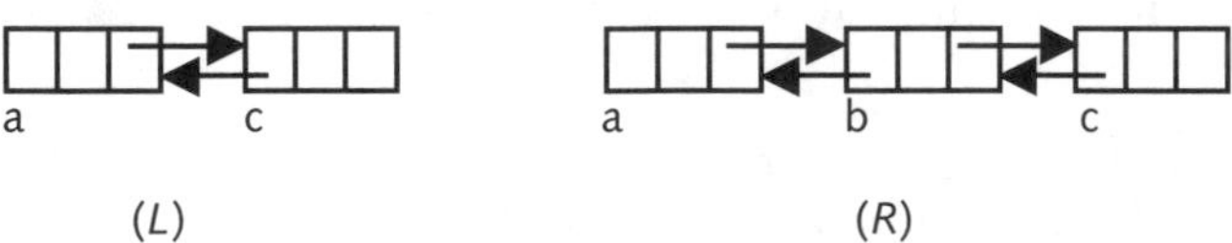

FIGURE 6.3 Given *L*, `a.insertAfter (aPoint)` yields *R*; given *R*, `b.remove ()` yields *L*.

```
b.remove();
```

the vertex b would be removed and the chain of vertices restored to configuration *L*.

The insertAfter method constructs a new vertex newV at the position indicated by the input point, and then inserts newV after this vertex. To link the new vertex into the chain, it is necessary to set newV's two link fields, and to update the next field of newV's predecessor (i.e., this vertex) and the prev field of its successor. Here is the method definition:

```
// method of Vertex class
protected Vertex insertAfter(PointGeometry p) {
  Vertex newV = new Vertex(new PointGeometry(p));
  Vertex prev = this;
  Vertex next = this.next();
    // link newV into the chain of vertices
  newV.prev = prev;
  newV.next = next;
  prev.next = next.prev = newV;
  return newV;
}
```

I will leave the implementation of the Vertex.remove method as an exercise.

Exercises

6.3 Why is the class Vertex's toString declared public? What error message does the Java compiler produce if toString is declared protected?

6.4 Draw the storage structure for the dynamic polygon poly as each of the following instructions are executed in turn:

```
DynamicPolygonGeometry poly =
  new DynamicPolygon(new PointGeometry(4, 5));
Vertex v = poly.vertex();
poly.insertAfterVertex(v, new PointGeometry(8, 9));
v = poly.insertAfterVertex(v,new PointGeometry(6,7));
v = v.next();
poly.removeVertex(v);
```

ESSENTIAL 6.5 Implement the Vertex.remove method.

Implementing Dynamic Polygons

We now have the machinery to implement our `DynamicPolygonGeometry` class, whose skeleton was given at the beginning of Section 6.2.2. A dynamic polygon contains two instance fields: The `vertex` field holds a reference to some `Vertex` in the polygon's vertex chain, and the `nbrVertices` field stores the number of vertices. Here is a mostly complete class definition:

```
public class DynamicPolygonGeometry
       implements AreaGeometry {

  protected Vertex vertex;
  protected int nbrVertices;

  public DynamicPolygonGeometry(PointGeometry point)
         throws NullPointerException {
    vertex = new Vertex(point);
    nbrVertices = 1;
  }

  public DynamicPolygonGeometry(PointGeometry[] points)
   throws NullPointerException, ZeroArraySizeException {
    if (points.length == 0)
      throw new ZeroArraySizeException();
    this.vertex = new Vertex(points[0]);
    this.nbrVertices = 1;
    Vertex v = this.vertex;
    for (int i = 1; i < points.length; i++)
      v = insertAfterVertex(v, points[i]);
  }

  public int nbrVertices() {
    return this.nbrVertices;
  }

  public PolygonIterator iterator() {
    return new DynamicPolygonIterator(this);
  }

  protected String toString() {
    return "dynamic polygon: " + verticesToString();
  }

  public Shape shape() {
    GeneralPath path = new GeneralPath();
    Vertex v = vertex();
    path.moveTo(v.point().getX(), v.point().getY());
```

```
    for (int i = 0; i < nbrVertices() - 1; i++) {
      v = v.next();
      path.lineTo(v.point().getX(),v.point().getY());
    }
    path.closePath();
    return path;
  }

  public void translate(int dx, int dy) {
    ...
  }

  public boolean contains(int x, int y) {
    return shape().intersects(x-0.01,y-0.01,.02,.02);
  }

  public boolean contains(PointGeometry p) {
    return contains(p.getX(), p.getY());
  }

  protected Vertex vertex() {
    return this.vertex;
  }

  protected Vertex insertAfterVertex(Vertex v,
                        PointGeometry newPoint) {
    ...
  }

  protected void removeVertex(Vertex v) {
    if (v == this.vertex)
      this.vertex = v.next();
    v.remove();
    —nbrVertices;
  }

  protected String verticesToString() {
    String res = "";
    Vertex v = vertex();
    for (int i = 0; i < nbrVertices - 1; i++) {
      res += v + ",";
      v = v.next();
    }
    res += v;
    return res;
  }
}
```

Observe that the DynamicPolygon.iterator method returns an instance of the DynamicPolygonIterator class. We will define this class in the next subsection.

Exercise

ESSENTIAL 6.6 Complete the definition of the DynamicPolygonGeometry class.

6.2.3 Polygon Iterators

Dynamic polygons are designed to be manipulated by means of iterators, objects that implement the PolygonIterator interface. Using polygon iterators, clients can visit a polygon's vertices in either sense of rotation, insert new vertices, remove existing vertices, and translate vertices to new positions. A client obtains an iterator for a dynamic polygon by sending the polygon an *iterator* message.

A polygon iterator is positioned at all times at some vertex of its underlying polygon. This is referred to as the iterator's **current vertex.** The current vertex's position in the plane is obtained using the iterator's point method. As the traversal proceeds, different vertices become the current vertex. The next and prev methods move the iterator from vertex to vertex: The next method moves it to the current vertex's successor, whereas the prev method moves it to the current vertex's predecessor. Successive calls to next cause the iterator to traverse the polygon's vertices in forward rotation; successive calls to prev cause traversal in backward rotation. The edge method returns the **current edge,** which connects the current vertex to its successor vertex.

An iterator's methods for modifying the underlying polygon operate on the current vertex. The insertAfter method inserts a new vertex immediately after the current vertex; the argument to insertAfter specifies the location of the new vertex, which becomes the iterator's current vertex. The iterator's remove method removes the current vertex, and moves the iterator to what had been its predecessor vertex (the method throws an exception if the vertex to be removed is the underlying polygon's *only* vertex). The moveTo and moveBy methods are used to move the current vertex to a new location in the plane. Here is the interface definition:

```
public interface PolygonIterator {
  public PointGeometry point();
    // EFFECTS: Returns position of the current vertex

  public LineSegmentGeometry edge();
    // EFFECTS: Returns the current edge.

  public void next();
    // MODIFIES: this
```

```
      // EFFECTS: Moves this iterator to the current
      //   vertex's successor.

    public void prev();
      // MODIFIES: this
      // EFFECTS: Moves this iterator to the current
      //   vertex's predecessor.

    public void insertAfter(PointGeometry p)
          throws NullPointerException;
      // MODIFIES: this, and the underlying polygon
      // EFFECTS: If p is null throws NullPointerException;
      //   else inserts a new vertex v, positioned at p,
      //   as the successor to the current
      //   vertex and makes v the current vertex.

    public void remove() throws IllegalStateException;
      // MODIFIES: this, and underlying polygon
      // EFFECTS: If nbrVertices()==1 throws
      //   IllegalStateException; else removes the current
      //   vertex and makes its predecessor the current
      //   vertex.

    public void moveTo(int x, int y);
      // MODIFIES: underlying polygon
      // EFFECTS: Moves the current vertex to (x,y).

    public void moveBy(int dx, int dy);
      // MODIFIES: underlying polygon
      // EFFECTS: Translates the current vertex by dx
      //   and dy.

    public int nbrVertices();
      //EFFECTS: Returns the number of vertices in the
      //   underlying polygon.
}
```

Translating Polygons

Let's look at two short examples illustrating the use of polygon iterators. The first example is a procedure that translates a polygon `poly` by `dx` units along the *x* axis and `dy` units along the *y* axis. It works by translating every vertex individually. The procedure obtains an iterator from the input polygon `poly` and uses it to visit all of the polygon's vertices. At each vertex, it applies the iterator's `moveBy` method to translate the vertex:

```
static void translatePolygon(DynamicPolygonGeometry poly,
                             int dx, int dy) {
  PolygonIterator iter = poly.iterator();
  for (int i=0; i<iter.nbrVertices(); i++, iter.next())
    iter.moveBy(dx, dy);
}
```

The test `i<iter.nbrVertices()` in the *for* loop ensures that every vertex is visited exactly once.

Building Regular Polygons

The second example involves the construction of **regular polygons,** simple polygons whose sides have equal length and meet at equal angles. Examples include the equilateral triangle and the square. We shall write the procedure `buildRegularPolygon` whose header has this form:

```
static DynamicPolygonGeometry
       buildRegularPolygon(int n, int rad,
                           PointGeometry center,
                           double twist)
```

The procedure returns an n–sided regular polygon centered at the point `center` and of radius `rad`. The polygon is rotated clockwise around its center by `twist` degrees. Figure 6.4 shows the regular pentagon produced by the following call:

```
buildRegularPolygon(5, 1, new PointGeometry(2, 2), 45);
```

The implementation of `buildRegularPolygon` proceeds in three steps. First, the procedure constructs a polygon `poly` and obtains an iterator for the polygon. At this stage, the polygon contains only a single "dummy" vertex that will eventually be removed. The second step iteratively inserts the polygon's `n` vertices. In each iteration, the procedure constructs a new trans-

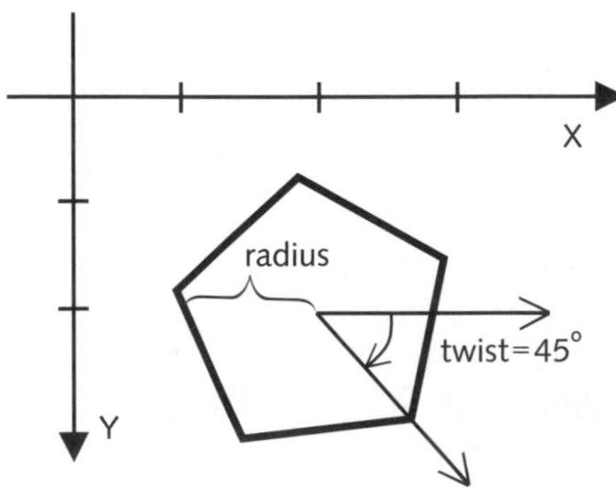

FIGURE 6.4 A regular polygon.

formable point p at the origin, translates p by the polygon's radius along the positive x axis, rotates p around the origin by the current rotation angle, translates p into position, and lastly inserts point p after the iterator's current vertex. In the third and final step, the procedure removes the dummy vertex and returns the resulting polygon poly. Here is the implementation:

```
static DynamicPolygonGeometry
buildRegularPolygon(int n, int rad, PointGeometry center,
                    double twist)
 throws NullPointerException {
    // step 1: build a new polygon and obtain iterator
  DynamicPolygonGeometry poly =
    new DynamicPolygonGeometry(center);
  PolygonIterator iter = poly.iterator();
    // step 2: insert the n vertices
  double twistInc = 360.0 / n;
  for (int i = 0; i < n; i++, twist += twistInc) {
    TransformablePointGeometry p =
      new TransformablePointGeometry();
    p.translate(rad, 0);
    p.rotate(twist);
    p.translate(center.getX(), center.getY());
    iter.insertAfter(p);
  }
    // step 3: remove the dummy vertex
  iter.next();        // advance iter to dummy vertex
  iter.remove();      // and remove it
  return poly;
}
```

In the above implementation, the polygon's initial dummy vertex, positioned at center, is required because empty polygons are disallowed. After the polygon's n real vertices have been inserted, this dummy vertex is removed.

Implementing Polygon Iterators

Now, we'll define the DynamicPolygonIterator class, which implements the PolygonIterator interface. The class defines two instance fields. The polygon field stores a reference to the iterator's underlying polygon. And the vertex field stores a reference to the iterator's current vertex. Here is the implementation:

```
public class DynamicPolygonIterator
       implements PolygonIterator {

    // the underlying polygon
  protected DynamicPolygonGeometry polygon;
```

```
  // the current vertex
protected Vertex vertex;

public DynamicPolygonIterator(DynamicPolygonGeometry poly)
       throws NullPointerException {
  // EFFECTS: If poly is null throws
  //   NullPointerException; else constructs this for
  //   the polygon poly and any current vertex.
  this.polygon = poly;
  this.vertex = poly.vertex();
}

public DynamicPolygonIterator(DynamicPolygonIterator iter)
       throws NullPointerException {
  // EFFECTS: If iter is null throws
  //   NullPointerException; else constructs this for
  //   iter's underlying polygon and current vertex.
  this.polygon = iter.polygon;
  this.vertex = iter.vertex;
}

public PointGeometry point() {
  return new PointGeometry(vertex.point());
}

public LineSegmentGeometry edge() {
  return new LineSegmentGeometry(vertex.point(),
                                 vertex.next().point());
}

public void next() {
  vertex = vertex.next();
}

public void prev() {
  vertex = vertex.prev();
}

public void insertAfter(PointGeometry p)
       throws NullPointerException {
  if (p == null) throw new NullPointerException();
  vertex = polygon.insertAfterVertex(vertex, p);
}
```

```
  public void remove() throws IllegalStateException {
    if (nbrVertices() == 1)
      throw new IllegalStateException();
    Vertex prevVertex = vertex.prev();
    polygon.removeVertex(vertex);
    vertex = prevVertex;
  }

  public void moveTo(int x, int y) {
    PointGeometry p = vertex.point();
    p.setX(x);
    p.setY(y);
  }

  public void moveBy(int dx, int dy) {
    PointGeometry p = new PointGeometry(vertex.point());
    moveTo(p.getX() + dx, p.getY() + dy);
  }

  public int nbrVertices() {
    return polygon.nbrVertices();
  }
}
```

The preceding implementation requires that `DynamicPolygonIterator` belong to the same package as the classes `DynamicPolygonGeometry` and `Vertex` because it uses their protected interfaces. The implementation does not break the encapsulation of the latter two classes; indeed, their protected interfaces were intended for just such use.

Exercises

ESSENTIAL 6.7 Revise the implementation of the `verticesToString` and `shape` methods of the `DynamicPolygonGeometry` class using polygon iterators.

ESSENTIAL 6.8 Define the `DrawDynamicPolygonPainter` class, which does for dynamic polygons what the `DrawPolygonPainter` class of Section 5.6.4 does for static polygons.

ESSENTIAL 6.9 Implement the `buildRegularPolygon` procedure as a static method of a class named `DynamicPolygons`. This class contains useful methods for manipulating polygons, just as the `java.util.Arrays` class contains useful methods for handling arrays.

Develop the graphical program `PaintRegularPolygon` that when called thus

```
> java PaintRegularPolygon n radius [twist]
```

paints a regular n-gon of specified radius and twist (twist is zero if the optional program argument is not supplied). Your polygon should be centered in the frame, and filled and stroked with your choice of colors.

6.10 A star-shaped polygon can be constructed by starting with a regular polygon, and then translating every other vertex along the line that passes through the vertex and the polygon's center. In the procedure `buildStarPolygon` that follows, the first four arguments determine a regular polygon. The fifth argument, named `tf` for *translation factor,* determines how far alternate vertices get translated toward or away from the polygon's center. In effect, the program argument `tf` determines the concavity of the resulting polygon. Here is the implementation:

```
public static DynamicPolygonGeometry
 buildStarPolygon(int n, int rad, PointGeometry center,
                  double twist, double tf)
     throws NullPointerException {
  DynamicPolygonGeometry poly =
   buildRegularPolygon(n, radius, center, twist);
  PolygonIterator iter = poly.iterator();
  for (int i = 0; i < iter.nbrVertices() / 2; i++) {
    PointGeometry p = iter.point();
    int dx = (int)((center.getX() - p.getX()) * tf);
    int dy = (int)((center.getY() - p.getY()) * tf);
    iter.moveBy(dx, dy);
    iter.next();
    iter.next();
  }
  return poly;
}
```

Add the `buildStarPolygon` procedure to your `DynamicPolygons` class, and then implement a graphical program `PaintStarPolygon` for painting star-shaped polygons:

```
> java PaintStarPolygon n radius tf
```

Experiment with different values of `tf`. What happens when the value of `tf` exceeds one?

In Exercise 6.9, you implemented regular polygons as a class method of a `DynamicPolygons` class. It is also possible to implement regular polygons through a `RegularPolygonGeometry` class that extends the `DynamicPolygonGeometry` class. The class is used to construct new regular polygons, which can then be manipulated using polygon iterators (the `RegularPolygonGeometry` class inherits the `iterator` method from its parent class). Here is the class skeleton:

```
public class RegularPolygonGeometry
       extends DynamicPolygonGeometry {
  public RegularPolygonGeometry(int n, int radius,
              PointGeometry center, double twist)
         throws NullPointerException,
                IllegalArgumentException
     // EFFECTS: If center is null throws
     //   NullPointerException; else if n<3 throws
     //   IllegalArgumentException; else constructs
     //   a regular n-gon of given center and twist.

  public RegularPolygonGeometry(int n, int radius,
                               PointGeometry center)
         throws NullPointerException,
                IllegalArgumentException
     // EFFECTS: If center is null throws
     //   NullPointerException; else if n<3 throws
     //   IllegalArgumentException; else constructs
     //   a regular n-gon with given center and
     //   zero twist.

  public RegularPolygonGeometry(int n, int radius)
         throws IllegalArgumentException
     // EFFECTS: If n<3 throws
     //   IllegalArgumentException; else constructs
     //   a regular n-gon centered at the origin
     //   and with zero twist.
}
```

Implement this class. Revise your `PaintRegularPolygon` program (Exercise 6.9) so that it builds a regular polygon using this class instead of the static method `buildRegularPolygon` of class `DynamicPolygons`.

6.12 Develop the interactive program `PlayDynamicPolygon` for building and editing a dynamic polygon using text commands. Your program maintains a current vertex in the polygon to which most of the commands apply. The polygon is displayed at all times and its current vertex is highlighted. No polygon exists when the program begins execution, but it creates a new one-vertex polygon when a vertex is first inserted. In the following description below, we use the phrase *empty polygon* to describe the program's state whenever no polygon exists (at startup, and whenever all the vertices are removed). Here are the commands supported by this program:

- **insert** ***x y***—inserts a new vertex at position (*x*,*y*) after the current vertex; the new vertex becomes the current vertex. If the polygon is empty, creates a new one-vertex polygon at (*x*,*y*).
- **remove**—removes the current vertex and makes its predecessor the current vertex; if no vertices remain, an empty polygon results.
- **moveto** ***x y***—moves the current vertex to the position (*x*,*y*); does nothing if the polygon is empty.
- **translate** ***dx dy***—translates the current vertex by *dx* and *dy;* does nothing if the polygon is empty.
- **next**—makes the current vertex's successor the new current vertex; does nothing if the polygon is empty.
- **previous**—makes the current vertex's predecessor the new current vertex; does nothing if the polygon is empty.
- **clear**—replaces the polygon by an empty polygon.
- **size**—prints the number of vertices in the polygon.
- **quit**—exits this program.

Here is a sample interaction:

```
> java PlayDynamicPolygon
? insert 10 10
? insert 50 50    // left diagram of Figure 6.5
? insert -25 50
? insert -50 0
? next            // middle diagram of Figure 6.5
? remove          // right diagram of Figure 6.5
? quit
```

Figure 6.5 depicts three stages during the preceding interaction. The current vertex is highlighted by a dot (the vertex's point is painted), and the axes' tick marks occur at 50 unit intervals.

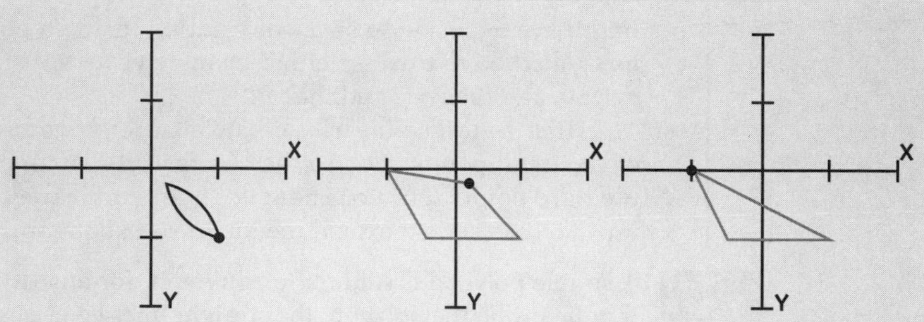

FIGURE 6.5 Interacting with a dynamic polygon.

[Hint: Your `PlayDynamicPolygon` program follows the *MyInteractiveProgram* template. The controller class maintains a field to hold the polygon and an iterator for the polygon (both fields are `null` whenever the polygon is empty). The controller class also provides a method that returns the current polygon and a method that returns the position of the current vertex. These two methods are required by the `PlayDynamicPolygon.paintComponent` method for display.]

ESSENTIAL 6.13 Define the class `TriangleGeometry`, an extension of the `DynamicPolygonGeometry` class, for building triangles. Your class defines only one method, a constructor that takes three noncollinear points and constructs a dynamic polygon with those three vertices:

```
public TriangleGeometry(PointGeometry a,
                        PointGeometry b,
                        PointGeometry c)
       throws NullPointerException,
              ColinearPointsException
   // EFFECTS: If a, b, or c are null throws
   //    NullPointerException; else if a, b, and c
   //    are colinear (on the same line) throws
   //    ColinearPointsException; else constructs
   //    triangle with vertices a, b, and c ordered
   //    in clockwise rotation (i.e., visiting its
   //    vertices in a forward traversal visits them
   //    in clockwise rotation).
```

As an example of clockwise rotation, suppose that points p0=(0,0), p1=(20,0), and p2=(20,20). Then, the triangles `t1` and `t2` produced by

```
TriangleGeometry t1 = new TriangleGeometry(p0,p1,p2)
TriangleGeometry t2 = new TriangleGeometry(p0,p2,p1)
```

both have a clockwise sense of rotation: using a polygon iterator's `next` method to traverse either triangle visits the vertices in the order `p0`, and then `p1`, and then `p2`.

[Hint: To test colinearity, create a `LineGeometry` object for two of the input points and use the `classifyPoint` method to classify the third point. Your `ColinearPointsException` class, which you must define, should extend the `RuntimeException` class.]

ESSENTIAL 6.14 A simple polygon is said to be **convex** if, for any two points a and b that lie inside the polygon, the straight line segment $\overline{ab}$ that connects a to b also lies inside the polygon. The first two polygons in Figure 6.6 are convex. However, the rightmost polygon in the figure is not convex because there exist points a and b inside the polygon for which the line segment $\overline{ab}$ leaves the polygon. It is noteworthy that in a convex polygon, the internal angle at every vertex is no greater than 180°.

A **supporting line** of a convex polygon P is a line that passes through some vertex of P, such that the interior of P lies entirely to the same side of the line. A supporting line is a line of tangency to the polygon. Suppose that p is any point that lies outside polygon P. There then are two unique supporting lines of polygon P that pass through point p. The **right supporting line** through p is the supporting line that passes through p and which lies to the right of polygon P's interior (see Figure 6.7). The **left supporting line** through point p is defined analogously.

Figure 6.7 depicts a process for discovering the right supporting line through point p. Traverse the polygon's edges in clockwise rotation until reaching some edge e, such that point p does not lie to the left of e (if we extend e into an infinite line, point p lies either to the right of or on this line). From edge e, continue traversing the polygon's edges in clockwise rotation until reaching some edge f, such that point p lies strictly to the left of edge f. The right supporting line through point p passes through the first endpoint of edge f (this first endpoint is labeled q in Figure 6.7).

The following procedure uses this strategy to find the right supporting line for a polygon through a point p. The procedure is not

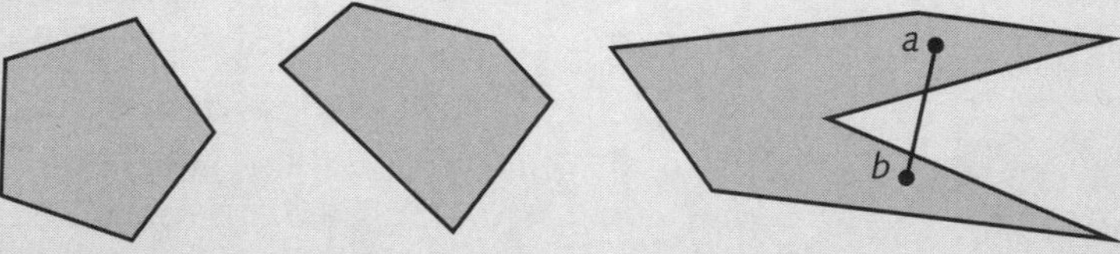

FIGURE 6.6 The first two polygons are convex, the last is not.

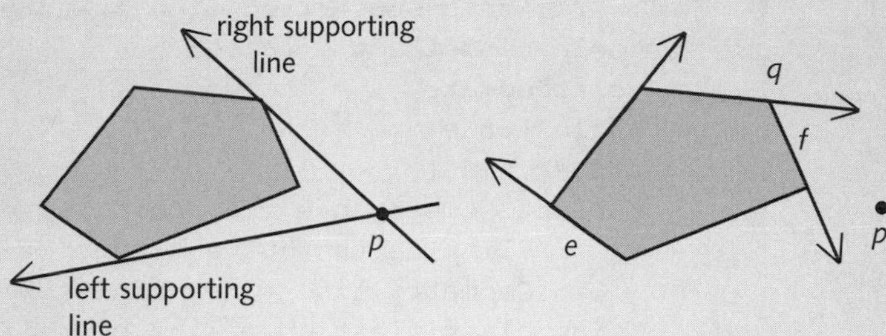

FIGURE 6.7 The left and right supporting lines through point p; and a process for discovering the vertex q through which the right supporting line passes.

passed the polygon directly; rather, it is passed an iterator for the polygon. Three preconditions are assumed:

- The polygon is convex and possesses at least three vertices, not all colinear,
- The input point `p` lies outside the polygon, and
- The polygon has clockwise rotation (this would be satisfied by the triangles produced by the `TriangleGeometry` class of the previous exercise).

The procedure guarantees the following two postconditions:

- The polygon iterator `iter` is made to point to some vertex through which passes the right supporting line through point `p`, and
- The procedure returns a `LineGeometry` object representing the supporting line.

Here is the procedure's definition:

```
public static LineGeometry
 rightSupportingLine(PolygonIterator iter,
                     PointGeometry p)
     throws NullPointerException {
    // REQUIRES: iter's underlying polygon is convex,
    //   has at least 3 noncolinear vertices, has
    //   clockwise rotation, and does not contain p.
    // MODIFIES: iter
    // EFFECTS: If iter or p is null throws
    //   NullPointerException; else iter is made to
    //   point to some vertex through which passes
    //   the right supporting line through point p, and
```

```
    //   this supporting line is returned.
  boolean pNotLeft = false;
  PointGeometry a = iter.point();
  while (true) {
    iter.next();
    PointGeometry b = iter.point();
      // line is the current edge of the polygon
    LineGeometry line = new LineGeometry(a, b);
    int classification = line.classifyPoint(p);
    if (pNotLeft &&
         (classification == LineGeometry.LEFT)) {
        // support point is found; set iter and
        // return the supporting line
      iter.prev();
      return new LineGeometry(p, iter.point());
    } else if (classification != LineGeometry.LEFT)
        // found some edge that p does not lie
        // to the left of
      pNotLeft = true;
      // advance to the next edge
    a = b;
  }
}
```

Note that the Boolean variable `pNotLeft` is set to true only when some edge *e* is discovered, such that point `p` does not lie to the left of *e*. Only after `pNotLeft` has been set is it possible to discover some vertex that supports the right supporting line.

For this exercise, add the `rightSupportingLine` procedure as a static method of your `DynamicPolygons` class. In addition, define the static method `leftSupportingLine` whose behavior is analogous to that of `rightSupportingLine`: when passed a polygon iterator and a point not on the polygon, it discovers the left supporting line through this point.

```
public static LineGeometry
 leftSupportingLine(PolygonIterator iter,
                    PointGeometry p)
     throws NullPointerException {
    // REQUIRES: iter's underlying polygon is convex,
    //   has at least 3 noncolinear vertices, has
    //   clockwise rotation, and does not contain p.
    // MODIFIES: iter
    // EFFECTS: If iter or p is null throws
    //   NullPointerException; else iter is made to
```

```
    //   point to some vertex through which passes
    //   the left supporting line through p, and
    //   this supporting line is returned.
```

6.15 Write the interactive graphical program `PlaySupportingLines` to test your two procedures from the previous exercise. Your program is called with two program arguments that determine a regular polygon `P`:

```
> java PlaySupportingLines nbrSides radius
```

Polygon *P* is convex because every regular polygon is convex. The program then repeatedly prompts the user for commands:

- **point *x y***—if the point (*x*,*y*) is contained in polygon *P*, the program displays *P* and prints the message (*x*,*y*) *lies inside the polygon* in the console window; however, if (*x*,*y*) lies outside *P*, the program displays polygon *P*, the point (*x*,*y*), and the two supporting lines through point (*x*,*y*).
- **quit**—exits this program.

You may want to paint the right supporting line red and the left supporting line green to distinguish between them.

ESSENTIAL 6.16 The **convex hull** of a set of points *S* is the smallest convex polygon *P* that contains every point in *S*. Here, polygon *P* is smallest in the sense that if *P′* is any convex polygon that contains the points of *S*, *P* is contained in *P′*. We use CH(*S*) to denote the convex hull of a point set *S*. See Figure 6.8.

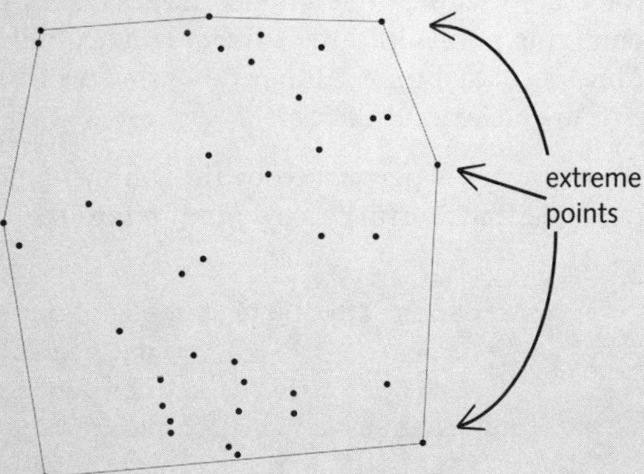

FIGURE 6.8 The convex hull of a point set.

The convex hull of a *finite* set of points *S* can be illustrated as follows. Imagine the plane to be a sheet of wood with a nail protruding from every point in *S*. Now stretch a rubber band so that it encloses all the nails, and then release it, allowing it to snap snug against the nails. The taut rubber band conforms to the convex hull boundary. Note that certain points in *S* serve as vertices of the convex hull where the interior angle is strictly less than 180°. These are known as **extreme points** of the convex hull. The remaining points of *S* lie either along the convex hull's edges or in the convex hull's interior. Although this is a *constructive* definition—we can in fact use a sheet of wood, nails, and a rubber band to build convex hulls in this way—it is not an approach we can employ using digital computers.

There are many interesting algorithms for constructing the convex hull of a finite point set *S*. In this exercise, we explore an incremental approach. Assume that *S* contains the points $p_0, p_{1,\ldots,} p_{n-1}$, where $n \geq 3$ (here, *S* might be implemented by an array or a vector). We let CH(i) denote the convex hull over the first i points; that is, CH(i) = CH({$p_0, p_{1,\ldots,} p_{n-1}$}). Our goal is to construct CH(n), which is the same as CH(S), the convex hull of *S*. Here is a high-level description of our algorithm:

```
convexHull(S={p0,p1,...,pn-1}) {
  H ← CH(3); // build the convex hull over {p0,p1,p2}
  for (int i = 3; i < n; i++)
    insertPointIntoHull(H, pi);    // H ← CH(H ∪ pi)
  return H;       // H is now CH(n)=CH(S)
}
```

We first construct the convex hull *H* over the first three points in *S*, which are assumed to be noncolinear. Then we iteratively insert the remaining points into the current convex hull *H*, thereby "growing" *H* one point at a time. At the end of this process, *H* is identical to the desired convex hull CH(*S*).

The real work is performed by the following procedure, which is responsible for inserting a new point *p* into the current convex hull `H`:

```
static void
  insertPointIntoHull(DynamicPolygonGeometry H,
                      PointGeometry p)
        throws NullPointerException
  // REQUIRES: H is a convex polygon with clockwise
  //   rotation and at least three vertices.
  // MODIFIES: H
  // EFFECTS: If H or p is null throws
```

```
//   NullPointerException; else makes H equal
//   to CH(H∪p), the convex hull of H and p.
```

Calculating the convex hull CH($H \cup p$) of a convex polygon H and a point p naturally falls into these two cases:

1. ***p* is contained in *H*.** Here p is absorbed by H; that is, CH($H \cup p$)=H. There is nothing to do in this case.
2. ***p* is not contained in *H*.** In this case, we discover the two supporting lines of H through point p. The two tangent points at which these supporting lines touch H divide the boundary of H into two chains of vertices, labeled the **near chain** and the **far chain** in Figure 6.9. To construct the convex hull CH($H \cup p$), we remove the near chain and replace it by the point p.

The following procedure handles the construction called for by case 2, in which H is a convex polygon and p is a point that lies outside H. The procedure produces the convex hull CH($H \cup p$) by modifying the input polygon H:

```
protected static void
 replaceInnerChain(DynamicPolygonGeometry H,
                   PointGeometry p)
        throws NullPointerException {
    // find left and right supporting lines
  PolygonIterator rightIter = H.iterator();
  rightSupportingLine(rightIter, p);
  PointGeometry rTangentPoint =
    rightIter.point();
  PolygonIterator leftIter = poly.iterator();
  leftSupportingLine(leftIter, p);
    // remove inner chain
```

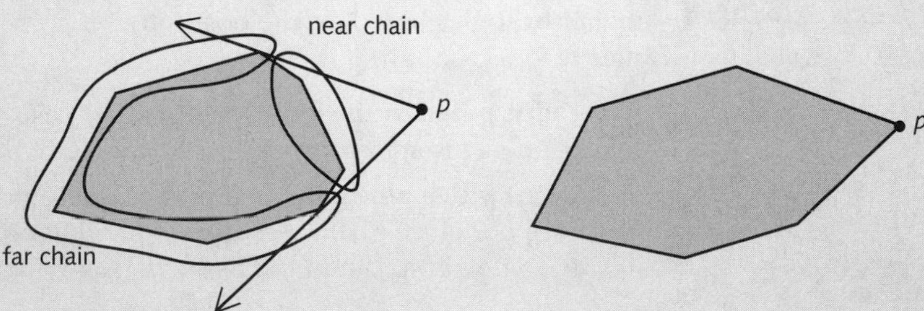

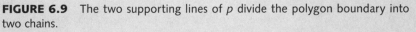

FIGURE 6.9 The two supporting lines of p divide the polygon boundary into two chains.

```
    leftIter.prev();
    while (!leftIter.point().equals(rTangentPoint))
      leftIter.remove();
      // insert point p
    leftIter.insertAfter(p);
}
```

We now have the machinery to construct convex hulls. Implement the static methods `convexHull`, `insertPointIntoHull`, and `replaceInnerChain`, and add them to the `DynamicPolygons` class. Here is the specification of the `convexHull` method:

```
static DynamicPolygonGeometry
 convexHull(PointGeometry[] points)
       throws NullPointerException,
              IllegalArgumentException,
              ColinearPointsException
  // EFFECTS: If points is null or some points[i]
  //   is null throws NullPointerException; else
  //   if points.length < 3 throws
  //   IllegalArgumentException; else if the
  //   first three points are colinear throws
  //   ColinearPointsException; else returns
  //   the convex hull of points.
```

Use your `convexHull` procedure in a program

```
> java PaintConvexHull n
```

that generates *n* random points, constructs the convex hull of the *n* points, and paints both the points and their convex hull. Figure 6.8 shows what the program displayed when I ran it with the program argument 40.

ESSENTIAL 6.17 In this exercise, you define a procedure for splitting a triangle *t* into smaller triangles based on the position of a point *p* contained in triangle *t*. Two cases are possible:

1. **Point *p* lies in the interior of *t*** (first case of Figure 6.10)—triangle *t* is split into the three triangles Δabp, Δbcp, and Δcap.
2. **Point *p* lies along the interior of some edge of *t*** (second case of Figure 6.10)—assuming that *p* lies along the edge *ab*, triangle *t* is split into the two triangles Δcap and Δbcp.

If point `p` coincides with some vertex of triangle `t`, it is not necessary to split `t` at all. This case is excluded by the following implementation of the `splitTriangle` procedure:

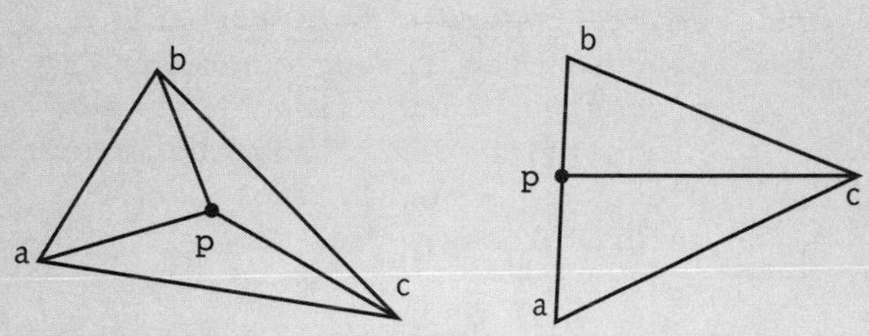

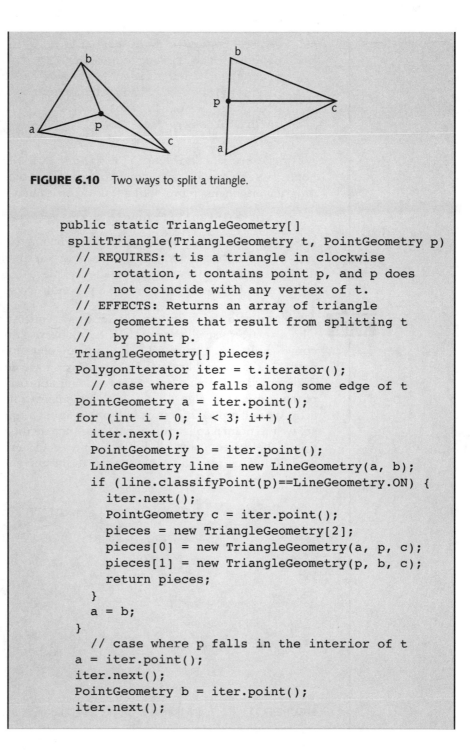

FIGURE 6.10 Two ways to split a triangle.

```
public static TriangleGeometry[]
 splitTriangle(TriangleGeometry t, PointGeometry p)
  // REQUIRES: t is a triangle in clockwise
  //   rotation, t contains point p, and p does
  //   not coincide with any vertex of t.
  // EFFECTS: Returns an array of triangle
  //   geometries that result from splitting t
  //   by point p.
  TriangleGeometry[] pieces;
  PolygonIterator iter = t.iterator();
    // case where p falls along some edge of t
  PointGeometry a = iter.point();
  for (int i = 0; i < 3; i++) {
    iter.next();
    PointGeometry b = iter.point();
    LineGeometry line = new LineGeometry(a, b);
    if (line.classifyPoint(p)==LineGeometry.ON) {
      iter.next();
      PointGeometry c = iter.point();
      pieces = new TriangleGeometry[2];
      pieces[0] = new TriangleGeometry(a, p, c);
      pieces[1] = new TriangleGeometry(p, b, c);
      return pieces;
    }
    a = b;
  }
    // case where p falls in the interior of t
  a = iter.point();
  iter.next();
  PointGeometry b = iter.point();
  iter.next();
```

```
        PointGeometry c = iter.point();
        pieces = new TriangleGeometry[3];
        pieces[0] = new TriangleGeometry(a, b, p);
        pieces[1] = new TriangleGeometry(b, c, p);
        pieces[2] = new TriangleGeometry(c, a, p);
        return pieces;
    }
```

For this exercise, add the `splitTriangle` to the `DynamicPolygons` class. Then, write a graphical program that takes eight integer program arguments representing four distinct points:

> java PaintSplitTriangle x_0 y_0 x_1 y_1 x_2 y_2 x_3 y_3

It is assumed that the point (x_3,y_3) is contained in the triangle t with vertices (x_0,y_0), (x_1,y_1), and (x_2,y_2). Your program should paint (using distinct colors) the two or three triangular pieces into which triangle t is split. Use the `splitTriangle` procedure to split triangle t.

ESSENTIAL 6.18 A **triangulation** of a finite point set S is a collection of triangles whose vertices use all the points of *S*, and whose union equals the convex hull of *S*. Figure 6.11 shows triangulations of a set of 12 points and a set of 24 points. In this exercise, we develop a procedure for triangulating a finite point set. Our approach is a variation of the incremental algorithm used to build convex hulls in Exercise 6.16. We will grow our convex hull one point at a time. While doing so, we maintain a collection of triangles representing the triangulation of the current convex hull. Each time we add a new point to the convex hull, we also add new triangles to the current triangulation.

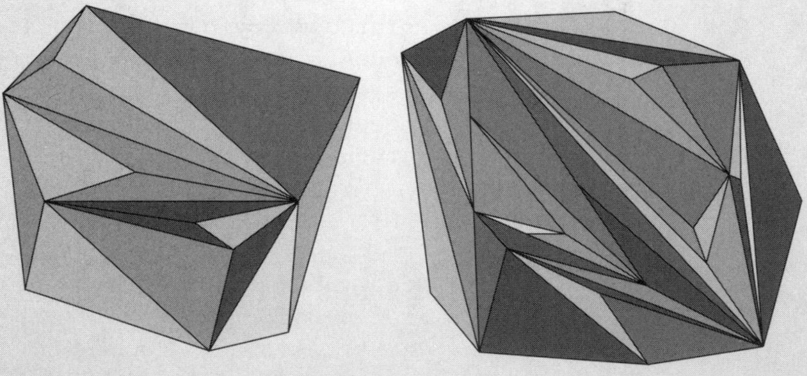

FIGURE 6.11 A triangulation of 12 points (left) and of 24 points (right).

The procedure returns a vector containing the triangles that make up a triangulation of the input array points. Here is the top-level procedure:

```
public static
 Vector triangulation(PointGeometry[] pts)
      throws NullPointerException,
             IllegalArgumentException,
             ColinearPointsException {
  // EFFECTS: If pts is null or pts[i] is null for
  //   some i throws NullPointerException; else if
  //   pts.length<3 throws IllegalArgumentException;
  //   else if the first three points are colinear
  //   throws ColinearPointsException; else returns
  //   a vector of triangles representing
  //   a triangulation of pts.
  if (pts.length < 3)
    throw new IllegalArgumentException();

  // container to hold triangles
  Vector triangles = new Vector();

  // construct CH(3) and add first triangle to
  //   the triangulation
  DynamicPolygonGeometry H =
    new TriangleGeometry(pts[0], pts[1], pts[2]);
  triangles.add(
    new TriangleGeometry(pts[0], pts[1], pts[2]));

  // for each i=4,...,pts.length, construct CH(i)
  //   and maintain current triangulation
  for (int i = 3; i < pts.length; i++)
    addNewTriangles(H, pts[i], triangles);
  return triangles;
}
```

The procedure

```
addNewTriangles(DynamicPolygonGeometry H,
                PointGeometry p,
                Vector triangles)
```

is called with the current convex hull H, a triangulation of H stored in the vector triangles, and a new point p to be inserted. The procedure adds triangles to, and removes triangles from, the vector `triangles` to account for the insertion of point `p`. As with our convex hull algorithm, there are two cases to consider: (1) point `p` is contained in `H`, and (2) point `p` lies outside `H`. You can see these two cases distinguished in the following implementation:

```
public static void
 addNewTriangles(DynamicPolygonGeometry hull,
                PointGeometry p,
                Vector triangles) {
  // REQUIRES: triangles is a triangulation of hull.
  // MODIFIES: triangles
  // EFFECTS: Revises triangles to account for the
  //   insertion of point p.
  if (hull.contains(p)) {  // case 1
    TriangleGeometry[] affectedTris =
      findAffectedTriangles(p, triangles);
    for (int i=0; i<affectedTris.length; i++) {
      TriangleGeometry t = affectedTris[i];
      TriangleGeometry[] pieces =
        splitTriangle(t, p);
      triangles.remove(t);
      for (int j = 0; j < pieces.length; j++)
        triangles.add(pieces[j]);
    }
  } else  // case 2
    splitFan(hull, p, triangles);
}
```

The rest of this exercise treats these two cases.

[Case 1] **Point *p* is contained in the convex hull of the current triangulation.** The triangles affected by point *p* are obtained by calling the `findAffectedTriangles` procedure, and then each such triangle is removed from the triangulation and replaced by its pieces.

The `findAffectedTriangles` procedure returns an array of those triangles that must be split into pieces based on the position of input point *p*. The procedure tests point *p* against each triangle of the triangulation in turn. Here are the four cases that can arise, and the action taken in each case:

- ***p* coincides with a vertex of some triangle**—return an array of length zero (no triangles need to be split into pieces).
- ***p* lies along an edge of exactly one triangle**—return an array containing only that triangle. In this case, point *p* lies along the convex hull boundary.

- ***p* lies along an edge shared by two triangles**—return an array containing only those two triangles.
- ***p* lies in the interior of exactly one triangle**—return an array containing only that triangle.

Here is the procedure's implementation:

```
protected static TriangleGeometry[]
 findAffectedTriangles(PointGeometry p,
                              Vector triangles) {
  // REQUIRES: p and triangles are not null, and
  //   p lies in at least one triangle.
  // EFFECTS: Returns an array of those triangles
  //   that contain p and must be split into either
  //   two or three pieces (as in Figure 6.10).
  TriangleGeometry[] affectedTris =
    new TriangleGeometry[2];
  int nbrAffectedTris = 0;
 nexttriangle:
  for (int i = 0; i < triangles.size(); i++) {
    TriangleGeometry t =
      (TriangleGeometry)triangles.get(i);
    if (t.contains(p)) {
      PolygonIterator iter = t.iterator();
        // if p coincides with a vertex of t,
        // then no triangles are affected by p
      for (int j = 0; j < 3; j++, iter.next())
        if (p.equals(iter.point()))
          return new TriangleGeometry[0];
        // if p lies along an edge of t, keep t
      PointGeometry a = iter.point();
      for (int j = 0; j < 3; j++) {
        iter.next();
        PointGeometry b = iter.point();
        LineGeometry line = new LineGeometry(a, b);
        if (line.classifyPoint(p)==LineGeometry.ON){
          affectedTris[nbrAffectedTris++] = t;
          if (nbrAffectedTris == 2)
             return affectedTris;
          else continue nexttriangle;
        }
        a = b;
      }
        // p lies in the interior of t,
```

```
            // so keep t and return
          TriangleGeometry[] resTris =
            new TriangleGeometry[1];
          resTris[0] = t;
          return resTris;
        }
    }  // end for loop
      // p lies on one triangle's edge along
      // the convex hull boundary
    if (nbrAffectedTris != 1)
       throw new IllegalStateException();
    TriangleGeometry[] resTris =
      new TriangleGeometry[1];
    resTris[0] = affectedTris[0];
    return resTris;
  }
```

[Case 2] **Point p lies outside the convex hull of the current triangulation.** The `addNewTriangles` procedure creates a "fan" of new triangles (see Figure 6.12). The procedure call

```
splitFan(H, p, triangles);
```

updates the convex hull `H` to make it represent the convex hull CH(`H`∪p), just as was done in our convex hull algorithm. Moreover, the triangles connecting point `p` to the edges of the inner polyline—the portion of `H` that faces point `p`—are added to the vector `triangles`. Here is an implementation for this procedure:

```
public static
 void splitFan(DynamicPolygonGeometry H,
               PointGeometry p,
               Vector triangles) {
```

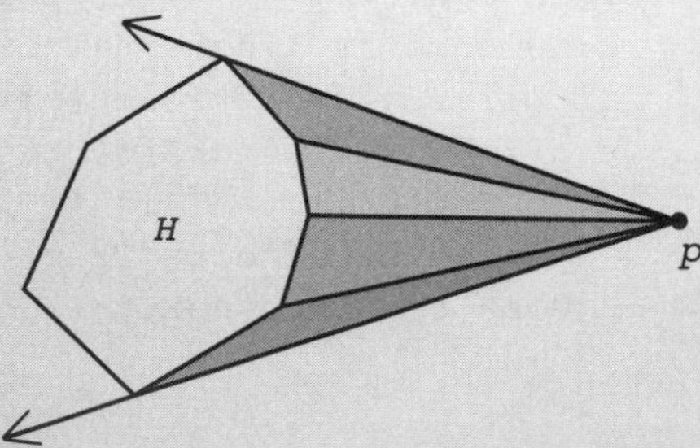

FIGURE 6.12 The fan of triangles between point p and the convex polygon H.

```
    // REQUIRES: H is convex, contains at least
    //    three vertices, and does not contain p.
    // MODIFIES: H, triangles
    // EFFECTS: Adds to triangles the fan of
    //    triangles between p and H, and changes H
    //    to CH(H∪p).
    // find left and right supporting lines
    PolygonIterator rightIter = H.iterator();
    rightSupportingLine(rightIter, p);
    PointGeometry rTangentPoint = rightIter.point();
    PolygonIterator leftIter = H.iterator();
    leftSupportingLine(leftIter, p);
      // build triangles and remove inner chain
    PointGeometry a = leftIter.point();
    leftIter.prev();
    while (!leftIter.point().equals(rTangentPoint)) {
      PointGeometry b = leftIter.point();
      triangles.add(new TriangleGeometry(a, b, p));
      a = b;
      leftIter.remove();
    }
    triangles.add(
     new TriangleGeometry(a,leftIter.point(),p));
      // insert point p
    leftIter.insertAfter(p);
  }
```

For this exercise, add the procedures presented in this exercise to your `DynamicPolygons` class. Then, write a program

```
> java PaintTriangulation n
```

that generates n random points in the frame, constructs a triangulation over the n points, and paints the triangulation. Figure 6.11 shows two of the images produced by this program.

6.2.4 Structure and Applicability of the Iterator Pattern

The iterator design pattern is used to access the elements of an aggregate without exposing its internal structure. An iterator provides a set of operations for traversing the underlying aggregate, and keeps track of the current position in the traversal (its traversal state). For example, an iterator for lists provides access to the elements in (say) list order while keeping track of the last element visited. An iterator for a binary tree provides operations for visiting a node's left child, right child, and parent node, while keeping track of the last node visited. In general, an iterator provides operations for visiting elements systematically, based on the structure of the aggregate and the needs of clients.

The iterator pattern takes the responsibility for access and traversal out of the aggregate object and places it into an iterator object. This results in several benefits. First, it allows variation in how an aggregate is traversed. For example, the polygon iterator defined in this chapter visits vertices in their order along a polygon boundary. It is also possible to define iterators that traverse a polygon's vertices in other ways, such as ordered from left to right across the plane, or ordered by distance from a fixed point in the plane. Complex aggregates (such as polygons) may be traversed in different ways. Iterators implementing different traversal policies may be developed as needed to accommodate the various requirements of clients.

A second benefit of the iterator pattern is that it simplifies the aggregate's interface. The aggregate need not provide operations for accessing its elements in every possible way that clients might require. Use of iterators also simplifies the task of the client's author, due to control abstraction. To traverse an aggregate, it isn't necessary to use the aggregate's interface. Rather, it is sufficient to work with the control abstraction supported by the iterator.

A further benefit is that any number of traversals may be pending on a given aggregate at the same time. Each traversal is represented by an iterator object with its own traversal state. We used this feature in the `replaceInnerChain` procedure for our convex hull construction of Exercise 6.16.

The class diagram of Figure 6.13 shows the structure of the iterator pattern. This design pattern includes five participants:

- ***Iterator* interface**—specifies the operations for accessing a given category of collections.
- ***ConcreteIterator* class**—implements the *Iterator* interface. Each *ConcreteIterator* object keeps track of its current position in the traversal of its underlying aggregate.
- ***Aggregate* interface**—specifies the operations for aggregates, which includes an operation for creating iterators.
- ***ConcreteAggregate* class**—implements the *Aggregate* interface.
- ***Client***—interacts with a *ConcreteAggregate* through the *Iterator* interface.

The multiplicity values in Figure 6.13 indicate that any number of *ConcreteIterator* objects may share the same underlying *ConcreteAggregate*. This captures the fact that any number of traversals may be pending on an aggregate at the same time.

The class boxes in the class diagram of Figure 6.13 are an elaboration of those we've encountered in previous class diagrams (see Appendix C). Each is divided into three compartments. The first compartment shows the class name. The second compartment shows relevant fields and their types (these

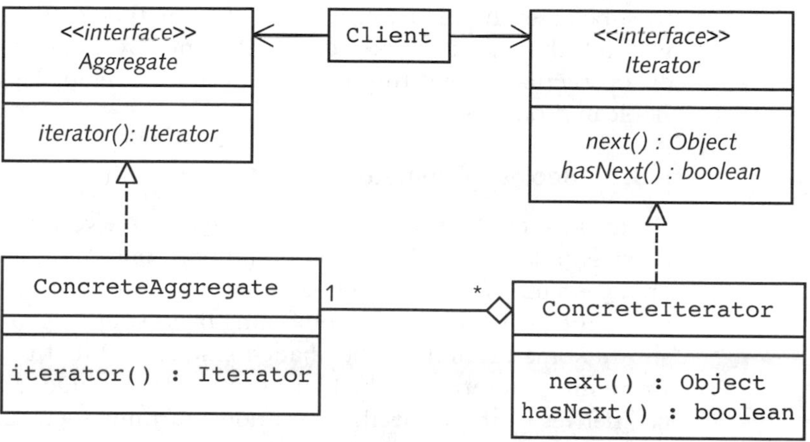

FIGURE 6.13 Structure of the iterator pattern.

compartments are empty in this particular class diagram). The third compartment of each class box indicates relevant operations and their return types. The *`Iterator`* interface defines two relevant operations, *`next`* and *`hasNext`*, where both are italicized to indicate that they are abstract operations of the *`Iterator`* interface. The *`next`* operation returns an `Object`, and the *`hasNext`* operation returns a `boolean`. The subclass *`ConcreteIterator`* provides an implementation for both operations. Similarly, the *`Aggregate`* interface specifies an *`iterator`* method that returns an iterator for the aggregate; each *`ConcreteAggregate`* subclass implements this method.

The polygon iterator presented in this section implements a slightly abbreviated version of the structure depicted in Figure 6.13. Our `PolygonIterator` interface corresponds to *`Iterator`* (in this figure), and our `DynamicPolygonIterator` class corresponds to *`ConcreteIterator`*. Our `DynamicPolygonGeometry` class provides both the implementation indicated by *`ConcreteAggregate`* and the interface promised by *`Aggregate`*. Note that the *`next`* and *`hasNext`* operations specified by *`Iterator`* do not appear with these names in our `PolygonIterator` class. Rather, these two operations stand for any number of methods for obtaining the current element, advancing the iterator, and testing for boundary conditions (e.g., whether the iterator has reached some last element).

6.3 The Template Method Design Pattern

The template method pattern is used to define an algorithm, some of whose details may vary from one use to the next. The method responsible for the algorithm, known as a **template method,** carries out the algorithm step by step. However, those steps of the algorithm whose details may vary are implemented by subclasses. In other words, a template method calls one or more abstract methods that may be implemented differently by different subclasses. The rest of this section applies this design pattern to develop classes for representing Boolean geometries.

6.3.1 Boolean Geometries

Up to now, the area geometries with which we've worked have been relatively simple: rectangles, ellipses, and polygons. Yet, there is a vast array of area geometries that are more complicated than rectangles, ellipses, or polygons, but can be formed by combining these simpler geometries. Figure 6.14 shows some examples. The shaded shapes in this figure are examples of **Boolean geometries,** which are geometries produced by combining area geometries by three specific operations: forming their union, their intersection, and their difference. These are known as **Boolean shape operations.** The first shape, called a *lune,* is formed by intersecting two filled circles. The second shape is obtained by subtracting a filled circle from a larger regular hexagon. The third shape is a "pear," whose body is the union of a filled circle and a filled noncircular ellipse, and whose two leaves are lunes; the pear as a whole is formed by the union of its two leaves and its body.

The Java 2D API supports Boolean shape operations through its `Area` class. This class, which implements the `Shape` interface, supports Boolean shape operations on area-enclosing shapes. The following skeleton for the `Area` class shows only those operations that we will require:

```
public class java.awt.geom.Area
       implements java.awt.Shape {
  public Area(Shape s)
    // REQUIRES: s is not null.
    // EFFECTS: Initializes this area from the shape s.

  public boolean contains(double x, double y)
    // EFFECTS: Returns true if this area contains
    //   the point (x,y); else returns false.
```

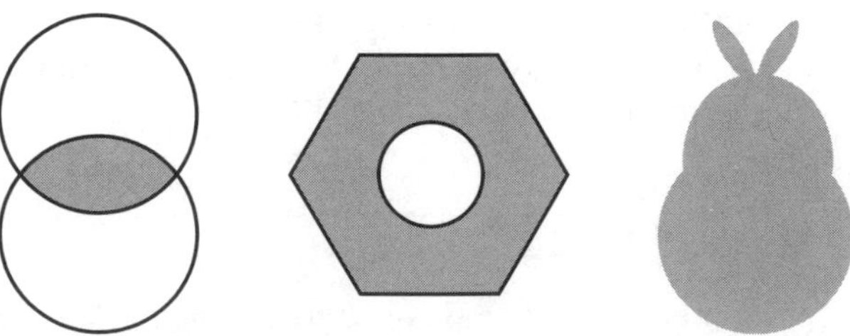

FIGURE 6.14 Three Boolean geometries.

```
  public void add(Area a)
    // REQUIRES: a is not null.
    // MODIFIES: this
    // EFFECTS: Sets the shape of this area to
    //   the union of this and a
    //   (i.e., this_post = this ∪ a).

  public void intersect(Area a)
    // REQUIRES: a is not null.
    // MODIFIES: this
    // EFFECTS: Sets the shape of this area to
    //   the intersection of this and a
    //   (i.e., this_post = this ∩ a).

  public void subtract(Area a)
    // REQUIRES: a is not null.
    // MODIFIES: this
    // EFFECTS: Sets the shape of this area to
    //   the difference of this and a
    //   (i.e., this_post = this − a).
}
```

Class `Area`'s Boolean shape operations `add`, `intersect`, and `subtract` are mutators—they modify the state of this object. Where `a1` and `a2` are `Area` objects, the procedure call

```
a1.intersect(a2);
```

modifies the state of `a1`, setting it to the intersection of the two areas that `a1` and `a2` represent prior to the procedure call. The state of object `a2` is not affected by the operation.

We can use `Area` objects to construct the intersection of two `AreaGeometry` objects `a` and `b`. Our strategy is to extract the shapes from `a` and `b`, convert these two shapes to `Area` objects, and then form their intersection. This strategy is used in the following procedure, which returns a shape representing the intersection of two area geometries:

```
static Shape shapeOfIntersection(AreaGeometry a,
                                 AreaGeometry b) {
  Area aArea = new Area(a.shape());
  Area bArea = new Area(b.shape());
  aArea.intersect(bArea);
  return aArea;
}
```

For example, the following code fragment produces the lune shape—the intersection of two filled circles—shown in Figure 6.14:

```
AreaGeometry topCircle =
   new EllipseGeometry(20, 20, 10, 10);
AreaGeometry bottomCircle =
   new EllipseGeometry(20, 26, 10, 10);
Shape lune = shapeOfIntersection(topCircle,bottomCircle);
```

Interestingly, the same strategy used by the `shapeOfIntersection` procedure can also be used to form the union or difference of two area geometries, the only difference being the Boolean shape operation that gets applied in the last step. Suppose that the desired Boolean shape operation is carried out by a procedure `applyOp` which, when called with two `Area` arguments, sets the first argument to represent their Boolean combination. We use `applyOp` to implement a procedure that generalizes the `shapeOfIntersection` procedure. The following procedure returns the union, intersection, or difference of its two arguments, depending on which of these three Boolean shape operations the procedure `applyOp` implements:

```
public Shape shape(AreaGeometry a, AreaGeometry b) {
  Area aArea = new Area(a.shape());
  Area bArea = new Area(b.shape());
  applyOp(aArea,bArea);
  return aArea;
}
```

The procedure `shape` defined previously is an example of a template method. It defines an algorithm, some of whose steps are not implemented; specifically, the operation specified by `applyOp` is left unimplemented. So where does the `applyOp` procedure get implemented? Answer: in the subclasses of the class to which method `shape` belongs. The idea of the template method pattern is to locate a template method in an abstract parent class. The child classes implement those abstract methods that the template method calls. In addition, the parent class *declares* the necessary abstract methods to ensure that its child classes provide implementations. In the context of this design pattern, these abstract methods are known as **hook methods.**

Let's apply the template method design pattern to our Boolean geometry problem. We'll include the `shape` procedure defined previously as a method belonging to an abstract `BooleanGeometry` class. This `BooleanGeometry` class also declares an abstract `applyOp` procedure. Subclasses of `BooleanGeometry` are responsible for implementing `applyOp`. We define three concrete subclasses of `BooleanGeometry`, one for each Boolean shape operation (see Figure 6.15). Here, `shape` is a template method and `applyOp` is its sole hook method.

Figure 6.15 indicates that a `BooleanGeometry` is composed of two area geometry objects, named `a` and `b` in the class diagram, whose combination forms the Boolean geometry. The third compartment of each class box indicates relevant operations and their return types. The `BooleanGeometry` class defines two relevant operations, `shape` and `applyOp`, where `applyOp`

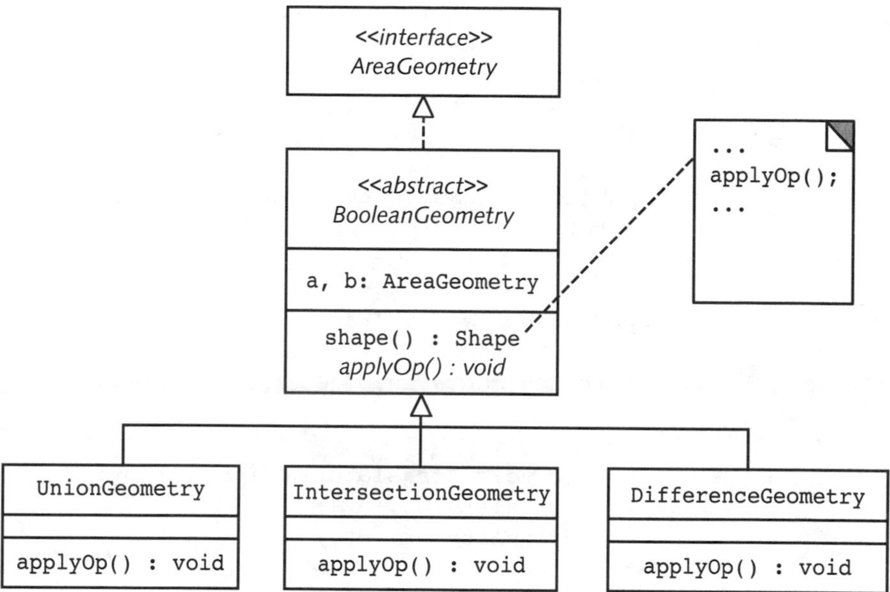

FIGURE 6.15 Boolean geometry classes use the template method.

is italicized to indicate that it is an abstract operation of the `BooleanGeometry` class. Each of the three concrete subclasses inherits its fields from its superclass `BooleanGeometry` and implements the `applyOp` operation. The note attached to the `BooleanGeometry.shape` method in Figure 6.15 shows the form of this method's implementation; specifically, the `shape` method calls the abstract `applyOp` method. This is the hallmark of the template method pattern: A template method calls one or more hook methods that are declared abstract within the template method's class.

Let us implement the `BooleanGeometry` class. Because a Boolean geometry encloses area, our class implements the `AreaGeometry` interface. This means that the `BooleanGeometry` class (or at least its descendants) is responsible for implementing the `contains`, `shape`, and `translate` methods. Here is the class definition:

```
public abstract class BooleanGeometry
      implements AreaGeometry {

  protected AreaGeometry a, b;

  protected BooleanGeometry(AreaGeometry a, AreaGeometry b)
          throws NullPointerException {
    // EFFECTS: If a or b is null throws
    //   NullPointerException; else constructs
    //   the Boolean combination of a and b.
```

```
    if ((a==null) || (b==null))
      throw new NullPointerException();
    this.a = a;
    this.b = b;
  }

  public boolean contains(int x, int y) {
    return shape().contains(x, y);
  }

  public boolean contains(PointGeometry p)
         throws NullPointerException {
    return contains(p.getX(), p.getY());
  }

  public void translate(int dx, int dy) {
    a.translate(dx, dy);
    b.translate(dx, dy);
  }

  // the template method shape expects the applyOp method to
  // be implemented by concrete descendants of this class.
  public Shape shape() {
    Area aArea = new Area(a.shape());
    Area bArea = new Area(b.shape());
    applyOp(aArea, bArea);
    return aArea;
  }

  // hook method required by the shape method.
  protected abstract void applyOp(Area aArea, Area bArea);
    // REQUIRES: aArea and bArea are not null.
    // MODIFIES: aArea
    // EFFECTS: Sets aArea to the Boolean combination
    //   of aArea and bArea.
}
```

The two-argument `contains` method delegates its work to the Boolean geometry's shape. This is the same approach taken in our implementation of the `PolygonGeometry.contains` method. Note that the `translate` method translates the Boolean geometry by translating each of its two parts.

The child classes implement the `applyOp` method declared by their parent class `BooleanGeometry`. Here is the definition of the `IntersectionGeometry` class, which represents the intersection of two area geometries `a` and `b`:

```
public class IntersectionGeometry extends BooleanGeometry {

  public IntersectionGeometry(AreaGeometry a,AreaGeometry b)
        throws NullPointerException {
    super(a, b);
  }

  protected void applyOp(Area aArea, Area bArea) {
    aArea.intersect(bArea);
  }
}
```

Exercise

ESSENTIAL 6.19 Implement the `UnionGeometry` and `DifferenceGeometry` classes.

6.3.2 Lunes

A lune is formed by the intersection of two disks (filled circles). In this subsection, we develop a short graphics program for painting lunes, and then encapsulate lunes by its own geometry class.

Painting Lunes

A lune is the intersection of two filled circles. Our lune-painting program assumes that the two circles are of equal radius and that their centers occur along the (vertical) *y* axis at equal distance from the origin. Figure 6.16 (left) illustrates the two parameters that determine a lune's shape and size. A lune's *radius* is the radius of each of the two circles, and its *offset* is the distance between the origin and each circle's center.

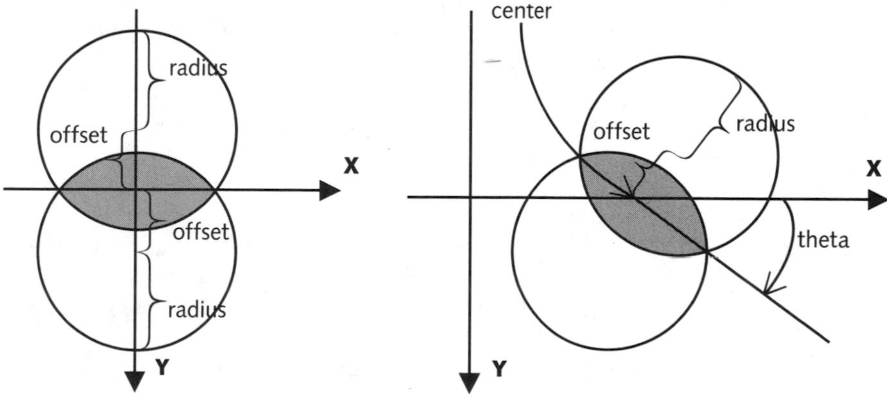

FIGURE 6.16 Parameters for describing lunes.

Our program follows the *MyGraphicsProgram* template, which requires us to define the `parseArgs`, `makeContent`, and `paintComponent` methods for parsing program arguments, creating graphics content, and painting graphics content, respectively. The `PaintLune` program is called with two program arguments specifying the lune's offset and radius values:

```
> java PaintLune offset radius
```

Here is the implementation of the `parseArgs` method:

```
// static fields of PaintLune class
protected static int offset, radius, diam;

// static method of PaintLune class
public static void parseArgs(String[] args) {
  if (args.length != 2) {
    String s="USAGE: java PaintLune offset radius";
    System.out.println(s);
    System.exit(1);
  }
  offset = Integer.parseInt(args[0]);
  radius = Integer.parseInt(args[1]);
  diam = 2 * radius;
}
```

The lune is stored in the `luneFigure` field of type `Figure`. It will be filled with the color forest-green (ours is an earthy lune). Our program's `makeContent` method is defined thus:

```
// field of PaintLune class
protected Figure luneFigure;

// method of PaintLune class
public void makeContent() {
  PointGeometry p =
      new PointGeometry(-radius, -radius-offset);
  AreaGeometry topCircle =
      new EllipseGeometry(p, diam, diam);
  p.translate(0, 2*offset);
  AreaGeometry botCircle =
      new EllipseGeometry(p, diam, diam);
  BooleanGeometry lune =
      new IntersectionGeometry(topCircle, botCircle);
  Painter painter =
      new FillPainter(new Color(33,140,33));
  luneFigure =
      new Figure(lune, painter);
}
```

In the following implementation of the paintComponent method, the last three instructions translate the rendering context to the center of the screen and paints the lune:

```
// method of PaintLune class
public void paintComponent(Graphics g) {
  super.paintComponent(g);
  Graphics2D g2 = (Graphics2D)g;
  g2.setRenderingHint(RenderingHints.KEY_ANTIALIASING,
                      RenderingHints.VALUE_ANTIALIAS_ON);
  Dimension d = getFrame().getContentSize();
  g2.translate((int)(d.width/2), (int)(d.height/2));
  luneFigure.paint(g2);
}
```

Exercise

6.20 Implement the PaintLune program described in this section.

A Lune Geometry Class

Here, we develop a class that encapsulates a lune geometry. To generalize the position and orientation of lunes, I'll introduce two more parameters for describing lunes, in addition to those of *offset* and *radius* presented earlier in the context of the PaintLune program. The *center* of a lune is the position of its center. The *theta* of a lune is the angle that its major axis makes with the right-pointing horizontal, measured in degrees. These parameters appear in the right diagram of Figure 6.16. Our LuneGeometry class provides a constructor that takes these parameters as values:

```
public LuneGeometry(PointGeometry center, int offset,
                    int radius, double theta)
```

The LuneGeometry class defines an instance field that stores a Boolean geometry representing the lune:

```
// field of LuneGeometry class
protected AreaGeometry lune
```

This lune field is set by a protected computeLune method based on the values of the class' remaining fields. Because a lune encloses area, our LuneGeometry class implements the AreaGeometry interface. Here is the class definition in its entirety:

```
public class LuneGeometry implements AreaGeometry {

  protected AreaGeometry lune;
  protected PointGeometry center;
```

```
protected int offset, radius;
protected double theta;

public LuneGeometry(PointGeometry center,
          int offset, int radius, double theta)
       throws NullPointerException {
  // EFFECTS: If center is null throws
  //   NullPointerException; else constructs a
  //   lune based on the supplied parameters.
  this.center = new PointGeometry(center);
  this.offset = offset;
  this.radius = radius;
  this.theta = theta;
  computeLune();
}

public Shape shape() {
  return lune.shape();
}

public void translate(int dx, int dy) {
  center.translate(dx, dy);
  computeLune();
}

public boolean contains(int x, int y) {
  return shape().intersects(x-0.01, y-0.01, .02, .02);
}

public boolean contains(PointGeometry p) {
  return contains(p.getX(), p.getY());
}

protected void computeLune() {
  // REQUIRES: center is not null.
  // MODIFIES: lune
  // EFFECTS: Sets lune to values in the center,
  //   offset, radius, and theta fields
  int diam = 2 * radius;
  TransformablePointGeometry topP =
   new TransformablePointGeometry(center.getX(),
                        center.getY()-offset);
  topP.rotate(theta, center);
  topP.translate(-radius, -radius);
  AreaGeometry topCircle =
    new EllipseGeometry(topP, diam, diam);
  TransformablePointGeometry botP =
```

```
        new TransformablePointGeometry(center.getX(),
                                       center.getY()+offset);
      botP.rotate(theta, center);
      botP.translate(-radius, -radius);
      AreaGeometry botCircle =
        new EllipseGeometry(botP, diam, diam);
      lune =
        new IntersectionGeometry(topCircle, botCircle);
    }
}
```

Exercises

6.21 What are the class invariants for the `LuneGeometry` class?

6.22 Describe the dimensions—position, width, and height—of each of the two circles whose intersection produces the following lune:

```
new LuneGeometry(new PointGeometry(10,20),100,120,45)
```

6.23 Generalize the `PaintLune` program so that it also takes three optional program arguments: *theta* specifies the lune's angle of rotation, and the integers *x* and *y* the position of its center:

```
> java PaintLune offset radius [theta [x y]]
```

The values of *theta*, *x*, and *y* are zero whenever the optional program arguments are not supplied.

6.24 Develop a `NutGeometry` class for representing nuts, such as the one pictured in the middle image of Figure 6.14, composed of a regular polygon from which a smaller circle is subtracted. The constructor is called with the position of the nut's center, the polygon's number of sides `n`, the polygon's radius (`outerRadius`), the circle's radius (`innerRadius`), and the regular polygon's twist:

```
public NutGeometry(PointGeometry center, int n,
  int outerRadius, int innerRadius, double twist)
       throws NullPointerException,
              IllegalArgumentException
  // EFFECTS: If center is null throws
  //   NullPointerException; else if n<=2, or
  //   innerRadius or outerRaidus are <= 0 throws
  //   IllegalArgumentException; else creates a
  //   nut with the specified parameters.
```

Your class should implement the `AreaGeometry` interface. You may want to model your class after our `LuneGeometry` class, and to form the nut as the Boolean difference of a `RegularPolygonGeometry` and an `EllipseGeometry`.

Also, write a graphical program called `PaintNut` that when called like this:

```
> java PaintNut n outerRadius innerRadius [theta [x y]]
```

paints an *n*-sided nut with specified radii and twist, and centered at the point (*x*,*y*): the default value for the twist is zero and the default center is the origin. What sort of geometry results when *innerRadius* is no less than *outerRadius*?

6.3.3 Constructive Area Geometry

To construct a lune in the previous section, we combined two basic geometries (ellipses). Yet, it is also possible to form the union, intersection, or difference of Boolean geometries as well as basic geometries. The process of constructing new shapes by applying Boolean shape operations to existing geometries—both basic and Boolean—is known as **constructive area geometry (CAG).**

The result of this process can be depicted as a binary tree of geometries known as a **CAG tree.** Figure 6.17 shows the CAG tree for an eye shape, constructed by subtracting a circle (representing the iris) from a lune, and then adding a circle of even smaller radius (the pupil). A CAG tree's leaf nodes—those nodes that have no children—represent basic area geometries such as ellipses, rectangles, and polygons. In contrast, each internal node denotes a Boolean shape operation *op* and represents the geometry obtained by applying *op* to the geometries represented by its two child nodes.

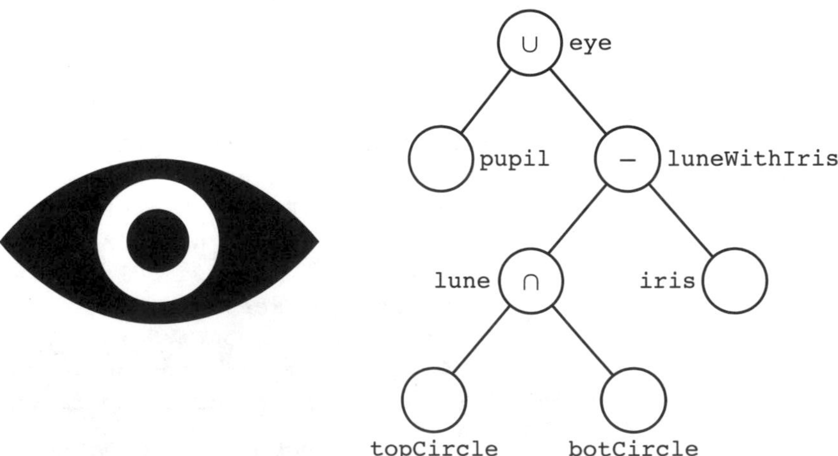

FIGURE 6.17 Using constructive area geometry to build an eye.

The CAG tree shown in Figure 6.17 can be constructed using the code fragment given next. Each node is labeled by the name of the corresponding variable in the code fragment. The code fragment includes several parameters specifying the eye's dimensions:

```
int lunerad,       // lune radius (see Figure 6.16)
    luneOffset,    // lune offset (see Figure 6.16)
    luneDiam,      // lune diameter: 2*luneRad
    irisRad,       // iris radius
    irisDiam,      // iris diameter: 2*irisRad
    pupilRad,      // pupil radius
    pupilDiam;     // pupil diameter: 2*pupilRad

AreaGeometry topCircle =
 new EllipseGeometry(-luneRad, -luneOffset-luneRad,
                    luneDiam, luneDiam);
AreaGeometry botCircle =
  new EllipseGeometry(-luneRad, luneOffset-luneRad,
                     luneDiam, luneDiam);
BooleanGeometry lune =
  new IntersectionGeometry(topCircle, botCircle);
AreaGeometry iris =
  new EllipseGeometry(-irisRad, -irisRad,
                     irisDiam, irisDiam);
BooleanGeometry luneWithIris =
  new DifferenceGeometry(lune, iris);
AreaGeometry pupil =
  new EllipseGeometry(-pupilRad, -pupilRad,
                     pupilDiam, pupilDiam);
BooleanGeometry eye =
  new UnionGeometry(pupil, luneWithIris);
```

Exercises

6.25 Write a Java application based on the *MyGraphicsProgram* template for creating eyes of the sort pictured in Figure 6.17. Your application is called with four program arguments:

```
> java PaintEye luneRadius luneOffset irisRad pupilRad
```

matching the parameters used in the code fragment given earlier. The eye pictured in Figure 6.17 was made using the following parameter settings:

```
luneRadius: 160
luneOffset: 120
```

```
irisRad: 30
pupilRad: 15
```

6.26 Write an interactive program `PlayBoolean` for constructing and displaying Boolean geometries. The program maintains a current Boolean geometry. Each text command describes a regular polygon that gets combined with the current Boolean geometry to form a new current Boolean geometry. The command also indicates whether the new Boolean geometry is formed by union, intersection, or difference. (Initially, the current Boolean geometry is null. The first command replaces this by the regular polygon that the command describes.) Here are the commands:

- **union *n radius***—forms the union of the current geometry with a regular *n*-sided polygon of specified radius, centered at the origin (at the center of the frame).
- **intersection *n radius***—forms the intersection of the current geometry with a regular *n*-sided polygon of specified radius, centered at the origin.
- **difference *n radius***—forms the difference of the current geometry with a regular *n*-sided polygon of specified radius, centered at the origin.
- **quit**—exits the program.

Figure 6.18 shows what is painted at three different points during the following sample interaction:

```
> java PlayBoolean
? union 4 100
? difference 6 60      // left figure of Figure 6.18
? union 4 40           // middle figure
? intersection 3 100   // right figure
? quit
```

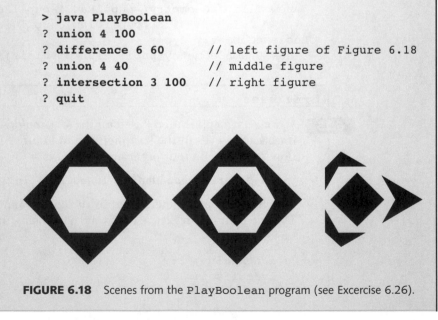

FIGURE 6.18 Scenes from the `PlayBoolean` program (see Excercise 6.26).

6.27 As things stand, the regular polygons specified in the `BooleanPlay` program are all centered at the origin and have zero degrees of twist. Add the following two commands to your program to make it possible to specify each regular polygon's center and twist:

- **twist** ***d***—subsequent polygons specified by the *union, difference,* and *intersection* commands have a twist of *d* degrees.
- **center** ***x y***—subsequent polygons specified by the *union, difference,* and *intersection* commands are centered at position (*x,y*).

The following transcript refers to Figure 6.19:

```
> java PlayBoolean
? union 4 100
? center 50 0
? union 4 100       // left figure of Figure 6.19
? twist 45
? difference 4 60   // middle figure
? center -25 0
? twist 10
? difference 8 20   // right figure
? quit
```

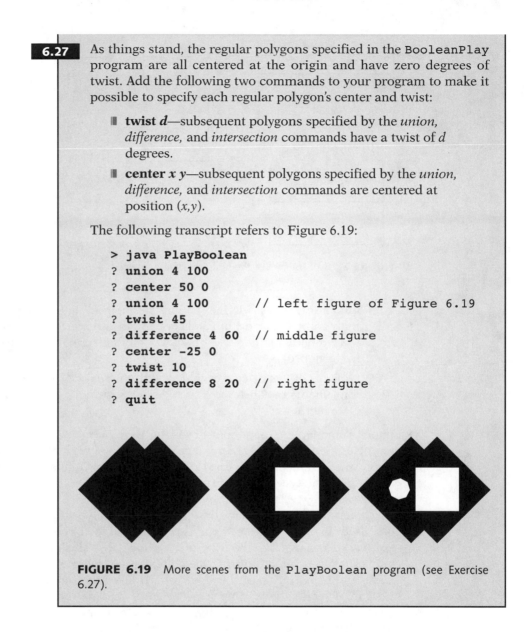

FIGURE 6.19 More scenes from the `PlayBoolean` program (see Exercise 6.27).

6.3.4 Structure and Applicability of the Template Method Pattern

The template method pattern is used to define an algorithm, some of whose steps are implemented by subclasses. The algorithm is carried out by a method known as a template method which calls one or more abstract methods (its hook methods). By implementing the hook methods, subclasses complete the algorithm in different ways. Figure 6.20 shows the structure of the template method pattern. There are two kinds of participants in this design pattern:

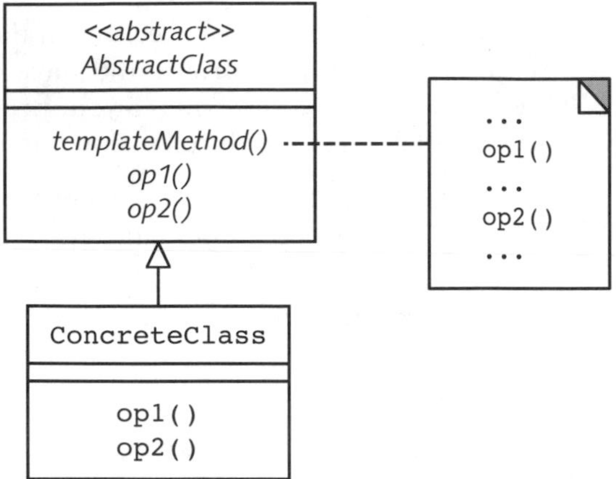

FIGURE 6.20 Structure of the template method pattern.

- ***`AbstractClass`***—defines a template method that implements a partially complete algorithm and specifies the abstract hook methods that the template method uses (the hook methods are named *`op1`* and *`op2`* in the figure).
- ***`ConcreteClass`***—classes that extend *`AbstractClass`*, each of which implements the abstract hook methods required by the inherited template method.

In our example, `BooleanGeometry` is the *`AbstractClass`*, and `shape` is its template method. Here `shape` depends on one hook method to apply the Boolean shape operation (`applyOp`), which in turn gets implemented by three different types of *`ConcreteClass`* (`UnionGeometry`, `IntersectionGeometry`, and `DifferenceGeometry`).

Under this design pattern, the algorithm realized by the template method is reused. Each *`ConcreteClass`* is responsible for implementing only the *abstract* operations that the template method calls. This minimizes both the effort that goes into authoring the child classes and the likelihood of erroneous implementation of the algorithm. It also guarantees that each child class implements the missing steps, because any *`ConcreteClass`* that fails to implement the abstract hook methods declared by its parent class *`AbstractClass`* will not be concrete and therefore cannot be instantiated.

6.4 The Composite Design Pattern

The composite pattern is used when you want to group a set of **primitive** objects together, thereby forming a **composite.** Because both primitives and composites can be grouped, it is possible to build hierarchies that extend to arbitrary depth. The key to this design pattern is an interface that gets implemented by both the primitives and the composites. This enables clients to treat both primitives and composites uniformly—both can be viewed as **components.**

Java's Abstract Window Toolkit (AWT) employs this design pattern to let you construct containment hierarchies of GUI components (containment hierarchies were discussed in Section 3.4.2). Examples of GUI components include buttons, lists, labels, text fields, and containers. Containers are components that can contain other components. Because containers are a kind of component, they themselves may be contained, thereby allowing components and containers to nest arbitrarily. The beauty of this design pattern is that containers behave like components. Thus, a client may send (say) a *repaint* message to a component without knowing whether the receiver is an atomic component such as a button or a label, or a container of other components.

In the rest of this section, we will apply this design pattern to the problem of representing composite figures, which are figures composed of simpler figures.

6.4.1 Composite Figures

Up to now, we've developed the means to construct primitive figures: blue rectangles, polygons outlined in green, purple Boolean geometries, and the like. In practice, however, the sort of figures we often work with are more complex, such as those depicted in Figure 6.21. Such **composite figures** are composed of simpler figures; each simpler figure may be a composite in its own right, composed of still simpler figures. What results is a hierarchy of figures whose leaves are primitive figures like those cited previously, and whose root is the composite figure that the hierarchy represents as a whole.

There are several advantages to working with composite figures. First, composite figures may be treated in many ways like primitive figures. You can define classes for creating faces or flowers, and you can paint instances of these classes into rendering contexts. A second advantage is that you can

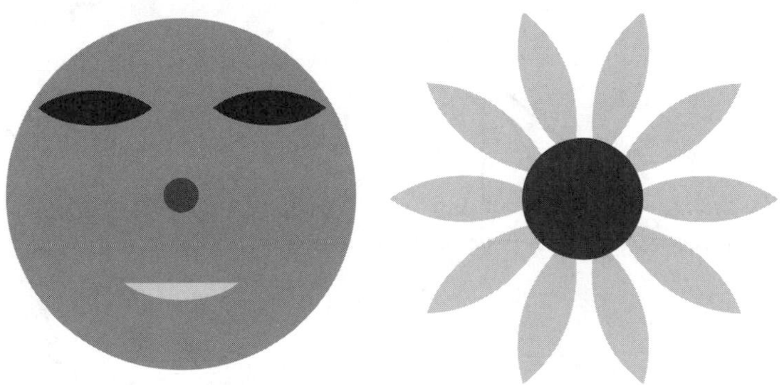

FIGURE 6.21 Two composite figures.

modify individual components without affecting the rest of the composite to which they belong. Thus, the color or shape of a face's eyes can be changed without affecting the rest of the face. Lastly, you can add new components to and remove existing components from composite figures. A stem can be added to a flower or the mouth removed from a face.

We define a `GroupNode` class for representing composite figures. A `GroupNode` object maintains a list of simpler figures which are its components. The following code fragment illustrates how we might use this class to construct the face shown in Figure 6.21:

```
GroupNode face = new GroupNode();
face.addChild(contour);
face.addChild(leftEye);
face.addChild(rightEye);
face.addChild(nose);
face.addChild(mouth);
```

In the code fragment, it is assumed that the variables `contour`, `leftEye`, `rightEye`, `nose`, and `mouth` reference instances of the `Figure` class; for example, `leftEye` and `rightEye` each reference a blue lune, and `mouth` references a green Boolean geometry formed by a circle minus a rectangle (you'll just have to imagine the colors). The hierarchy that results is shown in the left drawing of Figure 6.22.

Hierarchies of figures such as those of Figure 6.22 are known as **scene graphs.** The elements that comprise a scene graph are called **nodes.** The left scene graph of Figure 6.22 contains six nodes: the `GroupNode face` and its five components, all five of which are instances of the `Figure` class.

Within a scene graph, the components of a `GroupNode` are referred to as its **children.** Children are maintained in index order, where the first child has the index zero. The order of a group node's children is important because it affects the node's appearance when it is painted. Specifically, when a group node is painted, its children get painted in index order: Children with higher indexes are painted after—therefore on top of—children with lower indexes.

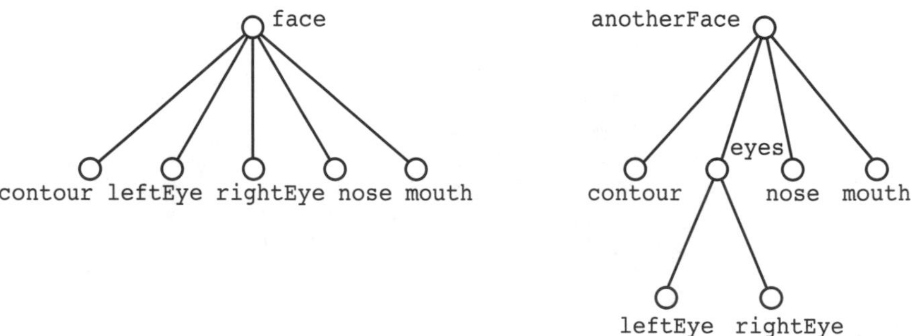

FIGURE 6.22 Two possible scene graphs for the face of Figure 6.21.

What behaviors do group nodes such as `face` support? First, it is possible to paint a `GroupNode` into a rendering context `g2`:

```
face.paint(g2);
```

It is also possible to add more children to a group node using its `addChild` method and to remove children using its `removeChild` method. In addition, you can access individual children: When called with the index of the child being sought, the `child` method returns a reference to that child. For example, the following code fragment gives the group node `face` a black left eye:

```
Figure eye = face.child(1);
eye.setPainter(new FillPainter(Color.black));
```

`GroupNode` objects also provide iterators for visiting its children in index order. For instance, we can outline all of `face`'s children in green using this code fragment:

```
Iterator iter = face.iterator();
while (iter.hasNext()) {
  Figure fig = (Figure)iter.next();
  fig.setPainter(new DrawPainter(Color.green));
}
```

The scene graph rooted at `face` is only two levels deep. Yet, because a `GroupNode` object can contain other `GroupNode`'s as children, scene graphs can extend to any depth. In the second scene graph of Figure 6.22, the child `eyes` of the root `anotherFace` is a `GroupNode`; its children are the figures `leftEye` and `rightEye`. This scene graph nests the group node `eyes` within the group node `anotherFace`. The following code fragment produces this scene graph:

```
  // build the composite figure eyes
GroupNode eyes = new GroupNode();
eyes.addChild(leftEye);
eyes.addChild(rightEye);
  // build the composite figure anotherFace
GroupNode anotherFace = new GroupNode();
anotherFace.addChild(contour);
anotherFace.addChild(eyes);
anotherFace.addChild(nose);
anotherFace.addChild(mouth);
```

The code fragment suggests that the children of a `GroupNode` may be either of two types: `GroupNode` or `Figure`. These two types share a common supertype, which we shall name `Node`. The `Node` type specifies the behavior that group nodes and figures have in common: Both `GroupNode` and `Figure` objects can be painted into rendering contexts. Accordingly, we define the `Node` interface like this:

```
public interface Node {
  public void paint(Graphics2D g2);
  // REQUIRES: g2 is not null.
  // EFFECTS: Paints this scene graph into
  //   the rendering context g2.
}
```

Because our `Figure` class already implements this `paint` method, we need only revise its header so that it declares that it implements the `Node` interface:

```
public class Figure implements Node {
  // same as before
  ...
}
```

We will also ensure that our `GroupNode` class, to be defined momentarily, also implements the `Node` interface.

Figure 6.23 shows that a `GroupNode` is made up of `Node` objects; these `Nodes` are the group node's children. The multiplicity symbol "*" along the edge connecting the `GroupNode` class box to the `Node` class box stands for *zero or more:* A `GroupNode` can have any number of children. The `GroupNode` class is used to represent composites. In contrast, the `Figure` class represents primitive components. The `Node` interface provides the interface shared by all components, both group nodes and figures.

Although the `Figure` and `GroupNode` classes both implement the `Node` interface, their interfaces also differ. Group nodes provide methods for adding, removing, and accessing children (some of the additional operations that the `GroupNode` class supports appear in its class box in Figure 6.23). In contrast, a figure provides accessors for its *geometry* and *painter* properties.

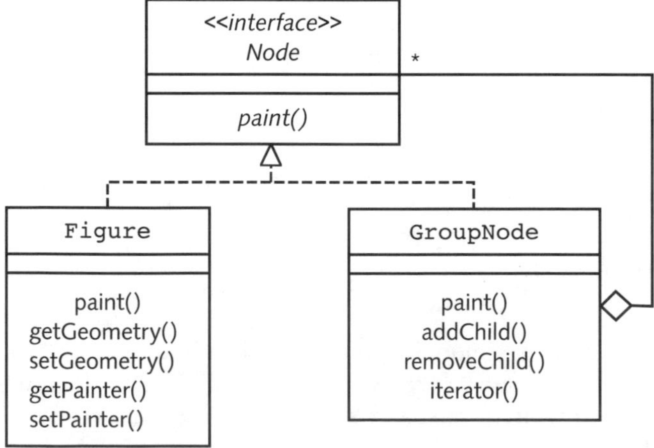

FIGURE 6.23 Class diagram for composite figures.

In the composite design pattern, all components share a common interface (`Node`), but it is also common for primitive components (`Figure`) and composites (`GroupNode`) to extend their respective interfaces.

Having considered how group nodes behave, we can turn to an implementation. We will store the children of a `GroupNode` in a vector, ordered by index. Here is the implementation:

```
public class GroupNode implements Node {

  protected Vector children;

  public GroupNode() {
    // EFFECTS: Creates a group node with no children.
    children = new Vector();
  }

  public int nbrChildren() {
    // EFFECTS: Returns the number of children.
    return children.size();
  }

  public void addChild(Node node, int i)
         throws NullPointerException,
                IndexOutOfBoundsException {
    //  MODIFIES: this
    //  EFFECTS: If node is null throws
    //    NullPointerException; else if 0 <= i  and
    //    i <= nbrChildren() inserts node as the i'th
    //    child and increases by one the index of every
    //    child whose index not less than i; else
    //    throws IndexOutOfBoundsException.
    if (node == null) throw new NullPointerException();
    children.add(i, node);
  }

  public void addChild(Node node)
         throws NullPointerException {
    // MODIFIES: this
    // EFFECTS: If node is null throws
    //   NullPointerException; else inserts node
    //   as the last child.
    addChild(node, children.size());
  }

  public void removeChild(int i)
         throws IndexOutOfBoundsException {
    //  MODIFIES: this
```

```
    //  EFFECTS: If 0 <= i < nbrChildren() removes the
    //    i'th child and decreases by one the index of
    //    every child whose index is greater than i;
    //    else throws IndexOutOfBoundsException.
    children.remove(i);
  }

  public Node child(int i)
        throws IndexOutOfBoundsException {
    // EFFECTS: If 0 <= i < size() returns the i'th child;
    //   else throws IndexOutOfBoundsException.
    return (Node)children.get(i);
  }

  public Iterator iterator() {
    // EFFECTS: Returns an iterator which visits this
    //   node's children in index order.
    return children.iterator();
  }

  public void paint(Graphics2D g2) {
    // REQUIRES: g2 is not null.
    // EFFECTS: Paints this scene graph into g2.
    Iterator iter = iterator();
    while (iter.hasNext()) {
      Node node = (Node)iter.next();
      node.paint(g2);
    }
  }
}
```

Most of class `GroupNode`'s methods are implemented by delegating to its vector `children`. Observe that the implementation of the `paint` method exploits the fact that any subtype of `Node` can be painted: The method sends `node` the *paint* message without having to determine whether `node` is a group node or a figure.

6.4.2 Building a Set of Axes

In this section, we define a class for representing a pair of axes in the plane. Our `Axes` class will serve as a graphical aid when we cover coordinate systems in the next section. A pair of axes is drawn as a two lines—a horizontal *x* axis and a vertical *y* axis—with tick marks appearing at regular intervals. In Figure 6.24, the axes cross at the origin (0,0), and the tick marks occur at 50-unit intervals (the face has radius 100). The scene graph shows that a pair of axes is represented by a group node named `axes` containing two children, `xAxis` and `yAxis`. In turn, each of `xAxis` and `yAxis` is a group node

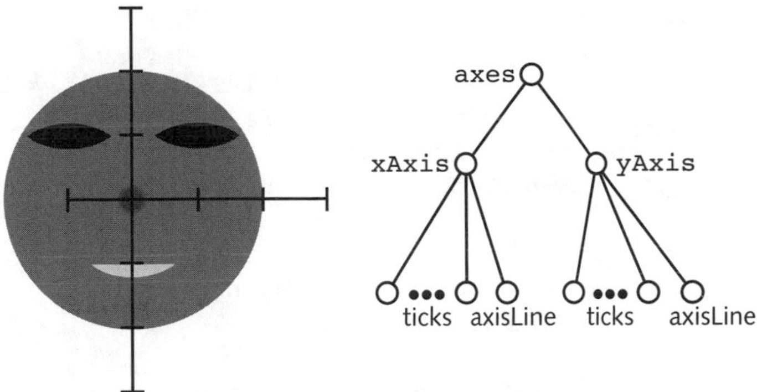

FIGURE 6.24 The scene graph for a pair of coordinate axes.

composed of a number of `Figure` objects representing the axis line and its multiple tick marks.

The four-argument constructor looks like this:

```
public Axes(Range xRange, Range yRange,
            int tickStep, Painter painter)
```

The `xRange` argument determines the extent of the *x* axis: The *x* axis extends from the point (*xMin,0*) to the point (*xMax,0*) where `xRange` is [*xMin..xMax*]. Analogous remarks apply to the `yRange` argument and the *y* axis. The `tickStep` argument indicates the interval between tick marks along both the *x* and *y* axes; the first tick mark occurs at the point (*xMin*,0) and (*yMin*,0) respectively. The argument `Painter` references the `Painter` object to be applied to every figure that makes up the pair of axes. For example, the following code fragment produces the pair of axes shown in Figure 6.24:

```
Range xRange = new Range(-50, 150);
Range yRange = new Range(-150, 150);
Painter black =
  new DrawPainter(Color.black, new BasicStroke(2));
Node axes = new Axes(xRange, yRange, 50, black);
```

To produce the face and axes shown in Figure 6.24, you can create a new group node and add the face and axes as children:

```
GroupNode faceAndAxes = new GroupNode();
faceAndAxes.addChild(face);
faceAndAxes.addChild(axes);
```

The `Axes` class provides a *tickStep* property whose value indicates the number of units between successive tick marks, and a *tickHeight* property whose value is half the length of a tick mark. A pair of axes is represented by this group node to which are added two children, the group nodes `xAxis` and `yAxis`, corresponding to the *x* and *y* axes. Here is the implementation:

```
public class Axes extends GroupNode {

  protected static int DefaultTickHeight = 2;
  protected static Range DefaultRange =
    new Range(-100, 100);
  protected static int DefaultTickStep = 50;

  protected int tickStep, tickHeight = DefaultTickHeight;
  protected Range xRange, yRange;
  protected Painter painter;

  public Axes(Range xRange, Range yRange,
              int tickStep, Painter painter)
   throws NullPointerException, IllegalArgumentException {
    // EFFECTS: If xRange, yRange, or painter is null
    //   throws NullPointerException; else if tickStep<=0
    //   throws IllegalArgumentException; else constructs
    //   a pair of axes whose x and y extents are given
    //   by xRange and yRange, the interval between tick
    //   marks is given by tickStep, and the axes are
    //   painted by painter.
    if ((xRange==null)||(yRange==null)||(painter==null))
      throw new NullPointerException();
    if (tickStep <= 0)
      throw new IllegalArgumentException();
    this.tickStep = tickStep;
    this.xRange = xRange;
    this.yRange = yRange;
    this.painter = painter;
    createAxes();
  }

  public Axes(Painter painter)
         throws NullPointerException {
    // EFFECTS: If painter is null throws
    //   NullPointerException; else constructs a pair
    //   of axes with x and y extents [-100..100], tick
    //   marks every 50 units, and painted by painter.
    this(DefaultRange, DefaultRange,
         DefaultTickStep, painter);
  }

  public int getTickStep() {
    // EFFECTS: Returns the interval between tick marks.
    return tickStep;
  }
```

```
public void setTickStep(int newTickStep)
       throws IllegalArgumentException {
  // MODIFIES: this
  // EFFECTS: If newTickStep <= 0 throws
  //   IllegalArgumentException; else sets the
  //   interval between tick marks to newTickStep.
  if (newTickStep <= 0)
    throw new IllegalArgumentException();
  tickStep = newTickStep;
  createAxes();
}

public int getTickHeight() {
  // EFFECTS: Returns the height of a tick mark.
  ...
}

public void setTickHeight(int newTickHt)
         throws IllegalArgumentException {
  // MODIFIES: this
  // EFFECTS: If newTickHt is negative throws
  //   IllegalArgumentException; else sets the height
  //   of tick marks to newTickHt.
  ...
}

protected void createAxes() {
  // REQUIRES: Instance fields are initialized.
  // MODIFIES: this.children
  // EFFECTS: Creates a new set of axes.
  if (nbrChildren() >= 2) {
    removeChild(1);
    removeChild(0);
  }
  GroupNode xAxis = createXAxis();
  GroupNode yAxis = createYAxis();
  addChild(xAxis, 0);
  addChild(yAxis, 1);
}

protected GroupNode createXAxis() {
  // REQUIRES: Instance fields are initialized.
  // MODIFIES: this.children
  // EFFECTS: Creates a new x axis.
  GroupNode xAxis = new GroupNode();
  for (int x = xRange.getMin(); x <= xRange.getMax();
                                          x += tickStep) {
```

```
        Geometry tick =
          new LineSegmentGeometry(0, tickHeight,
                                  0, -tickHeight);
        tick.translate(x, 0);
        xAxis.addChild(new Figure(tick, painter));
      }
      Geometry axisLine =
       new LineSegmentGeometry(xRange.getMin(), 0,
                               xRange.getMax(), 0);
      xAxis.addChild(new Figure(axisLine, painter));
      return xAxis;
    }

    protected GroupNode createYAxis() {
      // REQUIRES: Instance fields are initialized.
      // MODIFIES: this.children
      // EFFECTS: Creates a new y axis.
      ...
    }
}
```

Note that the protected `createAxes` method is used to create or recreate the pair of axes. If the axes already exist and must be recreated because the tick step or tick height has changed, `createAxes` removes the existing axes before constructing a new set of axes.

Exercises

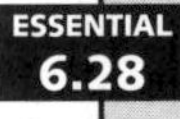

Complete the implementation of the `Axes` class. Write a program that produces a face with a pair of axes superimposed, as in Figure 6.24.

6.29 As things stand, the axes displayed by the `Axes` class are not labeled. Add the following methods to the `Axes` class for attaching the labels *X* and *Y*, and for removing these labels:

```
public void addLabels()
  // MODIFIES: this
  // EFFECTS: If the axes are currently labeled does
  //   nothing; else adds the labels X and Y to this set
  //   of axes, rendered using TextGeometry.DefaultFont.

public void addLabels(Font font)
  // MODIFIES: this
  // EFFECTS: If the axes are currently labeled does
  //   nothing; else if font is null throws
```

```
   //    NullPointerException; else adds the labels X and
   //    Y to this set of axes, rendered using font.

public void removeLabels()
   // MODIFIES: this
   // EFFECTS: If the axes are not currently labeled does
   //    nothing; else removes the labels from the axes.
```

Labeled axes appear in Figure 6.26. You may want to represent each label by a `Figure` whose geometry is a `TextGeometry` object; for instance, the label *X* might contain this geometry:

```
new TextGeometry(font, "X")
```

where `font` is supplied to the `addLabels` method (`TextGeometry`'s default font is used if `font` is not supplied). The *X* label may be added by adding such a figure as a child, and the *Y* label may be added similarly. To remove labels, remove the appropriate children. You might find it helpful to define a `boolean` field whose value indicates whether the axes are currently labeled.

6.30 Write a program `PaintFlower` to produce flowers like the one pictured in the Figure 6.21:

```
> java PaintFlower n radius
```

The resulting flower has *n* leaves spaced evenly along the circumference of the flower's face. The face has specified radius, and the leaves should be scaled such that their length slightly exceeds the diameter of the flower's face.

6.4.3 Transformable Composite Figures

We have seen that when a graphics object is painted into a rendering context (a `Graphics2D` object), the object is positioned and oriented with respect to a coordinate system known as *user space*. By default, user space coincides with Java's default coordinate system, in which the origin occurs in the upper-left corner of the drawing surface with *x* coordinate values increasing to the right and *y* coordinate values increasing down, and (in the case of screen graphics) both *x* and *y* coordinates are measured in pixels. The user space is determined by the rendering context's *transform* property and as such, can be changed. In fact, we have already done a bit of this: Some of our graphics programs have translated user space so that its origin lies in the center of the drawing surface, in order to center renderings in the frame (see Section 3.4.4).

In this section, we define a type of group node that encapsulates a coordinate system. The resulting `TransformGroup` class—a subclass of

GroupNode—defines a coordinate system within which its children are located. But before proceeding, we consider why such a class is useful. There are three principal reasons for defining new coordinate systems. First, doing so allows us to orient certain geometries in ways that are impossible when working in Java's default coordinate system. For example, a rectangle's sides are parallel to the coordinate system's x and y axes. Under the default coordinate system, this means that a rectangle's sides are parallel to the edges of the drawing surface. However, in a *rotated* coordinate system, the rectangle's sides are parallel to the rotated x and y axes, meaning that the rectangle itself is rotated (see Figure 6.26 for an example).

Second, we often define multiple coordinate systems for efficiency. You can locate a given node in different coordinate systems at the same time by creating multiple references to the node, each within its own coordinate system. Each reference is positioned and oriented independent of the other references. This avoids the need to make multiple *copies* of the same node, resulting in smaller scene graphs. Moreover, this facilitates scene graph editing: When the node is edited, such as painted a different color or assigned new children, the changes propagate automatically to every reference to the changed node. In Figure 6.30, you can add a pair of ears to the single group node representing a face, and all 25 faces find themselves endowed with ears.

Lastly, you can choose a coordinate system that is convenient for building scene graphs, independent of the larger scene or scenes in which the scene graph will eventually appear. Thus, you can construct a flower in a convenient coordinate system, such as one whose origin lies at the flower's center. Later, any number of flowers can be located in the coordinate system of a large scene, such as a meadow. Each flower is lifted from the coordinate system of its definition into that of the meadow.

The Behavior of Transform Groups

A TransformGroup object contains any number of nodes as children, and it provides methods for accessing its children and for adding and removing children. As such, we make the TransformGroup class an extension of the GroupNode class. Refer to instances of GroupNode or TransformGroup collectively as **grouping nodes.** Yet the TransformGroup class does more than its superclass: It defines a new coordinate system within which its children are positioned. See the class diagram of Figure 6.25.

A TransformGroup defines a new coordinate system relative to that of its parent node within the scene graph. The new coordinate system is a **child coordinate system** that is nested within its **parent coordinate system.** The parent coordinate system, in turn, may be nested within the coordinate system of *its* parent. The scene graph is viewed as a hierarchy of coordinate systems. At the root of the hierarchy is the top-level coordinate system. Each internal node of the hierarchy is a grouping node that defines its coordinate

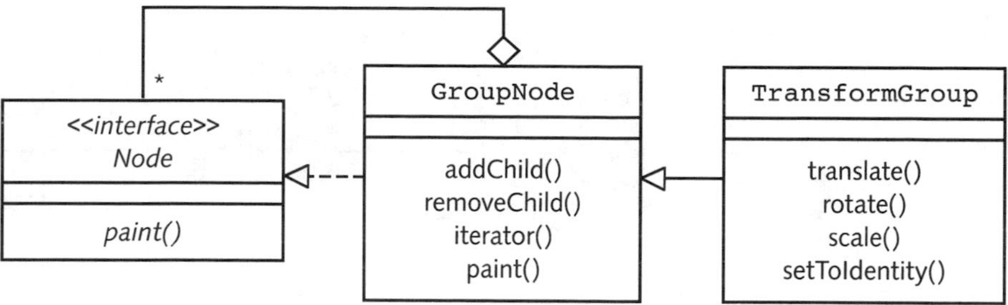

FIGURE 6.25 A `TransformGroup` node is a grouping node that defines a local coordinate system.

system in terms of the coordinate system of its parent node. The leaves of the hierarchy are `Figure` objects.

The children of a `TransformGroup` node are positioned and oriented relative to the node's coordinate system. When that coordinate system is translated, scaled, or rotated, the children are likewise translated, scaled, or rotated. The `TransformGroup` class provides several operations for specifying its coordinate system. We'll look at some examples of their use. These examples assume that the variable `squareFig` references a `Figure` object representing a square centered at the origin and 100 units to a side. This figure might be constructed thus:

```
Geometry geom = new RectangleGeometry(-50, -50, 100, 100);
Painter fillPainter = new FillPainter(Color.green);
Painter drawPainter = new DrawPainter(Color.red);
Painter painter =
  new MultiPainter(fillPainter, drawPainter);
Figure squareFig = new Figure(geom, painter);
```

The following code creates a new transform group and then adds `squareFig` as a child. The `TransformGroup`'s coordinate system is then rotated by 45° in the clockwise sense:

```
TransformGroup rNode = new TransformGroup();
rNode.addChild(squareFig);
rNode.rotate(45.0);
```

The first picture in Figure 6.26 shows the effect of painting `rNode` into a rendering context `g2`:

```
rNode.paint(g2);
```

The illustration includes two pairs of coordinate axes superimposed (the tick marks are set at 50-unit intervals). The black axes indicate the root coordinate system, whereas the gray axes indicate the coordinate system defined by `rNode` to which the square belongs. Note that the square's sides are aligned with the gray coordinate axes.

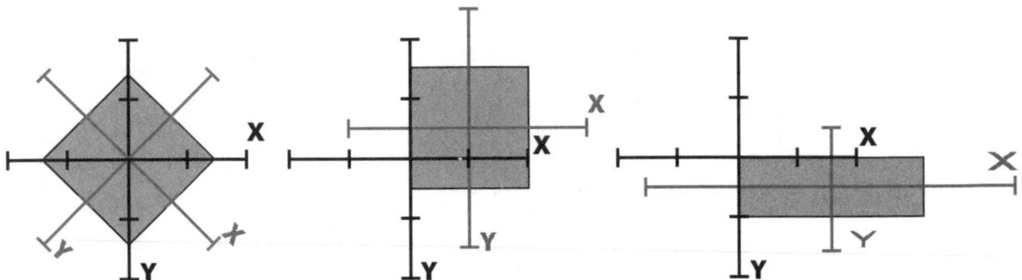

FIGURE 6.26 A square in a rotated, translated, and scaled-then-translated coordinate system.

It is also possible to translate a coordinate system. The following code fragment produces the second illustration in Figure 6.26.

```
TransformGroup tNode = new TransformGroup();
tNode.addChild(squareFig);
tNode.translate(50, -25);
tNode.paint(g2);
```

Scaling a coordinate system stretches or shrinks the units of measure and results in figures growing larger or smaller. The units in the *x* and *y* directions are scaled independently by separate numeric scale factors. The third illustration in Figure 6.26 was produced with the following code:

```
TransformGroup sNode = new TransformGroup();
sNode.scale(1.5, .5);
sNode.translate(50, 50);
sNode.addChild(squareFig);
sNode.paint(g2);
```

Here two transformations are applied in succession: The transform group `sNode` is first scaled, and then translated. Note that the axes and axis labels were scaled along with the square (although the axes do not appear in the code fragment, I added them as children of `sNode` to produce these figures). Observe also that, in this example, the transform group `sNode` was transformed *before* its child `squareFig` was added. Generally, you can add children to a transform group and specify the coordinate system in any order; what matters is the transform group node's state whenever it is painted.

It is of course possible to place any of the nodes constructed in the previous code fragments within a common grouping node. Here, the nodes `rNode` and `tNode` are made children of a common `GroupNode` object:

```
GroupNode scene = new GroupNode();
scene.addChild(rNode);
scene.addChild(tNode);
```

The result is a scene graph whose root node `scene` has the children `rNode` and `tNode`. When painted into a rendering context `g2`:

```
scene.paint(g2);
```

the scene graph displays the same square twice, each positioned and oriented independently. The scene graph in Figure 6.27 illustrates why a scene graph is not called a scene *tree*: It is possible for a node to belong as a child to any number of grouping nodes. In this example, the node **`squareFig`** belongs to two different transform groups (`rNode` and **`tNode`**). In general, a scene graph has the structure of what is known as a **directed acyclic graph,** a generalization of a tree. Note that any change made to the figure `squareFig` propagates to every instance. For example, the following expression suffices to paint *both* squares in Figure 6.27 magenta:

```
squareFig.setPainter(new FillPainter(Color.magenta));
```

Here is the skeleton for the `TransformGroup` class:

```
public class TransformGroup extends GroupNode {

  public TransformGroup()
    // EFFECTS: Constructs a new transform group having
    //   the same coordinate system as its parent node
    //   in the scene graph.

  public void rotate(double theta)
    // MODIFIES: this
    // EFFECTS: Rotates this coordinate system by theta
    //   degrees around its origin, from the x axis
    //   toward the y axis (i.e., clockwise in the
    //   default user space).

  public void rotate(double theta, PointGeometry center)
        throws NullPointerException
    // MODIFIES: this
```

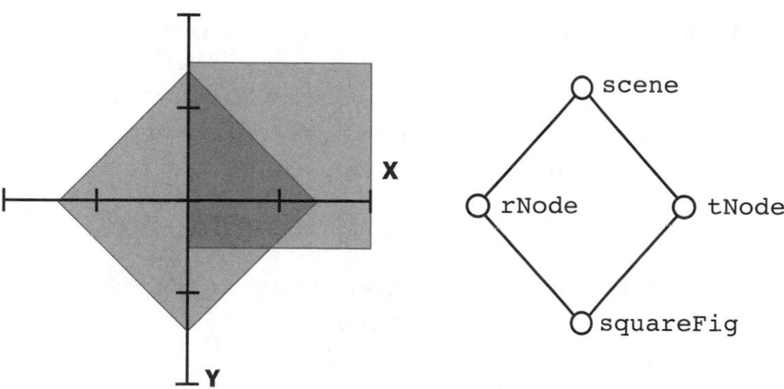

FIGURE 6.27 A scene graph and its rendering.

```
    // EFFECTS: If center is null throws
    //   NullPointerException; else rotates this
    //   coordinate system by theta degrees around
    //   center, from the x axis toward the y axis.

  public void scale(double sx, double sy)
         throws IllegalArgumentException
    // MODIFIES: this
    // EFFECTS: If sx or sy equals zero throws
    //   IllegalArgumentException; else scales this
    //   coordinate system by sx along x and sy along y.

  public void translate(double dx, double dy)
    // MODIFIES: this
    // EFFECTS: Translates this coordinate system by dx
    //   along x and dy along y.

  public void setToIdentity()
    // MODIFIES: this
    // EFFECTS: Restores this coordinate system to that
    //   of its parent node in the scene graph.

  public void paint(Graphics2D g)
    // EFFECTS: Paints this node's children in index
    //   order within its coordinate system.
}
```

Transforms and Rendering Contexts

To understand the implementation of the `TransformGroup` class requires some preliminaries. As we've seen, a transform group specifies a new coordinate system in terms of another coordinate system, specifically, that of its parent node in the scene graph. A group node represents its coordinate system by means of a **coordinate-system transformation,** more simply known as a **transform.** A transform captures the differences between two coordinate systems; it describes the steps needed to obtain one coordinate system from another.

Java provides the `java.awt.geom.AffineTransform` class for representing transforms. `AffineTransform`'s zero-argument constructor returns a new **identity transform,** which represents the same coordinate system as the original one. Subsequently, one changes the transform by applying such operations such as *translate*, *rotate*, and *scale*. For example, the following code fragment:

```
AffineTransform tform = new AffineTransform();
tform.rotate(Math.toRadians(45));
tform.translate(50, 100);
```

produces a transform `tform` representing a rotation by 45 degrees around the origin, followed by a translation by 50 units along the x axis and 100 units along the *y* axis. The `AffineTransform` class also provides a `setToIdentity` method that resets it to the identity transform. The following skeleton for the `AffineTransform` class specifies only those methods that we will need:

```
public class AffineTransform {

  public AffineTransform()
    // EFFECTS: Initializes this to identity transform.

  public void translate(double dx, double dy)
    // MODIFIES: this
    // EFFECTS: Translates this by dx along x and
    //   dy along y.

  public void rotate(double theta)
    // MODIFIES: this
    // EFFECTS: Rotates this by theta radians around
    //   the origin, from the x axis toward the y axis.

  public void rotate(double theta, double x, double y)
    // MODIFIES: this
    // EFFECTS: Rotates this by theta radians around
    //   (x,y), from the x axis toward the y axis.

  public void scale(double sx, double sy)
    // MODIFIES: this
    // EFFECTS: Scales this by sx along the x axis and
    //   sy along the y axis.

  public void setToIdentity()
    // MODIFIES: this
    // EFFECTS: Restores this to the identity transform.
}
```

We saw in Section 3.4.4 that a `Graphics2D` object has a *transform* attribute that determines the coordinate system in which rendering takes place. The value of this *transform* attribute is an `AffineTransform` object. Some of our previous graphics programs used this *transform* attribute to center graphics within the frame. Consider the following generic `paintComponent` procedure, which paints the node `scene` into the rendering context `g2`:

```
public void paintComponent(Graphics g) {
  super.paintComponent(g);
  Graphics2D g2 = (Graphics2D)g;
  Dimension d = getFrame().getContentSize();
  g2.translate((int)(d.width/2), (int)(d.height/2));
  scene.paint(g2);
}
```

Here, g2 is told to translate itself by half the dimensions of the frame. This repositions the origin of g2's coordinate system from the frame's upper-left corner to its center, so that scene gets painted in the center of the frame. The value of g2's *transform* attribute is modified by the *translate* message it is sent.

In general, whenever a Graphics2D object receives a message to transform its coordinate system, it responds by updating the value of its *transform* attribute. For instance, in response to the message

```
g2.translate(50,100)
```

the rendering context g2 sends its AffineTransform object a *translate* message.

The Graphics2D class provides several other methods in addition to translate for modifying its coordinate system. Its scale method is used to scale the coordinate system by the factors sx along the *x* axis and sy along the *y* axis:

```
// method of Graphics2D class
public void scale(double sx, double sy)
```

The rotate method is used to rotate the coordinate system by theta radians around the point (*x*,*y*):

```
// method of Graphics2D class
public void rotate(double theta, double x, double y);
```

For example, the following code fragment paints a rotated square in the center of the frame:

```
Dimension d = getFrame().getContentSize();
g2.translate((int)(d.width/2), (int)(d.height/2));
g2.rotate(Math.toRadians(45), 0, 0);
squareFig.paint(g2);
```

Here g2's coordinate system is first translated to the center of the frame, and then rotated by 45° around its frame-centered origin.

The Graphics2D class also provides the transform method, which takes a transform as input and applies the transform to its coordinate system:

```
// method of Graphics2D class
public void transform(AffineTransform tform)
```

One way to specify the coordinate system of a rendering context g2 is to set a transform tform as desired, and then to transform g2 by tform. For example, the following code has the effect of rotating g2's coordinate system by 45°, and then translating it by 50 units along the *x* axis and 100 units along the *y* axis. The resulting square is rotated, and then translated:

```
AffineTransform tform = new AffineTransform();
tform.rotate(Math.toRadians(45));
tform.translate(50, 100);
```

```
g2.transform(tform);
squareFig.paint(g2);
```

The `Graphics2D` class also provides the following methods for setting and getting its *transform* attribute, respectively:

```
// methods of Graphics2D class
public void setTransform(AffineTransform newTform)
public AffineTransform getTransform();
```

To summarize, a rendering context—that is, an instance of the `Graphics2D` class—has a *transform* attribute whose value is a `java.awt.geom.AffineTransform` object. This attribute specifies the coordinate system that is in force whenever a client renders into the rendering context. The rendering context provides a number of methods for modifying its coordinate system—for translating, scaling, rotating, restoring to identity, transforming by a given transform, and others. Whenever a graphics context receives any sort of transform-yourself message, it responds by transforming its `AffineTransform` object in the manner called for.

Implementing Transform Groups

We're at last in a position to implement the `TransformGroup` class. As we've seen, a `TransformGroup` object defines a new coordinate system relative to that of its parent node within the scene graph. It is natural to represent this transform using an instance of the `AffineTransform` class. Indeed, the `AffineTransform` class serves our `TransformGroup` class in the same way it serves the `Graphics2D` class: as a component used to represent and manipulate a coordinate system (see Figure 6.28).

The `TransformGroup` class stores its transform in the following field:

```
// field of TransformGroup class
protected AffineTransform tform;
```

The class defines only one constructor, which takes no arguments and produces a new transform group representing the identity transform:

```
public TransformGroup() {
  tform = new AffineTransform();
}
```

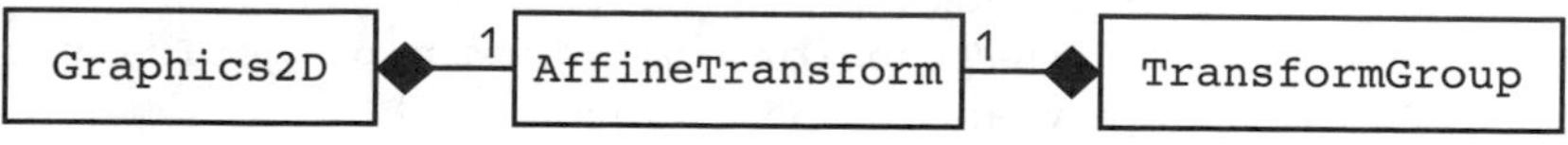

FIGURE 6.28 `Graphics2D` objects and `TransformGroup` objects each represent its coordinate system by an `AffineTransform`.

Thus, the coordinate system of a new transform group is the same as that of its parent node in the scene graph.

Over the course of its lifetime, a transform group responds to transform-yourself messages such as *translate, rotate,* and *scale*. In this manner, it comes to represent different coordinate systems over time. Such messages are implemented by delegation: they are forwarded to the `AffineTransform` component stored in the `tform` field. These various transformation-producing methods are implemented thus:

```
// methods of TransformGroup class
public void rotate(double theta) {
  tform.rotate(Math.toRadians(theta));
}

public void rotate(double theta, PointGeometry center)
       throws NullPointerException {
  tform.rotate(Math.toRadians(theta), center.getX(),
                                      center.getY());
}

public void scale(double sx, double sy)
       throws IllegalArgumentException {
  if ((sx == 0) || (sy == 0))
    throw new IllegalArgumentException();
  tform.scale(sx, sy);
}

public void translate(double dx, double dy) {
  tform.translate(dx, dy);
}

public void setToIdentity() {
  tform.setToIdentity();
}
```

Note that transform group rotations are specified in degrees, not radians.

The transform `tform` comes into play when the children of a `TransformGroup` node are painted: The children are painted in the transform group's coordinate system. Here is the implementation of the `paint` method:

```
// method of TransformGroup class
public void paint(Graphics2D g2) {
  AffineTransform oldTform = g2.getTransform();// step 1
  g2.transform(tform);                          // step 2
  super.paint(g2);                              // step 3
  g2.setTransform(oldTform);                    // step 4
}
```

The `paint` method proceeds in four steps. Where `g2` is the rendering context passed to `paint`, the method:

1. Obtains and saves a copy of `g2`'s transform. This saved transform represents the coordinate system of this node's parent node within the scene graph.
2. Applies this node's transform `tform` to the transform stored in `g2`. At the completion of this step, `g2` represents the coordinate system of this transform group.
3. Paints this node's children into `g2`. Because `TransformGroup`'s superclass is the `GroupNode` class, the method call

   ```
   super.paint(g2);
   ```

   paints this node's children in index order.
4. Restores `g2`'s former transform. This is necessary so that clients that call the `paint` method can assume that `g2`'s coordinate system has not changed.

Throughout the process of painting of the scene graph, the rendering context `g2` is used to convey the current coordinate system from each grouping node to its children. This is why restoring `g2`'s former transform (in step 4) is critical for correct display of scene graphs. Each grouping node is responsible for painting its children correctly, within its own coordinate system. To do so, it must be free to assume that the rendering context it passes to each of its children correctly reflects its own coordinate system. A grouping node has this guarantee only if none of its children alters `g2`'s *transform* attribute.

Consider an example. Using `TransformGroup` nodes, we can build scene graphs that locate a given input `node` within different coordinate systems. As an example, the following `LineOfNodes` class represents a group node with n children. Each child is a `TransformGroup` that contains `node` as a child. The n `TransformGroups` are translated along a given line: the first locates its origin at the point `pos`, and each successive transform group is translated by `dx` and `dy` relative to its predecessor. Here is the implementation of the class:

```
public class LineOfNodes extends GroupNode {
  public LineOfNodes(Node node, int n, PointGeometry pos,
                     int dx, int dy)
       throws NullPointerException {
    for (int i = 0; i < n; i++) {
      TransformGroup t = new TransformGroup();
      t.addChild(node);
      t.translate(pos.getX() + i*dx, pos.getY() + i*dy);
      addChild(t);
    }
  }
}
```

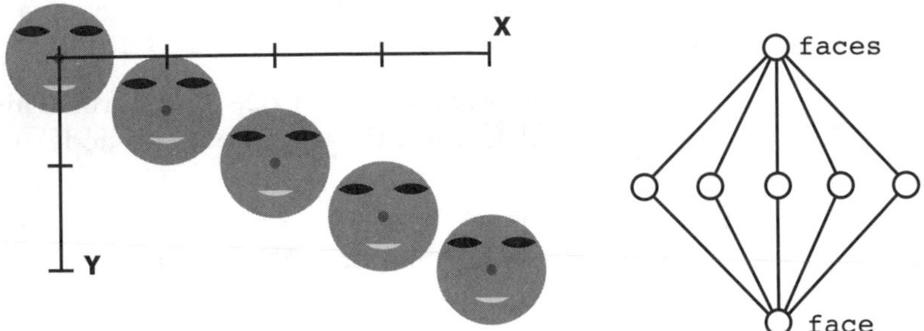

FIGURE 6.29 The group node faces contains five `TransformGroup` children, each of which contains face as its child.

Figure 6.29 shows the effect of painting a line of `face` nodes, where the axes' tick marks occur at 50-unit intervals. The following code fragment does the trick:

```
faces =
  new LineOfNodes(face,5,new PointGeometry(0,0),50,25);
faces.paint(g2);
```

Here, `face` is a `Figure` representing a face of radius 20. Figure 6.29 also shows the resulting scene graph. The five children of the grouping node `faces` are `TransformGroups`, each of which contains a single child, the node `face`.

Exercises

6.31 What is the purpose of the following class?

```
public class MatrixOfNodes extends GroupNode {
  public MatrixOfNodes(Node node, PointGeometry pos,
           int n1, int dx1, int dy1,
           int n2, int dx2, int dy2)
         throws NullPointerException {
    Node line =
      new LineOfNodes(node,  n1, pos, dx1, dy1);
    Node matrix =
      new LineOfNodes(line,  n2, pos, dx2, dy2);
    addChild(matrix);
  }
}
```

Write a program using the `MatrixOfNodes` class that produces the image in Figure 6.30. Where `face` is a `Figure` representing a face of radius 20, the matrix of faces shown in Figure 6.30 was produced with the following instruction:

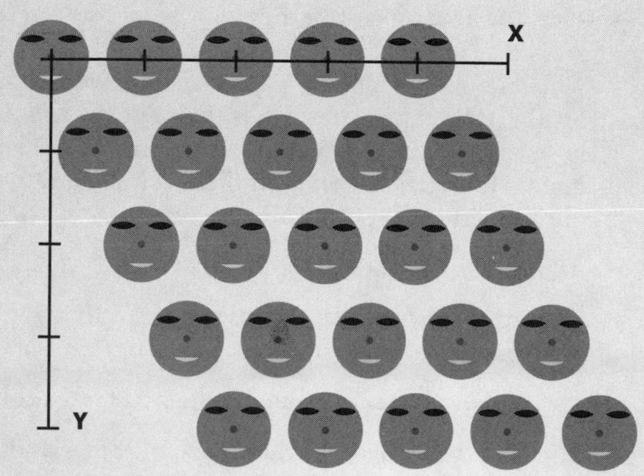

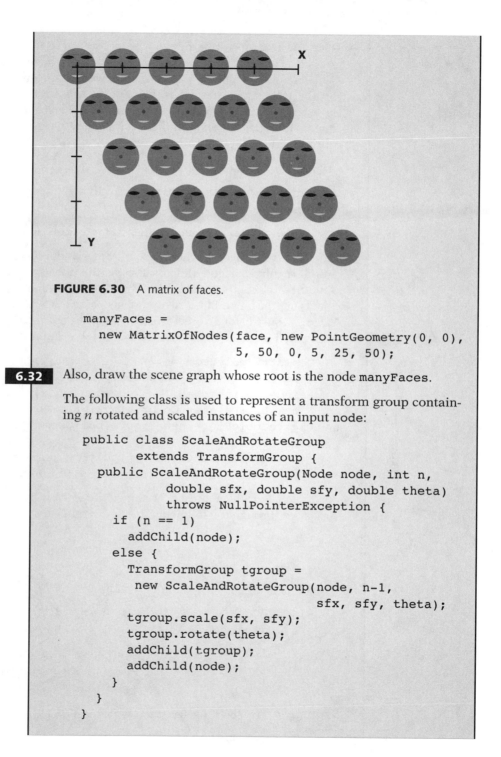

FIGURE 6.30 A matrix of faces.

```
manyFaces =
  new MatrixOfNodes(face, new PointGeometry(0, 0),
                         5, 50, 0, 5, 25, 50);
```

6.32 Also, draw the scene graph whose root is the node `manyFaces`.

The following class is used to represent a transform group containing *n* rotated and scaled instances of an input node:

```
public class ScaleAndRotateGroup
      extends TransformGroup {
  public ScaleAndRotateGroup(Node node, int n,
          double sfx, double sfy, double theta)
          throws NullPointerException {
    if (n == 1)
      addChild(node);
    else {
      TransformGroup tgroup =
       new ScaleAndRotateGroup(node, n-1,
                               sfx, sfy, theta);
      tgroup.scale(sfx, sfy);
      tgroup.rotate(theta);
      addChild(tgroup);
      addChild(node);
    }
  }
}
```

The first instance of `node` is not transformed. Each successive instance of `node` is obtained by scaling the previous instance by the scale factors `sfx` and `sfy` and rotating by `theta` degrees around the origin. In fact, this describes the net effect, but it does not explain how the constructor works or account for the scene graph it produces. To better understand these things, draw the scene graph produced by the following call:

```
new ScaleAndRotateGroup(node, 3, .5, .5, 45.0);
```

In addition, write a graphics program that renders a set of scaled and rotated regular polygons. The program is called like this:

```
> java PaintScaleAndRotate nbrSides radius n sfx sfy theta
```

The first two program arguments, *nbrSides* and *radius*, describe the initial regular polygon which serves as the node passed to `ScaleAndRotateGroup`'s constructor. The four remaining program arguments are the four additional arguments passed to `ScaleAndRotateGroup`'s constructor. In other words, the scene described by the generic program line might be constructed by the following code fragment:

```
Geometry polyGeom =
  new RegularPolygonGeometry(nbrSides, radius);
Painter painter =
  new DrawPainter(Color.black, new BasicStroke(4));
Figure polyFig = new Figure(polyGeom, painter);
Node scene =
  new ScaleAndRotateGroup(polyFig, n, sfx, sfy,
                          theta);
```

From left to right, Figure 6.31 shows the images produced by this program through the following three program calls:

FIGURE 6.31 Some figures made with the `PaintScaleAndRotate` program.

```
> java PaintScaleAndRotate 4 100 8 .707 .707 45
> java PaintScaleAndRotate 4 100 16 .9 .9 10
> java PaintScaleAndRotate 8 100 40 .95 .8 10
```

6.33 In this exercise, you develop a command-driven program for painting and transforming figures. The user assigns each figure a name when it is constructed and subsequently refers to figures by name. The user creates and names a new rectangle of specified dimensions using a command of this form:

define *name* rectangle *x y width height*

Ellipses are created and named similarly:

define *name* ellipse *x y width height*

When a new figure is constructed, it is assigned the current color; whenever painted, a figure is filled with its assigned color. The program maintains a current figure which gets selected by name:

select *name*

Transform commands apply only to the current figure. For example, a command of the form

```
rotate 45 10 20
```

rotates the current figure by 45° clockwise around the point (10,20).

The program displays all the figures created so far. In addition, it displays the axes indicating the current figure's coordinate system. (However, the program also provides an *axes* command for showing and hiding these axes.) Here is a summary of all the commands:

- **define *id* [rectangle | ellipse] *x y width height***—creates a new figure positioned at (*x*,*y*) and of specified *width* and *height*, and assigns it the name *id*. If a figure named by *id* already exists, that figure is replaced by the new figure. The figure is also assigned the current color and becomes the current figure.
- **color *red green blue***—updates the current color; the new color is specified by the integer color components $0 \le red, green, blue \le 255$.
- **select *id***—makes the figure named by *id* the current figure. If no figure is named *id*, does nothing.
- **rotate *theta x y***—rotates the current figure by *theta* degrees around (*x*,*y*).
- **translate *dx dy***—translates the current figure by *dx* and *dy*.

- **axes [*on* | *off*]**—shows or hides the axes associated with the current figure's coordinate system.
- **quit**—exits this program.

The following sample interaction is illustrated in Figure 6.32:

```
> java PlaySceneGraph
? color 200 100 100
? axes on
? define a rectangle -50 -50 100 100
? rotate -45 0 0      // left image of Figure 6.32
? color 0 0 255
? define b ellipse -25 -50 50 100
? translate 50 0      // middle image of Figure 6.32
? select a            // right image of Figure 6.32
```

[Hint: Represent the entire scene using a `GroupNode` named (say) `scene`. Whenever a new `Figure` is created, make it the child of a new `TransformGroup`, and then make that `TransformGroup` a child of `scene`. To display the scene, send `scene` the *paint* message. Your program must maintain a reference to the `TransformGroup` that contains the current figure. Whenever a *rotate* or *translate* command is issued, transform the current `TransformGroup` accordingly. Let the program's `paintComponent` method be responsible for displaying the axes. If the axes are visible, this method adds a set of axes as children of the current `TransformGroup` and then paints `scene`, and then removes the axes.]

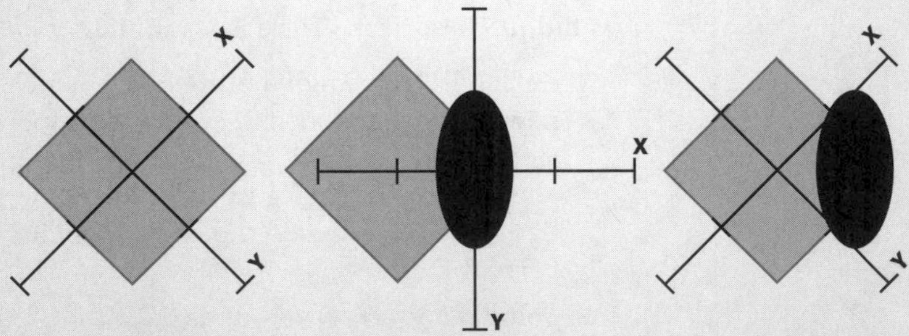

FIGURE 6.32 Images made with the `PlaySceneGraph` program.

6.4.4 Structure and Applicability of the Composite Pattern

The composite design pattern is used to construct hierarchies of primitives and composites while enabling clients to treat both primitives and composites uniformly. This design pattern comprises three elements (see Figure 6.33):

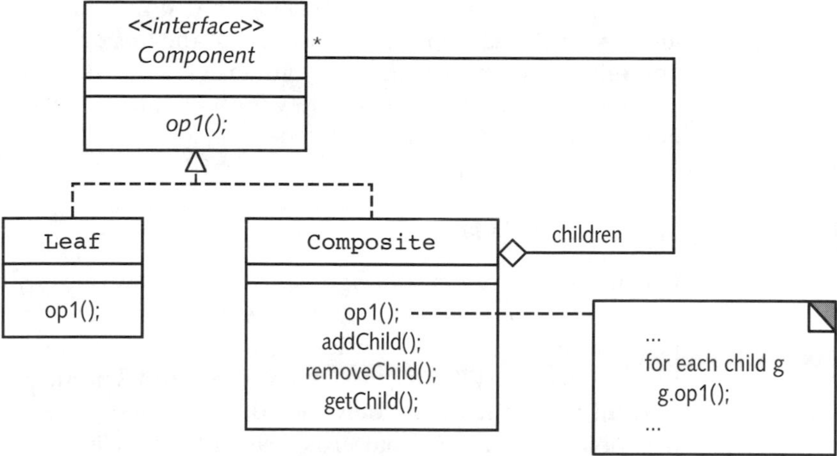

FIGURE 6.33 Structure of the composite design pattern.

- ***Component* interface**—specifies the interface common to all objects in the composition (in our example, the `Node` interface serves as *`Component`*).
- ***Leaf* classes**—each *`Leaf`* class implements *`Component`* and defines the behaviors for primitive objects in the composition. *`Leaf`* objects have no children in the composition. In our example, the `Figure` class is a *`Leaf`*.
- ***Composite* class**—implements *`Component`* and defines the behaviors for components with children. Our `GroupNode` class serves as *`Composite`*.

Clients interact with the objects in the composite using the *`Component`* interface. If the object is a *`Leaf`*, it handles the message directly; if the object is a *`Composite`*, it forwards the message to each of its children, and possibly performs additional work of its own. In Figure 6.33, the operation *`op1`* belongs to the interface shared by all components. The operations *`addChild`*, *`removeChild`*, and *`getChild`* that appear in the *`Composite`* class represent a set of operations for managing children. Any number of *`Leaf`* objects can extend the *`Component`* interface, even though only one *`Leaf`* appears in the figure. This design pattern makes it easy to add new kinds of *`Leaf`*s without affecting existing code. Specialized composites can also be devised by extending the *`Composite`* class, just as the `TransformGroup` class extends the `GroupNode` class in our application.

The fact that all objects implement a common *`Component`* interface helps simplify code because clients need not distinguish between leafs and composites. The exceptions to this occur when clients manage the children of a *`Composite`* object or use additional methods introduced by *`Leaf`* or *`Composite`* classes. A variation of the composite design pattern specifies the methods for managing a `Composite`'s children (such as the `addChild` and `removeChild` operations) as part of the `Component` interface. Doing so enlarges the interface shared by all objects in a composition. However, this is achieved at the expense of safety for it enables clients to send meaningless child-management messages to `Leaf` objects.

6.5 Classifying Design Patterns

Because there are many design patterns and new ones will be invented in the future, we need a way to organize them. The book *Design Patterns* organizes patterns using two classification schemes. The first classifies patterns according to purpose: *What is the pattern used for?* The three purposes are **creational, structural,** and **behavioral.** Creational patterns are used to create new objects. Structural patterns deal with how classes and objects are organized to form larger structures. Behavioral patterns are concerned with the responsibilities of objects and the collaboration between objects.

The second scheme classifies patterns by scope: whether a pattern applies primarily to classes or to objects. **Class patterns** deal with relationships between classes and interfaces, and their subtypes. Because class patterns are established through inheritance, they are static—they remain fixed throughout program execution. **Object patterns** deal with the relationships between objects. Object patterns are dynamic because the relationships between objects can change while a program runs.

To understand design patterns, it also helps to recognize that many patterns isolate some aspect of a system that is likely to change. This allows you to vary that aspect of the system without affecting other aspects. For example, consider the iterator pattern. By defining different iterator classes, you can vary the order in which the elements belonging to an aggregate are visited (i.e., the traversal policy). Yet clients are not otherwise affected when they use different kinds of iterators because each implements the interface that the client expects. In the pattern descriptions to follow, I'll point out (where relevant) how each pattern encapsulates change.

Consider the three design patterns covered so far. The iterator pattern provides access to an aggregate while hiding its implementation and internal structure. This is a behavioral pattern because it's concerned with collaboration between objects: The pattern describes how an iterator mediates interactions between its underlying aggregate and its clients. It is an object pattern because the relationship between an iterator and its aggregate is based not on inheritance but on message passing between the two objects. The iterator pattern is dynamic: Iterators maintain a traversal state that changes over time, and new iterators can be constructed at runtime. The iterator pattern is a behavioral object pattern.

The template method pattern defines an algorithm, some of whose steps are implemented by subclasses. Using a template method, we can implement an algorithm while allowing certain steps to vary. This is a behavioral class pattern. It is a class pattern because it is based on the inheritance relationship between classes: An abstract class defines the template method and its subclasses implement the abstract hook methods required by the template method. These relationships are static because the subclasses, which represent variations of the same algorithm, are defined prior to program execution.

The composite pattern is used to combine objects into hierarchies of primitives and composites while enabling clients to treat both primitives and composites uniformly. This is a structural object pattern because it provides a way to combine objects into more complex objects. The composite pattern is dynamic: It enables new primitives and composites to be constructed and combined on the fly.

The remainder of this section presents and classifies several additional design patterns—the factory method, adapter, observer, and strategy patterns—which, like those already covered, are quite common and useful.

6.5.1 The Factory Method Pattern

The **factory method pattern** is used when a client calls a method to create new objects without knowing what kind of objects to create. This decision is left to subclasses that implement the method in different ways. Using this design pattern, you can vary the actual type of objects that are created while ensuring that they implement a common interface that clients expect.

As an example, consider a GUI-based program for painting various kinds of graphical figures into an electronic canvas. One of the program's key abstractions is the **paint tool,** examples of which include brushes for freehand painting, buckets for filling regions, and tools for drawing curves. Each kind of tool is represented by its own class; for instance, we have `BrushTool`, `BucketTool`, and `CurveTool` classes. All of these classes implement a common `PaintTool` interface which the paint program uses to interact with its paint tools. The user selects a paint tool by clicking a button on a tool bar. In response, the program creates a new object to represent the selected tool. Unfortunately, the paint program doesn't know the actual type of tool to create. In fact, if the paint program is a framework to which new kinds of tools can be added, it doesn't even know the actual type of tools it supports.

The factory method pattern provides a solution. It places the knowledge of which kind of tool to create in the button. Every button is represented by an object that subtypes an abstract `ToolButton` class. The `ToolButton` class declares an abstract `createTool` method that every subclass implements. Whenever the user clicks a paint tool button, the program is notified of the event and handed a reference to the clicked button. The program then sends the button a *createTool* message in order to construct the corresponding `PaintTool` object. For example, a brush button is represented by an instance of the `BrushButton` class, and its `createTool` method creates a new `BrushTool` (see Figure 6.34). When the user clicks the brush button, the program is

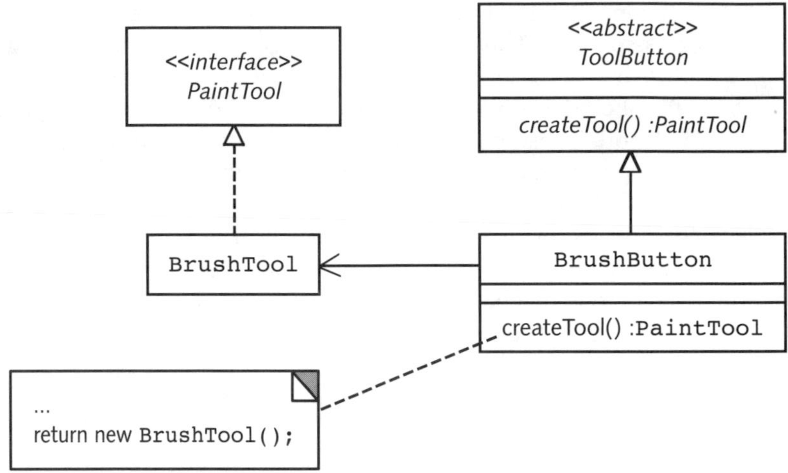

FIGURE 6.34 An example of the factory method pattern.

notified of the event and handed a reference to the clicked button stored in a variable named (say) `clickedButton`. The program responds by creating a new instance of the `BrushTool` class through the following instruction:

```
PaintTool currentTool = clickedButton.createTool();
```

The program doesn't know the actual type of tool it creates because this is the responsibility of `clickedButton`. Yet it can subsequently use `currentTool`—even without knowing its actual type—because the tool implements the `PaintTool` interface.

The `createTool` method is known as a **factory method** because it's responsible for manufacturing new objects. Four types are involved in this pattern:

- **an abstract *`Creator`* class**—specifies the factory method (in our example, the `ToolButton` is the *`Creator`* class).
- ***`ConcreteCreator`* classes**—each extends *`Creator`* and implement its factory method (`BrushButton` and any number of other subtypes of the `ToolButton` class).
- ***`Product`* interface**—specifies the interface of objects created by the factory method (`PaintTool`).
- ***`ConcreteProduct`* classes**—each implements the *`Product`* interface; objects created by the factory method are instances of *`ConcreteProduct`* (in our example, `BrushTool` and any number of other subtypes of `PaintTool`).

The factory method pattern reduces the dependence between a client and the classes that implement the objects it uses. This makes it easier to change the classes that the client uses—the client creates the object it uses through the factory method and handles the object according to its apparent type (*Product*) rather than its actual type (*ConcreteProduct*). It also hides from the client the details involved in deciding what classes to instantiate.

Factory methods are often called by template methods. To carry out its algorithm, a template method may require the services of new objects that it creates itself. However, the actual type of objects required depends on the subclasses that implement the template method (each subclass specializes the algorithm in its own way). The template method creates new objects by calling a factory method, thereby letting the subclasses decide what type of objects to create.

The factory method pattern is a creational pattern because it is used to create new objects. It is a class pattern because it describes an inheritance hierarchy of creators. Specifically, a parent class (*Creator*) specifies a factory method that gets implemented by one or more subclasses (*ConcreteCreator*). Often, this hierarchy of creators connects to a parallel inheritance hierarchy of products. In our example, `PaintTool` specifies the interface shared by all products, one of which is its subclass `BrushTool`. The hierarchy of creators connects to the hierarchy of products through the various implementations of the factory method `createTool`.

6.5.2 The Adapter Pattern

The **adapter pattern** is used to convert the interface of an object into a different interface that a client expects. This enables the client to use the object's services even though the object's interface is incompatible. The server object is not changed. Rather, the pattern interposes a new "adapter" between the client and the server object that adapts the interface of the latter to the requirements of the former. The adapter is analogous to a plug used to connect an electrical appliance to an incompatible outlet. The plug adapts the outlet—which provides the service of electricity—to the requirements of the appliance.

Under this design pattern, an *Adaptee* class provides the desired functionality but the wrong interface, and an *Adapter* class accesses *Adaptee*'s functionality while providing the interface that clients expect. Here is a description of the participants:

- ***Target* interface**—specifies the interface that *Client* expects.
- ***Client***—interacts with objects using the *Target* interface.
- ***Adaptee* class**—provides the desired functionality but an interface that needs to be adapted to *Target*.
- ***Adapter* class**—adapts the interface of *Adaptee* to the *Target* interface.

The adapter pattern is a structural pattern, and it appears in both object and class versions. In the object version, the *Adapter* object owns an *Adaptee* component. Here, *Adapter* implements the desired interface by converting the messages it receives into messages that its *Adaptee* component understands, thereby delegating the real work to *Adaptee*. We used this pattern in the design of our `TextGeometry` class (Exercise 5.20). The functionality for drawing text is provided by Java's `GlyphVector` class, but this class does not have the expected `Geometry` interface. Our design defines the `TextGeometry` class such that *it* provides the expected `Geometry` interface while using the services of the `GlyphVector` class to carry out its shape operation. In Figure 6.35, `TextGeometry` assumes the role of *Adapter*, and `GlyphVector` the role of *Adaptee*. The `Geometry` interface is the *Target* because it specifies the interface that clients expect.

In the class version of the adapter pattern, *Adapter* subclasses the *Adaptee* to inherit its implementation and implements the *Target* interface to provide the interface expected by clients. Figure 6.36 shows how we might have designed our `TextGeometry` class using this approach. Here again, the `TextGeometry` class is the *Adapter*, the `GlyphVector` is the *Adaptee*, and the `Geometry` interface is the *Target*.

The architecture depicted in Figure 6.36 is impractical because Java's `GlyphVector` class is abstract, requiring the `TextGeometry` class to provide far too much implementation of its own. The class version of the adapter pattern is more promising when the *Adaptee* is a concrete class. The main advantage of the class version is that it allows the *Adapter* to override some of *Adaptee*'s behaviors. The main disadvantage is that it commits the *Adapter* to a specific *Adaptee* (its superclass), thereby preventing *Adapter* from ben-

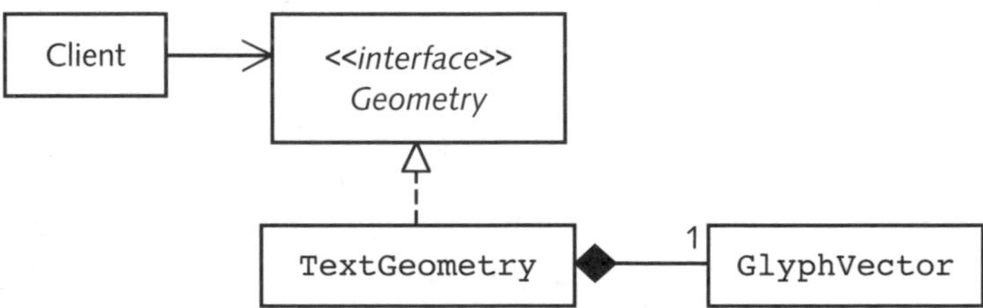

FIGURE 6.35 The `TextGeometry` class adapts `GlyphVector` (object version of the adapter pattern).

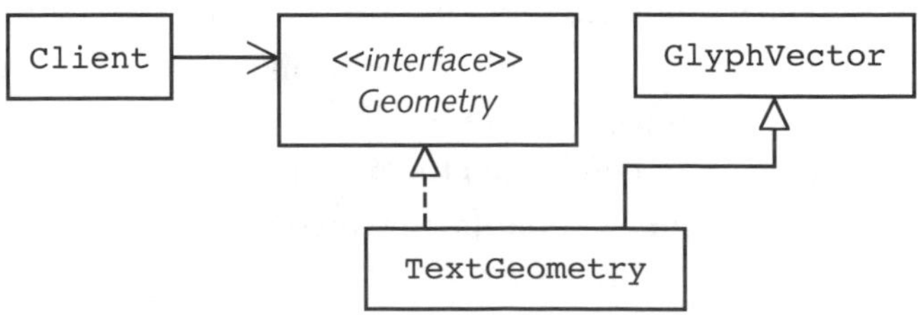

FIGURE 6.36 The `TextGeometry` class adapts `GlyphVector` (class version of the adapter pattern).

efiting from any of `Adaptee`'s subclasses. In contrast, the object version of the adapter pattern benefits from `Adaptee`'s subclasses through polymorphism—the `Adapter`'s component can be any subtype of `Adaptee`.

6.5.3 The Observer Pattern

The **observer pattern** is used when a change in an object's state is of interest to certain other objects. The object of interest is known as the **subject,** and the objects interested in the subject are its **observers.** When the subject's state changes, each of its observers is notified of the change so that it can respond. For example, the subject might be data capable of being displayed in different ways: as a spreadsheet, a bar graph, a pie chart, and so forth. Each of the data's observers displays the data in its own way. Whenever the data changes, each of its observers is notified so that it can update itself.

The subject maintains a list of its observers and provides methods for adding new observers to the list and for removing observers from the list. Whenever the subject's state changes, it notifies each of the observers on its list by calling the observer's `update` method. The subject supplies an argument to `update` that encapsulates its state change. Alternatively, the subject defines methods that observers use to query its new state. In this case, either the subject passes itself as an argument to `update`, or the observers maintain references to the subject.

Four types are involved in this design pattern:

- **`Subject` class**—maintains a list of `Observer` objects and provides methods for adding observers, removing observers, and notifying observers of changes in state in the `ConcreteSubject`.
- **`ConcreteSubject` classes**—objects whose state is of interest; each such class extends the `Subject` class.
- **`Observer` interface**—specifies an interface by which `ConcreteObservers` are notified of changes in state in the `ConcreteSubject`.
- **`ConcreteObserver` classes**—each `ConcreteObserver` class implements the `Observer` interface and provides the behaviors for responding to changes in the `ConcreteSubject`'s state.

In the class diagram of Figure 6.37, whenever the `ConcreteSubject`'s state changes, it calls its `notifyAll` method, which notifies each of its observers in turn.

Java's event model is based on the observer pattern. Components such as buttons, lists, and panels, generate events in response to user actions such as mouse clicks and item selections. Event listeners are objects that define methods (known as event handlers) for responding to events. In Java's event model, components play the role of subject and event listeners are their observers. Whenever a component generates an event, it notifies its observers, thereby giving them an opportunity to respond to the event. We will cover Java's event model in Section 7.2.

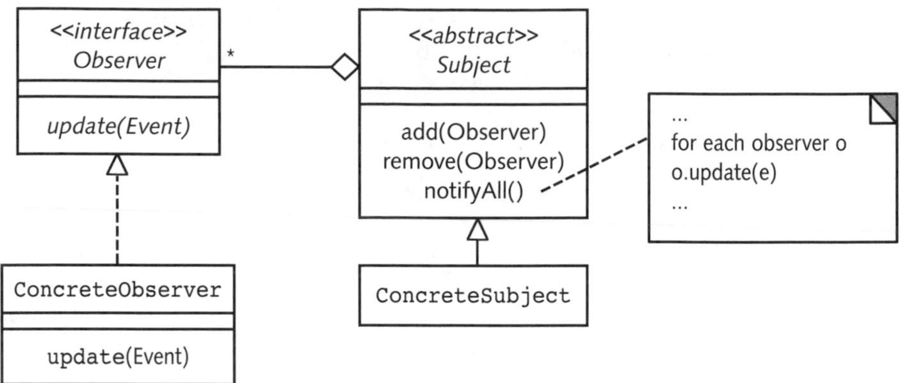

FIGURE 6.37 The observer pattern.

The main advantage of the observer pattern is that it minimizes the coupling between a subject and its observers. A subject knows only that it has a list of interested observers that implement the `Observer` interface; it knows nothing of the implementation or behavior of its observers. The subject is responsible for notifying its observers of significant state changes, and its observers for responding to those state changes. Thus, the observer pattern allows two aspects of the system to vary: the list of objects observing a subject, and their behaviors in response to change-in-state updates.

Lastly, note that just as a subject may have any number of observers, it is possible for a given observer to observe any number of subjects. Whenever the observer's `update` method is called, the argument to `update` indicates (at the very least) which subject underwent the change in state.

6.5.4 The Strategy Pattern

It is often the case that a problem can be solved in different ways. The strategy pattern encapsulates a family of different solutions as objects. Each object uses a different strategy to solve the problem, but because the objects provide a common interface, they can be used interchangeably by clients.

By way of example, there are different strategies for laying out components such as buttons, text fields, and lists, inside a container such as a window. For instance, a `FlowLayout` object arranges components from left to right in rows, whereas a `GridLayout` object places components in the rectangular cells of a grid. When a container arranges its components, it interacts with its layout manager through the `LayoutManager` interface which is implemented by all layout managers. The container uses its layout manager through a common interface without needing to know the layout manager's actual strategy (see Figure 6.38). We will cover Java layout managers in Section 7.4.

Three types are involved in the strategy pattern:

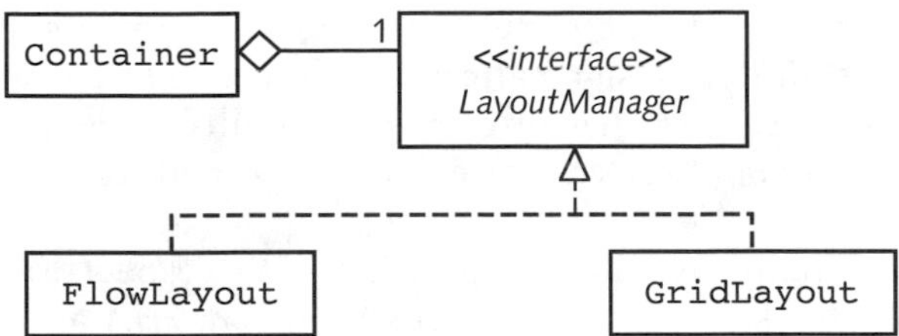

FIGURE 6.38 The Strategy pattern is used for component layout.

- ***Strategy* interface**—specifies the interface implemented by all *ConcreteStrategy* classes (in our example, the `LayoutManager` interface).
- ***ConcreteStrategy* classes**—each such class implements the *Strategy* interface and implements its own strategy (`FlowLayout` and `GridLayout`).
- ***Context* class**—maintains a reference to some *ConcreteStrategy* object, and invokes it through the *Strategy* interface to execute a strategy (`Container`).

A *ConcreteStrategy* generally requires information from the *Context* to perform its work. One approach is for the *Context* to pass the information whenever it calls the strategy. A second approach is for the *Context* to pass itself as an argument, thereby enabling strategies to query the *Context* directly for information. Java uses this second approach for component layout. When a container calls its layout manager, it passes itself as an argument. The layout manager then queries the container to obtain such information as the container's size and its list of components.

This pattern, classified as behavioral object, has several advantages. First, clients are simplified because they don't need to implement the often-complex algorithms realized by the strategies. A client invokes its actual strategy through the common *Strategy* interface. Second, strategies are interchangeable at runtime. Lastly, new strategies can be defined without affecting clients.

The strategy pattern allows an algorithm to vary independent of the clients that use it. Observe that the strategy pattern and template method patterns accomplish similar goals by different means. The strategy pattern uses delegation to vary an algorithm, whereas the template method pattern uses inheritance to vary certain steps of an otherwise fixed algorithm.

Summary

At its simplest, a design pattern is a solution to a recurring design problem. A pattern describes the generic problem it solves and a design solution: an arrangement of classes and objects, and the relationships and collaborations between them. A design pattern also describes the results and tradeoffs of using the solution. Design patterns are a record of the accumulated experience and wisdom of the software community. They continue to evolve—existing design patterns are often enhanced and refined, and new ones are invented.

Design patterns can be classified with respect to both *purpose* and *scope*. With respect to purpose, *creational patterns* are used to create new objects; *structural patterns* deal with how classes and objects are organized to form larger structures; and *behavioral patterns* are concerned with the collaborations among objects. With respect to scope, *class patterns* deal with the relationships between classes and interfaces and their subtypes, whereas *object patterns* emphasize the relationships between objects. In addition, most design patterns allow one aspect of a system to vary without affecting the other aspects of the system.

This chapter introduced the following design patterns, which are but a few of those in common use:

- The *factory method pattern* is used when a client creates new objects but does not know the actual type of objects to create (creational class pattern).
- The *adapter pattern* is used to convert the interface of a class into an interface that clients expect (structural pattern with both class and object versions).
- The *composite pattern* is used to combine objects into hierarchies of primitives and composites while enabling clients to treat both primitives and composites uniformly (structural object pattern).
- The *template method* pattern defines an algorithm, some of whose steps are implemented by subclasses (behavioral class pattern).
- The *iterator pattern* provides access to an aggregate while hiding its implementation and internal structure (behavioral object pattern).
- The *observer pattern* allows interested objects to observe state changes in a subject object (behavioral object pattern).
- The *strategy pattern* encapsulates each of a family of strategies and makes them available to clients through a common interface (behavioral object pattern).

CHAPTER

7

Object-Oriented Application Frameworks

Object-oriented application frameworks, known more simply as **frameworks,** are a form of design reuse. A framework is a set of classes and interfaces forming an application that the programmer customizes as desired. The goal is to simplify the development of applications in a particular application domain. Because frameworks are tied to a particular system or programming language, they are less abstract than design patterns. However, frameworks are usually large in scope and often contain design patterns as their architectural elements.

Frameworks have been developed for numerous application domains including multimedia, telecommunications, operating systems, distributed computing, business systems, and finance. In this chapter, we examine the Abstract Window Toolkit (AWT) and Swing, which make up Java's framework for building programs with **graphical user interfaces** (GUIs). Following the overview of Section 7.1, the remainder of this chapter delves into the main features of Java's GUI framework through the development of a number of programs. The chapter culminates in a program for drawing and editing various kinds of graphical shapes using modern interaction techniques. The purpose of this chapter is to introduce Java's framework for building GUIs, and to use this framework to illustrate characteristics of frameworks in general.

7.1 Building GUI-Based Programs in Java Using Frameworks

This section surveys the characteristics of frameworks in general, and provides an overview of Java's framework for creating programs with graphical user interfaces.

7.1.1 Characteristics of Frameworks

One of the main benefits of object-orientation is its support for reuse. We've seen that individual software components can be reused through inheritance and object composition and that software designs can be reused through design patterns. Frameworks support reuse at an even larger scale. A framework is a reusable software system in a particular application domain. To develop an application using a framework, the developer defines classes that connect to the framework, thereby customizing it.

An application that is based on a framework is molded and shaped by the framework. The framework determines the application's overall design and provides most or all of its software components. Even when you develop custom components for your application, the framework provides generic components you can base your custom components on, allowing you to focus on their application-specific behaviors while letting the framework handle the rest.

Frameworks support the reuse of both design and code. Design is reused because the framework prescribes your application's overall design. Generally, the resulting design implies an inversion of control. When you develop an application from scratch, even when you make use of a class library or toolkit, your application controls the flow of execution—it calls the objects whose services it requires. In contrast, when your application derives from a framework, the framework is responsible for the flow of execution. The framework invokes the application-specific behaviors that you as the application developer provide. One consequence is that you give up considerable control over your application's design when you use a framework. However, because the framework manages the generally complicated flow of execution, your development effort is made simpler and less time consuming, and the resulting product is likely to be more reliable and easier to understand and maintain.

Frameworks reuse code because they provide a library of useful components. Framework-supplied components can often be used directly without modification. Yet, frameworks also simplify the development of custom components. When specialized components are needed, the framework provides generic components that can be customized through inheritance and/or composition.

A framework defines **hot spots** where the developer's code connects to the framework. Each hot spot specifies rules that customizations should follow. The hot spots account for variation across different applications derived from the same framework. An application customizes a framework by implementing its hot spots, either through inheritance or composition.

When you customize a framework using inheritance, you develop an application-specific class that extends a class of the framework. You use this approach, for example, when you create a new component by extending one of Java's component classes such as `JFrame` or `JPanel`. Your new class inherits the often-extensive capabilities of its superclass, while adding new methods and overriding inherited methods that account for its distinctive behavior. Framework classes intended for customization often provide hook methods to be overridden by custom subclasses. For instance, you can develop a panel that paints whatever you like by defining a new class that extends the `JPanel` class and overrides the `paintComponent` method. To define custom classes through inheritance, the developer should be familiar with the framework's inheritance hierarchy. Because the developer must understand the classes being extended, customization via inheritance is sometimes referred to as a **white box** mechanism—the framework must be open to examination.

Frameworks are also customized by composition. In this case, the framework defines interfaces for components that can be plugged into the framework. The developer defines new components, or uses components supplied by the framework, that implement interfaces expected by the framework. Customization through composition frees you to focus on each new component's responsibilities without considering the framework's architecture. Because you can create custom components and reuse existing components without having to understand the framework beyond the interfaces that the components target, customization via composition is referred to as a **black box** mechanism.

Few frameworks are strictly white box or black box; most frameworks are customized using both inheritance and object composition. As we'll see, this is true of Java's framework for building GUI-based programs.

It is worth considering the relationship between frameworks and design patterns. Frameworks are usually large in scope and often contain design patterns as their architectural elements. Moreover, a framework induces certain patterns in the applications that derive from it because such applications conform to the framework's model. Patterns are especially significant at the framework's hot spots—those places that allow variation from one application to the next. This is because most design patterns provide the means to vary some aspect of a system while holding all other aspects of the system fixed. Customization through inheritance (white box) is often achieved using the template method pattern. The framework defines a template method for an algorithm, and custom child classes complete the algorithm by implementing the abstract hook methods that the template method calls. Customization through composition (black box) is often achieved using the strategy pattern. Here, the framework specifies an interface that a component implements in order to be plugged in. The developer defines a tailor-made component that implements the interface while providing a customized strategy.

Because frameworks are tied to a system and implemented in a programming language, they are less abstract than design patterns. Frameworks are also, in a sense, larger than design patterns, because they contain patterns. In contrast, design patterns are independent of any particular programming language. Patterns are intended to be implemented, but they may be implemented in many contexts and in most any language. A framework is a program, but a design pattern is an abstraction that can be realized by different programs in different languages.

Using frameworks provides numerous benefits, including:

- A framework captures expertise both in the application domain and in application programming. Through reuse, this expertise is made available to developers who need not be as well versed in either.
- It is generally possible to build complex applications much more efficiently using frameworks than from scratch.
- Applications derived from frameworks are generally reliable, because they benefit from the testing and effort that has gone into the framework.
- Applications based on a framework are relatively uniform. This means that they're likely to be compatible with each other, they're easier to maintain and extend, and they tend to provide similar user experiences such as look-and-feel and interaction conventions.

Using frameworks also has some drawbacks:

- Building a good framework is difficult and time consuming.
- Evolving a framework over time is a difficult and ongoing task. Moreover, framework evolution is usually indispensable due to changes in application requirements, advances in technology, and new insights into the application domain and the framework's design.
- As a framework evolves, applications based on it may need to change to benefit from improvements to, or to remain compatible with, newer versions of the framework.
- It may not be possible to customize a framework to exactly meet an application's requirements. Thus, it is sometimes necessary to modify an application's requirements to accommodate a framework's capabilities, or to evolve a framework to suit the application, or to choose a different framework for the application (or none at all).
- It can take considerable time and effort to learn a framework. (However, it can take even more effort to learn to develop similar applications from

scratch, and the effort needed to learn a framework can be amortized over many projects.)

- When you use a framework, you give up some control over the design of your application, usually including the program's flow of execution. (This inversion of control means that the framework calls upon application-specific objects rather than the reverse. The upside is that it allows the application developer to focus on the responsibilities of the objects she develops while ignoring their collaborations with the framework's objects.)

7.1.2 Java's AWT and Swing

The interactive programs we've developed so far in this book have been text-based: The user types into a console window and the input text is read and parsed using the `ScanInput` class. In contrast, users interact with GUI-based programs by such means as clicking, dragging, and selecting with the mouse, pushing buttons, selecting menu items, typing into text fields, and the like. Most programs in widespread use today sport graphical user interfaces.

Java's GUI framework comprises three main building blocks: components, layout managers, and event handling. Components, such as buttons, panels, dialog boxes, menus, text fields, and lists, are the visual widgets that respond to user actions. Components appear in containers, which are themselves a type of component. What results is a containment hierarchy, an example of which appears in Figure 3.4 near the start of Section 3.4. Layout managers arrange the components belonging to a container. For example, components can be arranged along a rectangular grid, or left to right like the lines of text in a paragraph, or within five regions laid out on the points of a compass (north, south, east, west, and center). Java's event model is used to associate event-handling behaviors with components. For instance, when the user pushes a button, the objects observing the button—so-called event listeners—respond to the button push.

The AWT, introduced in Java 1.0, provides the basic elements for GUI development. The components in the AWT are implemented in terms of **peer components** belonging to the local platform's native GUI system. For instance, a button is implemented using the button component of the Windows system when the Java program runs under Windows, and using the button component of the Macintosh system when it runs on the Macintosh operating system. Accordingly, the program has the look and feel of the environment it runs in. The advantage is that users accustomed to a certain platform are comfortable with the Java program's look and feel. But there are disadvantages to the AWT. Because some GUI systems are richer than others, it is necessary to program to a least common denominator: A program designed to run on every kind of system can employ only those features common to all systems. Even when a standard component is supported by all common GUI systems, its behavior may vary in subtle ways from one system to the next, making it difficult for programmers to ensure consistent behavior across platforms. For these reasons, the AWT was kept relatively simple, but this means it lacks many of the component types and sophisticated features supported by modern GUI environments.

These problems were addressed by Java 1.1 and Swing. Java 1.1 and higher allows the creation of so-called **lightweight components,** which are components that do not depend on the native GUI system. (In contrast, the components of the AWT are called **heavyweight components**—they depend on peer components that often consume considerable system resources.) Lightweight components are implemented entirely in Java code. When component functionality is handled by Java code, rather than by each platform's native GUI system, programs behave consistently across all platforms. Moreover, it is possible to create programs whose look and feel is the same across all platforms and can even be chosen and changed by the user at runtime.

Swing is Java's user interface library featuring lightweight components. Swing provides a much larger set of components than the AWT, and Swing components are generally more powerful and rich with features. Swing does not replace the AWT; rather, it builds upon the AWT. Nonetheless, in cases where the AWT and Swing provide similar services (and this is often the case), we will opt to use Swing in this chapter. Swing-based applications can be run by Java interpreters for Java 1.2 and higher, but it is only a matter of time before Swing-aware Web browsers become widespread.

The rest of this chapter explores the elements of Java's framework for creating GUI-based programs. Sections 7.2 through 7.4 cover the three main building blocks for building GUI-based programs—event handling, components, and layout managers. Sections 7.5 through 7.7 develop programs that explore how these building blocks may be used together, culminating in a GUI-based program for drawing and editing shapes such as polygons, rectangles, and ellipses.

7.2 Java's Event Model

This section presents an overview of Java's event model and then illustrates its use in a series of programs for editing sets of points in the plane and for manipulating polygons. The event model covered here applies to Java 1.1 and higher and is used by Swing and the AWT. We will not cover the earlier Java 1.0 event model, which is mostly obsolete.

7.2.1 Overview

Java's event model is based on the observer design pattern. The subjects are components that generate events in response to user actions. The observers are objects that are notified of events and given an opportunity to respond. For example, a push button may be a subject, and its observer an object that responds to button presses. The observer is notified whenever the user presses the button. Java's event model appears complicated because of the wide range of subjects and event types it provides and the variety of techniques available for customization. However, keep in mind that beneath its rich features, Java's event model follows the observer pattern.

In the context of Java's event model, subjects are known as **event sources** and observers are known as **event listeners.** Events are generated by GUI components in response to user actions. For instance, an event is generated whenever the user presses a button, types text into a text field and presses the Enter key, or selects an item from a menu or a list. GUI components are event sources. When an event source generates an event, it notifies every event listener registered with the event source. An event source also provides methods by which event listeners can register interest in its events.

An event source notifies a registered event listener of an event by calling one of the listener's **event handlers,** which are its methods for responding to events. The specific event handler that gets called depends on the nature of the event (many event listeners define more than one event handler). The event handler is passed an **event object** that encapsulates information relating to the event; the event handler uses the event object to learn about the event to which it must respond. Every event object includes a `getSource` method which reveals the component that generated the event (the event source), but otherwise event objects vary according to the type of event they represent. All event objects belong to subtypes of the `java.util.EventObject` class.

There are many different types of events, which is to be expected: Different event sources produce different kinds of information. For example, when the user presses a button—an instance of the `javax.swing.JButton` class—the button generates an **action event.** An `ActionEvent` object, which encapsulates an action event, stores such information as which button was pressed and which modifier keys (such as the Shift key or the Control key) were held down when the button was pressed. As another example, when the user clicks the mouse, the component on which the mouse was clicked generates a **mouse event.** The `MouseEvent` object captures such information as which mouse button the user pressed and the x and y coordinates of the clicked point in the component's coordinate system. We'll see other examples as the chapter proceeds; but for now, it is important to recognize that a Java program may contain any number of GUI components serving as event sources, and that each type of event source is capable of generating events of certain types but not others.

At this point in the discussion, it will be helpful to consider a concrete example. Let's suppose that we're developing an application that stores and displays a set of points in a panel. This application provides a button labeled *Triangulate* which, when clicked, causes the panel to construct and display a triangulation of the point set. (See Exercise 6.18 for more on triangulations, and Figure 7.12 for a picture of an application like the one I'm describing here.) We'll assume that the panel containing the point set is created with this instruction:

```
PointSetPanel panel = new PointSetPanel();
```

and that the *Triangulate* button is created with the following instruction:

```
JButton triangulateButton = new JButton("Triangulate");
```

When an event source generates an event, it notifies every event listener registered with the event source. Event sources provide methods that event listeners can use to register. In our example, the panel is interested in being notified whenever the *Triangulate* button is pressed. Hence, the panel registers as a listener of action events generated by the *Triangulate* button object. Registration is achieved by the following instruction:

```
triangulateButton.addActionListener(panel);
```

By registering with an event source, a listener also implicitly indicates the type of event in which it's interested. In our example, `panel` indicates interest in *action* events by registering via the button's `addActionListener` method, rather than through one of the other registration methods that the button provides. Here, `panel` will be notified of all action events that the *Triangulate* button generates, but it will not be notified of other types of events.

To register with an event source, an event listener object must be of the correct type. In our example, `panel` must be capable of listening for action events—more precisely, `panel` must implement the `ActionListener` interface:

```
public interface java.awt.event.ActionListener {
  public abstract void actionPerformed(ActionEvent e);
}
```

The fact that `panel` implements this interface is guaranteed by the signature of the button's `addActionListener` method, by which `panel` registers as a listener:

```
// method of JButton class
public void addActionListener(ActionListener obj);
```

Were `panel` not a subtype of the `ActionListener` interface, it would not be possible for `panel` to register as a listener of the button's action events (the compiler would flag any attempt to do so).

When an event source generates an event, it notifies every registered listener of the event. Specifically, the event source calls the appropriate event handler method of each of its registered listeners, passing an event object that encapsulates the event as argument. In our running example, when the user clicks the *Triangulate* button, the system sends `panel` the following message:

```
panel.actionPerformed(e)
```

where the argument `e` is an event object describing the button press that resulted in the event. Here, `panel` necessarily implements the `actionPerformed` method because it implements the `ActionListener` interface. Generally, when an event listener registers with an event source, the act of registration guarantees that the event listener implements the event handler method(s) by which the event source notifies it of events.

Event sources provide a method for deregistering listeners to parallel each of its methods for registering listeners. For example, buttons provide the following method for deregistering listeners:

```
// method of JButton class
public void removeActionListener(ActionListener obj);
```

The instruction:

```
triangulateButton.removeActionListener(panel);
```

removes `panel` from `triangulateButton`'s set of interested listeners; `panel` will no longer be notified of the button's action events until `panel` registers once again at some later time.

A listener's event handlers are its methods for responding to events. In the case of action events, listeners promise to implement only one event handler method, `actionPerformed`. (Later, we'll see other event listener interfaces that promise more than one event handler.) In our running example, the definition of the `PointSetPanel` class might take this form:

```
public class PointSetPanel extends JPanel
                     implements ActionListener {

  public void actionPerformed(ActionEvent e) {
    Object source = e.getSource();
    if (source == triangulateButton) {
      // respond to action events produced
      // by Triangulate button
      ...
    }
    // else handle action events generated
    // by other event sources
    // with which this panel is registered
    ...
  }

  // other methods
  ...
}
```

In the implementation of the `actionPerformed` method, the first instruction captures a reference to the source of the action event. It is generally

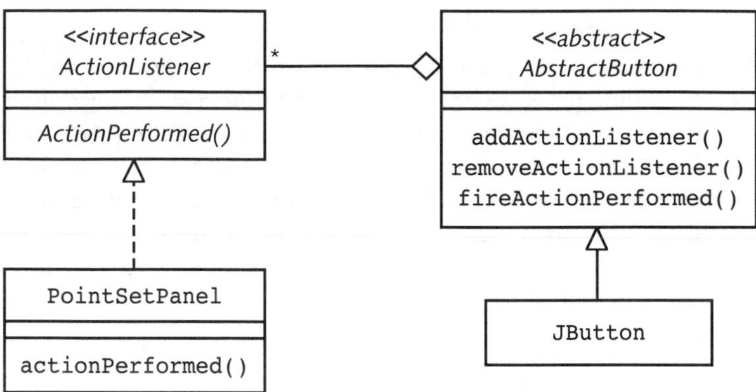

FIGURE 7.1 Java's event model is based on the observer design pattern (compare to Figure 6.37).

necessary to identify the source of an event when an event listener is registered with more than one source of the same type of event. In this case, `panel` may be registered with other buttons besides `triangulateButton`, and `panel`'s response to an action event depends on which button was pressed. Because the `getSource` method is defined in the `EventObject` class (which is a supertype for all event types), it is always possible to obtain the event source for any type of event.

The class diagram of Figure 7.1 shows the relationships among the classes discussed in the running example of this section. Here, the `JButton` class inherits its methods `addActionListener` and `removeActionListener` for registering and deregistering listeners from its abstract superclass `AbstractButton`. The `AbstractButton` class also defines the `fireActionPerformed` method which notifies all registered listeners whenever the button is clicked. Note that Figure 7.1 conforms to the class diagram for the observer design pattern (see Figure 6.37).

The sequence diagram of Figure 7.2 illustrates the object interactions discussed in our running example. In response to the user's click, `triangulateButton` sends itself a *fireActionPerformed* message, which in turn causes an *actionPerformed* message to be sent to the registered listener `panel`. The sequence diagram suggests that `panel` registers itself with the button. However, it is not necessary for an event listener to register itself with an event source, although *some* object must register the listener if it is to be notified of events.

7.2.2 Creating Point Sets

In Sections 7.2.2 though 7.2.5, we'll develop four GUI-based programs, each building on the previous ones. Our first program allows the user to add and delete points in a frame through mouse clicks. The points are rendered as small, colored disks. The second program (Section 7.2.3) extends the first one, in that it allows the user to move points around by dragging the mouse.

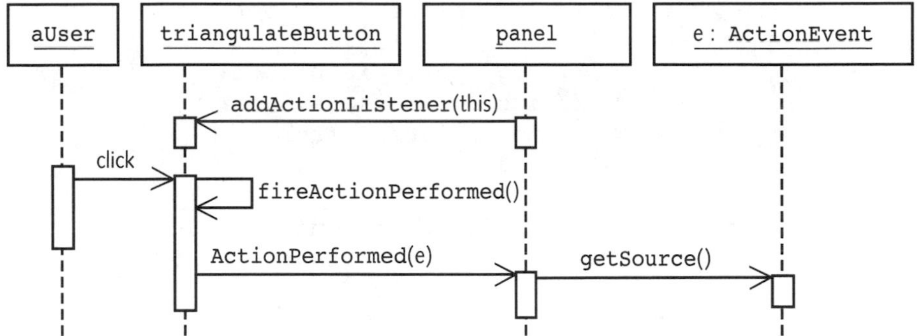

FIGURE 7.2 Sequence diagram for registering `panel` with the *Triangulate* button and later responding when the user clicks the button.

The third program is a simple polygon editor, which enables the user to create, delete, and reposition polygon vertices through mouse clicks and drags. The last program (Section 7.2.5) introduces an interface for manipulating figures, and reimplements the point-editing program of Section 7.2.3 using this interface. The purpose of these programs is to illustrate Java's event model. Note that these programs' reliance on Swing is limited to the use of panels (we'll explore the use of other Swing components in Section 7.3).

Our first GUI-based program is a primitive point set editor. The points appear in a frame as small, colored disks. To create new randomly colored points, the user clicks the mouse in the frame's background. To delete an existing point, the user clicks the point to be deleted.

Our program `ClickPoints` is a type of panel, an extension of Java's `JPanel` class. The user actions of interest are mouse clicks. Whenever the mouse is clicked in the `ClickPoints` panel, it generates a **mouse event,** an instance of the `java.awt.event.MouseEvent` class. In our implementation, the panel listens for the very mouse events it generates, so it registers itself as a listener of its own mouse events. This idiom—in which an object observes the very events it generates—is useful when the event-handling logic is fairly simple. Here is the structure of our `ClickPoints` class:

```
public class ClickPoints extends JPanel
                         implements MouseListener {

  // fields
  ...

  public static void main(String[] args) {
    ...
  }

  public ClickPoints() {
```

```
      // initialize this application
      ...
      // register this panel as a listener of
      // its own mouse events
      addMouseListener(this);
    }

    public void paintComponent(Graphics g) {
      // paint the current set of points into
      // the graphics context g
      ...
    }

    //
    // implement MouseListener interface
    //   this program responds only to mouse clicks;
    //   the remaining four event handlers of the
    //   MouseListener interface do nothing
    //
    public void mouseClicked(MouseEvent e) {
      // handle mouse clicks
      ...
    }
    public void mouseEntered(MouseEvent e) { }
    public void mouseExited(MouseEvent e) { }
    public void mouseReleased(MouseEvent e) { }
    public void mousePressed(MouseEvent e) { }

    // additional helper methods
    ...
  }
```

Listeners of mouse events (such as our `ClickPoints` class) must implement the `java.awt.event.MouseListener` interface. This interface specifies five methods which get called in response to various mouse actions applied to a component. For example, when the mouse is clicked on a component, the component generates a mouse event and notifies its registered listeners by calling each listener's `mouseClicked` method. Here is the definition of this interface:

```
public interface java.awt.event.MouseListener {
    // invoked when the mouse is clicked on a component
  public void mouseClicked(MouseEvent e);

    // invoked when the mouse enters a component
  public void mouseEntered(MouseEvent e);
```

```
    // invoked when the mouse exits a component
  public void mouseExited(MouseEvent e);

    // invoked when a mouse button is pressed
    // on a component
  public void mousePressed(MouseEvent e);

    // invoked when a mouse button is released
    // on a component
  public void mouseReleased(MouseEvent e);
}
```

Because the `ClickPoints` class implements the `MouseListener` interface, it must implement all five event-handler methods promised by this interface. However, because our application is interested only in events arising from mouse clicks, only the `mouseClicked` event handler boasts a nontrivial implementation; the other four event handlers promised by `MouseListener` have do-nothing bodies. Our program responds only to mouse clicks.

Let's complete the implementation of the `ClickPoints` class. As to its storage structure, we'll maintain the current set of points in a vector named `figures`. We'll also maintain a random-color generator to produce the points' colors:

```
// fields of ClickPoints class
protected Vector figures;
protected RandomColor rnd;
```

The following class definition includes the implementation of the public interface, but only the specification of the protected interface:

```
public class ClickPoints extends JPanel
                         implements MouseListener {

  protected Vector figures;
  protected RandomColor rnd;

  public static void main(String[] args) {
    JPanel panel = new ClickPoints();
    ApplicationFrame frame =
      new ApplicationFrame("ClickPoints");
    frame.getContentPane().add(panel);
    frame.show();
  }

  public ClickPoints() {
    setBackground(Color.black);
    figures = new Vector();
    rnd = new RandomColor();
```

```
    addMouseListener(this);
  }

  public void paintComponent(Graphics g) {
    super.paintComponent(g);
    Graphics2D g2 = (Graphics2D)g;
    g2.setRenderingHint(RenderingHints.KEY_ANTIALIASING,
                   RenderingHints.VALUE_ANTIALIAS_ON);
    Iterator iter = figures.iterator();
    while (iter.hasNext()) {
      Figure fig = (Figure)iter.next();
      fig.paint(g2);
    }
  }

  //
  // implement MouseListener interface
  //
  public void mouseClicked(MouseEvent e) {
    Figure clickedFig = findFigure(e.getX(), e.getY());
    if (clickedFig == null)   // no figure was clicked
      addFigure(e.getX(), e.getY());
    else
      removeFigure(clickedFig);
    repaint();
  }

  public void mouseEntered(MouseEvent e) { }
  public void mouseExited(MouseEvent e) { }
  public void mouseReleased(MouseEvent e) { }
  public void mousePressed(MouseEvent e) { }

  protected Figure findFigure(int x, int y) {
    // EFFECTS: If (x,y) is contained in some point
    //   figure returns that figure; else returns null.
    ...
  }

  protected void addFigure(int x, int y) {
    // MODIFIES: figures, rnd
    // EFFECTS: Adds a new randomly colored point figure
    //   at position (x,y).
    ...
  }

  protected void removeFigure(Figure fig) {
    // MODIFIES: figures
```

```
        // EFFECTS: Removes the point figure fig.
        ...
    }
}
```

To complete our implementation of the ClickPoints class, we need to implement its three protected methods. The methods for adding and removing point figures are straightforward. The addFigure method creates a figure representing a new point at (*x*,*y*) and adds the new figure to the vector figures:

```
// method of ClickPoints class
protected void addFigure(int x, int y) {
  PointGeometry point = new PointGeometry(x, y);
  Painter painter = new FillPainter(rnd.nextColor());
  figures.add(new Figure(point, painter));
}
```

And the removeFigure method removes from the vector figures the figure with which it's called:

```
// method of ClickPoints class
protected void removeFigure(Figure fig) {
  figures.remove(fig);
}
```

The remaining protected method, findFigure, is called with integer inputs *x* and *y* and returns some point figure that is close to the point (*x*,*y*), or null if no such figure exists. A point *p* is considered close to (*x*,*y*) if *p* lies no greater than some small, fixed distance *R* from (*x*,*y*). We can imagine centering a small disk of radius *R* on the point (*x*,*y*) and testing each of the points in the vector figures until finding some point *p* that lies inside this disk and then returning *p*. If none of the points lies inside this disk, the method returns null. The following implementation assumes the value *R*=3:

```
// method of ClickPoints class
protected Figure findFigure(int x, int y) {
  EllipseGeometry disk =
    new EllipseGeometry(x-3, y-3, 6, 6);
  Iterator iter = figures.iterator();
  while (iter.hasNext()) {
    Figure fig = (Figure)iter.next();
    PointGeometry p = (PointGeometry)fig.getGeometry();
    if (disk.contains(p))
      return fig;
  }
  return null;
}
```

Exercises

7.1 Write a program `ClickAndColorPoints` that behaves like `ClickPoints`, except that whenever the user clicks an existing point, the point is assigned a new random color instead of being deleted.

7.2 Write a program `ClickEllipses` that behaves like `ClickPoints`, except that it produces an ellipse, rather than a point, whenever the user clicks in the frame's background. Each ellipse is assigned a random color and a random width and random height each in the range [10..40].

ESSENTIAL 7.3 Define a `PointZoneGeometry` class that behaves like a `PointGeometry` yet which also provides `contains` methods for deciding whether an input point p lies within a given distance R of this point. Here, we refer to R as the *zone radius* property. For testing point containment, a point zone geometry behaves like a disk; otherwise, it behaves like a point. The following class skeleton specifies those methods that differ from the ones inherited from `PointGeometry`:

```
public class PointZoneGeometry
                  extends PointGeometry
                  implements AreaGeometry {
  public PointZoneGeometry(int x,int y,int radius)
         throws IllegalArgumentException
    // EFFECTS: If radius <= 0 throws
    //   IllegalArgumentException; else constructs
    //   a point at (x,y) and sets its zone radius
    //   to radius.

  public PointZoneGeometry(int x, int y)
    // EFFECTS: Constructs a point at (x,y) and
    //   sets its zone radius to 2.

  public PointZoneGeometry(PointGeometry p,
                           int radius)
   throws NullPointerException,
          IllegalArgumentException
    // EFFECTS: If p is null throws
    //   NullPointerException; else if radius <= 0
    //   throws IllegalArgumentException; else
    //   constructs a point at p and sets its
    //   zone radius to radius.
```

```
    public PointZoneGeometry(PointGeometry p)
           throws NullPointerException
      // EFFECTS: If p is null throws
      //   NullPointerException; else constructs a
      //   point at p and sets its zone radius to 2.

    public PointZoneGeometry()
      // EFFECTS: Constructs a point at the origin
      //   and sets its zone radius to 2.

    public boolean contains(int x, int y)
      // EFFECTS: Returns true if (x,y) lies within
      //   zone radius units from this point;
      //   else returns false.

    public boolean contains(PointGeometry p)
           throws NullPointerException
      // EFFECTS: If p is null throws
      //   NullPointerException; else if p lies
      //   within zone radius units from this point
      //   returns true; else returns false.

    public void setZoneRadius(int newR)
           throws IllegalArgumentException
      // MODIFIES: this
      // EFFECTS: If newR <= 0 throws
      //   IllegalArgumentException; else sets
      //   the zone radius to newR.

    public int getZoneRadius()
      // EFFECTS: Returns current zone radius.
}
```

For example, the following code fragment:

```
PointZoneGeometry p = new PointZoneGeometry(5,10,4);
if (p.contains(new PointGeometry(5, 12)))
  System.out.println("print me");
if (p.contains(new PointGeometry(30, 40)))
  System.out.println("don't print me");
```

prints only the string *print me* because the point (5,12) lies no more than 4 units from the point (5,10), whereas the point (30,40) lies more than 4 units from (5,10).

To implement one of the `contains` methods, you might consider constructing an ellipse to serve as the disk and then delegating the query to the ellipse. Revise the implementation of the `ClickPoints.findFigure` method so that it uses a point zone geometry instead of an ellipse geometry, and then try your `ClickPoints` pro-

7.2.3 Editing Point Sets

Our next GUI-based program, named `EditPoints`, is a point set editor that enhances the functionality of the previous program. Again, points appear in a panel as small, colored disks, and the user creates new randomly colored points by clicking in the panel's background. To delete an existing point, the user control-clicks the point to be deleted (presses the Control key while clicking the point). In addition, the user can use the mouse to drag an existing point to a new location—the point being dragged follows the cursor until the user releases the mouse button.

To implement this program, it is necessary to listen to events generated whenever the mouse button is pressed or released and whenever the mouse is dragged. We've seen that it's possible to listen to events arising from mouse button presses and releases by registering a `MouseListener` with a mouse event source (such as a panel). Unfortunately, mouse listeners are not notified of events arising from mouse motion. Java does, however, provide a different interface for listening to events arising from mouse motion. The `MouseMotionListener` interface is defined like this:

```
public interface java.awt.event.MouseMotionListener {
    // invoked repeatedly while the mouse is dragged
    // (with its button down) in a component
  public void mouseDragged(MouseEvent e);

    // invoked repeatedly while the mouse is moved
    // (with its button up) in a component
  public void mouseMoved(MouseEvent e);
}
```

As a source of mouse events, a panel provides the following methods for registering and deregistering listeners of events arising from mouse motion:

```
// methods of JPanel class
public void addMouseMotionListener(MouseMotionListener l)
public void
  removeMouseMotionListener(MouseMotionListener l)
```

A mouse motion listener is registered with a panel like this:

```
panel.addMouseMotionListener(aListener);
```

Subsequently, `aListener` is notified of mouse events due to mouse motion. Specifically, while the mouse is moved with its button is up, the system repeatedly sends the message:

```
aListener.mouseMoved(e)
```

where `e` encapsulates the mouse event. Similarly, while the mouse is dragged with its button down, the system repeatedly sends the message:

```
aListener.mouseMoved(e)
```

To summarize, there are two kinds of listeners for mouse events: *mouse listeners* are notified of mouse events arising from mouse button actions and component-boundary crossings, whereas *mouse motion listeners* are notified of mouse events arising from mouse motion. For our `EditPoints` program, we'll create one listener of each type and register both with the `EditPoints` panel. The `EditPoints` panel is a source of mouse events but it will not observe its own events; instead, two separately defined listener objects registered with the panel will listen.

To respond to mouse events, both listeners must access the state of the `EditPoints` class. In our implementation, we provide such access by defining the two listener classes as *inner classes* of `EditPoints`. This allows them to directly refer to the fields of the `EditPoints` class using the fields' names, without further qualification. Here is the implementation:

```
public class EditPoints extends JPanel {

  protected Vector figures;
  protected RandomColor rnd;
  protected Figure clickedFig;
  protected PointGeometry clickedPoint;

  public static void main(String[] args) {
    JPanel panel = new EditPoints();
    ApplicationFrame frame =
      new ApplicationFrame("EditPoints");
    frame.getContentPane().add(panel);
    frame.show();
  }

  public EditPoints() {
    setBackground(Color.black);
    figures = new Vector();
    rnd = new RandomColor();
    addMouseListener(new EditPointsMouseListener());
    addMouseMotionListener(
```

```
      new EditPointsMouseMotionListener());
  }

  public void paintComponent(Graphics g) {
    // same as method ClickPoints.paintComponent
    ...
  }

  //
  // the following three methods are defined the
  // same as their counterparts in class ClickPoints.
  //
  protected Figure findFigure(int x, int y) { ... }
  protected void addFigure(int x, int y) { ... }
  protected void removeFigure(Figure fig) { ... }

  //
  // inner class: mouse motion listener for mouse motion
  //
  class EditPointsMouseMotionListener
                extends MouseMotionAdapter {
    public void mouseDragged(MouseEvent e) {
      if (clickedFig != null) {
        clickedPoint.setX(e.getX());
        clickedPoint.setY(e.getY());
        repaint();
      }
    }
  }

  //
  // inner class: mouse listener for mouse button actions
  //
  class EditPointsMouseListener extends MouseAdapter {
    public void mouseReleased(MouseEvent e) {
      if (clickedFig == null)   // no figure was clicked
        addFigure(e.getX(), e.getY());
      else if (e.isControlDown())
        removeFigure(clickedFig);
      clickedFig = null;
      repaint();
    }

    public void mousePressed(MouseEvent e) {
      clickedFig = findFigure(e.getX(), e.getY());
      if (clickedFig != null)
```

```
            clickedPoint =
              (PointGeometry)clickedFig.getGeometry();
        }
      }
    }
```

Each of the two inner classes extends an **adapter class;** for instance, the `EditPointsMouseListener` class extends the `MouseAdapter` class (see Figure 7.3). The `MouseAdapter` class implements the five methods promised by the `MouseListener` interface as do-nothing methods:

```
public class java.awt.event.MouseAdapter
                       implements MouseListener {
  public void mouseClicked(MouseEvent e) { }
  public void mouseEntered(MouseEvent e) { }
  public void mouseExited(MouseEvent e) { }
  public void mousePressed(MouseEvent e) { }
  public void mouseReleased(MouseEvent e) { }
}
```

To define a new mouse listener class, you may extend the `MouseAdapter` class and override only those methods of interest. For example, the inner class `EditPointsMouseListener` extends `MouseAdapter` and overrides only the `MousePressed` and `MouseReleased` methods. The new subclass need not implement the remaining methods of the `MouseListener` interface because they are already implemented by `MouseAdapter`. Java provides the `MouseAdapter` class as a convenience. It is always possible to define a class that implements the `MouseListener` interface directly, without extending `MouseAdapter`, but such a class must implement all five methods declared by the `MouseListener` interface, even those methods it doesn't really need.

Similarly, Java provides the `MouseMotionAdapter` class to simplify the implementation of mouse motion listeners:

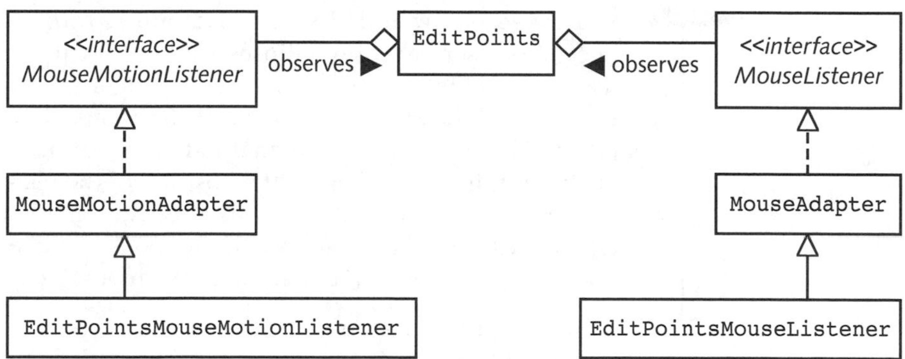

FIGURE 7.3 Structure of the `EditPoints` program.

```
public class java.awt.event.MouseMotionAdapter
                      implements MouseMotionListener {
  public void mouseDragged(MouseEvent e) { }
  public void mouseMoved(MouseEvent e) { }
}
```

As we've seen, Java defines two different interfaces for mouse event listeners: the `MouseListener` interface for events arising from mouse button actions and component-boundary crossings, and the `MouseMotionListener` interface for events arising from mouse motions. Why does Java provide two different interfaces for mouse event listeners when a single seven-method interface would suffice? The answer is, for efficiency. Because the mouse is typically moved so frequently, generating events every time it moves is CPU intensive. Java's event model is designed to avoid generating such expensive events if they're not needed. When an event source registers only `MouseListener` objects, the event source generates mouse events in response to mouse button actions and component-boundary crossings, but not in response to mouse motion. This is how our `ClickPoints` program of Section 7.2.2 works. Only if a `MouseMotionListener` object registers with an event source does the event source bother to generate mouse events in response to mouse motion. Our `EditPoints` program requires this extra work because it displays the continually changing position of points while they're dragged.

Exercises

7.4 Revise the implementation of `EditPoints` so that whenever a point is clicked or dragged to a new location, the point appears on top of (i.e., is painted after) any other points it happens to overlap. [Hint: The *layer ordering* of points is determined by their order in the vector `figures`.]

ESSENTIAL 7.5 Write a program `DragEllipses` which behaves like the `ClickEllipses` program of Exercise 7.2 but with the following difference: The user can drag ellipses to different positions. When the user presses the mouse button on some ellipse and drags the mouse, the ellipse follows the cursor until the mouse button is released. [Hint: The `mousePressed` method finds some ellipse that was clicked on (if any) and saves the position of the click. If an ellipse is currently being dragged, the `mouseDragged` method translates the ellipse by the difference between the mouse's current position and its previous position, and then saves the mouse's current position.]

ESSENTIAL 7.6 Write the program `SweepRectangles` for creating a collection of rectangles in the frame using mouse drags. When the mouse button is pressed, a new rectangle of initial width and height equal to zero is positioned at (x_0,y_0), the point of the mouse press. The rectangle is filled with a random color. As the mouse is dragged (with its button down), the position (x,y) of each mouse event determines one of the rectangle's corners—specifically, (x_0,y_0) and (x,y) are opposite corners of the rectangle under construction. The corner at (x_0,y_0) remains anchored, whereas the corner at (x,y) varies as the mouse is dragged. The final dimensions of the new rectangle are fixed by the position of the mouse release. While the mouse is being dragged, the frame should display all the rectangles previously created including the one under construction. [Hint: When the mouse is pressed, save the mouse event coordinates x_0 and y_0, create a new rectangle figure, and add it to the collection of figures. As the mouse is dragged, update the properties of the current rectangle and repaint the frame—this should repaint all the figures including the one under construction. You may want to define a protected helper method

```
// method of SweepRectangles class
protected void updateCurrentRectangle(int x, int y)
```

for updating the current rectangle's dimensions based on the initial click-down point (x_0,y_0) and the current position of the mouse at (x,y). Note that (x_0,y_0) may correspond to any one of the rectangle's four corners, depending on the values of x and y.]

7.2.4 Editing Polygons

In this section, we develop a GUI-based program for editing a polygon. The `EditPolygon` program displays the polygon in a panel and highlights its current vertex. Whenever the user clicks in the panel, a new vertex is created at the click point and inserted after the current vertex. The user can drag an existing vertex to a new location—the vertex being dragged follows the cursor until the user releases the mouse button. And the user can delete a vertex by control-clicking it (although the sole vertex of a one-vertex polygon cannot be deleted). Whenever a new vertex is created or an existing one is dragged, it becomes the current vertex; when a vertex is deleted, its predecessor becomes the current vertex.

The `EditPolygon` program is similar to the `EditPoints` program of the previous section insofar as a polygon's vertices can be thought of as the points of a point set. However, the programs' designs differ in a key way. As we've seen, the `EditPoints` class defines two inner classes to serve as listeners for its mouse events. In contrast, the `EditPolygon` program defines a separate listener class (named `PolygonListener`) to observe mouse events. This listener class is responsible for managing the polygon geometry.

The `EditPolygon` class is a panel that maintains a figure for the polygon and a figure for its current vertex in fields named `polygonFigure` and `vertexFigure`, respectively. Besides defining a constructor and a `paintComponent` method, the `EditPolygon` class defines a `setVertexPosition` method which the event listener uses to update the current vertex's position. Here is the definition of the `EditPolygon` class:

```
public class EditPolygon extends JPanel {

  protected Figure polygonFigure;
  protected Figure vertexFigure;
  final static PointGeometry InitialPoint =
    new PointGeometry(100, 100);

  public static void main(String[] args) {
    JPanel panel = new EditPolygon();
    ApplicationFrame frame =
      new ApplicationFrame("Edit Polygon");
    frame.getContentPane().add(panel);
    frame.show();
  }

  public EditPolygon() {
    setBackground(Color.black);
      // create the polygon and vertex figures
    Painter fill = new FillPainter(Color.blue);
    Painter draw =
      new DrawDynamicPolygonPainter(Color.green);
    DynamicPolygonGeometry poly =
      new DynamicPolygonGeometry(InitialPoint);
    polygonFigure =
      new Figure(poly,new MultiPainter(fill, draw));
    vertexFigure =
      new Figure(InitialPoint, new FillPainter(Color.red));
      // create and register the listener
    PolygonListener listener =
      new PolygonListener(this, poly);
    addMouseListener(listener);
    addMouseMotionListener(listener);
  }

  public void paintComponent(Graphics g) {
    super.paintComponent(g);
    Graphics2D g2 = (Graphics2D)g;
```

```
    g2.setRenderingHint(RenderingHints.KEY_ANTIALIASING,
                  RenderingHints.VALUE_ANTIALIAS_ON);
    polygonFigure.paint(g2);  // paint the polygon
    vertexFigure.paint(g2);   // paint current vertex
  }

  public void setVertexPosition(PointGeometry p) {
    vertexFigure.setGeometry(p);
  }
}
```

The `PolygonListener` class manipulates the polygon through a polygon iterator stored in its `iter` field. Because the `EditPolygon` class maintains a reference to the iterator's underlying polygon, changes to the polygon made through the iterator are automatically communicated to `EditPolygon`. Nonetheless, the listener must inform `EditPolygon` *when* such changes occur; it must also inform `EditPolygon` of the current vertex's position whenever it changes. Accordingly, `PolygonListener` maintains a reference to the `EditPolygon` panel. The `PolygonListener` class also defines a `boolean` field named `vertexBeingDragged`, whose value indicates whether some vertex is in the process of being dragged. Here is the class definition:

```
public class PolygonListener extends MouseAdapter
                   implements MouseMotionListener {
  protected PolygonIterator iter;
  protected boolean vertexBeingDragged;
  protected EditPolygon panel;

  public PolygonListener(EditPolygon panel,
                         DynamicPolygonGeometry poly) {
    this.panel = panel;
    iter = poly.iterator();
    panel.repaint();
  }

  public void mousePressed(MouseEvent e) {
    vertexBeingDragged = findVertex(e.getX(), e.getY());
  }

  public void mouseReleased(MouseEvent e) {
    if (vertexBeingDragged && e.isControlDown())
      removeVertex();
    else if (!vertexBeingDragged) {
      PointGeometry p =
        new PointGeometry(e.getX(), e.getY());
      insertNewVertex(p);
    }
```

```
    vertexBeingDragged = false;
    panel.repaint();
  }

  public void mouseDragged(MouseEvent e) {
    if (vertexBeingDragged) {
      moveVertex(e.getX(), e.getY());
      panel.repaint();
    }
  }

  public void mouseMoved(MouseEvent e) { }

  //
  // protected interface
  //
  protected boolean findVertex(int x, int y) {
    PointZoneGeometry disk = new PointZoneGeometry(x, y);
    for (int i=0;i<iter.nbrVertices(); iter.next(),i++) {
      PointGeometry p = iter.point();
      if (disk.contains(p)) {
        panel.setVertexPosition(p);
        return true;
      }
    }
    return false;
  }

  protected void insertNewVertex(PointGeometry p) {
    iter.insertAfter(p);
    panel.setVertexPosition(p);
  }

  protected void removeVertex() {
    if (iter.nbrVertices() > 1) {
      iter.remove();
      panel.setVertexPosition(iter.point());
    }
  }

  protected void moveVertex(int x, int y) {
    iter.moveTo(x, y);
    panel.setVertexPosition(new PointGeometry(x, y));
  }
}
```

7.2.5 Editing Points Revisited

Since introducing the `Figure` class in Section 5.6, we've taken care to distinguish between geometries and their appearance: A geometry implements the `Geometry` interface, whereas an appearance implements the `Painter` interface. The two are joined in `Figure` objects. Along the same lines, it's helpful to distinguish between operations involving geometries and operations involving figures. Our `EditPoints` program of Section 7.2.3 is an example of a program that mostly fails to maintain this distinction. When the user clicks to create new points, these are essentially geometric actions: The mouse is used to indicate locations in the plane. Yet, in response to a mouse click, the `EditPoints` program takes steps involving both geometry and appearance: It creates a new point geometry and a new randomly colored painter and then combines the two in a new figure.

In this section, we revisit the `EditPoints` program with an eye toward distinguishing between operations involving geometries and those involving appearances and figures. To do so, we introduce a new `FigureManager` interface that specifies operations for managing figures and appearances. A figure manager is designed to remove from its clients the responsibilities for wrapping geometries in figures and for managing figures generally. The use of a figure manager will not greatly simplify the point-editing application to be presented in this section, because this program was not very complicated to begin with; however, it will significantly simplify the programs that we develop later in this chapter.

Our new point-editing program, named `EditPointSet`, behaves the same as the `EditPoints` program from the user's perspective, but its design is different (see Figure 7.4). Our new program employs a figure manager, an instance of the `EditPointSetManager` class. Here, `EditPointSet` manipulates figures by sending messages to its figure manager, whereas it manipulates geometries directly: creating new point geometries and deleting existing ones, and translating point geometries to new locations. As in the case of the `EditPoints` class, the `EditPointSet` class is a panel that defines its two mouse listeners as inner classes.

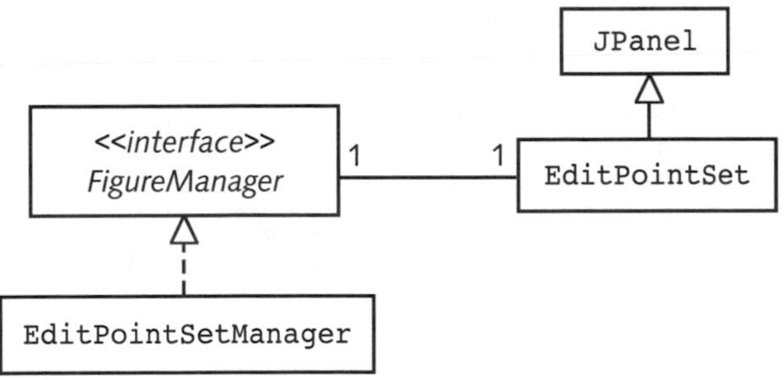

FIGURE 7.4 Structure of the `EditPointSet` program.

We'll consider the `FigureManager` interface first. This interface specifies the behaviors for wrapping geometries in figures—essentially assigning appearances to geometries—and for managing a collection of figures. At any given time, at most one of the geometries is considered the **selected geometry.** (For many applications, it is helpful to maintain a selected geometry to which certain operations apply by default; for example, most drawing programs support the notion of a selected geometry which may be translated, edited, assigned a new appearance, and so forth.) The `FigureManager` interface specifies a `select` operation for selecting a geometry from among those in the collection, and a `selected` operation for obtaining the selected geometry. The interface also declares an `add` operation which, when called with an input geometry, wraps the geometry in a figure and adds the figure to the collection. Again, the client is responsible only for providing geometries, whereas the figure manager is responsible for wrapping them in figures. The `remove` operation is called with a geometry and removes the geometry's figure from the collection. The `size` operation reports the number of geometries in the collection and the `get` operation allows geometries to be accessed by a zero-based index. A geometry can also be accessed using the `find` operation: when called with the *x* and *y* coordinates of some point *p*, `find` returns some geometry of the collection that is "hit" by point *p*.

Whenever the figure manager changes in some significant way, its client notifies it by sending the *updateManager* message. This can occur, for instance, when significant changes require the screen to be repainted. Lastly, the `FigureManager` interface specifies a `getFigures` operation that returns a node representing its collection of figures. Clients may use this operation to paint the figures through an instruction such as:

```
aFigureManager.getFigures().paint(g2);
```

where `g2` is a rendering context. Here is the definition of the `FigureManager` interface:

```
public interface FigureManager {
  public void select(Geometry g)
        throws IllegalArgumentException;
    // MODIFIES: this
    // EFFECTS: If g is null deselects the selected
    //   geometry (if any): else if g belongs to
    //   this collection selects g; else throws
    //   IllegalArgumentException.

  public Geometry selected();
    // EFFECTS: Returns the selected geometry if any;
    //   else returns null.

  public Node getFigures();
    // EFFECTS: Returns a node representing the set
```

```
    //   of figures.

  public void updateManager();
    // MODIFIES: this
    // EFFECTS: Any.

  public void add(Geometry g);
    // MODIFIES: this
    // EFFECTS: Wraps g in a figure and adds it to
    //   its collection.

  public void remove(Geometry g);
    // MODIFIES: this
    // EFFECTS: If g belongs to some figure in
    //   the collection, removes the figure;
    //   else does nothing.

  public Geometry get(int i)
        throws IndexOutOfBoundsException;
    // EFFECTS: If 0 <= i < size() returns the i'th
    //   geometry; else throws IndexOutOfBoundsException.

  public int size();
    // EFFECTS: Returns the number of geometries
    //   in this collection.

  public Geometry find(int x, int y);
    // EFFECTS: Returns some geometry in this collection
    //   hit by the point (x,y); returns null if no
    //   such geometry exists.
}
```

The postconditions promised by certain methods of the `FigureManager` interface are weak by design and are intended to be strengthened by classes implementing the interface. With respect to the `find` method, the notion of a point *p* *hitting* a geometry may mean that *p* is contained in the geometry or that point *p* is "close enough" to the geometry; or it may mean something else. Similarly, the effect of the `updateManager` method is essentially unspecified; a figure manager may be updated in whatever way an application requires.

The implementation of the `EditPointSet` class serves as a nontrivial example of how a figure manager can be used. Here is the class definition:

```
public class EditPointSet extends JPanel {

  protected FigureManager manager;
  protected PointGeometry clickedPoint;
```

```
public static void main(String[] args) {
  JPanel panel = new EditPointSet();
  ApplicationFrame frame =
    new ApplicationFrame("EditPointSet");
  frame.getContentPane().add(panel);
  frame.show();
}

public EditPointSet() {
  setBackground(Color.black);
  makeFigureManager(this);
  addMouseListener(new EditPointSetMouseListener());
      // the following mouse motion listener is
      // implemented as an anonymous inner class
      // (see the explanation below)
  addMouseMotionListener(new MouseMotionAdapter() {
           public void mouseDragged(MouseEvent e) {
             if (clickedPoint != null) {
               clickedPoint.setX(e.getX());
               clickedPoint.setY(e.getY());
               manager.updateManager();
             }
           }
         });
}

public void makeFigureManager(JPanel canvas) {
  manager = new EditPointSetManager(canvas);
}

public void paintComponent(Graphics g) {
  super.paintComponent(g);
  Graphics2D g2 = (Graphics2D)g;
  g2.setRenderingHint(RenderingHints.KEY_ANTIALIASING,
                 RenderingHints.VALUE_ANTIALIAS_ON);
  manager.getFigures().paint(g2);
}

class EditPointSetMouseListener extends MouseAdapter {
  public void mouseReleased(MouseEvent e) {
    if (clickedPoint == null) // no figure was clicked
      manager.add(new PointGeometry(e.getX(),e.getY()));
    else if (e.isControlDown())
      manager.remove(clickedPoint);
    clickedPoint = null;
    manager.updateManager();
  }
```

```
        public void mousePressed(MouseEvent e) {
          clickedPoint =
            (PointGeometry)manager.find(e.getX(), e.getY());
          manager.updateManager();
        }
      }
    }
```

The EditPointSet and EditPoints classes differ in how they manage figures. Because the EditPoints class manages figures on its own, it provides fields for storing figures as well as several protected methods for manipulating figures. In contrast, the EditPointSet class manages figures through the services of its figure manager, a reference to which is stored in its manager field. For example, the mouseReleased method of its mouse listener class adds new figures and deletes existing figures by sending its figure manager the *add* message and the *remove* message, respectively.

The EditPointSet class implements the mouse motion listener as an **anonymous inner class** which appears in the EditPointSet constructor. Specifically, the listener is the argument to the call to the addMouseMotion-Listener method. The anonymous class extends the MouseMotion-Adapter class which, as we've seen, provides do-nothing implementations for the methods declared by MouseMotionListener. The class overrides the mouseDragged method so that it tracks the point being dragged. Anonymous inner classes are useful when only a single instance of a class is needed (here, we need only one mouse motion listener). It is common to define event listeners as anonymous inner classes when only a single instance of a listener is required and the listener's methods can be defined concisely.

We'll turn next to the implementation of the EditPointSetManager class. This class defines three instance fields. The canvas field stores a reference to the panel in which points are drawn; whenever the manager is updated, it sends this panel a *repaint* message. The node field stores a group node whose children represent the points in the point set. And the rnd field stores a random-color generator used to produce the colors assigned to new points. Here is the class definition:

```
public class EditPointSetManager
       implements FigureManager {

  protected JPanel canvas;
  protected GroupNode node;
  protected RandomColor rnd;

  public EditPointSetManager(JPanel canvas) {
    this.canvas = canvas;
    node = new GroupNode();
    rnd = new RandomColor();
  }
```

```
public Node getFigures() {
  return node;
}

public void updateManager() {
  canvas.repaint();
}

public void add(Geometry p) {
  Painter painter = new FillPainter(rnd.nextColor());
  Figure fig = new Figure(p, painter);
  node.addChild(fig);
}

public void remove(Geometry p) {
  for (int i = 0; i < node.nbrChildren(); i++) {
    Figure fig = (Figure)node.child(i);
    Geometry g = fig.getGeometry();
    if (g == p) {
      node.removeChild(i);
      return;
    }
  }
}

public Geometry find(int x, int y) {
  PointZoneGeometry disk = new PointZoneGeometry(x,y);
  for (int i = node.nbrChildren()-1; i >= 0; i–) {
    Figure fig = (Figure)node.child(i);
    PointGeometry point =
      (PointGeometry)fig.getGeometry();
      if (disk.contains(point))
        return point;
  }
  return null;
}

public Geometry get(int i)
       throws IndexOutOfBoundsException {
  Figure fig = (Figure)node.child(i);
  return fig.getGeometry();
}

public int size() {
  return node.nbrChildren();
}
```

```
        // methods of FigureManager interface
        // not used by this application
      public void select(Geometry g)
             throws IllegalArgumentException { }
      public Geometry selected() { return null; }
    }
```

To summarize the material of this section, Java's event model is based on the observer pattern. Event sources (usually GUI components) are the subjects, and event listeners are their observers. When an event source triggers an event, each of its listeners is notified by a call to one of its event handlers. The event handler is passed an event object that encapsulates the event.

To customize event-handling behaviors, you define an event listener class. Your class should implement one of the interfaces expected by the event sources it observes. For instance, if your event listener is interested in action events generated by a button, it implements the `ActionListener` interface. This is an example of customization by composition (i.e., black box customization) because event listeners are components that get plugged in by implementing certain interfaces prescribed by the framework.

To customize event sources, you may extend GUI component classes provided by the framework. Your class is specialized by defining new behaviors and overriding inherited behaviors. For instance, the `EditPointSet` class, which represents an application-specific panel, was defined by extending Java's `JPanel` class. It overrides the `paintComponent` method and adds new behaviors of its own. This is an example of customization by inheritance (white box customization).

Exercises

7.7 Revise the implementation of the `EditPointSet` class so that the mouse listener currently realized by the inner `EditPointSet-MouseListener` class is implemented by an anonymous inner class.

ESSENTIAL 7.8 Write an `EditRectangles` program which behaves like the `Sweep-Rectangles` program of Exercise 7.6 but with two differences. First, you create new rectangles only by beginning a drag in the frame's background; if your drag begins inside an existing rectangle, no new rectangle is constructed. Second, if you control-click a rectangle, the rectangle is deleted (if the click occurs on top of more than one rectangle, only one of the rectangles is deleted). Your implementation should define an `EditRectanglesManager` class that implements the `FigureManager` interface. Your `EditRectan-gles` class uses the services of `EditRectanglesManager`.

7.3 Components

A graphical user interface may include buttons, panels, labels, text fields, scrollbars, drop-down lists, and other kinds of **components.** Related components are arranged within a **container.** Because containers are themselves a kind of component, a container can contain other containers, resulting in a hierarchy of components called a **containment hierarchy** (see Figure 3.4 for an example). At the root of a containment hierarchy lies the frame—the top-level window that appears on your desktop. The leaves of a containment hierarchy correspond to atomic components, which are noncontainer components such as buttons and labels.

In the AWT, Java's original component toolkit, component classes are subtypes of the abstract `java.awt.Component` class. One of its subclasses, `java.awt.Container`, represents containers. These two classes are related by the composite design pattern: `Container` is a subtype of `Component`, and a `Container` object is composed of zero or more instances of `Component` subtypes.

Swing grafts a new set of classes and interfaces onto the AWT. Swing defines an abstract `javax.swing.JComponent` class, which extends the AWTs `Container` class. Swing component classes are subtypes of this `JComponent` class (see Figure 7.5). Subtypes of the `JComponent` class represent lightweight components: they are fully implemented in Java rather than in terms of peer components belonging to the native GUI system. Figure 7.5 shows those GUI elements that we'll cover in the present chapter. This class diagram depicts but a small subset of the classes and interfaces that comprise the AWT and Swing.

By convention, the names of Swing components begin with the letter *J*. In many cases, the name of a Swing component is formed by prepending the letter *J* onto the name of the component's counterpart in the AWT. For example, push buttons are represented by the `Button` class in the AWT, and by the `JButton` class in Swing. In addition, Swing defines many component types that are not available in the AWT.

7.3.1 The *Component* and *Container* Classes

The abstract `java.awt.Component` class is the superclass of all GUI component classes, except for AWT components involving menus. The class provides color-valued *foreground* and *background* properties whose effect varies with the type of component. Components are capable of generating mouse events in response to both mouse button and mouse motion actions. Accordingly, the `Component` class defines the following methods for registering and deregistering listeners:

```
public void addMouseListener(MouseListener l);
public void removeMouseListener(MouseListener l);
public void
  addMouseMotionListener(MouseMotionListener l);
```

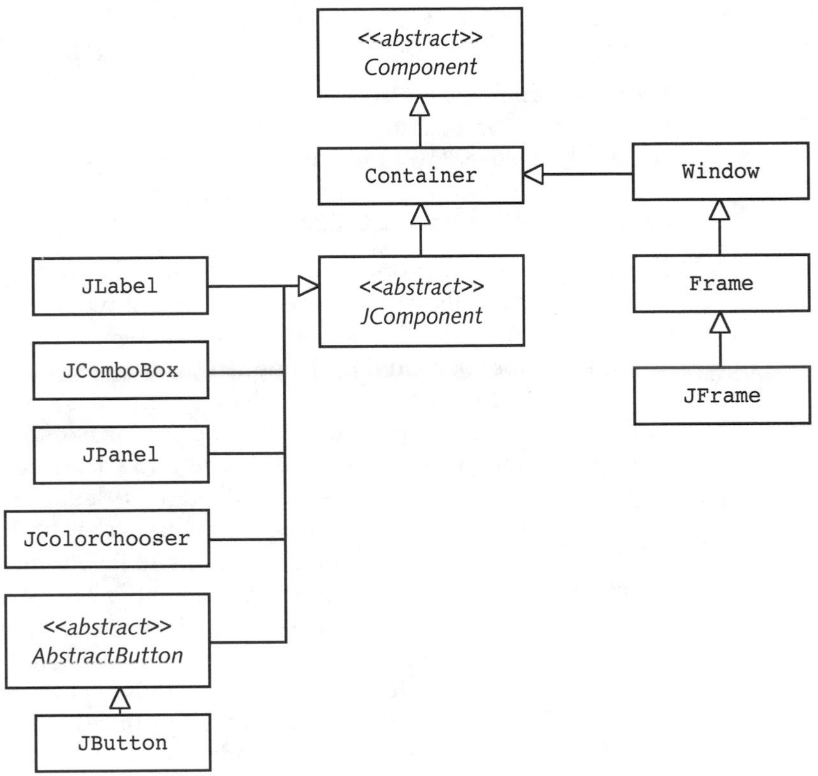

FIGURE 7.5 The GUI components used in this chapter.

```
public void
  removeMouseMotionListener(MouseMotionListener l);
```

The `java.awt.Container` class is used to build container objects to hold components. The class defines several overloaded `add` and `remove` methods for adding and removing components, respectively. One version of the `add` method adds a component to the end of this container; a second version adds a component at position `indx` (where zero-based indexing is assumed):

```
public void add(Component component);
public void add(Component component, int indx);
```

The `Con]tainer` class also defines `remove` methods for removing a component specified by component or by index:

```
public void remove(Component component);
public void remove(int indx);
```

The `getComponents` method returns an array holding the components in this container, and the `getComponent` method returns the component at a specific index:

```
public Component[] getComponents();
public Component getComponent(int indx);
```

The `Container` class also possesses a *layout* property whose value, a `LayoutManager` object, determines how this container's components are arranged. I'll cover layout managers in Section 7.4.

7.3.2 The *JComponent* Class

The `javax.swing.JComponent` class lies at the root of the Swing component hierarchy—all Swing components are subtypes of this class except for top-level containers such as frames. The `JComponent` class provides many useful behaviors beyond those supplied by its parent class `Container`. The `setToolTipText` method is used to specify a short string description (called a *tool tip*) that pops up when the cursor pauses over a component. The class defines a *border* property whose value describes a border. (Borders may be decorative such as raised, etched, or titled; nondecorative such as padding; or combinations of simpler forms.) The `JComponent` class provides a number of methods for giving hints to layout managers, such as the `setPreferredSize`, `setMimimumSize`, and `setMaximumSize` methods for specifying a component's best size, minimum size, and maximum size, respectively. The `JComponent` class also paints frame sequences more smoothly by means of double buffering (components are rendered to an off-screen buffer, which is then displayed all at once). The `JComponent` class provides numerous other services in addition to those just noted.

7.3.3 The *JPanel* Class

The `JPanel` class serves as a generic container for Swing components. A panel paints itself by painting its background, and then its border, and lastly its components. To add a component to a panel, you send the *add* message to the panel with the component as argument. For instance, the following command adds a new button to `aPanel`:

```
aPanel.add(new JButton("Press me"));
```

The various overloaded `add` methods are inherited from its supertype `Container`. Components are arranged within a panel (or within a container generally) based on the layout manager associated with the panel.

You use a panel when adding components to a top-level window (`JFrame`). First, you obtain the frame's content pane, which is a container for holding the frame's components. Then, you add a `JPanel` to the content pane, and then add components (including nested containers if desired) to the panel. The resulting code looks like this:

```
JPanel topPanel = new JPanel();
frame.getContentPane().add(topPanel);
// build and add new components to topPanel
...
```

Alternatively, you can create a new `JPanel` and make it the frame's content pane:

```
JPanel topPanel = new JPanel();
frame.setContentPane(topPanel);
// build and add new components to topPanel
...
```

7.3.4 The *JButton* Class

The `JButton` class is used to implement push buttons, three instances of which appear along the bottom of the dialog box in Figure 7.6. A button displays a text label and/or an icon corresponding to its *text* and *icon* properties. The class' four constructors can be used to initialize these two properties:

```
public JButton(String text, Icon icon);
public JButton(String text);
public JButton(Icon icon);
public JButton();
```

The *text* and *icon* properties (of type `String` and `Icon`, respectively) can also be set through the setter methods `setText` and `setIcon`.

When the user presses a button, the button triggers an action event and each `ActionListener` registered with the button is notified of the event through its `actionPerformed` method. Recall that the `ActionListener` interface is defined thus:

```
public interface java.awt.event.ActionListener {
  public void actionPerformed(ActionEvent e);
}
```

Accordingly, the `JButton` class provides `addActionListener` and `removeActionListener` methods for registering and deregistering observers. These two methods, as well as most of the `JButton` class' behaviors, are implemented in its parent class, `AbstractButton`.

7.3.5 The *JLabel* Class

The `JLabel` class is used to display text and images but allows the user to edit neither (components that allow the user to edit text subtype the `JTextComponent` class). The `JLabel` class has a *text* property and an *icon* property whose values are displayed by the label. The *font* property, inherited from the `Component` class, determines the text's font. The `JLabel` class also provides methods for aligning the label's contents within its bounds. Labels are often positioned next to other components in the same container in order to describe them; for instance, we might place a label beside a text field or a combo box, neither of which provides a descriptive label of its own.

7.3.6 The *JComboBox* Class

A combo box is a drop-down list of selectable items. In its editable form, it includes a field in which the user can edit items selected from the list, or enter new items and edit them (the items in the list are not affected in either case). By default, a combo box is noneditable, meaning that the user can select only items present in the list and cannot edit them. The programs in Figures 7.11 and 7.12 each include a combo box which appears as a box containing a downward-pointing triangle and the currently selected item. The drop-down list visible in Figure 7.11 contains a set of icons representing color chips. The user clicks one of them to select a new color.

The items in a combo box can be specified at the time of its construction. Two constructors are provided for this purpose:

```
public JComboBox(Object[] items);
public JComboBox(Vector items);
```

For example, the following code creates a combo box whose list displays four color names:

```
String[] colorNames = {"red", "green", "blue", "purple"};
JComboBox colorBox = new JComboBox(colorNames);
```

The class also provides a no-argument constructor for initializing a combo box with no items.

The items in a combo box are ordered by index, beginning with zero. Several methods are provided for determining the selected item. In particular, the `getSelectedItem` method returns the selected item and the `getSelectedIndex` returns the selected item's index:

```
public Object getSelectedItem();
public int getSelectedIndex();
```

The `getSelectedIndex` method returns −1 if the selection is not in the list (this can occur only in the case of editable combo boxes). Because *selectedItem* and *selectedIndex* are properties of the combo box, the following methods are available for selecting items:

```
public void setSelectedItem(Object obj);
public void setSelectedIndex(int indx);
```

The `setSelectedItem` method selects the first item if its input `obj` is not present in the list. In any case, items are ordinarily selected by the user rather than the program.

A combo box's list of items can be modified at runtime. The `addItem` method is used to add a new item to the end of the list, and the `removeItem` method to remove an item from the list:

```
public void addItem(Object obj);
public void removeItem(Object obj);
```

Other methods are provided for adding and removing list items by index.

A combo box generates an action event whenever the selection changes. Accordingly, the class provides `addActionListener` and `removeActionListener` methods. Registered action event listeners often define an `actionPerformed` method of the following form:

```
public void actionPerformed(ActionEvent e) {
  JComboBox source = (JComboBox)e.getSource();
  String item = (String)source.getSelectedItem();
  // process based on the selection item
  ...
}
```

Combo boxes are sometimes used without registering listeners at all. In such cases, the combo box represents a state variable that the user sets by selecting an item. The program queries the combo box for the current selection as necessary.

7.3.7 The *JColorChooser* Class

A `JColorChooser` provides a dialog box from which the user can select a color (see Figure 7.6). The dialog box is partitioned into a preview panel and a chooser panel. The preview panel displays the selected color. The chooser panel contains three tabbed panes allowing the user to select a color by (a) choosing from a table of color swatches, (b) setting color coordinates under the red-green-blue color model, and (c) setting color coordinates under the hue-saturation-brightness color model. If the dialog box is modal (meaning that the user must respond to the dialog box before continuing), it includes three buttons: *OK* to accept the new color selection and dismiss the dialog box, *Cancel* to dismiss the dialog box without accepting the new color selection, and *Reset* to revert the dialog box to the original color without dismissing it.

The `JColorChooser` class can be used in three ways. The easiest way is to call the following static method to display a modal dialog box:

```
public static Color showDialog(Component parent,
                               String title,
                               Color initialColor)
```

Here, `parent` is the parent component for the dialog box, `title` is the dialog box's title, and `initialColor` is the dialog box's initial setting when it appears (the `parent` argument can be `null` if the dialog box need not be displayed on top of its parent frame). The `showDialog` method returns when the user dismisses the dialog box: it returns the selected color if the user clicks the *OK* button, or it returns `null` if the user clicks the *Cancel* button or closes the dialog box by clicking its frame control. This is the approach we'll take when using the color chooser in this book. The color chooser evoked by the `showDialog` procedure appears in Figure 7.6.

A second (and more general) way to use the `JColorChoose` class is to call its static `createDialog` method to create a new dialog. This approach

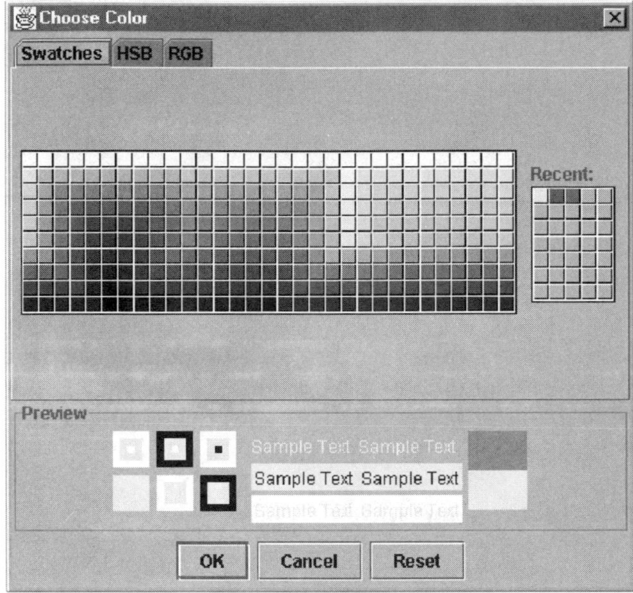

FIGURE 7.6 A color chooser.

allows one to create modal and nonmodal dialog boxes, to associate specific action listeners with the *OK* and *Cancel* buttons, and to create non-standard chooser panels. The last way to use this class is to add an instance of the `JColorChooser` class to any container. Property change listeners registered with the color chooser are notified whenever its *color* property changes.

7.4 Layout Managers

Layout managers are used to arrange components within a container. The `java.awt.LayoutManager` interface specifies the behavior common to all layout managers. Java defines a number of implementations of the `LayoutManager` interface; those that we'll use later in this chapter appear in the class diagram of Figure 7.7. The layout manager assigned to a container determines the placement of its components. You send a container the *setLayout* message to assign it a layout manager:

```
aContainer.setLayout(aLayoutManager);
```

The layouts with which we'll be concerned are the flow layout, grid layout, and border layout. It is noteworthy that the AWT and Swing define a number of other layouts besides these, of which the gridbag layout is the most flexible and powerful, and also probably the most cumbersome to use.

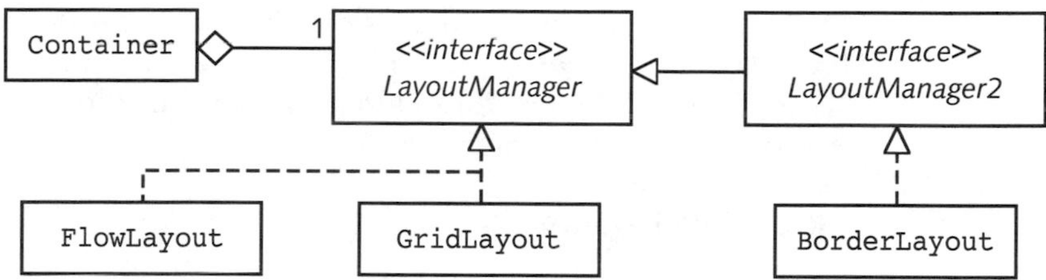

FIGURE 7.7 The layout managers used in this chapter.

7.4.1 Flow Layouts

A flow layout arranges components from left to right within a container and then from top to bottom as each row fills up, much as the words in a paragraph are placed by a text editor. The components are placed in the order they're added to the container. The following program produces the frame shown in Figure 7.8:

```
public class TryFlowLayout {
  public static void main(String[] args) {
    ApplicationFrame frame =
      new ApplicationFrame("Flow Layout");
    Container pane = frame.getContentPane();
    pane.setLayout(new FlowLayout(FlowLayout.LEFT));
    pane.add(new JButton("Button one"));
    pane.add(new JButton("Button two"));
    pane.add(new JButton("Button three"));
    pane.add(new JButton("Button four"));
    frame.show();
  }
}
```

Because the `TryFlowLayout` program registers no event listeners with the buttons, clicking the buttons has no effect. Within each row, the buttons are centered, left-justified, or right-justified depending on the argument passed to the `FlowLayout` constructor. The `FlowLayout` class defines the static constants `CENTER`, `LEFT`, and `RIGHT` to specify justification (the no-argument

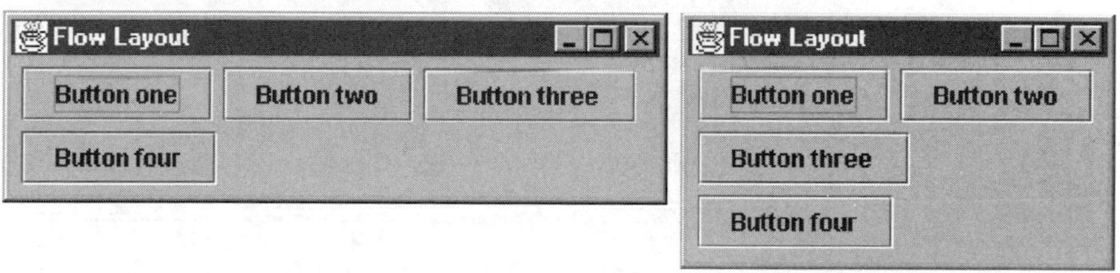

FIGURE 7.8 Flow layout.

`FlowLayout` constructor applies center justification). As is true of most of Java's layout managers, the components are rearranged whenever the container is resized. Figure 7.8 shows the arrangement of buttons for two different sizes of the enclosing frame.

7.4.2 Grid Layouts

A grid layout arranges components in a grid of rectangular cells of equal size. Each component is sized to occupy the entire space of its cell. When the container is resized, the cells are resized to fill the container, hence the components themselves are resized. The `GridLayout` constructor takes two positive integers specifying the number of rows and columns in the grid. The following program places six buttons within a 2×3 grid (see Figure 7.9):

```
public class TryGridLayout {
  public static void main(String[] args) {
    ApplicationFrame frame =
      new ApplicationFrame("Grid Layout");
    Container pane = frame.getContentPane();
    pane.setLayout(new GridLayout(2, 3));
    pane.add(new JButton("Button one"));
    pane.add(new JButton("Button two"));
    pane.add(new JButton("Button three"));
    pane.add(new JButton("Button four"));
    pane.add(new JButton("Button five"));
    pane.add(new JButton("Button six"));
    frame.show();
  }
}
```

The `GridLayout` class also provides a four-argument constructor:

```
public GridLayout(int rows,int cols,int hgap,int vgap);
```

The last two parameters are used to add extra space between components. The `hgap` parameter specifies the horizontal gap (in pixels) between adjacent columns, and the `vgap` parameter specifies the vertical gap between ad-

FIGURE 7.9 Grid layout.

jacent rows. The two-argument constructor sets both the horizontal gap and vertical gap to zero.

7.4.3 Border Layouts

A border layout divides a container into five areas: north, south, east, west, and center. Up to five components are placed in the container, at most one per area. The center area expands to occupy as much available space as possible, whereas each of the four remaining areas expands only as much as necessary to hold its component. When you add a component to a border layout, you specify the area where it belongs. For example, the instruction:

```
aContainer.add(aComponent, BorderLayout.SOUTH)
```

adds `aComponent` to `aContainer`'s south area. The `BorderLayout` class provides the static constants `NORTH`, `SOUTH`, `EAST`, `WEST`, and `CENTER` for identifying areas. The following program produces the frame shown in Figure 7.10:

```
public class TryBorderLayout {
  public static void main(String[] args) {
    ApplicationFrame frame =
      new ApplicationFrame("Border Layout");
    Container pane = frame.getContentPane();
    pane.setLayout(new BorderLayout());
    pane.add(new JButton("North"), BorderLayout.NORTH);
    pane.add(new JButton("South"), BorderLayout.SOUTH);
    pane.add(new JButton("East"), BorderLayout.EAST);
    pane.add(new JButton("West"), BorderLayout.WEST);
    pane.add(new JButton("Center"), BorderLayout.CENTER);
    frame.show();
  }
}
```

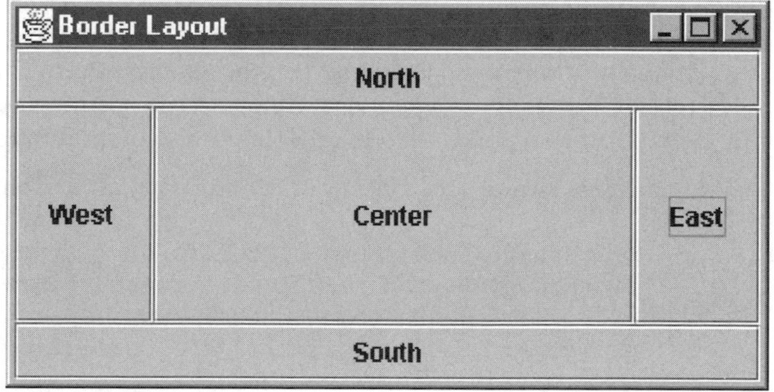

FIGURE 7.10 Border layout.

The order in which components are added is immaterial because their placement is determined by the second argument to the `add` method. The `BorderLayout` class also provides a two-argument constructor for adding space between components:

```
public BorderLayout(int hgap, int vgap);
```

Here, `hgap` specifies the horizontal gap in pixels, and `vgap` the vertical gap.

7.5 Components and Event Listeners

This section presents two relatively simple programs for displaying different colors in a panel. The purpose is to demonstrate the combined use of components and event listeners. Our first program lets the user select colors by clicking buttons. Our second program enhances the functionality of the first program: it lets the user select colors by clicking buttons and by selecting items from a combo box, and it records custom colors and presents them as items in the combo box for future selection.

7.5.1 Playing with Colors

Our `ColorPlay` program partitions the frame into two panels, based on the border layout manager. The center panel, which occupies most of the frame, displays the current color, and the south panel contains four buttons. The program looks like the one in Figure 7.11 but without the combo box control to the right of the buttons. Clicking the *red* button changes the color of the center panel (the canvas) to red. Clicking the *green* or *blue* button likewise changes the canvas' color. Clicking the *custom* button brings up a color chooser dialog box. When the user selects a color from the dialog box and dismisses it, the canvas is changed to the selected color; if the user cancels the dialog box, the canvas retains its old color.

Our implementation of the `ColorPlay` class creates a single event listener object and registers it with all four buttons. (Recall that a button generates an action event when it's pushed.) When the listener's event handler `actionPerformed` is called, it obtains a reference to the event source (one of the four buttons) and responds accordingly. Here is the program in its entirety:

```
public class ColorPlay extends ApplicationFrame {

  protected JPanel canvas, controls; // two main panels
  protected JButton redButton, greenButton,
                    blueButton, customButton;
  protected Color color;   // the current color

  public static void main(String[] args) {
    JFrame frame = new ColorPlay("Color Play");
```

```
    frame.show();
  }

  public ColorPlay(String title) {
    super(title);
    Container topPane = getContentPane();
    topPane.setLayout(new BorderLayout());
      // creates and adds the canvas panel to the frame
    canvas = new JPanel();
    topPane.add(canvas, "Center");
      // creates and adds the control panel to the frame
    controls = new JPanel();
    controls.add(redButton = new JButton("red"));
    controls.add(greenButton = new JButton("green"));
    controls.add(blueButton = new JButton("blue"));
    controls.add(customButton = new JButton("custom"));
    topPane.add(controls, "South");
      // creates an event listener and registers it
      // with the buttons
    addListeners();
    selectColor(Color.red);
  }

  protected void addListeners() {
    // REQUIRES: The four button fields are not null.
    // MODIFIES: the buttons
    // EFFECTS: Creates an action event listener and
    //   registers it with all four buttons.
    ActionListener l = new ActionListener() {
      public void actionPerformed(ActionEvent e) {
        Object source = e.getSource();
        if (source == redButton)
          selectColor(Color.red);
        else if (source == greenButton)
          selectColor(Color.green);
        else if (source == blueButton)
          selectColor(Color.blue);
        else selectColor();
      }
    };
    redButton.addActionListener(l);
    greenButton.addActionListener(l);
    blueButton.addActionListener(l);
    customButton.addActionListener(l);
  }
```

```
    protected void selectColor(Color color) {
      // REQUIRES: canvas is not null.
      // MODIFIES: color and canvas
      // EFFECTS: Sets the canvas background to color
      //   and repaints it.
      this.color = color;
      canvas.setBackground(color);
      repaint();
    }

    protected void selectColor() {
      // REQUIRES: canvas is not null.
      // MODIFIES: color and canvas
      // EFFECTS: Shows a color chooser dialog; if the
      //   user chooses a color from the dialog then
      //   selects the color; else does nothing.
      Color newColor =
        JColorChooser.showDialog(null,"Choose Color",color);
      if (newColor != null)
        selectColor(newColor);
    }
  }
```

Exercise

7.9 The `java.awt.event.ActionEvent` class defines the following method for obtaining a special string associated with the action event:

```
public String getActionCommand();
```

The string returned by `getActionCommand` is called the event's *command string*. When the event source is a button, the command string is the button's label. For instance, when the user presses the *red* button, the resulting event object contains the command string `"red"`. Revise the implementation of the `ColorPlay.addListeners` method so that the anonymous `ActionListener` distinguishes buttons by the event's command string.

7.5.2 Recording Colors

Our next program, `ColorRecord`, extends the functionality of `ColorPlay`. In addition to the four color-selection buttons, the `ColorRecord` program provides a combo box control containing a list of icons. Each icon is a square of solid color known as a **color chip.** The user can choose a color by selecting its color chip from the combo box. Initially, the combo box contains only three color chips for red, green, and blue. However, whenever the user selects a new color from the color chooser dialog box, a color chip for the color is added to the combo box. Figure 7.11 shows the `ColorRecord` program after four new colors have been added. The combo box's drop-down list is open because the user is currently choosing an item from it; otherwise, the list window would be closed.

Our implementation of `ColorRecord` includes two versions of the `selectColor` method for selecting a color by argument and from a color chooser dialog box, respectively:

```
protected void selectColor(Color color);
protected void selectColor();
```

These methods behave like their counterparts in the `ColorPlay` program. Our program defines three additional methods for managing colors. Because color chips are accessed by index in the combo box, it is necessary to map an index to a color whenever a combo box item is selected. The following method takes care of this:

```
protected Color indexToColor(int colorIndx)
  // REQUIRES: 0 <= colorIndx < nbrColors()
  // EFFECTS: Returns the color at index colorIndx.
```

The number of recorded colors is returned by the `nbrColors` method:

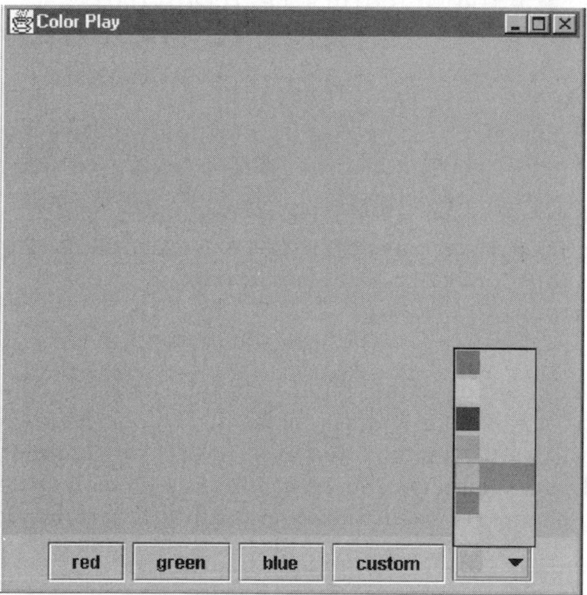

FIGURE 7.11 The `ColorRecord` program.

```
protected int nbrColors()
  // EFFECTS: Returns number of colors currently stored.
```

Lastly, the addColor method records a new color and adds a new color chip to the combo box:

```
protected void addColor(Color color)
  // REQUIRES: color is not null.
  // MODIFIES: vector colors, combo box colorsComboBox.
  // EFFECTS: Adds color to the end of vector colors,
  //   and creates a chip for color and adds
  //   it to the end of colorsComboBox.
```

To implement these three protected methods, the ColorRecord class defines a field named colors whose value, a Vector, stores Color objects in the same order as their color chips appear in the combo box. Here are the relevant definitions:

```
// fields of ColorRecord class
  // combo box of color chips
protected JComboBox colorsComboBox;
  // colors[i] stores the color of the chip at
  // index i of colorsComboBox
protected Vector colors;

// methods of ColorRecord class
protected Color indexToColor(int colorIndx) {
  return (Color)colors.get(colorIndx);
}

protected int nbrColors() {
  return colors.size();
}

protected void addColor(Color color) {
  Icon chip = makeChip(CHIP_SIZE, CHIP_SIZE, color);
  colorsComboBox.addItem(chip);
  colors.add(color);
}
```

The makeChip method builds and returns a new color chip of specified size and color. A color chip is represented by an ImageIcon object, which is a (typically small) image often used to decorate components. The ImageIcon class implements the Icon interface, which specifies behaviors for drawing pictures of fixed width and height. Here is the method definition:

```
// method of ColorRecord class
protected Icon makeChip(int w, int h, Color color) {
  // REQUIRES: w,h > 0, and color is not null.
```

```
    // EFFECTS: Returns a new chip of width w, height h,
    //   and filled with color.
    BufferedImage im =
      new BufferedImage(w,h, BufferedImage.TYPE_INT_RGB);
    Graphics2D g2 = im.createGraphics();
    g2.setPaint(color);
    g2.fill(new Rectangle2D.Float(0, 0, w, h));
    return new ImageIcon(im);
  }
```

The `makeChip` method creates a `BufferedImage` representing an image of specified size and type, and then obtains a rendering context `g2` for the image. Using `g2`, the entire image is filled with paint of the input `color`. Lastly, a new `ImageIcon` is constructed from the painted image and returned.

Here is the definition of the `ColorRecord` class:

```
public class ColorRecord extends ApplicationFrame {

  protected JPanel canvas, controls;
  protected JButton redButton, greenButton,
                    blueButton, customButton;
  protected JComboBox colorsComboBox;
  protected Color color;
  protected Vector colors = new Vector();
  protected static final int CHIP_SIZE = 16;

  public static void main(String[] args) {
    JFrame frame = new ColorRecord("Color Record");
    frame.show();
  }

  public ColorRecord(String title) {
    super(title);
    Container topPane = getContentPane();
    topPane.setLayout(new BorderLayout());
    canvas = new JPanel();
    topPane.add(canvas, "Center");
    controls = new JPanel();
    controls.add(redButton = new JButton("red"));
    controls.add(greenButton = new JButton("green"));
    controls.add(blueButton = new JButton("blue"));
    controls.add(customButton = new JButton("custom"));
    colorsComboBox = new JComboBox();
    controls.add(colorsComboBox);
    topPane.add(controls, "South");
    addColor(Color.red);
    addColor(Color.green);
    addColor(Color.blue);
```

```
    selectColor(Color.red);
    addListeners();
  }

  protected void addListeners() {
    redButton.addActionListener(
                new ColorButtonListener(0));
    greenButton.addActionListener(
                new ColorButtonListener(1));
    blueButton.addActionListener(
                new ColorButtonListener(2));

    customButton.addActionListener(new ActionListener() {
      public void actionPerformed(ActionEvent e) {
        selectColor();
      }
    });

    colorsComboBox.addActionListener(new ActionListener(){
      public void actionPerformed(ActionEvent e) {
        int colorIndx = colorsComboBox.getSelectedIndex();
        selectColor(indexToColor(colorIndx));
      }
    });
  }

  protected void selectColor(Color color) {
    this.color = color;
    canvas.setBackground(color);
    repaint();
  }

  protected void selectColor() {
    Color newColor =
     JColorChooser.showDialog(null,"Choose Color",color);
    if (newColor != null) {
      addColor(newColor);
      colorsComboBox.setSelectedIndex(nbrColors()-1);
    }
  }

  protected class ColorButtonListener
           implements ActionListener {
    int colorIndx;

    public ColorButtonListener(int colorIndx) {
      this.colorIndx = colorIndx;
    }
```

```
      public void actionPerformed(ActionEvent e) {
        colorsComboBox.setSelectedIndex(colorIndx);
      }
    }

    // the following methods were already defined
    // in the text
    protected void addColor(Color color) {...}
    protected Color indexToColor(int colorIndx) {...}
    protected int nbrColors() {...}
    protected Icon makeChip(int w, int h, Color color) {...}
  }
```

Each of the controls is observed by its own event listener. In particular, the *red*, *green*, and *blue* buttons are each observed by an instance of the inner `ColorButtonListener` class. This class is constructed with the index of some color. Its `actionPerformed` method selects its index from the combo box, which in turn selects the corresponding color and color chip.

Exercises

7.10 Suppose we had implemented the `actionPerformed` method of the inner class `ColorButtonListener` like this:

```
public void actionPerformed(ActionEvent e) {
  selectColor(indexToColor(colorIndx));
}
```

How would this affect the behavior of our `ColorRecord` program? Try it out.

7.11 Revise the implementation of `ColorPlay` so that each button has its own listener. In particular, the *red*, *green*, and *blue* buttons should each be observed by an instance of a class whose constructor takes a color. When a listener's `actionPerformed` is called, it selects its color.

ESSENTIAL 7.12 Develop a GUI-based program `SweepFigures` partitioned into two panels: a panel to serve as a canvas in the center area and a panel of controls in the south area. The user sweeps out figures in the canvas as described in the `EditRectangles` program of Exercise 7.8 with one difference: The figures may be either rectangles or ellipses. The control panel contains two controls. A combo box control contains the items `"rectangle"` and `"ellipse"`. Whenever the user sweeps out a new figure, the combo box's current selection determines whether the resulting figure is a rectangle or an ellipse. The control box also contains a *clear* button which, when pushed, removes all current rectangles and ellipses and clears the canvas.

ESSENTIAL 7.13 Revise your `SweepFigures` program so that whenever the user presses the mouse button inside some figure and then drags, the figure follows the cursor until the mouse button is released. Thus it is possible to translate figures via mouse drags. (If the mouse button is pressed in more than one figure, just one of the figures is dragged.) As before, the user presses the button in the background and then drags in order to sweep out a new figure.

7.6 Triangulate: A Point-Set Triangulation Program

In this section, we develop a GUI-based program for building and displaying triangulations of point sets (Figure 7.12). The user interacts with our program in two ways: through mouse actions in the main canvas to edit the point set and through the controls along the bottom of the frame. Point-editing is achieved the same as in our `EditPointSet` application of Section 7.2.5: The user clicks to create new points, drags to move points, and control-clicks to delete points.

The control panel along the bottom of the frame contains four controls. When the user clicks the *Triangulate* button, the program displays a triangulation of the current set of points. The *Clear* button removes the current triangulation, but has no effect on the current point set. The rightmost control

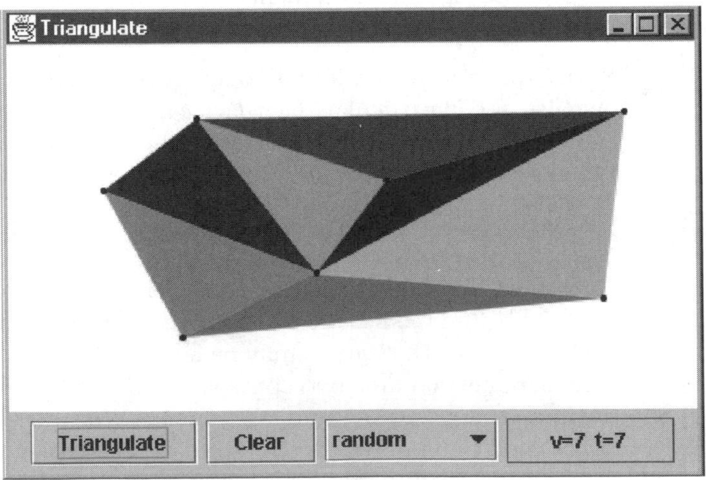

FIGURE 7.12 The `Triangulate` program.

is a label indicating the number of points v in the current point set and the number of triangles t in the current triangulation.

The remaining control, a combo box (whose *random* item appears in the figure), guides construction of the triangulation. Recall from Exercise 6.18 that when you triangulate a point set, the order of the input points determines the resulting triangulation. The combo box is used to specify the ordering of input points. Three items are available. The *random* item orders the input points randomly. If the *Triangulate* button is clicked repeatedly, you'll generate a series of often-different triangulations of the current point set. The *user-defined* item orders the input points in the order they were created by the user. Lastly, the *sorted* item sorts the input points from left to right.

Two things are noteworthy about our program's design, which appears in the class diagram of Figure 7.13. First, a `Triangulate` object, a type of frame, contains two panels: a `TriangulateCanvas` in which points are created and triangulations are displayed and a `TriangulateControlPanel` which contains the program's controls. Second, we use the `EditPointSet` program of Section 7.2.5 as part of the design. Indeed, the class diagram of Figure 7.4 is embedded in that of Figure 7.13, with only one difference: Because the figure manager `TriangulateManager` adds new behaviors, the canvas collaborates with it directly, rather than through the `FigureManager` interface.

We'll tackle the implementation of our program starting with the `Triangulate` class. This class represents a frame partitioned into two panels by a border layout manager: The canvas panel is added to the center area and the control panel is added to the south area. As we've seen, the center area expands to fill as much space as possible whereas the south area expands only as much as necessary to contain its component, which is why the canvas occupies the lion's share of the frame in Figure 7.12. Here is the class definition:

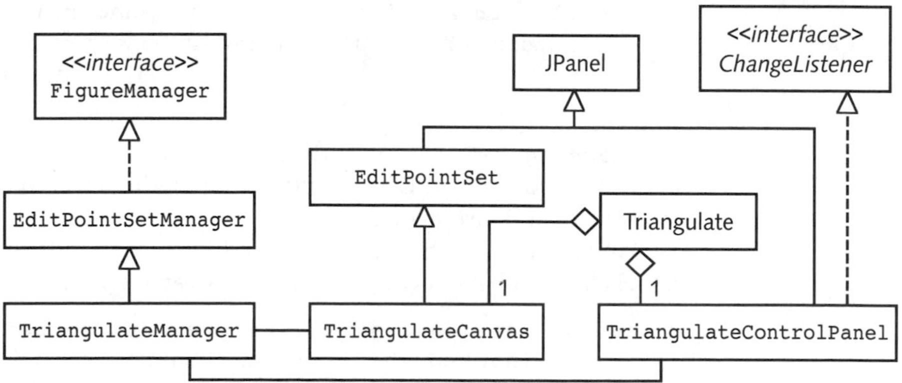

FIGURE 7.13 Structure of the `Triangulate` program.

```
public class Triangulate extends ApplicationFrame {

  public static int D_WIDTH = 500, D_HEIGHT = 450;

  public static void main(String[] args) {
    JFrame frame =
      new Triangulate("Triangulate", D_WIDTH, D_HEIGHT);
    frame.show();
  }

  public Triangulate(String title,int width,int height) {
    super(title, width, height);
    Container topPane = getContentPane();
    topPane.setLayout(new BorderLayout());
    TriangulateCanvas canvas = new TriangulateCanvas();
    TriangulateControlPanel controlPanel =
      new TriangulateControlPanel(canvas.getManager());
    topPane.add(canvas, "Center");
    topPane.add(controlPanel, "South");
  }
}
```

The `TriangulateCanvas` class is responsible for editing points and painting triangulations. The task of editing points is handled by its superclass `EditPointSet`, whereas the task of painting triangulations is handled by the figure manager. Here is the class definition:

```
public class TriangulateCanvas extends EditPointSet {
  public void makeFigureManager(JPanel canvas) {
    manager = new TriangulateManager(canvas);
  }

  public TriangulateManager getManager() {
    return (TriangulateManager)manager;
  }
}
```

The `makeFigureManager` method is a factory method defined in the parent class `EditPointSet`. By overriding this method, `TriangulateCanvas` installs its own figure manager.

We turn next to the control panel. Figure 7.13 indicates that the control panel class implements the `ChangeListener` interface, which is defined thus:

```
public interface javax.swing.event.ChangeListener {
    // invoked when this listener's subject
    // undergoes a change in state
  public void stateChanged(ChangeEvent e);
}
```

A change listener registers with a source of *change events*. Whenever a significant change of state occurs in the source, it notifies each registered change event listener by calling the listener's `stateChanged` method. This conforms to the event model we've worked with throughout this chapter.

As a listener of change events, our control panel registers with the figure manager. Whenever the triangulation managed by the figure manager changes, the figure manager generates a change event, in response to which the control panel's `stateChanged` method is called. Likewise, whenever the figure manager creates a new point or deletes an existing point, it generates a change event, again in response to which the control panel's `stateChanged` method is called. The `stateChanged` method responds by updating the control panel's message label that reports the current number of points and triangles.

The sequence diagram of Figure 7.14 depicts in greater detail the interactions that occur when the user presses the *Triangulate* button and triangulation of the current point set is possible. The *Triangulate* button's listener calls `addTriangulation` method to build the triangulation. If `addTriangulation` returns without throwing an exception, the listener then updates the figure manager. In turn, the figure manager repaints the canvas, and then sends itself a *fireStateChanged* message indicating that it must inform its listeners of a change in its own state. In response, the figure manager calls the control panel's `stateChanged` method.

The scenario takes a different course if the user clicks the *Triangulate* button when a triangulation is not possible (e.g., when the point set contains fewer than three points). In this case, the `addTriangulation` method throws an exception which is caught by the *Triangulate* button's listener. In response, the listener object updates its message label to inform the user of the problem. This "abnormal" scenario is not depicted in Figure 7.14.

Our implementation of the control panel class defines a field holding a reference to the figure manager and a field for each of the four components (two buttons, a label, and a combo box). Here is the class definition:

```
public class TriangulateControlPanel extends JPanel
                                 implements ChangeListener {

  protected TriangulateManager manager; // figure manager
  protected JButton tButton,         // triangulate button
                    cButton;         // color button
  protected JLabel msgLabel;            // message label
  protected JComboBox pointOrderBox;    // point ordering

  public TriangulateControlPanel(TriangulateManager mngr) {
      // register this panel as a listener of
      // the manager's change events
    this.manager = mngr;
    manager.addChangeListener(this);
      // create buttons, register their listeners, and
```

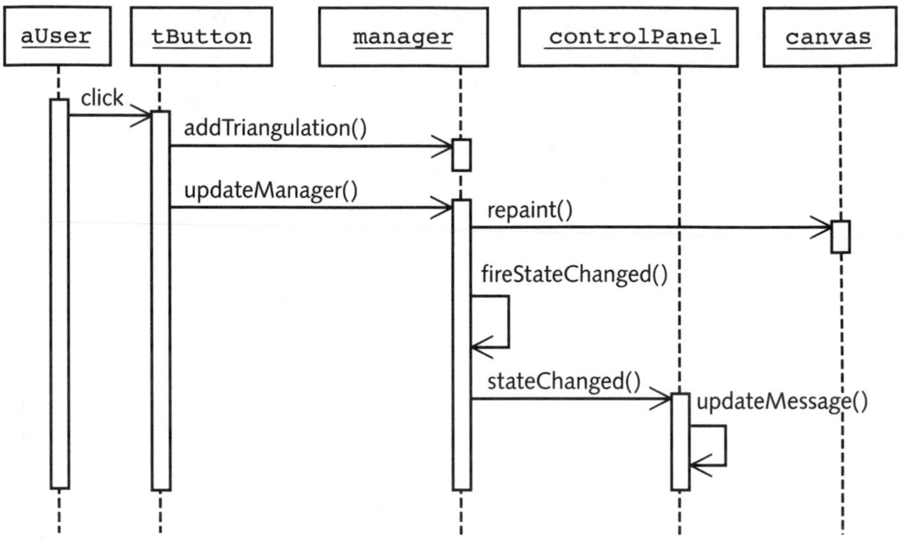

FIGURE 7.14 Sequence diagram for creating a new triangulation.

```
      // add them to panel
    add(tButton = new JButton("Triangulate"));
    tButton.addActionListener(new TriangulateListener());
    add(cButton = new JButton("Clear"));
    cButton.addActionListener(new ClearListener());
      // create point-order combo box and add it to
      // this panel
    pointOrderBox = new JComboBox();
    pointOrderBox.addItem("user-defined");
    pointOrderBox.addItem("random");
    pointOrderBox.addItem("sorted");
    add(pointOrderBox);
      // create message label and add it to this panel
    msgLabel = new JLabel();
    Border border =
      BorderFactory.createLineBorder(Color.blue);
    msgLabel.setBorder(border);
    msgLabel.setHorizontalAlignment(SwingConstants.CENTER);
    msgLabel.setPreferredSize(tButton.getPreferredSize());
    updateMessage();
    add(msgLabel);
  }

  //
  // implement ChangeListener interface
  //
```

```
  public void stateChanged(ChangeEvent e) {
    updateMessage();
  }

  protected void updateMessage() {
    // MODIFIES: msgLabel
    // EFFECTS: Sets label's text to number of points
    //   and triangles.
    String res = "v=" + manager.nbrVertices();
    int nbrTriangles = manager.nbrTriangles();
    if (nbrTriangles > 0)
      res += "  t=" + nbrTriangles;
    msgLabel.setForeground(Color.black);
    msgLabel.setText(res);
  }

  protected void updateMessage(String msg) {
    // MODIFIES: msgLagel
    // EFFECTS: Sets label's text to msg.
    msgLabel.setForeground(Color.red);
    msgLabel.setText(msg);
  }

  //
  // action listener classes for the Triangulate and
  // Clear buttons
  //
  class TriangulateListener implements ActionListener {
    public void actionPerformed(ActionEvent evt) {
      try {
        String pointsOrdering =
          (String)pointOrderBox.getSelectedItem();
        manager.addTriangulation(pointsOrdering);
        manager.updateManager();
      } catch (IllegalArgumentException e) {
        updateMessage("Too few points");
      } catch (ColinearPointsException e) {
        updateMessage("Colinear points");
      }
    }
  }

  class ClearListener implements ActionListener {
    public void actionPerformed(ActionEvent evt) {
      manager.removeTriangulation();
      manager.updateManager();
    }
  }
}
```

The TriangulateManager class manages two kinds of figures: points created by the user and triangles belonging to the current triangulation. The behaviors for handling points are supplied by its parent class, EditPointSetManager, but TriangulateManager supplies its own code for managing triangles. Triangles are stored in a GroupNode field named triangulation; the triangles are the group node's children. In response to the *getFigures* message, the manager constructs and returns a new group node with two children: (i) the node it inherits containing the points, and (ii) the node triangulation containing the triangles. If no triangulation exists at the time, the getFigures method returns only the node containing the points.

The TriangulateManager class also defines a changeListener field which references the registered change listener, of which there can be only one. When it receives an *updateManager* message, the class generates a change event by calling its fireStateChanged method, which in turn calls the listener's stateChanged method. These interactions appear in Figure 7.14. Here is the class definition:

```
public class TriangulateManager
       extends EditPointSetManager {

  protected GroupNode triangulation;
  protected ChangeListener changeListener;

  public TriangulateManager(JPanel canvas) {
    super(canvas);
  }

  //
  // override methods of FigureManager interface
  //
  public void updateManager() {
    super.updateManager();
    fireStateChanged();
  }

  public Node getFigures() {
    if (triangulation == null)
      return node;
    else {
      GroupNode topNode = new GroupNode();
      topNode.addChild(triangulation);
      topNode.addChild(node);
      return topNode;
    }
  }
```

```
//
// adding a change listener and implementing
// ChangeListener interface
//
public void addChangeListener(ChangeListener listener){
  changeListener = listener;
}

protected void fireStateChanged() {
  if (changeListener != null)
    changeListener.stateChanged(new ChangeEvent(this));
}

//
// methods used by TriangulateControlPanel class
//
public void addTriangulation(String pointOrdering)
       throws IllegalArgumentException,
              ColinearPointsException {
  // REQUIRES: node, triangulation, pointOrdering are
  //   not null.
  // MODIFIES: this
  // EFFECTS: If points contains no more than two
  //   points throws IllegalArgumentException; else
  //   if the first three points are colinear throws
  //   ColinearPointsException; else triangulates
  //   by ordering the input points according to
  //   pointOrdering and adds the triangles to
  //   the node triangulation.
  PointGeometry[] points = extractPoints();
  arrangePoints(points, pointOrdering);
  Vector triangles =
    DynamicPolygons.triangulation(points);
  triangulation = new GroupNode();
  for (int i = 0; i < triangles.size(); i++) {
    Geometry g = (Geometry)triangles.get(i);
    Painter painter = new FillPainter(rnd.nextColor());
    triangulation.addChild(new Figure(g, painter));
  }
  updateManager();
}

public void removeTriangulation() {
  // MODIFIES: this
  // EFFECTS: Removes the triangulation and
```

```
    //   updates the manager.
    triangulation = null;
    updateManager();
  }

  public int nbrVertices() {
    // EFFECTS: Returns the number of points
    //   in the point set.
    return node.nbrChildren();
  }

  public int nbrTriangles() {
    // EFFECTS: If triangulation exists returns the
    //   number of triangles; else returns zero.
    if (triangulation != null)
      return triangulation.nbrChildren();
    else return 0;
  }

  //
  // protected interface
  //
  protected PointGeometry[] extractPoints() {
    // REQUIRES: node is not null.
    // EFFECTS: Returns an array of the points
    //   in the point set.
    PointGeometry[] points =
      new PointGeometry[node.nbrChildren()];
    for (int i = 0; i < node.nbrChildren(); i++)
      points[i] = (PointGeometry)get(i);
    return points;
  }

  protected void arrangePoints(PointGeometry[] points,
                               String ordering) {
    // REQUIRES: points, ordering is not null.
    // MODIFIES: points
    // EFFECTS: Orders points according to the protocol
    //   ordering; does nothing if ordering is neither
    //   "sorted" nor "random".
    if (ordering.equals("sorted"))
      Arrays.sort(points);
    else if (ordering.equals("random"))
      Collections.shuffle(Arrays.asList(points));
  }
}
```

Exercises

7.14 The points produced by the `Triangulate` program are painted random colors. Revise the program so that the points are painted white. [Hint: Override the `add` method in the `TriangulateManager` class.]

7.15 As things stand, the `Triangulate` program paints the point set on top of the triangulation. Revise the program so that the triangulation is painted on top of the points.

7.16 Why isn't it necessary for the action listener registered with the *Clear* button to call the `updateMessage` method? How does the message label get updated?

7.7 DrawPad: A Drawing Program

In this section, we develop a GUI-based program for drawing and editing graphical figures. The program, named *DrawPad*, appears as a frame partitioned into two panels: a control panel containing a number of buttons and a panel that serves as the canvas in which the user draws figures. The control panel contains three kinds of buttons. The user presses a **shape button,** labeled *Polygon*, *Rectangle*, and *Ellipse* in Figure 7.15, to create or edit specific kinds of figures. The user presses the **pointer button** to select, translate, or delete a figure. Specifically, having pressed the pointer button, the user clicks a figure to select it and bring it to the foreground; drags a figure to translate it; or control-clicks a figure to delete it. The selected figure is highlighted (the ellipse, which is selected in Figure 7.15, is highlighted by the outline of its bounding box). The **color button** is used to bring up a color chooser dialog box for selecting a new color. The new color is applied to the selected figure, if any; in addition, the color is applied to any figures created subsequently. The draw program's behavior will be described in greater detail as we proceed. You might also want to use the program before delving into its design and implementation.

Our program design encompasses three class diagrams. The first diagram focuses on the program's GUI components and its figure manager (Figure 7.16), and the second diagram focuses on the various event listeners that may be registered with the canvas at different times (Figure 7.18). The third class diagram presents various strategies for highlighting different types of graphical figures (Figure 7.20). The three diagrams are connected by the `Tool` interface. Each of the canvas' event listeners implements the `Tool` interface; the events generated by the canvas (in response to user mouse actions) are observed by instances of subtypes of `Tool`. I've divided the following exposition into three sections. Section 7.7.1 presents *DrawPad's* components and figure manager; Section 7.7.2 presents *DrawPad's* event listeners (the `Tool` interface and its subtypes); and Section 7.7.3 presents strategies for highlighting figures.

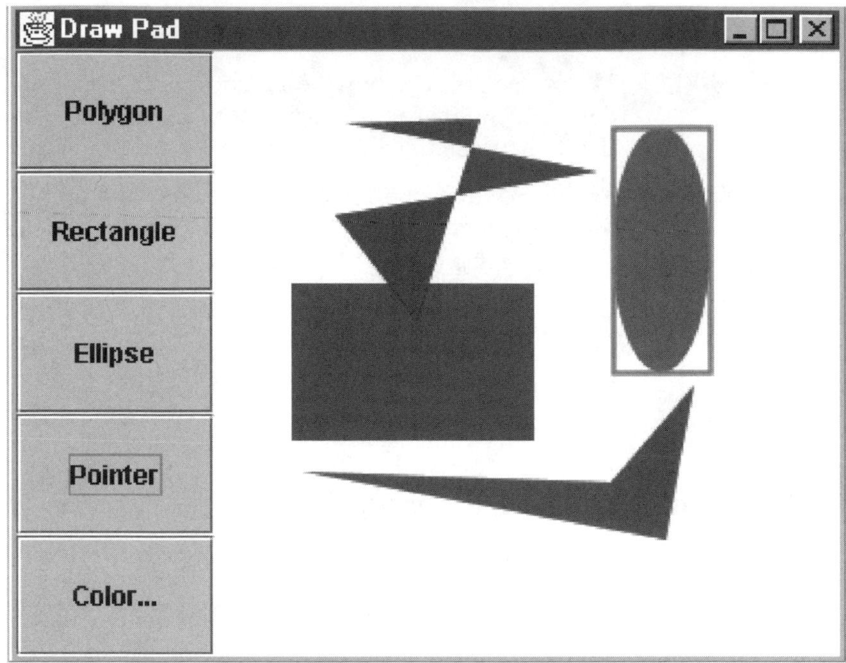

FIGURE 7.15 The `DrawPad` program.

7.7.1 DrawPad's Components and Figure Manager

`DrawPad` is a frame whose content pane is partitioned into two panels: a `ControlPanel` whose buttons are used to manage figures and choose drawing tools, and a `DrawCanvas` panel in which the user draws and edits figures (see Figure 7.16). When the user presses one of the control panel's buttons, the button registers the appropriate mouse event listener with the canvas (for example, if the user presses the *Rectangle* button, the button registers a listener that translates the user's actions into processes for creating and editing rectangles). All such listeners implement the `Tool` interface. The program uses a `DrawPadManager` object to manage figures; the `DrawPad-Manager` class implements the `FigureManager` interface. To repaint itself, the canvas obtains the current set of figures from the figure manager.

In this section, we implement the design of Figure 7.16. We begin with the `DrawPad` class, which defines the static `main` method where execution begins. A `DrawPad` is a frame containing a control panel and a canvas:

```
public class DrawPad extends ApplicationFrame {

  public static final int DEFAULT_WIDTH = 500,
                          DEFAULT_HEIGHT = 450;
```

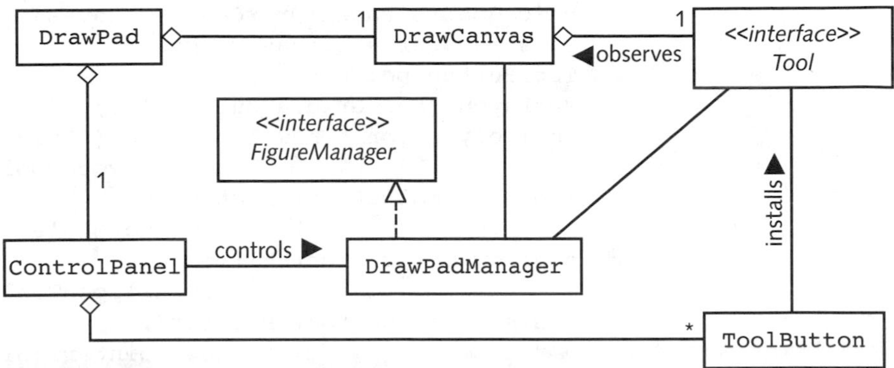

FIGURE 7.16 Components of the DrawPad program.

```
    protected DrawCanvas canvas;

    public static void main(String[] args) {
      JFrame frame =
       new DrawPad("DrawPad",DEFAULT_WIDTH,DEFAULT_HEIGHT);
      frame.show();
    }

    public DrawPad(String title, int width, int height) {
      super(title, width, height);
      Container topPane = getContentPane();
      topPane.setLayout(new BorderLayout());
      topPane.add(canvas = new DrawCanvas(), "Center");
      topPane.add(new ControlPanel(canvas), "West");
    }
  }
```

The control panel is a vertical panel along the left side of the frame containing several shape buttons, a pointer button, and a color button (Figure 7.15). The shape buttons and the pointer button are each represented by a `ToolButton` object. The `ToolButton` constructor creates a new button and registers a listener with the button. That is why the `ControlPanel` constructor below does not appear to register a listener with each of these buttons. However, the color button, which controls the color of shapes, is not an instance of the `ToolButton` class, so the `ControlPanel` constructor creates and registers a listener for its color button. Here is the code for `ControlPanel`:

```
  public class ControlPanel extends JPanel {

    protected DrawPadManager manager;
    protected JButton colorButton;
```

```
    public ControlPanel(DrawCanvas canvas) {
      this.manager = canvas.getManager();
      ToolButton polyButton;
      setLayout(new GridLayout(5, 1));
      add(polyButton = new ToolButton("Polygon",
                            new PolygonTool(canvas)));
      add(new ToolButton("Rectangle",
                            new RectangleTool(canvas)));
      add(new ToolButton("Ellipse",
                            new EllipseTool(canvas)));
      add(new ToolButton("Pointer",
                            new PointerTool(canvas)));
        // install the polygon tool initially
      polyButton.doClick();
        // color button
      colorButton = new JButton("Color...");
      colorButton.setBackground(manager.getColor());
      add(colorButton);
      colorButton.addActionListener(new ActionListener() {
        public void actionPerformed(ActionEvent e) {
          Color oldColor = manager.getColor();
          Color newColor =
            JColorChooser.showDialog(null, "Choose Color",
                                     oldColor);
          if (newColor != null) {
            manager.setColor(newColor);
            colorButton.setBackground(newColor);
          }
        }
      });
    }
  }
```

In the `ControlPanel` constructor, the listener registered with `colorButton` is an instance of an anonymous inner class. This listener implements the `ActionListener` interface—it implements the `actionPerformed` method. When the user clicks the color button, the call to `JColorChooser.showDialog` brings up a color chooser dialog box, which the user then uses to select a new color. When she selects a color and dismisses the dialog box, the call to `showDialog` returns the selected color. If the selected color is not `null`, meaning that the user did not cancel the dialog box, the listener informs the figure manager of the change in color and sets the color button's background to the new color (the button's background color is used to inform the user of the current color).

A `ToolButton` is a button associated with a tool (recall our terminology: A *tool* is an event listener registered with the canvas for manipulating shapes). When the user clicks a tool button, the button installs its tool with the canvas. Here is the implementation:

```
public class ToolButton extends JButton {

  protected Tool tool;

  public ToolButton(String text, Tool tool) {
    super(text);
    this.tool = tool;
    addActionListener(new ToolButtonListener());
  }

  class ToolButtonListener implements ActionListener {
    public void actionPerformed(ActionEvent e) {
      tool.install();
    }
  }
}
```

The sequence diagram of Figure 7.17 shows the interactions that result when the user selects a new tool by pressing a tool button. When the new tool (`theNewTool`) receives an *install* message in response to a button press,

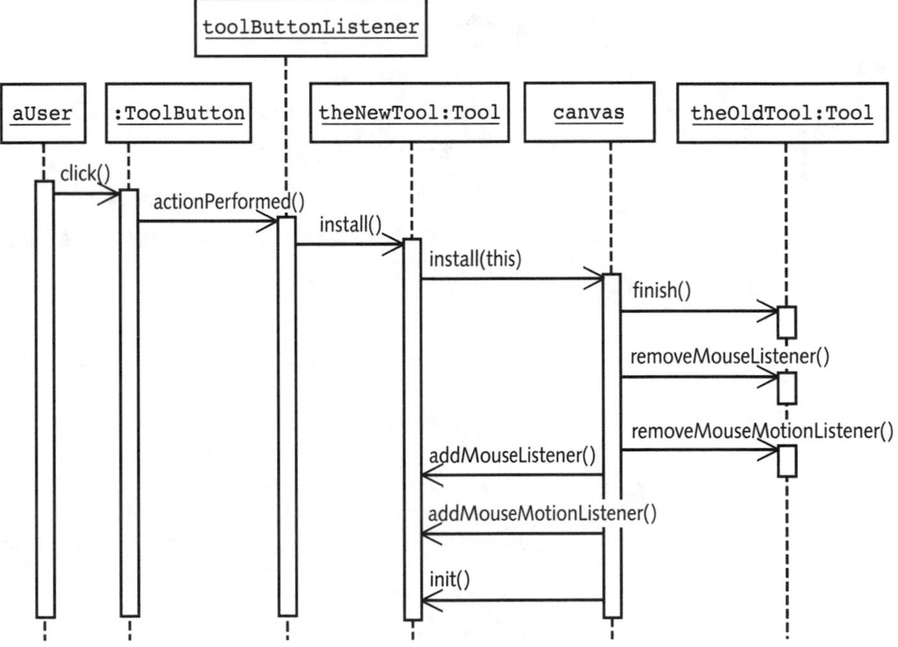

FIGURE 7.17 Sequence diagram for installing a tool in the canvas.

it forwards an *install* message to the canvas, passing itself as an argument. In response, the canvas installs the new tool: it deregisters the current tool (`theOldTool`) as a listener of mouse events, and registers the new tool as a listener of mouse events. In addition, the old tool is given an opportunity to clean up (`finish`) and the new tool an opportunity to initialize itself (`init`). These interactions involving tools and the canvas will be spelled out in code shortly when we define the `Tool` interface and the `DrawCanvas` class.

In addition to owning a control panel, the `DrawPad` application owns a canvas, the panel in which drawing occurs. The `DrawCanvas` class defines an `install` method for registering a new listener (a tool) and for deregistering the current listener. The behavior of `install` is depicted in the sequence diagram of Figure 7.17. The `DrawCanvas` class overrides the `paintComponent` method for rendering the current set of figures, which it obtains from the figure manager. The class also defines a `getManager` method which the current listener uses to obtain a reference to the figure manager. Here is the class definition:

```
public class DrawCanvas extends JPanel {

  public static final Color DefaultColor = Color.blue;

  protected Tool currentTool;
  protected DrawPadManager manager;
  protected Figure currentFigure;

  public DrawCanvas() {
    setBackground(Color.black);
    currentTool = null;
    manager = new DrawPadManager(this);
    manager.setColor(DefaultColor);
  }

  public DrawPadManager getManager() {
    return manager;
  }

  public boolean install(Tool tool) {
    if (currentTool == tool)
      return false;
    else if (currentTool != null) {
      currentTool.finish();
      removeMouseListener(currentTool);
      removeMouseMotionListener(currentTool);
    }
    currentTool = tool;
    addMouseListener(currentTool);
    addMouseMotionListener(currentTool);
    currentTool.init();
```

```
    return true;
  }

  public void paintComponent(Graphics g) {
    super.paintComponent(g);
    Graphics2D g2 = (Graphics2D)g;
    g2.setRenderingHint(RenderingHints.KEY_ANTIALIASING,
                        RenderingHints.VALUE_ANTIALIAS_ON);
    manager.getFigures().paint(g2);
  }
}
```

Let's turn to the DrawPadManager class, which manages the figures for our drawing program. This class implements the FigureManager interface of Section 7.2.5. For our drawing application, what are the responsibilities of a figure manager? The figure manager maintains a collection of figures, arranged in the order in which they get painted. In this **layer ordering,** each figure lies in its own layer, and figures are painted from the bottommost layer upward. When rendered, each figure appears on top of—and possibly obscures—those figures that lie in lower layers. For example, in Figure 7.15, the five-vertex polygon lies in a higher layer than the rectangle.

The figure manager also keeps track of the selected geometry and the figure to which it belongs. In response to the *getFigures* message, the manager returns a group node that represents the current collection of figures, as well as any highlights. The highlight (if any) is created by the strategy stored in the figure manager's hilightStrategy field. Various strategies are necessary because different geometric types may be highlighted in different ways. In Figure 7.15, the ellipse is highlighted by an outline of its bounding box, but we'll see later that other highlighting strategies are possible.

The DrawPadManager class defines five instance fields. The canvas field stores a reference to the canvas. The node field stores a group node whose children are the figures in layer order (i.e., sending node a *paint* message renders the figures from bottom to top). The currentFigure field stores a reference to the selected figure (which is some child of node), or null if no figure is selected. The currentColor field stores the current color, which gets applied when new figures are constructed. Lastly, the hilightStrategy field holds the current strategy for highlighting figures. The following definition of the DrawPadManager class omits the implementation of several methods, which are left as an exercise:

```
public class DrawPadManager implements FigureManager {

  protected DrawCanvas canvas;
  protected GroupNode node;
  protected Figure currentFigure;
  protected Color currentColor;
  protected HilightStrategy hilightStrategy;
```

```
public DrawPadManager(DrawCanvas canvas) {
  this.canvas = canvas;
  node =  new GroupNode();
}

public void select(Geometry g)
       throws IllegalArgumentException {
  // MODIFIES: this
  // EFFECTS: If g is not in this collection throws
  //   IllegalArgumentException; else if g is not null
  //   makes g the current geometry and moves its
  //   figure to the topmost layer; else no geometry
  //   is made current.
  if (g == null) {
    currentFigure = null;
    return;
  }
  int indx = findFigureIndex(g);
  if (indx < 0) throw new IllegalArgumentException();
  else {
    currentFigure = (Figure)node.child(indx);
    node.removeChild(indx);
    node.addChild(currentFigure);
  }
}

public Geometry selected() {
  // EFFECTS: Returns the current geometry if any;
  //   else returns null.
  if (currentFigure != null)
    return currentFigure.getGeometry();
  else return null;
}

public Node getFigures() {
  // EFFECTS: Returns a node whose chidlren
  //   represent the set of figures,
  //    including any highlights.
  GroupNode n = new GroupNode();
  n.addChild(node);
  Node hilight =
    hilightStrategy.makeHilight(selected());
  if (hilight != null)
    n.addChild(hilight);
  return n;
}
```

```
public void updateManager() {
  // EFFECTS: Repaints the canvas.
  canvas.repaint();
}

public void add(Geometry g) {
  // MODIFIES: this
  // EFFECTS: Creates a new figure with geometry g
  //   and a painter based on the current color
  //   and adds figure at the top layer.
  Painter painter = makePainter(getColor());
  node.addChild(new Figure(g, fill));
}

public void remove(Geometry g) {
  // MODIFIES: this
  // EFFECTS: Removes from this collection
  //   a figure with geometry g;
  //   does nothing if no such figure exists.
  int indx = findFigureIndex(g);
  if (indx >= 0) {
    node.removeChild(indx);
    if (selected() == g)
      select(null);
  }
}

public Geometry get(int i)
      throws IndexOutOfBoundsException {
  // EFFECTS: Returns the figure at index i.
  Figure fig = (Figure)node.child(i);
  return fig.getGeometry();
}

public int size() {
  // EFFECTS: Returns the number of figures
  //   in this collection.
  return node.nbrChildren();
}

public Geometry find(int x, int y) {
  // EFFECTS: Returns the geometry that contains the
  //   point(x,y) whose figure lies in the highest
  //   layer; returns null if no such geometry exists.
  ...
}
```

```
    public Color getColor() {
      // EFFECTS: Returns the current color.
      ...
    }

    public void setColor(Color newColor) {
      // MODIFIES: this
      // EFFECTS: Sets the current color to newColor,
      //   and if there exists a selected figure,
      //   changes its color to newColor.
      ...
    }

    public void setHilightStrategy(HilightStrategy s) {
      // REQUIRES: s is not null.
      // MODIFIES: this
      // EFFECTS: Sets the hilight strategy to s.
      this.hilightStrategy = s;
    }

    protected int findFigureIndex(Geometry g) {
      // EFFECTS: Returns the index of the figure
      //   whose geometry is g if
      //   such a figure exists; else returns -1.
      ...
    }

    protected Painter makePainter(Color color) {
      // EFFECTS: Returns a new painter based on color.
      Painter draw = new DrawDynamicPolygonPainter(color);
      Painter fill = new FillPainter(color);
      return new MultiPainter(fill, draw);
    }
}
```

Observe that the postconditions for some of `DrawPadManager`'s methods, as described by the effects clauses, are stronger than those specified by the `FigureManager` interface. For example, `FigureManager.find` promises to report some geometry that is "hit" by the input point (x,y), whereas `DrawPadManager.find` reports the topmost geometry that contains (x,y). Note also that `DrawPadManager` implements three public methods of its own (`getColor`, `setColor`, and `setHilightStrategy`), in addition to those specified by the `FigureManager` interface.

The implementation of `getFigures` is interesting. This method does not simply return the group node referenced by the field `node`. Rather, it constructs and returns a new group node whose first child is `node` and whose second child is a node that highlights the selected figure, if any. The state of `node` is not changed by the operation.

Exercise

ESSENTIAL 7.17 Complete the implementation of the DrawPadManager class.

7.7.2 DrawPad's Event Listeners

The user's actions in the canvas—mouse clicks and drags—are interpreted by whichever tool is registered with the canvas at the time. For instance, if the pointer tool is active, mouse clicks are used to select figures; if the polygon tool is active, mouse clicks are used to create or delete vertices. Every tool is a listener of mouse events, but they differ in their response to events. The present section implements the `Tool` interface and its various subtypes that appear in Figure 7.18.

The `Tool` interface promises three kinds of behavior. First, every tool implements the event-handler methods specified by the `MouseListener` and `MouseMotionListener` interfaces. Second, every tool provides the `init` and `finish` methods for use whenever the tool gets installed in the canvas and deinstalled from the canvas. Lastly, every tool implements the factory method `makeHilightStrategy` for creating a highlighting strategy appropriate to the tool's geometry (for example, the `EllipseTool` creates a `BoundingBoxStrategy` that highlights an ellipse by rendering the outline of its bounding box). Here is the definition of the `Tool` interface:

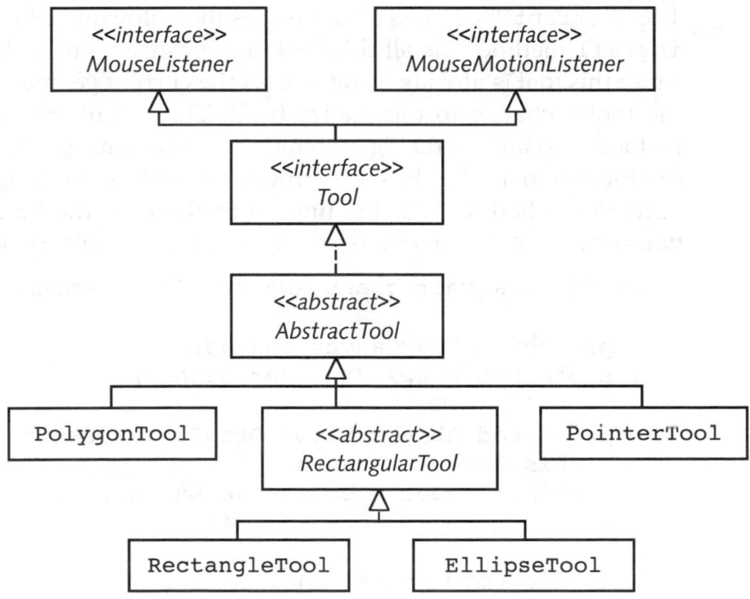

FIGURE 7.18 Structure of the `Tool` interface subtypes.

```
public interface Tool extends MouseListener,
                              MouseMotionListener {
  public abstract void install();
    // EFFECTS: Installs this tool in the canvas.

  public abstract void init();
    // MODIFIES: this
    // EFFECTS: Any (initializes this tool).

  public abstract void finish();
    // MODIFIES: this
    // EFFECTS: Any (cleans up this tool).

  public abstract HilightStrategy makeHilightStrategy();
    // MODIFIES: this
    // EFFECTS: Returns a highlighting strategy
    //   appropriate to the type
    //   of geometries handled by this tool.
}
```

The sequence diagram of Figure 7.17 shows the roles of the `init` and `finish` methods when a new tool is installed. Note that the postconditions for these methods are unrestricted: A tool can initialize and terminate itself in any way whatsoever.

Much of a tool's behavior is implemented in the `AbstractTool` class, which implements the `Tool` interface. This abstract class maintains a reference to the canvas it listens to and a reference to the figure manager it uses. The `AbstractTool` class also provides the following default behavior for the `install` method: Install this tool in the canvas, but if the install fails (because this tool is already installed), set the current geometry to `null` and give the tool a chance to reinitialize itself. The default behavior for the `init` method is to inform the figure manager of the appropriate highlighting strategy for this tool. The class also provides default do-nothing behaviors for the `finish` method and for the unused methods of the `MouseListener` and `MouseMotionListener` interfaces. Here is the resulting class definition:

```
public abstract class AbstractTool implements Tool {

  protected DrawCanvas canvas;
  protected DrawPadManager manager;

  protected AbstractTool(DrawCanvas canvas) {
    this.canvas = canvas;
    this.manager = canvas.getManager();
  }

  public void install() {
    if (!canvas.install(this)) {
      finish();
```

```
      manager.select(null);
      init();
    }
  }

  public void init() {
    manager.setHilightStrategy(makeHilightStrategy());
  }

  public void finish() { }
  public void mouseEntered(MouseEvent e) { }
  public void mouseExited(MouseEvent e) { }
  public void mouseClicked(MouseEvent e) { }
  public void mouseMoved(MouseEvent e) { }
}
```

Concrete subclasses of `AbstractTool` must implement the remaining mouse listener methods (`mousePressed`, `mouseReleased`, and `mouseDragged`) and the factory method `makeHilightStrategy` declared by the `Tool` interface. Note that subclasses of `AbstractTool` have access to the canvas and the figure manager via the protected `canvas` and `manager` fields, respectively.

We'll attack the definition of class `AbstractTool`'s subtypes beginning with the `PointerTool` class. A pointer tool is used to select, move, and delete figures. Here is a user-oriented description of its behaviors:

- When the user selects the pointer tool, the current figure (if any) is deselected and the cursor is changed to an arrow icon (in contrast, when a shape-defining tool is active, the cursor appears as a crosshairs icon).
- If the user clicks a figure, the figure gets selected and is highlighted; if the user clicks the background (outside any figure), the current figure (if any) is deselected.
- While the user drags a figure, the figure follows the cursor; when she releases the mouse button, the figure remains at its final position. However, if she releases the mouse button while pressing the Control key, the figure is deleted.

Here is the definition for the `PointerTool` class:

```
public class PointerTool extends AbstractTool {

  protected Geometry currentGeometry;
  protected PointGeometry lastPoint;

  public PointerTool(DrawCanvas canvas) {
    super(canvas);
  }
```

```
    public void init() {
      super.init();
      manager.select(null);
      canvas.setCursor(Cursor.getDefaultCursor());
      manager.updateManager();
    }

    public HilightStrategy makeHilightStrategy() {
      return new OutlineStrategy();
    }

    public void mousePressed(MouseEvent e) {
      currentGeometry = manager.find(e.getX(), e.getY());
      manager.select(currentGeometry);
      if (currentGeometry != null)
        lastPoint = new PointGeometry(e.getX(), e.getY());
      manager.updateManager();
    }

    public void mouseDragged(MouseEvent e) {
      if (currentGeometry != null) {
        int x = e.getX();
        int y = e.getY();
        int dx = x - lastPoint.getX();
        int dy = y - lastPoint.getY();
        currentGeometry.translate(dx, dy);
        lastPoint.setX(x);
        lastPoint.setY(y);
        manager.updateManager();
      }
    }

    public void mouseReleased(MouseEvent e) {
      if ((currentGeometry != null) && e.isControlDown()) {
        manager.remove(currentGeometry);
        currentGeometry = null;
      }
      lastPoint = null;
      manager.updateManager();
    }
  }
```

The `PointerTool.currentGeometry` field stores a reference to the selected geometry, if any. The `lastPoint` field is used to translate the current geometry during mouse drags. This field records the most recent position of the mouse. As the mouse is dragged, the `mouseDragged` method calculates the amount to translate by subtracting the most recent position from the mouse's new position. The manager is updated over the course of the mouse drag so that it has a chance to repaint the canvas.

`PointerTool`'s implementation of the `makeHilightStrategy` method returns a strategy that outlines the current geometry. We'll cover this and other highlighting strategies in Section 7.7.3.

Next, we consider tools for drawing rectangular shapes (rectangles and ellipses). In general, a shape-drawing tool is used both for drawing new figures and for editing the current figure. In the case of a tool for drawing *rectangular* shapes, the user manipulates the corners of the figure's bounding box, which is displayed. Here are the behaviors common to all rectangular tools:

- When the user selects a shape-drawing tool, the selected figure remains selected if its type is compatible with the tool's type (e.g., if the figure is an ellipse and the selected tool is an ellipse-drawing tool); otherwise, the selected figure is deselected. Also, the cursor is changed to a crosshairs icon.
- If some figure is selected, the user can drag any one of its corners to a new location. The corner follows the cursor, while the opposite corner remains anchored in place. This is how rectangular figures are reshaped.
- The selected figure is highlighted by its bounding box (a rectangle). This highlight is particularly useful for locating the "corners" of ellipses for reshaping.
- If no figure is selected, the user may sweep out a new figure. The click-down point fixes one corner, and then the user drags and releases to position the opposite corner.
- If the resulting rectangular geometry has width or height equal to zero, the geometry is removed.

The definition of the abstract `RectangularTool` class is somewhat complex, but this is mitigated by two factors. First, because so much implementation appears in this class, the definition of its subtypes is rather simple. Second, the design makes use of two design patterns: the template method and the factory method patterns (see Figure 7.19). The `init` method of class `RectangularTool` is a template method. The `init` method determines whether the tool is capable of editing the selected figure. It performs this check by calling the abstract `canEdit` method, which gets implemented by `RectangularTool`'s subclasses. Here the template method (`init`) defines an algorithm, one of whose steps (`canEdit`) is implemented by child classes.

The `makeRectangularGeometry` method is a factory method. It gets called by the `mousePressed` method whenever the user begins to sweep out a new figure. Because `mousePressed` doesn't know the actual type of geometry to construct, it leaves this decision to the child class' implementation of the `makeRectangularGeometry` method. Hence, the `RectangularTool` class provides an interface for creating new objects while letting its subclasses

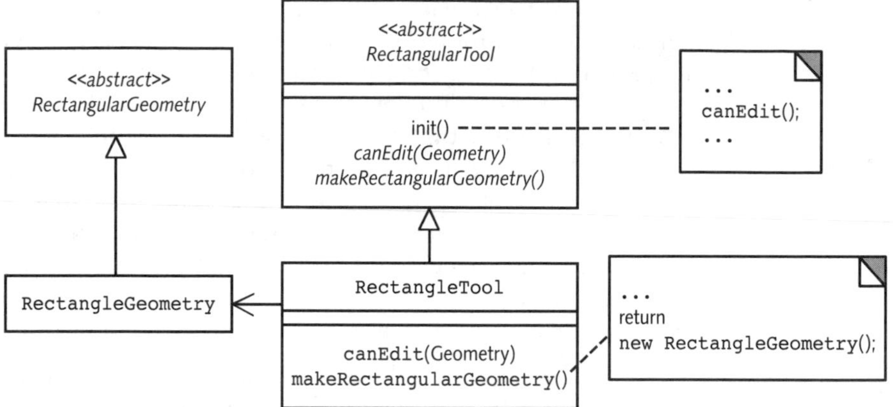

FIGURE 7.19 The template method and factory method patterns are used in the design of rectangular tools.

decide what type of object to create. Our use of the template method and factory method patterns is apparent in the class diagram of Figure 7.19.

The following implementation of the `RectangularTool` class defines two fields. The `geometry` field stores the geometry that the tool is currently editing. The `anchor` field comes into play whenever the user sweeps out a new figure or reshapes an existing figure by dragging one of its corners. In both cases, `anchor` stores the position of the opposite corner, that is, the corner that remains anchored in place. Here is the class definition:

```
public abstract class RectangularTool
                extends AbstractTool {

  protected RectangularGeometry geometry;
  protected PointGeometry anchor;

  public RectangularTool(DrawCanvas canvas) {
    super(canvas);
  }

  public void init() {
    super.init();
    canvas.setCursor(Cursor.getPredefinedCursor(
                        Cursor.CROSSHAIR_CURSOR));
    Geometry geom = manager.selected();
    if (!canEdit(geom)) {
      manager.select(null);
      geometry = null;
    } else
      geometry = (RectangularGeometry)geom;
    manager.updateManager();
  }
```

```
public void finish() {
  if ((geometry != null) &&
      ((geometry.getWidth() == 0) ||
       (geometry.getHeight() == 0))) {
    manager.select(null);
    manager.remove(geometry);
    geometry = null;
  }
}

public HilightStrategy makeHilightStrategy() {
  return new BoundingBoxStrategy();
}

//
// abstract methods
//
public abstract RectangularGeometry
  makeRectangularGeometry(PointGeometry p,int w,int h);
  // REQUIRES: p is not null,
  //   and w and h are nonnegative.
  // EFFECTS: Returns a new rectangular geometry with
  //   position p, width w, and height h.

public abstract boolean canEdit(Geometry geom);
  // EFFECTS: Returns true if this tool is capable
  //   of editing geom; returns false if geom is
  //   null or otherwise cannot edit geom.

public void mousePressed(MouseEvent e) {
  PointGeometry firstPoint =
    new PointGeometry(e.getX(), e.getY());
  if (geometry == null) {
    anchor = firstPoint;
    geometry = makeRectangularGeometry(anchor, 0, 0);
    manager.add(geometry);
    manager.select(geometry);
  } else
    anchor = oppositeCorner(firstPoint);
  manager.updateManager();
}

public void mouseDragged(MouseEvent e) {
  if (anchor != null) {
    PointGeometry curPoint =
      new PointGeometry(e.getX(), e.getY());
    updateRectangularGeometry(anchor, curPoint);
    manager.updateManager();
  }
}
```

```
  public void mouseReleased(MouseEvent e) {
    if (anchor == null) return;
    PointGeometry curPoint =
      new PointGeometry(e.getX(), e.getY());
    updateRectangularGeometry(anchor, curPoint);
  }

  protected void
    updateRectangularGeometry(PointGeometry p1,
                              PointGeometry p2) {
    // REQUIRES: p1, p2, and geometry are not null.
    // MODIFIES: geometry
    // EFFECTS: Updates the dimensions of geometry such
    //   that p1 and p2 are made opposite corners.
    int x = Math.min(p1.getX(), p2.getX());
    int y = Math.min(p1.getY(), p2.getY());
    int width = Math.abs(p2.getX() - p1.getX());
    int height = Math.abs(p2.getY() - p1.getY());
    geometry.setPosition(new PointGeometry(x, y));
    geometry.setWidth(width);
    geometry.setHeight(height);
  }

  protected PointGeometry
          oppositeCorner(PointGeometry p) {
    // REQUIRES: p and geometry are not null.
    // EFFECTS: Returns null if p is not near (within 3
    //   pixels of) one of geometry's corners; else
    //   where p is near corner c, returns the corner
    //   of geometry that is opposite c.
    PointGeometry res = new PointGeometry();
    int minX = geometry.getPosition().getX();
    int maxX = minX + geometry.getWidth();
    Range xRange = new Range(p.getX()-3, p.getX()+3);
    if (xRange.contains(minX)) res.setX(maxX);
    else if (xRange.contains(maxX)) res.setX(minX);
    else return null;
    int minY = geometry.getPosition().getY();
    int maxY = minY + geometry.getHeight();
    Range yRange = new Range(p.getY()-3, p.getY()+3);
    if (yRange.contains(minY)) res.setY(maxY);
    else if (yRange.contains(maxY)) res.setY(minY);
    else return null;
    return res;
  }
}
```

Observe where the `RectangularTool` class calls its two abstract methods. Its factory method `makeRectangularGeometry` is called by the `mousePressed` method whenever no geometry is currently selected (i.e., when the condition `geometry==null` is true). This code executes whenever the user presses the mouse button to begin sweeping out a new rectangle or ellipse. The template method `canEdit` is called by the `init` method whenever a rectangular tool is installed in the canvas. The `init` method uses `canEdit` to decide whether the tool is capable of editing the selected figure—if not, the selected figure is deselected and the tool is configured to construct a new figure from scratch.

The concrete subclasses of `RectangularTool` promise to implement the abstract `makeRectangularGeometry` and `canEdit` methods. Here is the definition of the `RectangleTool` class:

```
public class RectangleTool extends RectangularTool {
  public RectangleTool(DrawCanvas canvas) {
    super(canvas);
  }

  public RectangularGeometry
   makeRectangularGeometry(PointGeometry p,int w,int h){
    return new RectangleGeometry(p, w, h);
  }

  public boolean canEdit(Geometry g) {
    return (g instanceof RectangleGeometry);
  }
}
```

Lastly, we turn to the `PolygonTool` class for creating and editing polygons. This tool behaves like our polygon edit listener of Section 7.2.4 but with one caveat: Our polygon tool is used not only to edit polygons, but also to create and destroy them. Here is a user-oriented description of its behaviors:

- When the user selects the polygon tool, the selected figure remains selected if it's a polygon; otherwise, the selected figure is deselected. Also, the cursor is changed to a crosshairs icon.
- If some polygon is selected, the user clicks the canvas background to create a new vertex immediately after the current vertex (the new vertex becomes the current vertex); control-clicks a vertex to delete it (the vertex's predecessor becomes the current vertex, but if the deleted vertex is the only vertex, the polygon is destroyed); and drags vertices to move them to new locations.
- The selected polygon is highlighted by its outline, and its current vertex is highlighted by a brightly colored point.
- If no polygon is selected, the user clicks the canvas background to construct a new one-vertex polygon at the click-point.
- If the resulting polygon has fewer than three vertices, it's removed.

Not surprisingly, our implementation of the `PolygonTool` class is similar to that of the `PolygonListener` class of Section 7.2.4. Both classes define an `iter` field that holds a polygon iterator for the selected polygon, and both classes define a `boolean vertexBeingDragged` field which is `true` only while the user is dragging some vertex. Nonetheless, the two classes differ in three ways. First, being a kind of tool, `PolygonTool` extends the `AbstractTool` class. Second, the `PolygonTool` class uses a figure manager (it inherits the `manager` field from its superclass `AbstractTool`). So, for example, wherever `PolygonListener` repaints the canvas, our `PolygonTool` class instead updates its figure manager. Lastly, the protected interface of `PolygonTool` is somewhat more elaborate than that of `PolygonListener` because polygon tools must not only edit polygons, but also create and destroy them. Interestingly, their respective event-handlers `mousePressed`, `mouseReleased`, and `mouseDragged` have essentially the same implementation: their differences in behavior are accounted for by the protected methods they call upon. Here is the definition of our `PolygonTool` class:

```
public class PolygonTool extends AbstractTool {

  protected PolygonIterator iter;
  protected boolean vertexBeingDragged;

  public PolygonTool(DrawCanvas canvas) {
    super(canvas);
  }

  public void init() {
    super.init();
    canvas.setCursor(Cursor.getPredefinedCursor(
                             Cursor.CROSSHAIR_CURSOR));
    iter = null;
    Geometry geom = manager.selected();
    if (!(geom instanceof DynamicPolygonGeometry))
      manager.select(null);
    else {
      DynamicPolygonGeometry poly =
        (DynamicPolygonGeometry)manager.selected();
      iter = poly.iterator();
    }
    manager.updateManager();
  }

  public void finish() {
    if ((iter != null) && (iter.nbrVertices() <= 2))
      removePolygon();
  }

  public HilightStrategy makeHilightStrategy() {
    return new PolygonHilightStrategy(this);
  }
```

```
public void mousePressed(MouseEvent e) {
  vertexBeingDragged = findVertex(e.getX(), e.getY());
}

public void mouseReleased(MouseEvent e) {
  if (vertexBeingDragged && e.isControlDown())
    removeVertex();
  else if (!vertexBeingDragged) {
    PointGeometry p = new PointGeometry(e.getX(),e.getY());
    insertNewVertex(p);
  }
  vertexBeingDragged = false;
  manager.updateManager();
}

public void mouseDragged(MouseEvent e) {
  if (vertexBeingDragged) {
    moveVertex(e.getX(), e.getY());
    manager.updateManager();
  }
}

protected boolean findVertex(int x, int y) {
  if (iter == null)
    return false;
  PointZoneGeometry disk = new PointZoneGeometry(x, y);
  for (int i=0; i<iter.nbrVertices(); iter.next(),i++){
    PointGeometry p = iter.point();
    if (disk.contains(p))
      return true;
  }
  return false;
}

protected void insertNewVertex(PointGeometry p) {
  if (manager.selected() == null)
    makeNewPolygon(p);
  else
    iter.insertAfter(p);
}

protected void removeVertex() {
  if (iter.nbrVertices() == 1)
    removePolygon();
  else
    iter.remove();
}

protected void moveVertex(int x, int y) {
  iter.moveTo(x, y);
}
```

```
    protected void makeNewPolygon(PointGeometry p) {
      Geometry poly = new DynamicPolygonGeometry(p);
      manager.add(poly);
      manager.select(poly);
      init();
    }

    protected void removePolygon() {
      Geometry poly = manager.selected();
      manager.remove(poly);
      init();
    }

    protected PointGeometry selectedVertexPosition() {
      if (iter != null) return iter.point();
      else return null;
    }
}
```

The `PolygonTool` class defines the `selectedVertexPosition` method for use by the highlighting strategy. When a polygon is highlighted, the strategy calls this method to obtain the current vertex's position.

Exercises

ESSENTIAL 7.18 Implement the `EllipseTool` class.

ESSENTIAL 7.19 As it stands, the `DrawPad` program has two kinds of tools: drawing tools (for rectangles, ellipses, and polygons) and a pointer tool. Are there any behaviors that all drawing tools have in common, but that nondrawing tools (such as the pointer tool) lack? Suppose you were to define an `AbstractDrawingTool` class to serve as a supertype for all drawing tools. How would you revise the class diagram of Figure 7.18 to accommodate this new class? As the `DrawPad` program evolves, is it likely that you would discover additional behaviors for the `AbstractDrawingTool` class?

7.7.3 DrawPad's Highlighting Strategies

Whenever the canvas gets repainted, it asks the figure manager for a group node representing the scene. This group node includes a child depicting the highlight for the selected figure, if any. The figure manager manufactures this highlight using its highlight strategy. Specifically, it calls its highlight strategy's `makeHilight` method which returns a node depicting the highlight. The figure manager then adds this node to the group node that represents the scene as a whole.

There are different strategies for producing highlights. When the pointer tool is in use, the selected figure is highlighted by drawing its outline using a thick red stroke. When a rectangular tool is used, the selected figure—a rectangle or an ellipse—is highlighted by the outline of its bounding box. This enables the user to easily select any of the figure's corners for reshaping. When the polygon tool is in use, the selected polygon is highlighted by its outline; in addition, its current vertex is highlighted by a brightly colored point.

The figure manager does not implement the logic for manufacturing highlights. Rather, it delegates this task to its highlight strategy, which implements the `HilightStrategy` interface. This interface specifies the `makeHilight` method for manufacturing new strategies. Each of the three different strategies that appear in Figure 7.20 implements the `makeHilight` method in its own way.

When a tool is installed with the canvas, the tool assigns the appropriate highlight strategy to the figure manager. To accomplish this, each tool implements the `makeHighlightStrategy` method so that it returns the desired highlight strategy. When a tool is installed, its `init` method assigns to the figure manager the strategy returned by `makeHilightStrategy`. For instance, when the user clicks the *Pointer* tool, `PointerTool's init` method calls `makeHilightStrategy` which manufactures an instance of `OutlineStrategy` and then assigns the `OutlineStrategy` to the figure manager. This design uses the strategy design pattern to produce highlights and the factory method pattern to manufacture highlight strategies (see Figure 7.20).

Let's now implement `HilightStrategy` and its subtypes. The `HilightStrategy` interface specifies the `makeHilight` method, which gets called with a geometry `g` and returns a node representing a highlight for `g`. The `HilightStrategy` interface also defines a static painter (a red 3-pixel-wide stroke). This painter is available to help standardize the highlights produced by subclasses. Here is the interface definition:

```
public interface HilightStrategy {
  public final static Painter DefaultHilightPainter =
    new DrawDynamicPolygonPainter(Color.red,
                                 new BasicStroke(3));

  public Node makeHilight(Geometry g)
         throws ClassCastException;
    // EFFECTS: If g is null returns null; else if g's
    //    type is not compatible with this strategy
    //    throws ClassCastException; else returns
    //    a node representing a highlight for g.
}
```

The `OutlineStrategy` class is used to highlight the input geometry's outline. The default painter that it inherits determines the highlight's appearance. Here is the definition:

```
public class OutlineStrategy implements HilightStrategy {
  public Node makeHilight(Geometry g)
```

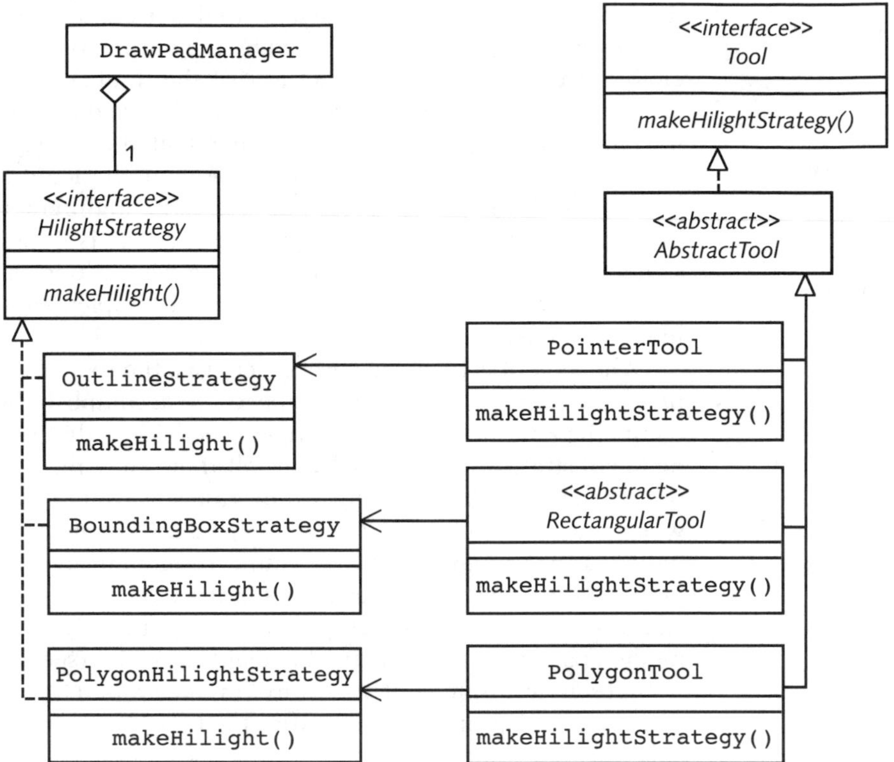

FIGURE 7.20 Highlights are based on the factory method and the strategy design patterns.

```
          throws ClassCastException {
      if (g == null)
        return null;
      else
        return new Figure(g, DefaultHilightPainter);
    }
  }
```

The `BoundingBoxStrategy` class highlights the bounding box of the input geometry. The input geometry should be a rectangular geometry; if it is not, the `makeHilight` method throws an exception:

```
  public class BoundingBoxStrategy
         implements HilightStrategy {
    public Node makeHilight(Geometry g)
          throws ClassCastException {
      if (g == null)
        return null;
      else {
        RectangularGeometry r = (RectangularGeometry)g;
```

```
        return
         new Figure(r.boundingBox(),DefaultHilightPainter);
      }
    }
  }
```

The PolygonHilightStrategy class highlights a polygon by stroking its outline and painting a point at the position of the polygon's current vertex. The class defines a tool field that references the PolygonTool that manipulates the polygon. The makeHilight method queries the polygon tool for the position of the polygon's current vertex. Here is the class definition:

```
public class PolygonHilightStrategy
       implements HilightStrategy {

  public final static Painter DefaultVertexPainter =
         new FillPainter(Color.white);

  protected PolygonTool tool;

  public PolygonHilightStrategy(PolygonTool tool) {
    this.tool = tool;
  }

  public Node makeHilight(Geometry g)
         throws ClassCastException {
    if (g == null)
      return null;
    else {
      GroupNode node = new GroupNode();
      node.addChild(new Figure(g, DefaultHilightPainter));
      Geometry vertexPos = tool.selectedVertexPosition();
      if (vertexPos != null)
        node.addChild(
          new Figure(vertexPos, DefaultVertexPainter));
      return node;
    }
  }
}
```

Our *DrawPad* program is designed to simplify the task of adding new shape-drawing tools. Examples include tools for building such geometries as round rectangles, points, lines, and curves. These are the steps you take to add a new shape-drawing tool:

- Define a class for the new geometry if the class is not already defined. This class should implement the `AreaGeometry` interface.
- Define a class to represent a tool for creating and editing instances of the geometry. This class should implement the `Tool` interface.
- Define a highlight strategy class for the tool if an appropriate strategy does not already exist.
- Modify the `ControlPanel` class such that it:
  (a) creates a new `ToolButton` for the new tool and adds the button to itself, and
  (b) adjusts its layout manager to accommodate this new button.

Some of the exercises that follow ask you to explore this process.

Exercises

ESSENTIAL 7.20 To the *DrawPad* program add a new tool for creating and editing round rectangles (see Exercise 5.19 for the specification of the `RoundRectangleGeometry` class). The tool's behavior should parallel those of the rectangle tool and the ellipse tool. Each new round rectangle should have a corner width and corner height of 50 pixels.

7.21 Revise your implementation of the tool in the previous exercise so that the corner width and corner height of each round rectangle depend on its width and height, respectively. Specifically, the corner width should equal the larger of (a) 20 pixels or (b) 0.25 times the round rectangle's width. Similarly, the corner height should equal the larger of 20 pixels and 0.25 times the rectangle's height. [Hint: Your `RoundRectangleTool` class may override the `updateRectangularGeometry` method.]

ESSENTIAL 7.22 Implement the `LineSegmentZoneGeometry` class, which does for line segments what the `PointZoneGeometry` class does for points (see Exercise 7.3). A line segment zone is a line segment that implements the `AreaGeometry` interface. A line segment zone L contains a given point p if the distance between p and L is no greater than some value R. Here, R is referred to as the **zone radius.** You can imagine that line L is enclosed by a neighborhood of points whose distance from L is no greater than R. Any point that belongs to this neighborhood is considered to be contained in L. The following class skeleton specifies those methods that differ from those of the parent class:

```
public class LineSegmentZoneGeometry
        extends LineSegmentGeometry
        implements AreaGeometry {
```

```
public LineSegmentZoneGeometry(int x0, int y0,
                int x1, int y1, int zoneRadius)
       throws IllegalArgumentException
  // EFFECTS: If radius <= 0 throws
  //    IllegalArgumentException; else constructs
  //    the line segment (x0,y0)-(x1,y1) with
  //    the specified zone radius.

public LineSegmentZoneGeometry(int x0, int y0,
                               int x1, int y1)
  // EFFECTS: Constructs the line segment
  //    (x0,y0)-(x1,y1) zone radius of 2 pixels.

public LineSegmentZoneGeometry(PointGeometry p0,
                               PointGeometry p1,
                               int radius)
       throws NullPointerException,
              IllegalArgumentException
  // EFFECTS: If p0 or p1 is null throws
  //    NullPointerException; else if radius <= 0
  //    throws IllegalArgumentException; else
  //    constructs the line segment from p0 to p1
  //    with specified zone radius.

public LineSegmentZoneGeometry(PointGeometry p0,
                               PointGeometry p1)
       throws NullPointerException
  // EFFECTS: If p0 or p1 is null throws
  //    NullPointerException; else if radius <= 0
  //    throws IllegalArgumentException; else
  //    constructs the line segment from p0 to p1
  //    with zone radius of two pixels.

public boolean contains(int x, int y)
  // EFFECTS: Returns true if the point (x,y) is
  //    no greater than zone radius pixels from
  //    (some point in) this line segment;
  //    else returns false.

public boolean contains(PointGeometry p)
               throws NullPointerException
  // EFFECTS: If p is null throws
  //    NullPointerException; else returns true
  //    if point p lies no greater than zone
```

```
    //   radius pixels from (some point in) this
    //   line segment; else returns false.

  public void setZoneRadius(int newR)
          throws IllegalArgumentException
    // MODIFIES: this
    // EFFECTS: If newR <= 0 throws
    //   IllegalArgumentException; else sets
    //   the zone radius to newR.

  public int getZoneRadius()
    // EFFECTS: Returns the current zone radius.
}
```

The method `Line2D.ptSegDist` returns the distance between a line segment and an input point. This method is used in the following implementation of the two-argument `contains` method, which you may want to include in your class definition:

```
// method of LineSegmentZoneGeometry class
public boolean contains(int x, int y) {
  Line2D shape = (Line2D)shape();
  return (shape.ptSegDist(x, y)<=getZoneRadius());
}
```

ESSENTIAL 7.23 To the *DrawPad* program add a tool for drawing line segments. Here is how the line-drawing tool is used:

- When the user selects the tool, the selected figure remains selected if it's a line segment; otherwise, the selected figure is deselected. Also, the cursor is changed to a crosshairs icon.
- If some line segment is selected, the user may drag either of its two endpoints to a new location. The other endpoint remains anchored in place.
- If no line segment is selected, the user defines a new line segment by dragging the mouse. The first endpoint is located where the drag begins, and the second endpoint where it ends.

The *DrawPad* program is designed to work with area geometries. Consequently, your line segment tool should create `LineSegmentZoneGeometry` objects. Each object's zone radius determines how close to a line segment the user must click to select it with the *Pointer* tool. A value of about four pixels works well.

7.24 To the *DrawPad* program add a control for setting a figure's outline color, independent of its fill color. Whenever a new figure is created, it's assigned a painter that fills with the current fill color and strokes with the current outline color. Your control may be a button whose behavior parallels that of class `ControlPanel`'s `colorButton`.

7.25 To the *DrawPad* program add a combo box control for specifying the stroke width in pixels. The combo box's items are the numeric strings `"1"`, `"2"`, `"3"`, and `"4"`. When a new figure is created, it's assigned a painter that fills with the current fill color and strokes with the current outline color and stroke width. You should also place a label near the combo box identifying its function.

Summary

An object-oriented application framework is a reusable software system in a particular application domain. The framework captures and allows reuse of expertise, both in the application domain and in programming. To develop an application using a framework, the developer defines classes that customize the framework. A framework is customized at its hot spots—places which allow variation across applications. Customization is achieved through inheritance (white box) and through composition (black box), depending on the rules governing use of each hot spot.

An application's overall design is prescribed by the framework on which it is based. Usually this design implies an inversion of control—code supplied by the framework calls the components supplied by the application. Although the developer gives up some control over the design of the application, using a framework generally simplifies and facilitates the development of complex, reliable software. Moreover, although it can take considerable time and effort to learn a framework, it is often less than what is required to build applications from scratch, and the effort can be amortized over many projects.

The Abstract Window Toolkit (AWT) and Swing make up Java's framework for building programs with graphical user interfaces. This framework comprises three main building blocks: components, layout managers, and the event model. Components, such as buttons, panels, dialog boxes, menus, text fields, and lists, are the visual widgets with which users interact. Components appear in containers, which are themselves a type of component. Layout managers arrange the components belonging to a container. And the event model associates event-handling behaviors with components.

APPENDIX A

Reading and Parsing User Input

Quite a few of the programs described in this book depend on input from the standard input stream, which is typically connected to input from the keyboard. For this purpose, I've written a class called `ScanInput` which provides methods for reading numbers and strings. Here is a short example of the class' use:

```
public class TryScanInput {
  public static void main(String[] args) {
    try {
      ScanInput in = new ScanInput();
      System.out.print("Please enter your first name: ");
      String name = in.readString();
      System.out.print("Enter an integer: ");
      int a = in.readInt();
      System.out.print("Enter any number: ");
      float b = in.readFloat();
      String res =
        "Don't you know " + a + " * " + b + " is ";
      res += (a*b) + ", " + name + "!";
      System.out.println(res);
    } catch (NumberFormatException e) {
      System.out.println("I can multiply only numbers!");
    } catch (IOException e) {
      System.out.println("unexpected i/o exception");
    }
  }
}
```

Here are two sample transcripts, where user input is in bold:

```
> java TryScanInput
Please enter your first name: Arianna
Enter an integer: 4
Enter any number: 2.5
Don't you know 4 * 2.5 is 10.0, Arianna!
```

```
> java TryScanInput
Please enter your first name: Phyllis
Enter an integer: 18
Enter any number: David
I can multiply only numbers!
```

The `ScanInput` class reads from the input stream sequentially. It assumes that input tokens are separated by sequences of whitespace characters, which include spaces, tabs, and newlines. Moreover, the string returned by the `readString` method is a maximal-length sequence of nonwhitespace characters. On reaching the input

```
thisIsARidiculousString
```

a call to the `readString` method returns the string *thisIsARidiculousString*, even though as English speakers we parse this into five words. Along the same lines, on reaching the input

6.3–7.42

a call to the `readFloat` method fails because this string is a badly formed number. However, if the input appears as

6.3 –7.42

a call to `readFloat` reads 6.3; if followed by a second call to `readFloat`, the value –7.42 is read next. Here is the specification for `ScanInput`:

```
public class ScanInput {

  public ScanInput(Reader inReader)
    // REQUIRES: inReader is not null.
    // EFFECTS: Constructs a new ScanInput whose input
    //   comes from inReader.

  public ScanInput()
    // EFFECTS: Constructs a new ScanInput whose input
    //   comes from the standard input System.in.

  public String readString() throws IOException
    // MODIFIES: this
    // EFFECTS: If i/o exception throws IOException;
    //   else returns the next string in the input
    //   stream (a string is a maximal-length sequence
    //   of nonwhitespace characters); returns the empty
    //   string if at end-of-file.

  public int readInt()
        throws IOException, NumberFormatException
    // MODIFIES: this
```

```
    // EFFECTS: If i/o exception throws IOException;
    //   else if the next string in the input stream is
    //   badly formed throws NumberFormatException; else
    //   returns the integer the next string denotes.

  public double readDouble()
        throws IOException, NumberFormatException
    // MODIFIES: this
    // EFFECTS: If i/o exception throws IOException;
    //   else if the next string in the input string is
    //   badly formed throws NumberFormatException; else
    //   returns the double that the next string denotes.

  public float readFloat()
        throws IOException, NumberFormatException
    // MODIFIES: this
    // EFFECTS: If i/o exception throws IOException;
    //   else if the next string in the input stream is
    //   badly formed throws NumberFormatException; else
    //   returns the float that the next string denotes.

  public boolean eof()
    // EFFECTS: Returns true if at end-of-file;
    //   else returns false.
}
```

Note that we can create a `ScanInput` object attached to any reader using the one-argument constructor. In particular, we can create a `ScanInput` attached to a file named *filename* with the following expression:

```
ScanInput in = new ScanInput(new FileReader("filename"));
```

The class definition follows:

```
public class ScanInput {

  protected static final int MAX_STRING_LEN = 512;

  protected Reader in;
  protected boolean eof;
  protected OneCharBuf buf;

  public ScanInput(Reader inReader) {
    in = new BufferedReader(inReader);
    eof = false;
    buf = new OneCharBuf();
  }
```

```
public ScanInput() {
  this(new InputStreamReader(System.in));
}

public String readString() throws IOException {
  char[] buf = new char[MAX_STRING_LEN];
  char c;
  int count = 0;
  skipWhitespace();
  if (eof()) return new String();
  for (c = readChar(); !isWhitespace(c) && !eof();
                                        c = readChar())
      buf[count++] = (char)c;
  return new String(buf, 0, count);
}

public int readInt()
       throws NumberFormatException, IOException {
  String s = readString();
  return Integer.parseInt(s);
}

public double readDouble()
       throws NumberFormatException, IOException {
  String s = readString();
  return Double.parseDouble(s);
}

public float readFloat()
       throws NumberFormatException, IOException {
  return (float)readDouble();
}

public boolean eof() {
  return eof;
}

//
// protected methods
//
protected char readChar() throws IOException {
  char c = (char)0;
  int cint;
  if (buf.isFull())
    c = buf.get();
  else {
```

```
        cint = in.read();
        if (cint == -1) eof = true;
        else c = (char)cint;
      }
      return c;
    }

    protected void unreadChar(char c) {
      if (buf.isFull())
        throw new Error("internal error");
      else
        buf.set(c);
    }

    protected boolean isWhitespace(char c) {
      return Character.isWhitespace(c);
    }

    protected void skipWhitespace() throws IOException {
      char c = (char)0;
      do {
        c = readChar();
      } while (isWhitespace(c) && !eof());
      if (eof()) eof = true;
      else unreadChar(c);
    }

    //
    // nested class for managing one-character buffer
    static class OneCharBuf {
      char c;
      boolean isFull = false;
      void set(char c) {
        this.c = c;
        isFull = true;
      }
      char get() {
        isFull = false;
        return c;
      }
      boolean isFull() {
        return isFull;
      }
    }
  }
```

APPENDIX B

Our Graphics Program Framework

The graphics programs presented through Chapter 6 (prior to the introduction of Java's GUI framework in Chapter 7) are based on two different program templates. The *MyGraphicsProgram* template (Section 3.5) serves as the model for static graphics programs, and the *MyInteractiveProgram* template (Section 4.5) serves as the model for graphics programs with which the user is able to interact. Both program templates require the programmer to define a new class that extends the `ApplicationPanel` class. In the case of static graphics programs, this new class (named `MyGraphicsProgram` in Figure B.1) overrides the `makeContent` method and the `paintComponent` methods, for creating graphics content and painting graphics content, respectively.

In the case of interactive graphics programs, the new class (named `MyInteractiveProgram` in Figure B.1) overrides the `paintComponent` method. In addition, it is necessary to define an auxiliary class that controls interactions and maintains graphics content (this class is named `MyInteractiveProgramController` in Figure B.1). The `MyInteractiveProgram` class, which remains responsible for painting itself, owns its controller as a component; whenever the program must repaint itself, it queries its controller for information about the current graphics content. In turn, the controller maintains a reference to the frame to which it sends a *repaint* message whenever the graphics content changes.

Here are the definitions of the `ApplicationPanel` and `ApplicationFrame` classes:

```
public class ApplicationPanel
       extends javax.swing.JPanel {

    // the frame that owns this application
  protected ApplicationFrame frame;

    // to be overridden if the subclass takes
    // program arguments
  static public void parseArgs(String[] args) {
```

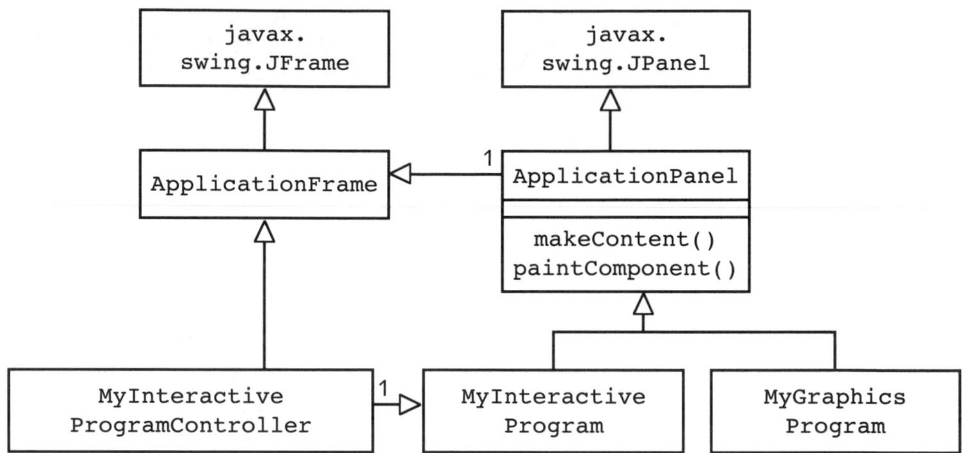

FIGURE B.1 Our graphics program framework.

```
    // EFFECTS: Processes program arguments, if any.
  }

  public void makeContent() {
    // MODIFIES: this
    // EFFECTS: Constructs the graphics content.
  }

  protected void setFrame(ApplicationFrame frame) {
    // MODIFIES: this
    // EFFECTS: Sets this panel's frame.
    this.frame = frame;
  }

  protected ApplicationFrame getFrame() {
    // EFFECTS: Gets this panel's frame.
    return this.frame;
  }
}

public class ApplicationFrame extends JFrame {

  public static String DEFAULT_TITLE = "My Frame";
  public static int DEFAULT_WIDTH = 400;
  public static int DEFAULT_HEIGHT = 400;

  public ApplicationFrame(String title, int width,
                                      int height) {
```

```
    // REQUIRES: title is non-null, and width and
    //   height are positive.
    // EFFECTS: Constructs a new frame with given
    //   title and size.
    super(title);
    setSize(width, height);
    center();
    addWindowListener(new WindowAdapter() {
      public void windowClosing(WindowEvent e) {
        dispose();
        System.exit(0);
      }
    });
  }

  public ApplicationFrame(String title) {
    // REQUIRES: title is non-null.
    // EFFECTS: Constructs a new frame of given title
    //   and default size.
    this(title, DEFAULT_WIDTH, DEFAULT_HEIGHT);
  }

  public ApplicationFrame(int width, int height) {
    // REQUIRES: width and height are positive.
    // EFFECTS: Constructs a new frame of given size.
    this(DEFAULT_TITLE, width, height);
  }

  public ApplicationFrame() {
    // EFFECTS: Constructs a new frame of default size.
    this(DEFAULT_TITLE, DEFAULT_WIDTH, DEFAULT_HEIGHT);
  }

  public void center() {
    // EFFECTS: Centers this frame within the screen.
    Dimension screenSize =
      Toolkit.getDefaultToolkit().getScreenSize();
    Dimension frameSize = getSize();
    int x = (screenSize.width - frameSize.width) / 2;
    int y = (screenSize.height - frameSize.height) / 2;
    setLocation(x, y);
  }

  public void setPanel(ApplicationPanel panel) {
    // MODIFIES: this
    // EFFECTS: Adds panel to this frame.
    Container contentPane = getContentPane();
```

```
    contentPane.add(panel);
    panel.setFrame(this);
    panel.setPreferredSize(getContentSize());
    pack();
  }

  public Dimension getContentSize() {
    // EFFECTS: Returns the size of this frame's
    //   content pane.
    Dimension d = getSize();
    Insets insets = getInsets();
    int w = d.width - insets.left - insets.right;
    int h = d.height - insets.top - insets.bottom;
    return new Dimension(w, h);
  }
}
```

A Notational Summary of UML

The Unified Modeling Language (UML) is a notation for expressing object-oriented designs. The notation, which is mainly graphical, comprises various kinds of diagrams for presenting different views of a design. UML diagrams are useful for understanding, implementing, communicating, and documenting a design—they serve as a blueprint for the system. Moreover, diagrams are intended to be modified and enhanced throughout the analysis and design process. Since being adopted in 1997 as a standard by the Object Management Group (OMG), a consortium of companies promoting the use of standardized object systems, UML is gaining broad acceptance as the modeling language of choice. The bibliography cites several good books for learning more about UML.

This book uses only a small subset of the UML to illustrate system designs. We use **class diagrams** to show the static structure of systems. A class diagram identifies classes and shows how they are related. Objects that exist while the system executes are instances of these classes, and the links between objects correspond to associations between their respective classes.

We also use **sequence diagrams** to show the dynamic structure of systems—how the system behaves over time. A sequence diagram shows how objects interact in a given scenario, while emphasizing the order in which messages are sent between objects.

C.1 Class Diagrams

A class diagram shows the classes relevant to a portion of a system, as well as the relationships between the classes. A class is represented most simply as a box that encloses the class' name. For more detail, the box may include a compartment for key attributes and a compartment for key methods. The attributes and methods may be typed if desired. The class name may be preceded with a stereotype that further characterizes the class; examples include <<*abstract*>> or <<*interface*>>. Elements that are abstract (including the names of abstract classes and interfaces) appear in italic.

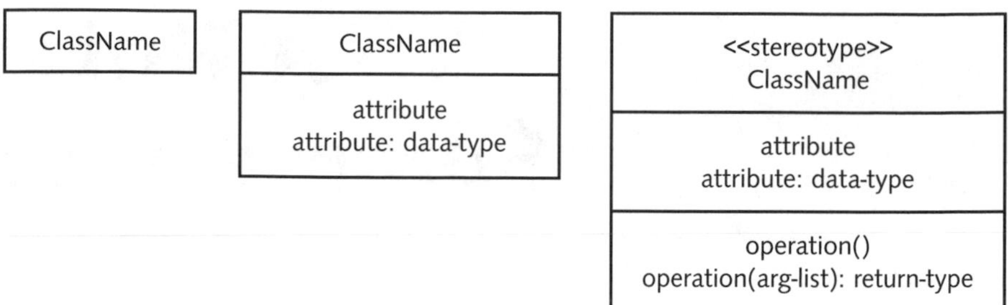

There is an association between two classes if it is possible for instances of one of the classes to create or send messages to instances of the second class. An association is shown by a line that connects the two class boxes. The association may be named, and the solid triangle that accompanies the name indicates the perspective of the speaker. For instance, in the following class diagram, if *association name* is replaced by the word *approves*, the diagram indicates that `Class1` approves `Class2`, or equivalently, that `Class2` is approved by `Class1`.

One-way navigability may be shown by attaching an arrow to one end of the line; messages may be sent only in the direction indicated by the arrow. The next diagram indicates that instances of `Class3` may send messages to instances of `Class4`, but not the reverse. If the arrows are omitted, navigability is either two-way—instances of either class can send messages to instances of the other class—or left unspecified.

Multiplicity values (also called cardinality constraints) may be included at either or both ends of a line linking two class boxes. The multiplicity values indicate the number of objects involved in the relationship. The variables that appear in the following notation represent non negative integers:

n	exactly *n*
a..b	from *a* to *b* inclusive where $a \le b$
a,b,c	only the values *a, b,* or *c*
n.. *	*n* or more
*	shorthand for 0..* (that is, zero or more)

The next diagram shows that an instance of `Class5` is associated with between four and seven instances of `Class6`, and that an instance of `Class6` is associated with exactly one instance of `Class5`.

Composition is a kind of association that models the whole-part relationship between classes. Objects of one class (the composite) own instances of the second class (its components). A component belongs to only one composite, and the component's lifetime is controlled by the composite. Composition is shown by including a filled diamond on the composite's end. In the following diagram, a `Class7` object owns one or more instances of `Class8`.

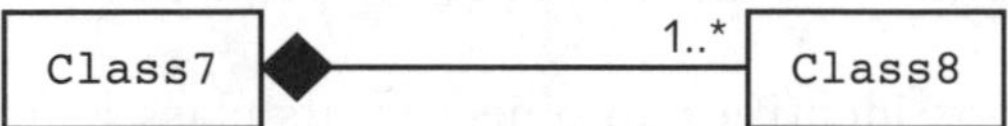

Aggregation is another kind of association that models the whole-part relationship between classes. Aggregation is sometimes considered a weak form of composition in which an aggregate whole may share its parts with other classes, although the UML does not specify the precise semantics. Aggregation is shown by including a hollow diamond on the whole's end. The class diagram below shows that a `Class9` object contains two `Class10` objects. The multiplicity values also indicate that a `Class10` object may be shared by any number of `Class9` objects.

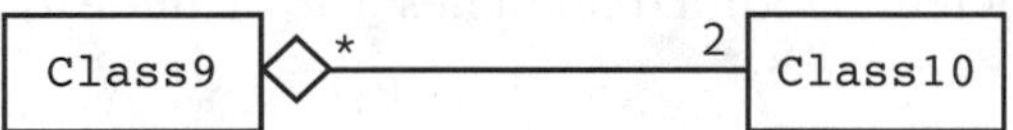

Inheritance is shown by including a hollow triangle on the parent class' end of the line joining two classes. A solid line is used to show extension and a dashed line to show implementation of an interface. In the next diagram, classes `Class12` and `Class13` both extend `Class11`, and `Class13` imple-

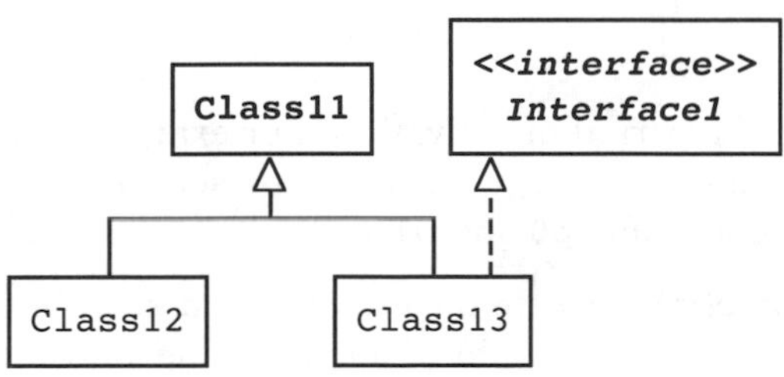

ments Interface1.

C.2 Sequence Diagrams

A sequence diagram shows how objects interact under a given scenario. The diagram is organized temporally to focus on the time-ordered sequence of messages between objects. A sequence diagram consists of a series of columns, one for each participating object. An object is identified by an object box whose label names the object's class. From each object box there descends a dashed vertical line called the object's lifeline. A message is shown by a horizontal arrow from the sending object's lifeline to the receiving object's lifeline. Time passes as you move from the top of the diagram to the bottom, so the messages are sequenced in time from top to bottom.

An object box identifies an object by its class name, underlined and preceded by a colon. If two or more objects of the same class are involved or, more generally, if it's desirable to note the names of objects, objects may be named by the underlined pair *object : class*. It is often useful to show the time intervals during which an object is active. An object becomes active when it receives a message. It remains active while performing the work necessary to respond to the message, which may involve sending messages of its own to itself and/or other objects. The object becomes inactive when it finally responds to the message it was sent originally, although it may of course be activated again later. Activations of objects are depicted by thin rectangles (or "candlesticks") whose span

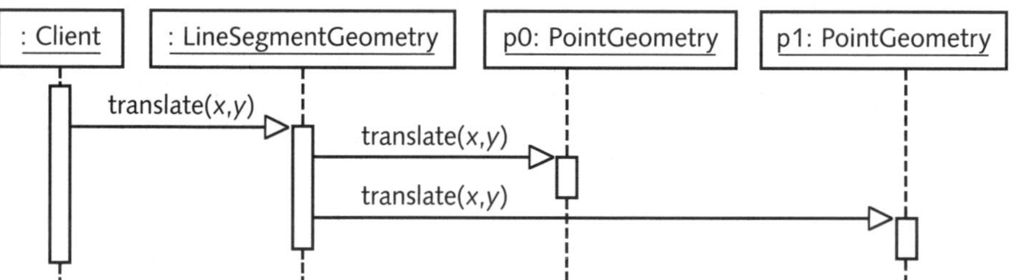

corresponds to the period of activation. For example, when a line segment receives a *translate* message, it responds by sending *translate* messages to each of its two endpoints `p0` and `p1`.

Interactions sometime involve the creation and destruction of objects. The creation of an object is shown by placing its object box at the receiving end of the message that creates it. The destruction of an object is indicated by a large X at the end of its final activation. Although Java's garbage collector may reclaim the object at a later time, an object is effectively destroyed when it is no longer referenced. As an example, when a polygon is asked whether it contains some point (*x*,*y*), it responds by constructing a new

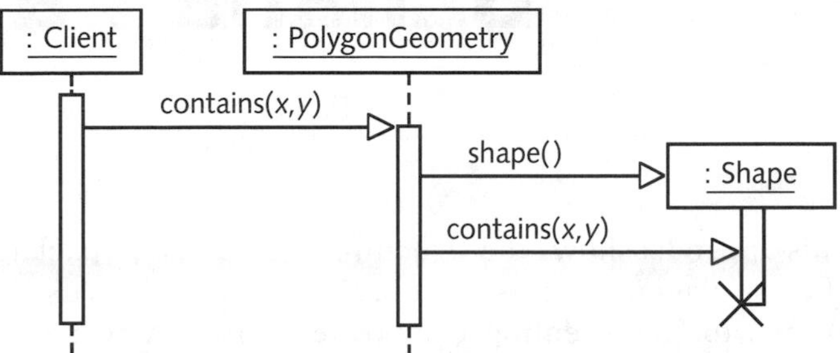

shape representing itself and sending this shape a *contains* message. Once the shape has reported whether it contains the input point, it is no longer needed.

APPENDIX D

Structure of the Banana Package

This appendix shows the structure of the banana package through a series of class diagrams. At its most basic, the package is used to construct scene graphs for representing composite figures. A scene graph is a directed acyclic graph whose elements are nodes. A scene graph's internal nodes—those with children—are grouping nodes, instances of the GroupNode class and its subtypes. The TransformGroup node is a grouping node that defines a new coordinate system in terms of the coordinate system of its parent node in the scene graph. The Axes class is a grouping node that creates a pair of coordinate axes. A scene graph's leaf nodes are figures (instances of the Figure class). A figure consists of at most one geometry and painter. Section 6.4 covers scene graphs in more detail.

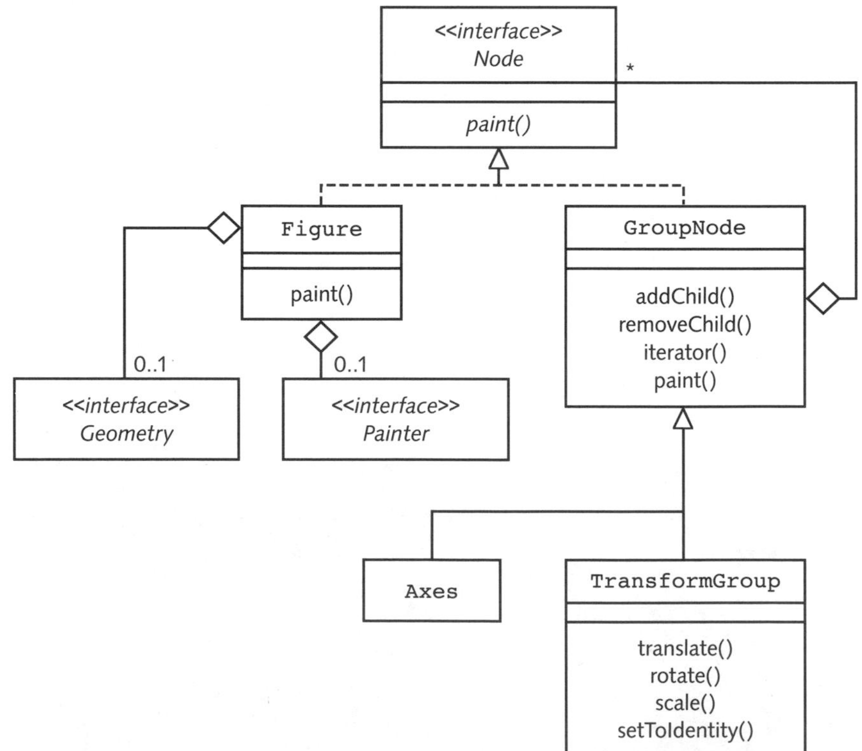

Geometry is one of the two key components of a figure. An area geometry is a geometry that encloses area, and a rectangular geometry is an area geometry that is described by an enclosing rectangle (Sections 5.4.2 and 5.4.3). A polyline geometry describes a path in the plane composed of straight line segments (Section 4.3.2), and a polygon geometry describes a closed polyline (Section 5.3.1). A dynamic polygon is a polygon that can be edited: new vertices inserted, old vertices removed, and existing vertices translated (Section 6.2.2). Triangle geometries prove useful in our triangulation algorithm of Section 6.2. Other kinds of geometries include text geometries (Exercise 5.20), point geometries (Section 3.2.1), line segment geometries (Exercise 3.3), infinite line geometries (Section 5.2.3), and various kinds of rectangular geometries: rectangle (Section 3.2.2), ellipse (Section 4.4.2), and round rectangle (Section 5.4.2) geometries.

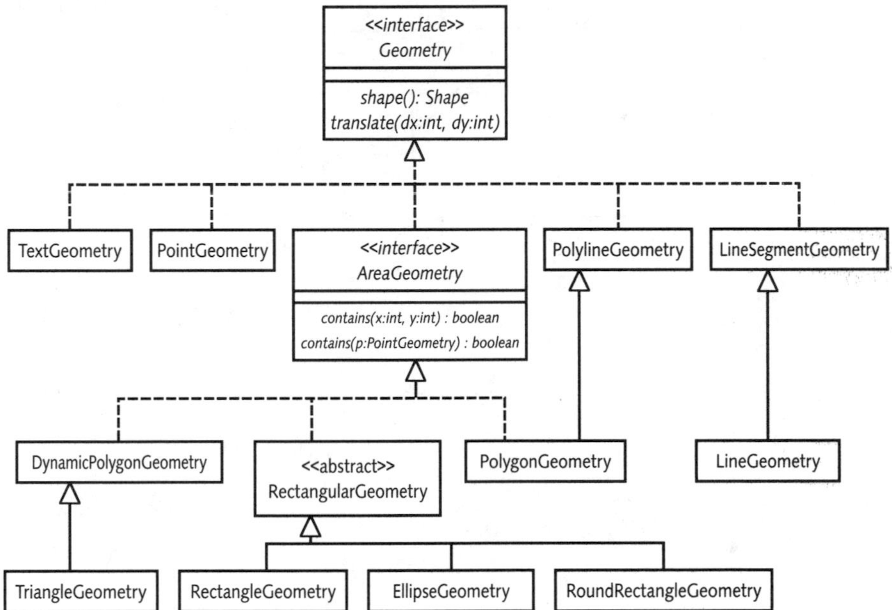

A dynamic polygon is composed of one or more vertices (Section 6.2.2). In turn, a vertex references a point that fixes its location in the plane, and two vertices (its predecessor and successor in the polygon). Clients manipulate dynamic polygons using polygon iterators (Section 6.2.3). A Boolean geometry is formed by combining two area geometries by means of the Boolean shape operations union, intersection, or difference (Section 6.3.1).

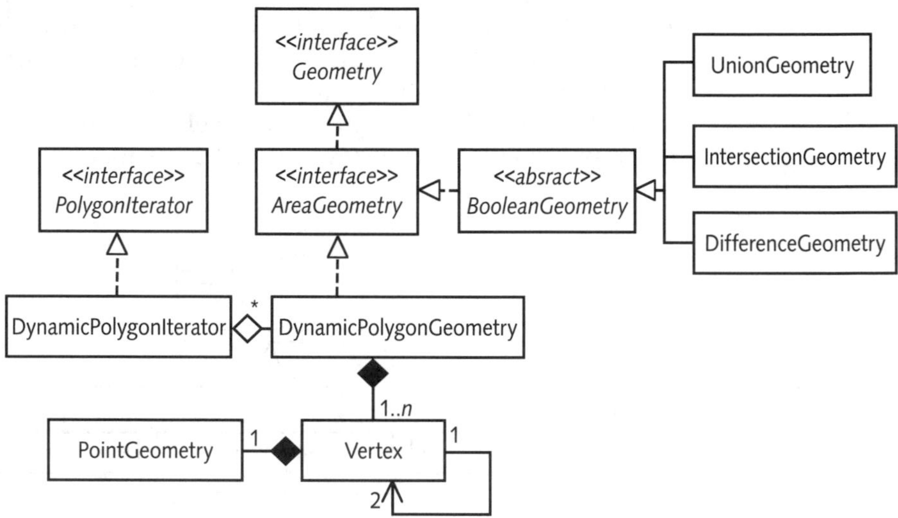

A figure is composed of a geometry and a painter. The `Painter` type, which is covered in Section 5.6, specifies a `paint` method for rendering a geometry into a graphics context. The specific type of painter determines the appearance, for instance, whether the geometry is filled with blue or stroked with green. The abstract `PaintPainter` class implements a *paint* property for its subclasses. The `FillPainter` and `DrawPainter` classes are used for filling and drawing geometries, respectively. The `DrawPolygonPainter` and `DrawDynamicPolygonPainter` classes are used to stroke static and dynamic polygons, respectively. (The `DrawPainter` class does not suffice for any polygon whose outline departs from its shape, such as a one-vertex polygon that gets rendered as a looping curve that links the vertex to itself.) The `MultiPainter` class is used to build a series of painters for composing rendering effects. When both components of a multipainter are `PaintPainter` types, the multipainter represents a series of two painters; when either of a multipainter's components is another multipainter, it represents a series of more than two painters.

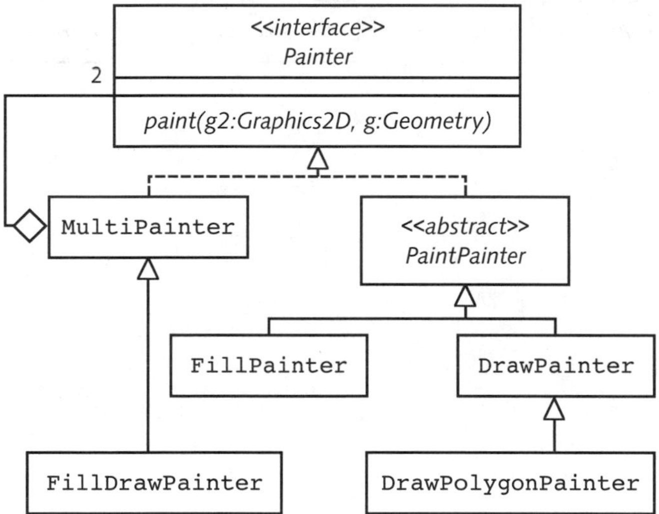

Random-value generators are useful for producing graphics that exhibit randomness. The `RandomInt` class, which provides random integers drawn from given ranges of numbers, uses Java's `Random` class to obtain random numbers. The `RandomIntInRange` class produces random integers drawn from a fixed range. The `RandomPoint` class produces random points guaranteed to lie within fixed bounds, and the `RandomRectangle` class produces random rectangles that also lie within fixed bounds. The `RandomColor` class generates random colors. These various random-value generators are covered in Section 4.2.

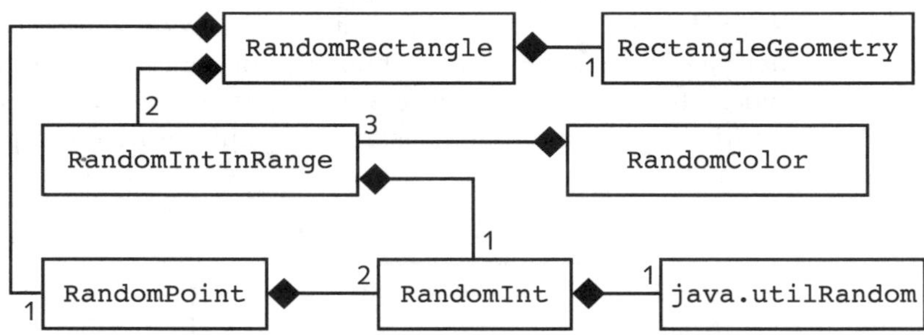

The following hierarchical overview of the `banana` package indicates the section or exercise in which each class and interface is introduced. Those classes and interfaces whose names are not fully qualified belong to the `banana` package. Indentation indicates extension; for instance, the `DifferenceGeometry` class extends the `BooleanGeometry` class. Because the `banana` package evolves over the course of the book, some classes acquire their supertypes well after they are introduced. For example, the `PointGeometry` class eventually implements both the `java.lang.Comparable` and `Geometry` interfaces. However, when introduced in Section 3.2.1, the `PointGeometry` class implements neither of these interfaces.

Class Hierarchy

- class Assert . . . . Sec. 2.2.1
- class Attribute . . . . Ex. 3.4
- class BooleanGeometry (implements AreaGeometry) . . . . Sec. 6.3.1
  - class DifferenceGeometry . . . . Ex. 6.19
  - class IntersectionGeometry . . . . Sec. 6.3.1
  - class UnionGeometry . . . . Ex. 6.19
- class Dictionary . . . . Ex. 4.21
- class DynamicPolygonGeometry (implements AreaGeometry) . . . . Sec. 6.2.2
  - class RegularPolygonGeometry . . . . Ex. 6.11
  - class TriangleGeometry . . . . Ex. 6.13
- class DynamicPolygonIterator (implements PolygonIterator) . . . . Sec. 6.2.3
- class DynamicPolygons . . . . Ex. 6.9
- class Figure (implements Node) . . . . Sec. 5.6.1
- class GroupNode (implements Node) . . . . Sec. 6.4.1
  - class Axes . . . . Sec. 6.4.2
  - class TransformGroup . . . . Sec. 6.4.3
- class LineSegmentGeometry (implements Geometry) . . . . Ex. 3.3
  - class LineGeometry . . . . Sec. 5.2.3
  - class LineSegmentZoneGeometry (implements AreaGeometry) . Ex. 7.21
- class MultiDrawPainter (implements Painter) . . . . Ex. 5.35
- class MultiPainter (implements Painter) . . . . Sec. 5.6.3
  - class FillDrawPainter . . . . Ex. 5.34
- class PaintPainter (implements Painter) . . . . Sec. 5.6.2
  - class DrawPainter . . . . Sec. 5.6.2
    - class DrawDynamicPolygonPainter . . . . Ex. 6.8
    - class DrawPolygonPainter . . . . Sec. 5.6.4

class FillPainter . . . . Sec. 5.6.2
class PointGeometry (implements java.lang.Comparable,Geometry) . Sec. 3.2.1
class PointZoneGeometry (implements AreaGeometry) . . . . Ex. 7.3
class TransformablePointGeometry . . . . Sec. 5.2.2
class PolylineGeometry (implements Geometry) . . . . Sec. 4.3.2
class PolygonGeometry (implements AreaGeometry). . . . . Sec. 5.3.1
class RandomColor . . . . Ex. 4.14
class RandomInt . . . . Sec. 4.2.2
class RandomIntInRange . . . . Sec. 4.2.3
class RandomPoint . . . . Sec 4.2.4
class RandomPointInRectangle . . . . Ex. 4.13
class RandomRectangle . . . . Sec. 4.2.5
class Range. . . . . Ex. 3.2
class Rational (implements java.lang.Comparable) . . . . Sec. 4.4.3
class RectangularGeometry (implements AreaGeometry) . . . . Sec. 5.4.2
class EllipseGeometry . . . . Sec. 4.4.2
class RectangleGeometry . . . . Sec. 3.2.2
class RoundRectangleGeometry . . . . Ex. 5.19
class ScanInput. . . . . Ex. 3.2, Appendix A
class Sort . . . . Sec. 5.5.2
class TextGeometry (implements Geometry). . . . . Ex. 5.20
class java.lang.Throwable (implements java.io.Serializable)
class java.lang.Exception
class java.lang.RuntimeException
class ColinearPointsException . . . . Ex. 6.13
class FailedConditionException. . . . . Sec. 2.2.1
class ZeroArraySizeException. . . . . Sec. 2.3

Interface Hierarchy

interface Geometry . . . . Sec. 5.4.3
interface AreaGeometry . . . . Sec. 5.4.3
interface Node . . . . Sec. 6.4
interface Painter. . . . . Sec. 5.6
interface PolygonIterator . . . . Sec. 6.2.3

BIBLIOGRAPHY

Abelson, Harold, Gerald Sussman, and Julie Sussman. 1997. *Structure and Interpretation of Computer Programs*. 2nd ed. New York: McGraw-Hill.

Arnold, Ken, James Gosling, and David Holmes. 2000. *The Java Programming Language.* 3rd ed. Boston: Addison Wesley.

Bailey, Duane. 2000. *Java Structures: Data Structures in Java for the Principled Programmer.* Boston: McGraw-Hill.

Booch, Grady, James Rumbaugh, and Ivar Jacobson. 1999. *The Unified Modeling Language User Guide*. Reading, MA: Addison Wesley.

Budd, Timothy. 1999. *Understanding Object-Oriented Programming with Java.* Reading, MA: Addison Wesley.

Foley, James, Andries van Dam, Steven Feiner, John Hughes, and Richard Phillips. 1994. *Introduction to Computer Graphics.* Reading, MA: Addison Wesley.

Friedman, Daniel, Mitchell Wand, and Christopher Haynes. 2001. *Essentials of Programming Languages.* 2nd ed. Cambridge, MA: MIT press.

Gamma, Erich, Richard Helm, Ralph Johnson, and John Vlissides. 1995. *Design Patterns: Elements of Reusable Object-Oriented Software.* Reading, MA: Addison Wesley.

Geary, David. 1998. *Graphic Java: Mastering the JFC.* 3rd ed. Upper Saddle River, NJ: Prentice Hall.

Hardy, Vincent. 1999. *Java 2D API Graphics.* Upper Saddle River, NJ: Prentice Hall.

Horstmann, Cay, and Gary Cornell. 2000. *Core Java 2 Vol. 1: Fundamentals.* Upper Saddle River, Prentice Hall.

Jia, Xiaoping. 2000. *Object-Oriented Software Development Using Java: Principles, Patterns, and Frameworks.* Reading, MA: Addison Wesley.

Liskov, Barbara, with John Guttag. 2001. *Program Development in Java: Abstraction, Specification, and Object-Oriented Design.* Reading, MA: Addison Wesley.

Meyer, Bertrand. 1997. *Object-Oriented Software Construction.* 2nd ed. Upper Saddle River, NJ: Prentice Hall.

Pooley, Rob, and Perdita Stevens. 1999. *Using UML: Software Engineering with Objects and Components.* Harlow, England: Addison Wesley.

Richter, Charles. 1999. *Designing Flexible Object-Oriented Systems with UML.* Indianapolis, IN: Macmillan Technical Publishing.

Rumbaugh, James, Ivar Jacobson, and Grady Booch. 1999. *The Unified Modeling Language Reference Manual.* Reading, MA: Addison Wesley.

Vlissides, John. 1998. *Hatching Patterns: Design Patterns Applied.* Reading, MA: Addison Wesley.

INDEX